HONG KONG SAR:
IN PURSUIT OF DOMESTIC AND INTERNATIONAL ORDER

Hong Kong SAR: In Pursuit of Domestic and International Order

Edited by

Beatrice Leung and Joseph Cheng

The Chinese University Press

ISBN 962–201–785–1

THE CHINESE UNIVERSITY PRESS
The Chinese University of Hong Kong
Sha Tin, N. T., Hong Kong
Fax: +852 2603 6692
+852 2603 7355
E-mail: cup@cuhk.edu.hk
Web-site: http://www.cuhk.edu.hk/cupress/w1.htm

Printed in Hong Kong

Contents

Preface

On 18–19 September 1996, an international conference titled "Hong Kong in Transition: Political Order, International Relations and Crisis Management" was held at the new campus of Lingnan College at Tuen Mun, Hong Kong. Under the main theme of the conference there were two concurrent sub-themes throughout the two days of the conference. After a review process, twelve selected papers presented in Theme I on *Changing International Relations and Crisis Management in Hong Kong After 1997* are compiled into this volume with the title altered into *Hong Kong SAR: In Pursuit of Domestic and International Order*. We must thank Centre for Asian Pacific Studies, Lingnan College for sponsoring the conference and the financial support in publishing this book. Our gratitude also goes to the staff of The Chinese University Press who took care of each step of its production. To Mr. Sundara Rajan Ramanatha Iyer who had done a wonderful job in the meticulous copy-editing, and Miss Mei Leung of Centre for Asian Pacific Studies of Lingnan College who contributed her valuable help in liaising with the publisher and contributors, and we are responsible for all mistakes.

Contributors

Brian BRIDGES is Associate Professor in the Department of Politics and Sociology, Lingnan College, Hong Kong. His research interests include Northeast Asian politics and international relations as well as European relations with Asia. His publications include *Japan and Korea in the 1990s* and, as co-author, *Pacific Asia in the 1990s*.

Andrew BYRNES is Associate Professor of Law and Director of the Centre for Comparative and Public Law in the Faculty of Law, the University of Hong Kong, where he teaches in the areas of international law, public law and human rights. He has written a number of articles on international human rights law, in particular in relation to women and human rights, and the UN Convention on the Elimination of All Forms of Discrimination against Women. He has worked with local and international human rights groups raising Hong Kong issues before the UN treaty bodies, as well as with human rights groups in Hong Kong.

Gerald CHAN is Senior Lecturer of International Relations in the Department of Politics, Victoria University of Wellington, New Zealand, and co-editor of *Political Science* journal, the July 1997 issue being a special issue on political studies in East Asia.

Joseph Y. S. CHENG is Chair Professor of Political Science at the City University of Hong Kong, and is the founding editor of the *Hong Kong Journal of Social Sciences*. He now serves as the Director of the Contemporary China Research Centre at the university. He has published extensively on Chinese politics, Chinese foreign policy, and Hong Kong's political development. His recent publications include *The Other Hong Kong Report 1997*.

CHEUNG Chor-yung is Lecturer in the Division of Social Studies, City University of Hong Kong. His research interests include Hong Kong Politics and Political Philosophy. He was twice an Administrative Officer of the Hong Kong Government and was a journalist with the British Broadcasting Corporation in London for seven years.

KAN Chak-yuen is Ph.D. candidate in the Department of Economics and Finance, City University of Hong Kong.

Jane C. Y. LEE is Chief Executive of Hong Kong Policy Research Institute, a non-government non-profit-making think-tank in Hong Kong. Dr. Lee specializes in political development and public administration in Hong Kong. Her most recent book is *Public Administration in NICs*.

Beatrice LEUNG is Programme Director and Associate Professor in the Faculty of Social Sciences, Lingnan College, Hong Kong. Her research interests include church and state relations including China's relations with world religions. Her publications include *Sino-Vatican Relations: Problems in Conflicting Authority* and, as editor, *Church and State Relations in 21st Century Asia*.

LIN Tzong-biau is Dean and Professor in the College of Management, National Chung Cheng University, Chia Yi, Taiwan.

Roda MUSHKAT is Professor of Law at the University of Hong Kong, where she has been teaching since 1979 in the subjects of Public International Law, Jurisprudence, Law and Society, Constitutional and Administrative Law, and Conflict of Laws. She has been affiliated as a visiting scholar with some of the world's leading law schools. Dr. Mushkat has published extensively in the areas of international refugee law, international environmental law, international law of war, human rights and legal theory. She is considered to be the principal authority on issues pertaining to Hong Kong's international legal status and personality, and has written *One Country, Two International Legal Personalities* and numerous papers on the topic.

TING Wai is Associate Professor in the Department of Government and International Studies, Hong Kong Baptist University. His research interests are on Chinese politics and international relations. His most recent publications include a monograph on "The External Relations and International Status of Hong Kong."

WONG Hung is Lecturer in the Division of Social Studies, City University of Hong Kong. His main research interests are labour studies, poverty and social security with particular reference to the working class in Hong Kong and China. He has published *Research on Expenditure Pattern of Low Expenditure Households in Hong Kong* and as co-author, *Disempowerment and Empowerment — An Exploratory Study on Low-Income Households in Hong Kong*.

Timothy Ka-ying WONG is Research Officer at the Hong Kong Institute of Asia-Pacific Studies, The Chinese University of Hong Kong. His research interests include cross-Taiwan-straits relations and social and political development in Taiwan and Hong Kong. He has published a number of books and articles, in Chinese and in English, on his research field.

Michael YAHUDA is Professor of International Relations at the London School of Economics and Political Science. He is the author of more than a hundred scholarly articles on aspects of Asian international politics, especially on Chinese politics and foreign policy. He is the author of five books, the most recent being *Hong Kong: China's Challenge*.

Ren YUE is Assistant Professor in the Department of Politics and Sociology, Lingnan College, Hong Kong. His research interests include international relations and comparative foreign policy.

Introduction

Beatrice Leung

Change, as a blessing or a curse, is a reality. Owing to continuous changes, in whatever context or form, opportunities for progress or shift points for regression are created. Persons, organizations or nations in designing strategies to manage change and its impact have to put the most important component of the design in the correct perspective: how to maintain the old order amid possible instability, uncertainty and complexity, and at the same time, create a new order out of the old to respond to the change.

Since 1 July 1997, Hong Kong has become a Special Administrative Region (SAR) of the People's Republic of China (P.R.C.). The change of its political status from a British colony to a special region of China has induced stress and pressure adversely affecting economic prosperity and political stability in the territory. China's resumption of Hong Kong's sovereignty, however, also presents opportunities for the community to maximize the benefits of China's economic development. As such, the ramifications of the political change in 1997 need not necessarily be negative. Whether Hong Kong can continue to flourish as a major international centre depends very much on how it can effectively manage the political, economic, social, psychological, or sociological changes.

Political Change and Politics

To effectively manage change, societies or communities must have sufficient capacity to maintain current political, social and economic order, to modify the impact arising from ecological changes, and to control the degree and extent of change. Sufficient capacity is a relative term: one can determine what is sufficient and what is not, only from one's perspective;

other people may disagree with one's judgement. Nevertheless, there are indicators that can be employed to reveal the level of sufficiency of the capacity: for example, crime rate, suicide rate, the number of annual emigration, the drainage of assets, frequency and intensity of protests, and indices of public confidence, etc.

While the level of sufficiency is readily measurable, the measurement can be meaningless: while the capacity level may be high according to the indicators, the public may still feel highly insecure or disgruntled. In the political arena, political games are played to achieve the personal goals of the participants. Thus, when irresponsible politicians try to maximize personal benefits at the expense of the community, they may manipulate the political sentiments of the public to misinterpret newly adopted political and economic measures that can effectively resolve problems in society as arrangements that deprive the citizens of their rights or induce regression.

Researchers in the field of political psychology find manipulation of sentiment both feasible and widely practised. In Western democracies, voters are found to be both rational and emotional. In some situations, emotions play a more critical role in determining policies the public chooses to support. This seems to be unavoidable, for passion (or emotional response) is what draws individuals to politics. Indeed, for policy issues to become a significant component of electoral choice, issues must evoke voters' emotion and sentiments because most human beings are not mere information processors who make decisions based solely on objective evaluation of benefits and costs incurred in the adoption or rejection of particular policies. Thus, to scholars who consider symbols an essential part of politics, issue voting is symbolic politics which is "associated with diffuse and emotionally laden reactions to issues."[1] Inevitably, newly adopted political and economic measures in Hong Kong, before or after 1997, that can effectively resolve problems in society may be misinterpreted by the public as undesirable if their emotion-dominated political leaders hold them as such.

Governor Patten's electoral reform package introduced in 1993 and passed as law on 30 June 1994 is an important example. As Jermain Lam

---

[1] George Rabinowitz and Stuart E. MacDonlad, "A Directional Theory of Issue Voting," *American Political Science Review*, Vol. 83, No. 1 (1989), pp. 93–121.

noted, the reform, rather than producing a harmonious effect on Hong Kong's political development, has "exacerbated political antagonisms and polarized the conflicts among political actors. Antagonism between Hong Kong citizens and mainland China has led to mutual distrust and alienation; antagonism between liberal and conservative groups has led to adversarial politics; antagonism between the British and mainland Chinese governments has led to a legitimacy crisis and power vacuum in the territory."[2]

In the absence of trust between political actors, the eventual establishment of a provisional legislature by China in 1997 is a natural outcome of adversarial politics. One can claim that Governor Patten is responsible; others may hold him simply incompetent. Regardless of the judgement, his electoral reform package and his way of pushing it through the political process had become the source of conflict and antagonism in Hong Kong. Yet, when he initially introduced the reform package, the public, under the influence of symbolic politics and his personal charm, was generally supportive.[3]

Obviously, politicization can be an important factor adversely affecting the stability of the community and thus its capacity to effectively cope with environmental changes. However, we need to know more about what is going on and how decisions that generate the most benefits and less expenses can be made so as to maximize our capacity to cope with these changes.

This demands further research on various issues. For example, if voters are non-rational or irrational, representative democracy may create opportunities for ambitious politicians to monopolize power, to suppress the minority, or, in extreme, to turn the community into a fascist system. Thus, to justify the introduction of representative democracy, many political leaders have claimed that democracy in Hong Kong is feasible and desirable because Hong Kong residents are rational beings, at least in terms of their economic track record. This argument is in line with public choice theorists' proposition that "Most, if not all, economic and political agents

---

[2] Jermain T. M. Lam, "Chris Patten's Constitutional Reform Package: Implications for Hong Kong's Political Transition," *Issues and Studies* (July 1993), pp. 55–74.

[3] *Ibid.*

obey the maxims of consistency and coherence leading to the maximization of utility."[4]

Yet, to psychologists, the human animal is "often controlled by emotions and desires that do not fit the model of calculating rationality."[5] Research conducted by experimental psychologists indicate that "human rationality is bounded limitations on memory and computational capabilities and that the cognitive machinery underlying human judgement and decision making is often inconsistent with the maxims of rationality."[6]

With reference to the prospect theory, which dictates that human beings have both risk-aversive and risk-taking tendencies, Quattrone and Tversky conducted a series of experiments with hundreds of undergraduate students of the Stanford University and the University of California to evaluate the implications of risk-aversive and risk-seeking behaviours for politics. They found that, firstly, while subjects are generally risk-aversive in a situation under which gains are more certain, they are more risk-seeking when loss is quite certain. This finding implies that in the political arena, voters tend to support the re-election of incumbents when the overall political and economic conditions are generally satisfactory, and to reject (and support challengers) when they are not. In short, given the tendencies, challengers have better chance of beating incumbents only when the overall political and economic condition deteriorates.[7]

Secondly, Quattrone and Tversky found that subjects were not as consistent as the rationality theory predicted. Specifically, their experiments indicated that the ways of presenting information affected decision making of the subjects: for example, according to the Federal Bureau of Investigation's crime statistics in 1982, 2.76% of American black citizens and 0.68% of American white citizens were arrested for serious crimes, with the law obedience rate of the black community at 97.24%, and that of the white community at 99.32%. When subjects were informed of the rate of arrests, they generally considered the crimes among blacks as more serious, but when the law obedience rates were presented, they considered

---

[4] George A. Quattrone and Amos Tversky, "Contrasting Rational and Psychological Analyses of Political Choice," *American Political Science Review*, Vol. 82, No. 3 (1988), pp. 719–36.

[5] *Ibid.*, p. 719.

[6] *Ibid.*, p. 720.

[7] *Ibid.*

the difference between the two racial communities to be very small.[8] This human perception phenomenon, explained by the so-called ratio-difference principle, can be taken as a basis for drawing one important political implication: successful politicians may be those who are more effective in applying the ratio-difference principle in framing political information in ways that induce desirable responses from voters. More importantly, this finding furnishes a basis for questioning the general validity of the rationality theory which is based on the premise that human beings are consistent.

In sum, research on political behaviour indicates that voters are not necessarily rational actors, and that their behavioural tendencies may result in non-rational or irrational voting. Thus, the argument that democracy in Hong Kong is feasible because Hong Kong residents are rational is misleading. Firstly, to introduce or not to introduce representative democracy is a constitutional policy. Therefore, the making of the decision is merely a function of politicking: he who has the most political influence could decide on when, how, and to what extent democracy shall be introduced. It is not a matter of logic or "truth."

Secondly, the necessary condition for ensuring the persistence of mass-based democracy is not voter rationality. Instead, as many political culture scholars have noted, the basic element required is a sense of interpersonal trust. On the findings in *The Civic Culture*, a classic by Almond and Verba,[9] Inglehart[10] states:

> interpersonal trust is a prerequisite to the formation of secondary associations, which in turn is essential to effective political participation in any large democracy. A sense of trust is also required for the functioning of the democracy rule for the game: one must view the opposition as a loyal opposition, who will not imprison or execute if you surrender political power but can be relied upon to govern within the law and to surrender political power reciprocally if your side wins the next election."[11]

---

[8] *Ibid.*

[9] Gabriel A. Almond and Sidney Verba, *The Civic Culture: Political Attitudes and Democracy in Five Nations* (Princeton: Princeton University Press, 1963).

[10] Ronald Inglehart, "The Renaissance of Political Culture," *American Political Science Review*, Vol. 82, No. 4 (1988), pp. 1203–30.

[11] *Ibid.*

Thus, those supporting democratization may conduct research on the sense of interpersonal trust in Hong Kong and, in view of their findings, argue for democracy.

After all, personal wishes or expectations are often unrealistic or inaccurate. For example, while some politicians had argued in the 1980s that Hong Kong residents were politically apathetic, one million people marched in the streets in 1989 to protest for democracy in China. While other politicians averred that Hong Kong residents were prepared for Legislative Council (Legco) direction election, less than 40% of the registered voters cast their ballots in the 1991 Legco election. These and other examples reflect that systematic research that lives up to the rigorous standard of social scientific investigation has to be pursued to identify the patterns of political behaviour, as well as their causes and effects, so as to furnish a basis for explaining, and possibly predicting the occurrence of political events.

As Kuan and Lau noted, "the political context in Hong Kong today is a unique experience in human history": unique in the sense that it is "an unprecedented experiment with a planned transfer of sovereignty involving the enclosure of a capitalist system into a socialist system."[12] In this process of planned transfer of sovereignty, new issues emerge, redistribution of political power becomes inevitable, and political norms and values undergo modification. "For the ordinary Hong Kong citizen, the political world has become less familiar than before, or even confusing. Learning and adjustment are called for. Thus the political culture in Hong Kong is in flux."[13] In such a changing context, Kuan and Lau noted, "more fundamental issues need to be addressed while greater caution in interpretation is in order."[14]

In conclusion, research evidence is essential to develop a better understanding of a variety of issues which can be a source of wisdom, and act

---

[12] Kuan Hsin-chi and Lau Siu-kai, "The Civic Self in a Changing Polity: The Case of Hong Kong," in *Hong Kong: The Challenge of Transformation*, edited by Kathleen Cheek-Milby and Miron Mushkat (Hong Kong: Centre of Asian Studies, University of Hong Kong, 1989).

[13] *Ibid.*, p. 92.

[14] *Ibid.*

as substitute for politicking, make rational choices for the community as to how to effectively respond to environmental changes.

Management of Change

Politics is on the one hand an art, and on the other a craft as is the management of change. There are ways to systematically maintain current political, social and economic order, modify the impact of ecological changes, and control the degree and extent of changes. These include assessing the current situation; diagnosing the nature of the problems arising from domestic or international change; identifying the distant and proximate causes of the problems; clarifying the complex relationships among those causes; reviewing the strengths and weaknesses of the parties concerned, as well as those of the disinterested parties — be they governmental, economic, or political — and their abilities and resources for coping with the problems; determining the strategies and tactics of responding to or controlling the changes; and finally evaluating the effectiveness of those strategies and tactics.

Where there is a will, there will be a way. To researchers in the field of conflicts' resolution, there are always creative solutions to problems. For example, according to Leung and Nagel,[15] whereas political issues and problems in China are complicated, efforts to "super-optimize" can be fruitful: that is, to find solutions to a problem by which all parties concerned will be better off. The reunification issue is discussed to illustrate that even highly politicized problems in China are amenable to super-optimal solutions. Specifically, as Leung and Nagel noted, some reunification options have been proposed: negotiation between Kuomintang (KMT) and the Chinese Communist Party (CCP) on equal footing; KMT's military take-over; CCP's military take-over; the "one country, two systems" formula, convergence by democratization, and incremental convergence through trading and communication. Yet, neither party finds the alternatives desirable in terms of optimal satisfaction. By employing their super-optimal solution approach,

---

[15] Beatrice K. F. Leung and Stuart S. Nagel, "Super-Optimizing China: Reunification as an Example," *International Journal of Public Administration*, Vol. 16, No. 9 (1993), pp. 1459–81.

reunification and democratization can be made feasible and all parties concerned are better off. The specific proposals are that Taiwan should introduce a wholesale buy-out scheme that costs US$30 billion, that a new republic be established, and that legislative powers should be shared among the majoritarian and non-majoritarian institutions. Together, these arrangements could ensure stability and result in democratization.

Yet, as Leung and Nagel pointed out, formulating a super-optimal solution (SOS) is different from having it adopted: the former involves engineering feasibility, while the latter, political feasibility. The underlying assumptions of the analysis by Leung and Nagel are that, firstly, all parties concerned are rational actors in that they are consistent in the pursuit of adopted goals and that they consistently choose the most effective means to accomplish stated ends. And secondly, they are also vitally concerned with the policy problems examined. It follows from these assumptions that the parties involved may consider themselves players in a non-zero-sum game pursuing the greatest possible benefits for all. As such, it is further assumed that the SOS would be adopted.

In reality, these assumptions may be invalid: players may not share the same objective and/or consider themselves the players in a positive-sum game, and thus they may not accept the goal of making everyone better off; players may be non-rational, or even irrational, actors. For example, due to such psychological forces as sense of insecurity and need for power, Jiang Zemin and his followers may be unwilling to step down, although they genuinely wish to achieve the historical mission. If so, the probability of having the proposed SOS adopted by them is close to zero. By the same token, if Taiwan leaders are in fact concerned only with maintenance of their political influence in Taiwan, they would have little interest in pushing for a wholesale buy-out scheme, which, to them, would generate little benefits but consume much of Taiwan's resources. In this light, whereas the engineering feasibility of the so-called super-optimal solutions presented by Leung and Nagel is affirmative, political feasibility is not.

In short, problems can be resolved only when participants are vitally concerned and have the commitment to cope with the problems. Similarly, while there are ways to systematically maintain current political, social and economic order, modify the impacts arising from ecological changes, and control the degree and extent of changes, the will to manage change is needed.

The Passion for Excellence

The will to act is closely related to the passion for excellence.[16] Thus, there is the need for Hong Kong to pay serious attention to the issue of excellence so that the capacity to cope with change can be improved. While excellence is a relative term and thus is difficult to define, we can use the term to describe the performance of the community that is not only good at maintaining current economic, political and social order, but also innovative and especially adroit at continually responding to change of any sort in the greater China context.

To enhance excellence, we need to focus on developing and keeping a vision, practise effective leadership, foster innovation at all levels of the community, and improve relations with external (interested and disinterested) parties which can assert political or economic impact upon the community. To focus and develop a vision is to maintain the essence of the community, political leaders need to inculcate the belief in the real existence of a common purpose in the community. Excellence demands a sense of purpose, a vision, and a communicated uniqueness that can turn people on to make Hong Kong a better place for all. Yet, in reality, most leaders often fail to communicate a vision and motivate people to pursue a common purpose. Regarding leadership, a major mission of today's pre-transition leadership is reshaping current mainstream culture for achieving a common purpose. Regarding innovation, the challenge is to assume the legitimate responsibility of living a bit dangerously and taking risks. Most societies have their greatest success when there are citizens who dare to take reasonable risks. The entrepreneurial spirit in Hong Kong has indeed been a crucial factor in the economic success of the community. The willingness of the citizenry to do things in different ways should be fostered. After all, excellence relies on this type of grassroots creativity. Regarding improving relations with external parties, the success of a society depends ultimately on how well it responds to its partners and enemies, real or potential. Cooperation can result in win-win outcomes while opposition in lose-lose outcomes. Hong Kong's economic cooperation with China in the past decades has been fruitful. Cooperation in other areas, particularly political and social, is likely to generate similar effects, provided it is not at the expense of the self-respect of Hong Kong's citizens.

---

[16] Margaret G. Hermann, "Ingredients of Leadership," in *Political Psychology*, edited by Margaret G. Hermann (San Francisco: Jossey-Bass Publishers, 1986).

In short, Hong Kong's capacity to cope with change relies very much on political leaders who can instil and maintain excellence in the community. This is possible when they introduce a degree of vision in every aspect of planning and communicate it effectively, and lead the citizenry to be the best by facilitating their quest to make a living while making a worthwhile contribution to the community. It would also provide a role model by thinking beyond the immediate and daring to be creative and innovative, and focus on interested and disinterested parties who may be the stakeholders in the well-being of Hong Kong. In the context of 1997 political change-over, leadership which strives to develop a passion for excellence in the community is necessary.

Strategic Management

Hong Kong's capacity for coping with change relies also on strategic management. A strategy can be viewed as a means of enabling leaders to guide the adaptation of the community to changing environments. Strategies seek to define the relationship between a community and its environment, and provide guidance for making decisions. Strategic management, therefore, involves analysis of both the community and its environment, and deciding on appropriate response to environmental changes.

The current strategic management literature emphasizes the importance of translating strategy into operational terms.[17] Failure to establish compatibility between strategic direction and the various components of operational control is of great concern to strategic management theorists. If control and feedback activities were not oriented to serve the furtherance of strategy, its successful implementation would be in doubt. Strategic management departs most from earlier strategic planning theory in its recognition that successful implementation is primarily a behavioural process in which the commitment of necessary persons is attained. In addition, theorists now emphasize that anticipatory activities are fallible and that entities, be they communities or organizations, must be able to perceive and respond quickly to changing conditions. Accordingly, strategic management theory has grown to include efforts to influence

---

[17] Alan J. Rowe, Richard O. Mason, Karl E. Dickel, Richard B. Mann and Robert J. Mockler, *Strategic Management: A Methodological Approach*, 4th edition (Reading, Mass.: Addison-Wesley Publishing Co., 1994).

behaviour with the intent of creating a strategic culture in which change is accepted as a normal state, conflict is managed to reduce the impediments to change, and values reflect a desire to achieve long-range performance. Thus, strategic management calls for leadership to include futuristic, creative thinking, emphasizing tacit understanding and qualitative methods while recognizing the legitimacy of political rationality. Moreover, strategic decisions should be guided by analysis of a broad ranging, speculative and futuristic nature. As such, political leaders in Hong Kong subscribing to strategic management should recognize that the perception of problems as interrelated spheres is essential to successfully anticipate future states, set directions and implement strategy.

Efforts to apply strategic management to the Hong Kong context raise inevitable questions about the locus, not merely analysis, of leadership itself. In organizations, strategic management is intended to serve those at the apex of authority, especially the CEO, and there are no counterparts to the Governor, the SAR Chief Executive, legislators, judges, and various political participants. Therefore, a different approach must be considered.

Research that reveals the nature and application characteristics of the appropriate approach is required. More importantly, the research should also take the passion for excellence into account. Specifically, as mentioned earlier, the enhancement of excellence requires developing and maintaining a vision, practising effective leadership, fostering innovation at all levels of the community, and improving relations with external (interested and disinterested) parties which can assert political or economic impact upon the community. All these imply the necessity of a philosophy for determining the principles to be adopted to guide decision-making.

A researcher, Ian Scott, argued in 1996 that Hong Kong was in turbulence and "turbulence in the Hong Kong environment dates specifically to the decision taken by Britain and China in September 1982 to negotiate on the future of the territory."[18] According to Scott, "the fears of the Hong Kong Chinese over their future within a communist polity provide the context of turbulence."[19] Then, "turbulence in the Hong Kong environment ... stems from four major sources: a mistrust of Chinese intentions after 1997;

---

[18] Ian Scott, "Policy-Making in a Turbulent Environment: The Case of Hong Kong," *International Review of Administrative Sciences*, Vol. 5, No. 2 (1986).

[19] *Ibid.*, p. 452.

the belief of some — most significantly, the civil servants — that they will be detrimentally affected by the agreement; the intervention of China and Britain in the affairs of the territory; and the mobilization of new groups into the policy process."[20] Moreover, "an important additional source of turbulence may be the inability of the present policy-making system to develop effective strategies to deal with environmental challenges."[21]

Scott's findings are in line with the argument here that how Hong Kong should be ruled in what ways to protect or advance the rights of which groups for what reasons and to what extent and at the expense of which groups is essentially a politically philosophical question deserving serious attention.

Public Philosophy

In the United States, many policy-makers and researchers have often overlooked the significance of public philosophy, which is "any set of principles and criteria above and beyond the reach of government and statesmen by which the decision of government are guided and justified"[22] and by which what the government should do and should not do are defined. Since public philosophy is the political formula — i.e. the "legal and moral basis, or principle, on which the power of the political class rests"[23] — it may generate substantial impact, positive or negative, upon society.

In the late 19th Century, as Lowi reckoned, liberalism-conservatism had been the source of the public philosophy in the United States. At that time, conservatism was committed to a discriminating defence of the social order against change and reform, and liberalism for reform and popular participation in government.[24] A new public philosophy has been in place since the 1930s. According to Lowi, it is "interest-group liberalism" because it sees as both necessary and good that the policy agenda and the

---

[20] *Ibid.*, p. 454.

[21] *Ibid*, p. 454.

[22] Theodore J. Lowi, "The Public Philosophy: Interest-Group Liberalism," in *Classic Readings in American Politics*, edited by Pietro S. Nivola and David H. Rosenbloom (New York: St. Martin's Press, 1986).

[23] *Ibid.*, p. 262

[24] *Ibid.*

public interest be defined in terms of the organized interests in society.[25] Lowi noted that "the new public philosophy is the source of important new political pathologies in America."[26] Together, the pathologies create a crisis of public authority. Under interest-group liberalism, the government no longer controls the society, while no single interest group controls the government.

Lowi's critique furnishes a basis for Hong Kong residents to critically evaluate the issue of public philosophy in the era of political change-over. In the 1980s, the essential issue was representative democracy versus administrative consultation. With the passage of the Basic Law and the introduction of direct election in 1991, the issue has become one of the redistribution of political power within the polity: the empowerment of the Legco versus the monopoly of power by the Governor-in-Council and the Chief Secretary Committee. While the two issues are the source of public philosophy in Hong Kong, both, in the light of Lowi's discussion, are obviously secondary and even misleading.

The issues are secondary because the fundamental problem that emerged after the signing of the Sino-British Joint Declaration was the basis on which to decide the authority of the government to perform functions, rather than (1) whether Hong Kong should have a "Government by the People" which is not necessarily a "Government of and for the people" and (2) whether Hong Kong should have more of its public authority reserved to representatives of some segments of the population. In other words, the key issue is the search for a set of principles and criteria for guiding and justifying the making of government decisions, instead of who shall have how much power to govern! After all, the issue of why public authority should be exercised must be resolved before deciding on who should have the authority.

The two issues are misleading because the 1997 political arrangement has fundamentally changed the nature of governance of and in Hong Kong and thus the essential issue is how to redefine the nature, scope and functions of the Hong Kong Government, both before and after 1997, rather than who should play what political roles to advance various interests. By shifting the focus of attention to how interests should be protected or

---

[25] *Ibid.*, p. 271.
[26] *Ibid.*, p. 268.

maintained, insufficient preparation for maximizing the contribution of local public authority to the socio-economic development in both Hong Kong and the mainland will become probable. The consequences may be disastrous. In short, the pressing need to develop a new public philosophy for Hong Kong becomes obvious. After all, if the political leadership is to develop and maintain a vision and inculcate the belief in the real existence of a common purpose in the community, there must be a basis on how the public authority should be prescribed and exercised to facilitate the pursuit of defining the vision and the common purpose.

Organization of the Book

After the signing of the Sino-British Joint Declaration, which spelled out the arrangements to turn Hong Kong into a Special Administrative Region of China, many scholars and commentators have conducted research to diagnose the various types of problems confronting the community. Their findings enhance our understanding of, for example, the nature and ramifications of the problems arising from the political change, the various causes and consequences of those problems, as well as the complex relationships among those causes and consequences, and the concerns of the various interested parties and their responses to those problems. Yet, little effort has been expended to research on how Hong Kong can systematically and effectively manage the changes resulting from the political change-over. This book seeks to remedy this lacuna.

The book is divided into two parts: the first, comprising seven chapters, reviews the issues concerning the pursuit of domestic order; the second, of five chapters, explores issues pertinent to maintaining relationships with various parties in the international arena.

In Chapter 1, Cheung notes that the question of legitimacy is firmly on the agenda of Hong Kong's transitional politics. Scholars such as Ian Scott have argued that, the British Hong Kong Government is undergoing an enduring crisis of legitimacy. Yet, Cheung's analysis reveals that this argument is misleading. Based on his review of recent empirical researches on the political values of the people of Hong Kong, Cheung concludes that at the justification level of legitimacy, the people of Hong Kong believe that since the government is regarded as relatively fair and trustworthy, they are ready to subscribe to its authority, provided that it consults the people, respects political opposition, keeps its power under check, upholds individual freedom and the rule of law, and positively guards the civil liberties of the people. At the same time, there is general support for speeding up the process of democratization in Hong Kong, though this does not amount to a full-scale support for popular sovereignty or for making the selection of government mainly dependent on popular choice by elections. Finally, Cheung concludes that it is possible to discern a distinct Hong Kong identity emerging; an identity which is different from the traditional monistic, harmony-conscious, and submissive Chinese identity. As the political values constituting this identity would play a major role in the legitimacy of the Hong Kong SAR Government, the Hong Kong SAR authorities will probably find that ignoring this emerging identity will not be only extremely unwise, but will also likely be at their peril.

In Chapter 2, Michael Yahuda draws our attention to some overlooked but important points pertinent to Hong Kong's pursuit of order and effective management of change. Yahuda notes that within China, the reversion of the sovereignty of Hong Kong is presented as a major rectification of a historic wrong. However, China's leaders realize that if they fail to preside over a smooth transition, the consequences would be serious and far-reaching. After all, if the "one country, two systems" concept failed in the relatively favourable circumstances of Hong Kong, Beijing would no longer have a viable policy for the peaceful reunification with Taiwan and it would be left with force as the only conceivable option. Yet, according to Yahuda, some leaders and the majority of citizens of China still know very little about Hong Kong. For example, at the popular level and even among intellectuals, a common view is that the people of Hong Kong are to some extent tainted by having lived under British capitalist colonial rule. Hence they are regarded as corrupt and to have especially corrupting influence on the mainland, as they are alleged to bribe officials and exploit their disadvantaged fellow countrymen. Thus, even Li Ruihuan publicly admitted that the Chinese leaders had a dangerously insufficient understanding of Hong Kong. Such insufficient understanding is further complicated by the leaders' overlooking of the potential impact of the Hong Kong SAR upon China. As Yahuda points out, by following the precepts of the Basic Law that was endorsed by its own National People's Congress, Beijing would leave Hong Kong to operate under the rule of law, with its apolitical and clean civil service and with a degree of democracy and basic freedoms that before too long would be desired by many in China. In other words, Hong Kong could become the trigger or the catalyst for another movement for political reform in China. How Hong Kong can become the catalyst that will enable China to complete its integration into the modern world has been overlooked by political leaders and the citizenry of Hong Kong. Yahuda's theme indeed redirects our attention to an important point: to manage change, we need to focus not only on our domestic issues and problems. By examining our relationships with external parties, we might very well find ways to increase our capacity to cope with change.

After 1979, when China started to open up the country to the outside world and liberalize its economy, Hong Kong quickly became the new centre of activities. As a result, Chinese firms in Hong Kong have mushroomed. In Chapter 3, T. B. Lin and C. Y. Kan make an attempt to review the past development and the present situation of the Chinese firms in Hong Kong, as well as analyse and project their role in and likely impact on the Hong Kong economy during the transition period before and after 1 July 1997. Lin and Kan find that the increasing participation by Chinese companies in Hong Kong is mutually beneficial. For example, the Chinese companies can expand their business horizon, learn the working of the capitalist system and raise the much needed capital overseas while the Hong Kong business people can cooperate with the Chinese bureaucrat-turned business people and at the same time create new opportunities for the local investors. To Lin and Kan, the Chinese firms have played a positive role in the development of the Hong Kong economy. Nevertheless, the presence of Chinese firms in Hong Kong may have negative impact: for example, the Chinese firms may bring with them bad business practices, such as back-door operations, corruption and so on into Hong Kong. The overall conclusion of the study by Lin and Kan is that the Chinese firms in Hong Kong will continue to work to the advantage of the economy during and after the transition period, simply because they are charged with the political mission to maintain the declared twin goal of stability and prosperity of Hong Kong.

In Chapter 4, Wong Hung analyses the crisis of marginalization of labour in Hong Kong. Being a process of labour subordination, marginalization is a worldwide phenomenon. According to Wong, the marginalization of workers of Hong Kong can be exemplified by three trends in recent years: the rise of structural unemployment, the changing labour market and employment relation, and the increasing poverty and inequality. Then, causes of marginalization crisis of Hong Kong workers can be identified at three levels: global, regional and local. At the global level, flexible accumulation of capital becomes a worldwide trend as a post-Fordist capitalistic mode of production. Economic reunification of the regional political economy between China and Hong Kong, and the unlimited supply of surplus workers in China are two important factors at the regional level. At the local level in Hong Kong, impotence of the workers and the increasing authority of Capital also contribute to the marginalization crisis of Hong Kong labour. The relocation of different circuit of migration of capital and labour in Zhujiang Delta Open Zone and Hong Kong is a result of both the economic reforms in China and the changing international division of labour. Hong Kong now performs its role as a secondary World City in the regional political economy. The new functions performed by Hong Kong in the region are the fundamental causes of its changing labour market. The economic reunification of Hong Kong and China is thus an underlying factor for the above changes, which in turn is an accelerating factor in the marginalization crisis of Hong Kong labour. Unfortunately, in the short term, the marginalization crisis may induce new waves of discontentment and critical awareness among workers. In the long term, it may increase political aspiration and awareness of the marginal workers. As a long-term political impact, the marginalization crisis may reactivate class politics, thus posing a threat to the stability of Hong Kong. As Wong concludes, there is the need for the government to introduce reforms in social welfare, housing and education to alleviate the impending marginalization crisis.

In Chapter 5, Beatrice Leung discusses the triangular relations between China, Vatican and Hong Kong in the context of the ideological and political conflicts between China and the Catholic Church. The role of Hong Kong Church as a "bridge" in the triangular relationship is discussed and its developments and implications upon China illustrated. Unfortunately, the revival of Catholic life in China poses a threat to the CCP's ideological stability. While Hong Kong Catholics are prepared for their transfer to a Communist rule, they are working out a strategy for crisis management by switching the bridge enterprise away from Hong Kong. The triangular relationship is gradually transforming into a bilateral relationship between China and the Vatican.

In Chapter 6, Ren Yue examines the role of non-governmental organizations (NGOs) in Hong Kong's political, social and economic life which has received little attention from researchers. Ren points out that the majority of Hong Kong's NGOs have developed since the 1970s when the territory emerged rapidly as one of the major international centres in trade, finance, shipping and the service sectors. Ren's telephone interviews with 38 NGOs conducted in August 1996 reveal that in general, the NGOs in Hong Kong are fairly active in their respective fields and that NGOs, with their enormous information resources, their expertise in various fields, and in some cases, their popular support from the grassroots level, have become actively involved in almost every aspect of life in Hong Kong. The NGOs' efforts to deliver services have been recognized by more and more people in Hong Kong. Often, their efforts are fruitful. For example, as Ren reported, partly due to the efforts of NGOs such as Amnesty International, Human Rights Watch, and some women and children's rights organizations, the human rights record in Hong Kong has improved substantially in recent years. How the NGOs can continue to exert influence in Hong Kong after 1997 is still uncertain. While the statutory right for NGOs to operate is guaranteed, political constraints are also present. Ren reports that while non-political organizations are more optimistic about the future, the politically active NGOs are uncertain or hold a relatively pessimistic view. An in-depth policy analysis needs to be conducted to find ways to ensure that NGOs continue to provide services.

In Chapter 7, Andrew Byrnes notes that there are many in Hong Kong's international and local business community who are concerned about the limitations on the enjoyment of such existing rights and freedoms such as freedom of expression and the media, freedom of movement, and freedom from arbitrary action at the hands of government. To Byrnes, the fear that these rights may be eroded is a factor at the back of many business people's minds, and one which is a destabilizing factor in planning for the future. Thus, the continuation of the human rights guarantees contained in international treaties applicable to Hong Kong has been an important and contentious issue, while the continuation of the guarantees themselves and the acceptance of international supervision in the form of reporting to the United Nations assume considerable symbolic importance. China has refused to submit reports as required by the International Covenant on Civil and Political Rights (ICCPR) and the International Covenant on Economic, Social and Cultural Rights (ICESCR). Byrnes's analysis reveals that the reasons for the refusal so far by the Chinese authorities to undertake to submit reports under the ICCPR and ICESCR after 1997 do not seem to lie in any deep-seated or principled objection to the international supervision of national law and practice by independent expert bodies. Rather, China maintains that it is not a "State party" to the Covenants, it is not required to report because the Covenants impose that obligation only on "States parties." Byrnes' in-depth analysis furnishes a legal basis for compelling China to submit reports under the two Covenants in a manner similar to Britain before 1997.

In Chapter 8, Roda Mushkat makes an attempt to demonstrate that within the context of prevailing international legal norms, the multilateral treaties currently applicable to Hong Kong should remain intact through the transition and beyond. She notes that the dynamism of the Hong Kong economy is due to a flexible economic structure and a high degree of integration into the international capitalist economy. Fortunately, the Hong Kong SAR as a unit in the "one country, two systems" configuration, is set to enjoy a wide latitude in the management of external affairs, including a capacity to establish and maintain treaty relationships. Moreover, both the British Government and its Chinese counterpart in the Joint Liaison Group are concerned with maintaining Hong Kong's international legal continuity, and their positive actions have resulted in the enhancement of post-transition applicability of a long list of treaties. Yet, as Mushkat notes, where connection between Hong Kong integration into the world economy and legal continuity is absent, China's attitude may prove less elastic.

In Chapter 9, Jane Lee and Gerald Chan recognize that the extent to which the concept of "one country, two systems" is applied in matters of external relations and foreign affairs is an area not fully explored in academic circles. The objective of the chapter is to investigate into the strategy adopted by the Hong Kong Government which enables it to achieve the greatest possible extent of autonomy in Hong Kong's relations with international organizations, the United States, and Taiwan. The tying together of two different systems, a socialist one in mainland China and a capitalist one in Hong Kong, to form a single entity under the diplomatic umbrella of the P.R.C. carries interesting implications for the development of Hong Kong's international relations. The authors strive to illustrate the potential dilemmas confronting Hong Kong and their analysis reveals that, firstly although Hong Kong's participation in international organizations is likely to remain largely intact, Hong Kong has to provide intergovernmental links with the British Commonwealth for political reasons. Secondly, issues concerning human rights, individual freedoms, and democratic reform may become the most sensitive areas affecting Sino-U.S. and Hong Kong–U.S. relations, while the current strategy of the Hong Kong Government is to avoid making comments and curbing local attempt to lobby U.S. support for the development of democratic institutions in the territory. And thirdly, while Hong Kong has been playing an important role in bridging the relations between China and Taiwan, the Hong Kong Government seems to enjoy the least autonomy, among all other issues, in its relations with Taiwan and thus it is clearly an area in which the SAR's pragmatic economic interests will be subordinated to the political principles of national sovereignty.

In Chapter 10, Timothy Wong reviews the evolution of the state in Taiwan and examines the uncertainty across the Taiwan Strait. His analysis reveals that Taipei's new mainland policy on the one hand urges the P.R.C. to normalize cross-strait relations by making the P.R.C. recognize Taiwan as a political equal and, on the other hand, launches the so-called "pragmatic diplomacy" to break its current international isolation, as well as to define the cross-strait relations through participation in the international community. Wong's analysis further reveals that there are several structural factors that serve to constrain Taipei from taking an even more radical state position and policy, including Beijing's threat of force, the short electoral cycle of Taiwan, Taiwan's pluralized and localized social and political interests, Taiwan's heavy economic dependency upon the mainland, the huge economic interests of Taiwan in Hong Kong which will revert to mainland China in 1997, and the rising influence of Beijing in the international community. Wong argues that a more reasonable and comprehensive way to manage the crisis on the current cross-strait conflicts should be not to allow each side to go its own way and step up confrontation. Moreover, Hong Kong has been helplessly squeezed by the political conflicts between mainland China and Taiwan and as it will come under Beijing's sovereignty after 1997, any cross-strait tension is likely to strain Hong Kong's future development.

In Chapter 11, Ting Wai reviews Sino-American and China–Hong Kong relations and analyses how the interactions between the two nations affect the future development of Hong Kong. Ting notes that during the Cold War era, the conflicts and confrontation between the P.R.C. and the U.S. did not have any detrimental effect on the political order and economic prosperity of Hong Kong. Yet, the change of sovereignty would bring political difficulties for Hong Kong in the post-Cold War period, with the continual Sino-U.S. conflict resulting from their mutually damaging perceptions and policy orientations. His analysis shows that it is quite clear that the U.S. Government wants to help consolidate an area in which it can make a contribution: the rule of law in Hong Kong. While it is difficult to predict the political future of Hong Kong after it becomes a part of China, because political development in China is full of uncertainties, and it is uncertain that whether the high degree of autonomy of Hong Kong would be infringed upon by the Chinese, Ting points out that Western countries including the U.S., Britain and Japan can help check and balance the behaviour of the P.R.C. Ting concludes that it is wise for China as well as Western nations to adopt a more cautious attitude not to involve Hong Kong in their political conflicts.

In Chapter 12, Brian Bridges endeavours to focus on the implications for European economic and political interests in the transition of Hong Kong. Bridges argues that clearly of paramount importance to European commercial interests is the need for Hong Kong to retain its open, market economy system, including the free flow of capital, and that stability and democracy within the territory are the most important European political interests in Hong Kong. To Bridges, Hong Kong is likely to continue to play its multiple roles as a commercial facilitator for China's modernization and by extension as a positive conduit for European commercial activity, if the principles laid down in the Joint Declaration and the Basic Law designed to maintain the free market system and a favourable attitude towards business are faithfully implemented.

Part 1
Domestic Order

1

Legitimacy, Legitimacy Crisis, and Transitional Politics in Hong Kong[1]

Cheung Chor-yung

Introduction: Legitimacy and Stability

For decades, social scientists have been impressed by Hong Kong's ability to maintain political stability without undergoing a process of democratization in the face of rapid economic development since World War II. Two sociologists, Ambrose Y. C. King and Lau Siu-kai have, perhaps, contributed most in accounting for this "intriguing issue."[2] King's thesis of "administrative absorption of politics"[3] and Lau's thesis of the "minimally-integrated social-political system"[4] have become standard explanations of Hong Kong's post-war stability. While King concentrates on the colonial administration's ability to institute administrative changes in response to

---

[1] I am grateful to Peter C. Y. Cheung and the editors for their comments on an earlier draft of this chapter.

[2] Lau Siu-kai and Kuan Hsin-chi comment that the Hong Kong Government's ability to maintain continuous and stable rule for about 150 years is "[t]he most intriguing issue in any discourse on the nature of governance in Hong Kong." See Lau Siu-kai and Kuan Hsin-chi, *The Ethos of the Hong Kong Chinese* (Hong Kong: The Chinese University Press, 1988), p. 18.

[3] Ambrose Y. C. King, "Administrative Absorption of Politics in Hong Kong: Emphasis on the Grass Roots Level," in *Social Life and Development in Hong Kong*, edited by Ambrose Y. C. King and Rance P. L. Lee (Hong Kong: The Chinese University Press, 1981), pp. 127–46.

[4] Lau Siu-kai, *Society and Politics in Hong Kong* (Hong Kong: The Chinese University Press, 1982).

or in anticipation of relevant socio-economic development in order to attain an integration of interests between the governors and the governed, Lau tries to argue that Hong Kong's stability has been sustained by a unique constellation of historical circumstances, such as China's reluctance to see Hong Kong's status quo altered; a non-indigenous and noncommittal local population until recently; a politically apathetic and largely self-sufficient Chinese community; and, the ability, albeit limited, of the British bureaucracy to develop linkages to integrate the largely secluded polity with the apolitical society.

However, political instability could either be the consequence of a state's inability to rule or loss of its right to rule. While it is obvious that a state's ability to rule is, in some way, related to its right to rule, the two are, nevertheless, distinct.[5] Of late, political scientists have become increasingly interested in the question of legitimacy concerning the last years of British rule in Hong Kong,[6] a question perhaps most pertinent to students of politics whose subject is, in the final analysis, a study of power relations and authority.

Seymour Martin Lipset once remarked that "a crisis of legitimacy is a crisis of change."[7] The biggest political issue concerning Hong Kong's recent development is, undoubtedly, the agreed change of sovereignty as

---

[5] This theoretical distinction is also supported by Lau Siu-kai and Kuan Hsin-chi's empirical study in their "Hong Kong People's Attitude towards Political Authority and the Legitimacy of the Colonial Government," in *Hong Kong Politics in the Transitional Period*, edited by Lau Siu-kai (Hong Kong: Wide Angle Press, 1993), p. 401 (in Chinese).

[6] The most comprehensive study, adopting a historical approach, is Ian Scott's *Political Change and the Crisis of Legitimacy* (Hong Kong: Oxford University Press, 1989). For more recent contributions, see Ian Scott, "Political Transformation in Hong Kong: From Colony to Colony," in *Hong Kong–Guangdong Link: Partnership in Flux*, edited by Alvin Y. So and Reginald Kwok Yin-wang (Hong Kong: Hong Kong University Press, 1995), pp. 189–223 and Jermain T. M. Lam, "The Political Culture of Voters: Reflection on the Legitimacy of the Hong Kong Government," in *25 Years of Social and Economic Development in Hong Kong*, edited by B. Leung and T. Wong (Hong Kong: Hong Kong University Press, 1994), pp. 236–51.

[7] Seymour Martin Lipset, "Social Conflict, Legitimacy and Democracy," in *Legitimacy and the State*, edited by William Connolly (Oxford: Basil Blackwell, 1984), p. 89.

provided for under the Sino-British Joint Declaration. It is therefore not surprising to see that as this change of supreme political power is approaching, people begin to wonder whether the departing colonial regime's right to rule has become untenable.

The leading scholar in exploring this issue is Professor Ian Scott.[8] Scott believes that the crisis of legitimacy in the transition period in Hong Kong stems from the loss of autonomy of the Hong Kong Government as both the current and future sovereign powers, Britain and China, begin to interfere substantially in matters affecting the future of Hong Kong. This interference is inevitable, given the fact that China has never recognized Hong Kong as a separate entity in the negotiations on its future and the Joint Declaration mandates both Britain and China to initiate changes in Hong Kong's affairs to secure a smooth transition. The controversial development of representative government in Hong Kong during the transition period is a prominent example in this respect.

According to Scott, the problem of loss of autonomy of the Hong Kong Government is complicated by the issue of consent, as the emerging middle class in Hong Kong, with their rising democratic aspirations, begins to lose faith in the colonial government's ability to protect their interests and to satisfy their demands for greater democracy in the face of Chinese intervention and opposition. This, according to Scott, results in an enduring crisis of legitimacy for the colonial regime.

One of Scott's major contributions to the political studies of Hong Kong is that through his analysis, he puts the question of legitimacy firmly on the agenda of Hong Kong's transitional politics. As reflections on political legitimacy should be on the *grounds*, not the causes, of a government's authority,[9] it is imperative to understand systematically the political values held most dearly by the people of Hong Kong in this period in order to see how the governments of Hong Kong, future and current, can justify their right to rule in the light of these values.

That would be a daunting task for any student of politics to accomplish. I would not pretend that the space of this chapter, nor my current competence in the subject, would allow me to adequately tackle this enormously

---

[8] See Ian Scott, *Political Change and the Crisis of Legitimacy.*

[9] See Michael Oakeshott, "The Authority of the State," in *Religion, Politics and the Moral Life*, edited by Timothy Fuller (New Haven and London: Yale University Press, 1993), Chapter 5.

interesting question. Instead, what I modestly propose is to offer a number of observations from recent studies on the question of legitimacy and transitional politics of Hong Kong.

Firstly, I would argue that if recent empirical researches on the political values of the people of Hong Kong are of any substance, it is misleading to suggest that the British Hong Kong Government is undergoing an enduring crisis of legitimacy.

The transition period has created various problems of governance for the Hong Kong Government, not the least its inability to make authoritative decisions alone on issues straddling 1997. It is also not to be denied that the authority of the colonial government is, naturally, declining. But it would be more appropriate to describe these challenges as putting the Hong Kong Government in a potential crisis situation, the mishandling of which could indeed deprive the colonial administration of its right to rule at this sensitive time.

Secondly, I wish to argue that the Hong Kong Government has, by and large, been able to maintain its authority at an acceptable level in the last years of the transition partly because of the implementation of Governor Christopher Patten's controversial constitutional reform proposals of 1992.[10] Patten's reform could be regarded as a response by the British side to adapt to new grounds of legitimacy in the light of changing political values in Hong Kong. This was one of the last major attempts by the British side to maintain its right to rule. Intentional or not, these changes would create important hurdles for the future Hong Kong Special Administrative Region (HKSAR) Government to overcome before it can acquire a decent level of legitimacy among the people of Hong Kong.

Thirdly, the fact that British rule is alien in Hong Kong should make it an easy target of attack by Chinese patriots. Also, with the resumption of sovereignty by the Chinese Government, it is natural to expect a rise of pro-China sentiment among the people of Hong Kong. Although the potential threat of Chinese patriotism has always been there, it is interesting to note that, on its own, it has never been able to shake the foundation of British rule in Hong Kong. This is so, partly because out of larger strategic and national considerations, successive Chinese authorities have been

---

[10] "The Governor's Annual Address to the Legislative Council," in *Hong Kong Hansard: Reports of the Sittings of the Legislative Council of Hong Kong*, 7 October 1992, paras. 101–147.

reluctant to see the collapse of British rule in Hong Kong. Equally important is that, even many patriotic Chinese in Hong Kong have recently
started to embrace an emerging Hong Kong identity. While the shape and
content of this identity is still developing, it is fair to say that it identifies
itself more with political pluralism, civil liberties, and tolerance than with
uncritical acceptance of Chinese patriotism. I would contend that this will
have important bearings both on the future central government's policy
towards the HKSAR, and on the legitimacy of the HKSAR Government.

David Beetham's Framework of Legitimacy

Before analysing the political values of the people of Hong Kong, it may
perhaps be useful to look at a conceptual framework of legitimacy as
expounded by the British political theorist, David Beetham. In his interesting and perceptive book *The Legitimation of Power*,[11] Beetham points out
that "[t]he key to understanding the concept of legitimacy lies in the
recognition that it is multi-dimensional in character. It embodies three distinct elements or levels, which are qualitatively different from one another.
The first and most basic level of legitimacy is that of rules. Power can be
said to be legitimate in the first instance if it is acquired and exercised in
accordance with established rules."[12]

Legal validity on its own, however, is not sufficient to secure
legitimacy, as the rules governing the power relations are themselves in
need of justification. Therefore, according to Beetham, the second level of
legitimacy requires that power is legitimate to the extent that the rules of
power can be justified in terms of beliefs and values about common interest
and reciprocal benefit shared by both the dominant and the subordinate
groups in a polity.[13] As for the third level of legitimacy, Beetham argues
that it involves the demonstrable expression of consent on the part of the
subordinate to the particular power relation in which they are involved,
through actions which provide evidence of consent. Beetham believes that
such actions have a publicly symbolic or declaratory force, in that they
constitute an express acknowledgement on the part of the subordinate of

---

[11] David Beetham, *The Legitimation of Power* (Basingstoke: Macmillan
Education, 1991).

[12] *Ibid.*, pp. 15–16.

[13] *Ibid.*, p. 17.

the position of the powerful, which the latter are able to use as confirmation of their legitimacy to third parties not involved in the relationship, or those who have not taken part in any expression of consent.[14] While I agree that the three levels of legitimacy in Beetham's framework are distinct, it is also clear that it is the second level which is central to the justification of the government's right to rule. The first level of legal validity is about the authenticity of rules. When a rule is deemed to be authentic, it must be authoritative. Yet, if an authoritative rule is persistently deemed to be unjust by the people who are obligated to subscribe, sooner or later, the appropriateness or authority of the rule itself will be questioned. Therefore, the people's concept of justice and political values will determine their evaluation of the system of rules which is crucial to legitimacy.

Similarly, although consent acts as an open confirmation of the authority of the system of rules regulating a polity's power relations, consent will only be given if the rules are deemed to be authentic and are consistent with the political values of those who give their consent. Therefore, a study of the question of legitimacy in Hong Kong necessarily presupposes an understanding of the political values of the people of Hong Kong.

Political Values of the People of Hong Kong and Legitimacy

The signing of the Joint Declaration on the question of Hong Kong in 1984 heralded the formal beginning of the transition period. The Joint Declaration provides that China will resume the exercise of sovereignty over Hong Kong with effect from 1 July 1997. Somewhat paradoxically, the Chinese Government which has never recognized the unequal treaties between Britain and the Qing Dynasty on Hong Kong, formally accepted the legal legitimacy of the British rule in the territory for the first time since the end of the dynastic period in China by the signing of the Joint Declaration, which states that the British "will be responsible for the administration of Hong Kong with the object of maintaining and preserving its economic prosperity and social stability"[15] in the transition period.

---

[14] *Ibid.*, p. 18.

[15] See Provision 4 of the *Joint Declaration of the Government of the United Kingdom of Great Britain and Northern Ireland and the Government of the People's Republic of China on the Question of Hong Kong.*

This undoubtedly has given the British side a legal authority over the administration of Hong Kong until 1997 even though Britain and China are at loggerheads over the future of Hong Kong. For example, even though the Chinese Government accuses the Patten reform as contravening the Joint Declaration, the Basic Law, and the agreements reached by the foreign ministers of Britain and China over Hong Kong's political development,[16] China has time and again reiterated its recognition of Britain's sole authority in the administration of Hong Kong until 1997 even after Christopher Patten unilaterally implemented his reform.[17] However, legal validity alone cannot justify the claim that the Patten reform helps to legitimize the Hong Kong Government's rule. Instead, a number of recent empirical researches have shed light on the political values upheld by the people of Hong Kong which are essential to the legitimacy of the Hong Kong Government.

Among the most important findings in these researches, I think three political values are worthy of particular attention. They are the confidence of the people of Hong Kong in the Hong Kong Government (both in terms of trust, fairness and ability); their moderate aspiration for greater and faster democracy; and their high regard for civil liberties.

Lau Siu-kai and Kuan Hsin-chi have found that the most relevant factor in support of the Hong Kong Government's legitimacy is people's trust in

---

[16] For a detailed account of the Chinese position on this controversy, see "Facts about a Few Important Aspects of Sino-British Talks on 1994–95 Electoral Arrangements in Hong Kong," *Chinese Law and Government*, Vol. 29, No. 1 (Jan.–Feb. 1996), pp. 21–50.

[17] Christopher Patten never fails to remind people of this. See, for example, *South China Morning Post* (*SCMP*), 27 March 1996. It must be pointed out that the Joint Declaration has also given China a formal and legal say on Hong Kong affairs before 1997 via the Sino-British Joint Liaison Group, the Land Commission, and other consultative channels. As 1997 approaches, China's interference in Hong Kong affairs has become more prominent. All these have undermined the authority of the Hong Kong Government. But given the legal recognition of the right to rule up to 30 June 1997, the Hong Kong Government's legal authority in respect of the governance of Hong Kong up to the change-over of sovereignty has never been definitively challenged.

the political system and the government.[18] Although, with the advent of the transfer of sovereignty, the level of trust the people have in the Hong Kong Government has been declining, it is still maintained at a reasonable level. For instance, in 1992, Lau and Kuan found that 45% of the people still had a reasonable level of trust in the government, though the figure in 1985 was 72.1%. Also, even though Hong Kong's political system has been evolving relatively rapidly since the 1980s towards limited democratization, the majority of the people, ranging from 56.3% to 75% in the transition period between 1985 to 1992 had consistently thought that the political system in this colony was, though not perfect, by far the best under the circumstances of Hong Kong.

It is important to note that according to Lau and Kuan's surveys, it seems that British colonial rule in Hong Kong has been successful in shaping the political culture of the people into accepting that it is a relatively fair government system which is free from personalized attributes. This is shown by the fact that 54% of the people surveyed believed that a good system was more important, whereas only 11.6% thought that a good leader was. As regards people's perception of the fairness of the Hong Kong Government, only 18.1% complained of the unfairness of the government, while 23.5% were satisfied and 51.4% found the government's performance above average.[19]

The career civil servants' perceived ability to rule Hong Kong was also evident in Lau and Kuan's surveys. A total of 72% of the people agreed that Hong Kong should continue to be ruled by the civil servants.[20] According to another survey in 1994 carried out by Ming Sing, the Hong Kong Government enjoyed even higher political trust (61.3%) than the directly elected Legislative Council (Legco) members (60.4%).[21] Christopher Patten, the Governor, has consistently scored around 55%, 61% and 61% for political trust, working ability, and closeness to the people respectively in the past

---

[18] Lau Siu-kai and Kuan Hsin-chi, "Hong Kong People's Attitude towards Political Authority and the Legitimacy of the Colonial Government," p. 412.

[19] *Ibid.*, pp. 389 and 412–13.

[20] *Ibid.*, p. 386.

[21] See Ming Sing's unpublished paper, "Public Support for Chris Patten's Reform and Democratization in Hong Kong," 1996, p. 43.

four years.[22] All these point to the fact that the people of Hong Kong value the government system because they think that it is fair and trustworthy, and because they trust the civil servants.

In many scholarly researches on political beliefs of the people of Hong Kong during the transition period, there is a loud and clear message that the people want greater democracy. In Lau and Kuan's 1992 survey, almost 60% of the people wanted further development of democracy in Hong Kong.[23] In Ming Sing's survey in 1994, 71% of the voting public agreed that Hong Kong should speed up its democratization process.[24] However, a closer look would reveal that the aspiration for democracy does not really undermine the legitimacy of the so-called executive-led government. Rather, there are evidences to suggest that this non-elected government is regarded as quite democratic.

In a survey conducted by Rowena Kwok and Elaine Chan a week prior to the September 1995 Legco elections, after which a wholly elected Legco was formed for the first time in Hong Kong's history, 47.2% of the respondents regarded the present political arrangement in Hong Kong as democratic. This was about 10% more than those who regarded it as undemocratic.[25] The reason for this, apparently, lies in the fact that more people in Hong Kong regard "government by consultation" as democratic. In Kwok and Chan's survey, 35.8% of the people agreed with this, very much in line with Lau and Kuan's surveys from 1988 to 1992, where 35.9% to 44.2% of the people surveyed held the same belief, leading those who held that democracy was "government by elections" by a margin of over 10% on an average.[26] In Ming Sing's survey, the top three most important

---

[22] *Ming Pao*, 8 July 1996.

[23] Lau Siu-kai and Kuan Hsin-chi, "Hong Kong People's Attitude towards Political Authority and the Legitimacy of Colonial Government," p. 386.

[24] Ming Sing, "Public Support for Chris Patten's Reform and Democratization in Hong Kong," p. 38.

[25] Rowena Kwok and Elaine Chan, "Political Culture and Prospects of Democratization in Hong Kong" (paper presented at a conference on the 1995 Legco elections at The Chinese University of Hong Kong on 17 and 18 May 1996, pp. 10–11). This paper will be published in a forthcoming book *Institutional Change and the Political Transition in Hong Kong*, edited by Ian Scott (Macmillan).

[26] Lau Siu-kai and Kuan Hsin-chi, "Hong Kong People's Attitude towards Political Authority and the Legitimacy of Colonial Government," pp. 386–87.

properties of democracy regarded by the respondents were freedom (23.5%), the rule of law (16.4%), and consultative government (14.7%).[27] Again, none of these properties is directly related to elections.

Although the aspiration for democracy does not seem to undermine the legitimacy of the colonial government, it does demonstrate that the people of Hong Kong believe that the power of the government should be checked. In 1992, 50.1% of the people agreed with this, with only 36.1% dissenting.[28] In addition, in 1995, close to 85% of the people believed that the government should let political parties of different convictions exist, while about 75% of them thought that even if government's efficiency were at stake, citizens should be allowed to participate in public affairs.[29] Again, it is clear that the ability to rule is regarded as different from the right to rule, though to the people of Hong Kong, the concept of political participation means something less than universal suffrage and direct political accountability of the government.

In addition to the support for political opposition and the right to participate, recent empirical researches also found that the people of Hong Kong were zealous of their civil liberties. I have already referred to Ming Sing's findings that freedom and the rule of law were the two most highly regarded properties of democracy as seen by the people.

If the government is expected to respect people's freedom and the rule of law, certainly the people's political inclination is for limited government. In the same survey, Ming Sing found that to secure individual freedom was the goal most cherished by the people of Hong Kong in the run-up to 1997. In Kwok and Chan's survey in 1995, there was almost universal agreement that everyone was entitled to freedom of speech, over 61% of the people supported the right to demonstrate even if such action might cause inconvenience to others.[30]

In summary, it seems clear from recent empirical researches that at the justification level of legitimacy, the people of Hong Kong believe that since

---

[27] Ming Sing, "Public Support for Chris Patten's Reform and Democratization in Hong Kong," p. 40.

[28] Lau Siu-kai and Kuan Hsin-chi, "Hong Kong People's Attitude towards Political Authority and the Legitimacy of Colonial Government," p. 398.

[29] Rowena Kwok and Elaine Chan, "Political Culture and Prospects of Democratization in Hong Kong," p. 11.

[30] *Ibid.*, p. 17.

the government is regarded as relatively fair and trustworthy, they are ready to subscribe to its authority, provided that the government consults the people, respects political opposition, keeps its power under check, upholds individual freedom and the rule of law, and guarantees the civil liberties of the people. At the same time, there is a general support for speeding up the process of democratization in Hong Kong, though this does not amount to a large scale support for popular sovereignty or making the selection of government dependent mainly on popular choice by elections.

In respect of the third level of legitimacy, namely the expression of consent, with the gradual development of elections in the Legco, political participation in Hong Kong is certainly on the rise. In 1981, before the introduction of elections at the District Board and Legco levels, only 6,195 voters turned out to vote in the Urban Council elections. Yet in 1995, when the Legco had all its members selected by direct or indirect elections, almost 1.34 million votes were cast, though the overall turnout rates remained modest.[31] While it is true that for the majority, participation seldom goes beyond voting, it is nevertheless safe to say that the tremendous increase in the absolute number of people participating in the evolving political system during the transition period vindicates the assumption that the people of Hong Kong have been responding quite well to the opening up of the political system and their participation is, if not a clear and active expression of consent to the political development here, evidence of a support for it.

An Enduring Crisis of Legitimacy?

In view of the empirical findings and analysis in the above section, it seems implausible to contend that the Hong Kong Government is suffering from an enduring crisis of legitimacy, a claim most persuasively advocated by Ian Scott.[32] Scott's main arguments are that a crisis of legitimacy often

---

[31] Kuan Hsin-chi, "Escape from Politics: Hong Kong's Predicament of Political Development?" (1996), p. 21. This paper will appear in *International Journal of Public Administration*, Vol. 21 (Summer 1998).

[32] Ian Scott, *Political Change and the Crisis of Legitimacy.*

represents two related problems: firstly, the withdrawal of consent or acquiescence to government actions by a significant proportion of the governed; and, secondly, the loss of governmental autonomy. Both problems would seriously undermine a government's ability to make and implement authoritative decisions. It should be clear that, in theory, the loss of autonomy is a much more serious problem for legitimacy than consent withdrawal, as while a loss of autonomy is a loss of authority and it is impossible to have legitimacy without authority,[33] it is almost impossible to have the consent of all even for a highly legitimate government.

Scott believes that the crisis of legitimacy in the transition period of Hong Kong stemmed initially from a loss of autonomy of the Hong Kong Government, as both Britain and China have interfered in matters affecting the future of the territory after 1982. These matters range from constitutional and economic development, to the granting of franchises and other infrastructural and social policies.[34] Scott further contends that, with the growth of democratic aspiration among the middle class in Hong Kong and the loss of confidence in the Hong Kong Government's ability to withstand Chinese encroachment on Hong Kong's constitutional, political and human rights development, the crisis becomes an enduring one.

Indeed, Scott argues that the earlier part of the transition period (1984–1989) witnessed an erosion of legitimacy on the part of the colonial administration as the rising democratic aspirations of the people of Hong Kong were frustrated by the colonial administration's acquiescence to China's conservative approach to political reform in Hong Kong. Their demands for more responsive decision-making process were denied by the British and Chinese Governments in the Daya Bay Nuclear Plant incident in 1986; and their concern about freedom of speech was foolishly threatened by the government's enactment of the Public Order (Amendment) Bill in 1987 which, among other things, made the publication of "false news" an

---

[33] Therefore, when Anthony B. L. Cheung says that Hong Kong's Legco "has the legitimacy but not the real power," he is confused about the concept of legitimacy. See Cheung, "The Civil Service in Transition," in *The Other Hong Kong Report 1995*, edited by Stephen Y. L. Cheung and Stephen M. H. Sze (Hong Kong: The Chinese University Press, 1995), p. 79.

[34] Ian Scott, *Political Change and the Crisis of Legitimacy*, Chapter 8.

offence.[35] After the proclamation of the Basic Law in 1990, Scott thinks that the "high degree of autonomy" as guaranteed under the Joint Declaration becomes nothing but a sham, for "[t]he Basic Law is a profoundly antidemocratic document,"[36] which would bar full direct elections to all Legco seats at least until 2007.[37] In addition, Scott believes that the Basic Law provides for the erosion of Hong Kong's autonomy as the HKSAR, among other things, will come directly under the Central People's Government. The Chief Executive will be appointed by the Chinese Government, and the Legco, instead of holding the executive accountable, will owe its existence to the Chief Executive as the latter can dismiss the former. Also, Article 18 of the Basic Law provides for direct interference of the central government in Hong Kong if the Standing Committee of the National People's Congress decides to declare Hong Kong to be in a state of turmoil.[38] Scott's analysis is more persuasive if we apply it to the earlier part, particularly before the June 4 Beijing crackdown in 1989, of the transition period when the British side was adopting the so-called convergence strategy whose main architect was Sir Percy Cradock, the foreign policy adviser to the then British Prime Minister, Mrs. Margaret Thatcher. In essence, the convergence strategy believes that given the great disparity of power between Britain and China over the future of Hong Kong, cooperation through tough negotiation between the two sovereign powers is the best way to secure the best possible future for Hong Kong. Any unilateral action by the British side would only be counter-productive as

---

[35] *Ibid.*, Chapter 7. The "false news" clause was subsequently taken out in January 1989.

[36] Ian Scott, "Political Transformation in Hong Kong," p. 202.

[37] According to the Basic Law, only up to half, i.e. 30, of the HKSAR Legco seats will be directly elected before 2007. After 2007, if Hong Kong wants to increase the number of directly elected seats, it needs the approval of two-thirds of all Legco members, half of whom are themselves not directly elected, together with the agreement of the HKSAR Chief Executive, who, again, is not directly elected.

[38] Ian Scott, "Political Transformation in Hong Kong," p. 199.

any such democratic reform would stand no chance to stick after the change-over.[39] Scott is certainly right in saying that this strategy would only lead to loss of the Hong Kong Government's, and indeed the British Government's, autonomy over the important issue of constitutional development in Hong Kong in accordance with their interpretation of the promises made in the Joint Declaration, particularly those promises regarding a high degree of autonomy and the structure of the future political system in the HKSAR. The reason for this is simple. By according cooperation with China the highest priority, and avoiding unilateral action almost at any cost, Britain in effect would have given a veto power to China and would be perceived by the people of Hong Kong not only as losing its capacity to make authoritative decisions, but also as increasingly irrelevant.

But with the change in British policy over Hong Kong after the June 4 incident (which not only shocked the conscience of the people of Hong Kong, but also demonstrated vividly that civil liberties in Hong Kong after 1997 could be blatantly violated by an authoritarian regime which was ready to order its troops to shoot at its people who organized peaceful protests), and the appointment of a political heavyweight, the former Tory Party Chairman, Christopher Patten as the new Governor in 1992, the British side seems to be determined to regain that autonomy before 1997 by risking confrontation with China if necessary to speed up democratization. The Hong Kong Government, under the leadership of Patten, who effectively becomes the main policy-maker on Hong Kong's constitutional future on the British side, has again become a central authoritative player in the political development of Hong Kong, at least before the change of sovereignty. Thus, Scott's analysis, and the so-called enduring crisis of legitimacy of the Hong Kong Government, has become less appropriate and tenable in the Patten era.

Patten's Political Reform and Legitimacy

I do not think it is necessary to recall all the details concerning the Patten

---

[39] For a fuller exposition of the rationale behind the convergence strategy, see Sir Percy Cradock's memo to the House of Commons' Foreign Affairs Committee in *China Law and Government*, Vol. 29, No. 1 (Jan.–Feb. 1996), pp. 51–56.

reform in this chapter, as they are well known already.[40] I would only touch on the strategy adopted by Patten in introducing and implementing his reform proposals so as to strengthen the legitimacy of the Hong Kong Government in the last years of British rule.

As the first level of legitimacy is about legal validity, the Patten reform had to be designed in accordance with the Joint Declaration and the Basic Law, both of which are the legal foundations of the future HKSAR. Both documents are understandably written in general terms. Also, since the British Government had previously adopted a convergence strategy with the Chinese side over Hong Kong's political development, the Basic Law deliberately remains open to the question of the formation of the first HKSAR Legco in anticipation of working out the details with the British side. It is precisely these grey areas which allowed Patten the room to give the documents a liberal interpretation and to introduce his constitutional package without violating the provisions of these two documents.

Patten is very conscious of the need not to go beyond the established legal limits in his proposals, which is why time and again, he reminds people that his democratic reform is "wholly in line with the letter and the spirit of the Joint Declaration and the Basic Law, and other understandings

---

[40] See Note 10. The design of the Patten reform is meant to open the channel of participation in the Legco elections as far, open and fair as possible within the parameters of the Joint Declaration and the Basic Law. Patten could not touch the 20 directly elected seats as this is specifically provided for in the Basic Law. What he proposed to do was: (1) to enlarge the franchise of the 9 new functional constituencies by allowing all working people in Hong Kong to have the right to vote for a candidate in the constituency to which his profession belongs; (2) in the traditional 21 functional constituencies, voting would be on individual rather than on corporate basis, thus expanding the franchise in these areas by more than 5 times; (3) all appointed seats in the District Boards and the two municipal councils would be abolished, making all their members returned by direct elections, except those *ex-officio* members in the New Territories District Boards and Heung Yee Kuk's elected representatives in the Regional Council; (4) the Election Committee, which would elect 10 Legco members, would be composed of all directly elected District Board members, making the Election Committee elections more suscep-tible to public control; and (5) an independent Boundary and Election Commission would be formed to ensure fairness in defining the boundaries for constituencies and other electoral arrangements.

between Britain and China." Patten further argues that no respectable legal opinion contradicts his claims on this issue.[41]

China was infuriated when Patten announced his proposals without prior consultation with Beijing. The Chinese Government would have preferred a more conservative interpretation of the documents for fear of losing control over Hong Kong's political development. They regarded Patten's initiatives as illegitimate. Although the two sides entered into seventeen rounds of negotiations between April and November 1993 to try to reach an agreement, the gulf between them proved too great for compromise. Beijing began preparation to set up a so-called "second stove" by creating an appointed Preliminary Working Committee (PWC) which, in effect, was meant to be a shadow government with the aim to dismantling what would have been established by the Patten reform and other British measures deemed to be contrary to the Basic Law.

Notwithstanding this, what is important is that even though the Patten reform was under constant virulent attacks from China, there is little evidence that the people of Hong Kong regarded the reform as illegitimate. In fact, Patten first made public his proposals in Hong Kong and submitted them for approval to the Legco which could reject them. Instead, the Legco endorsed it by a vote of 32 to 24 on 30 June 1994. Although the last Legco under British rule will not survive the Chinese resumption of their sovereignty over Hong Kong, it is far more representative and perceived as more fair than the Chinese proposed Provisional Legco which was selected by a 400-member Selection Committee many of whose members were electing themselves into the Provisional Legco. The democrats in Hong Kong, who won over half of the seats in the 1995 Legco elections, and many people of Hong Kong have already indicated their opposition to the creation of the Provisional Legco. The Democratic Party even goes so far as to refuse any dealing in affairs related to the Provisional Legco.[42]

---

[41] See Patten's speech, "Change Is Not on Our Agenda," *SCMP*, 11 July 1996.

[42] For the Democratic Party's stance on the Provisional Legco, see *Outspoken*, 15 January 1996, p. 9, in Chinese. For the Bar Association's stance, see *SCMP*, 9 July 1996. Patten is always ready to challenge the legality and necessity of the proposed Provisional Legco. Time and again he challenges the Chinese authorities to "justify their actions, demonstrate their legality, and defend the credibility of whatever replacement is proposed" for the 1995 Legco. See *SCMP*, 11 July 1996.

Given the fact that political opposition, political participation, and civil liberties are important political values upheld by the people of Hong Kong, anything less than a liberal interpretation of the promises of the Joint Declaration would be regarded as, to use Patten's phrase, "hollowing out" of the Joint Declaration.[43] Although an executive-led government is still acceptable, a consultative government without political opposition and a regression in democratic development would probably make it very difficult for the current and future Hong Kong Governments to govern the territory. What is more, with this liberal and unilateral approach apparently matching the political aspirations of the people of Hong Kong, Britain could have an onus to intervene with the post-1997 political development in Hong Kong if the Chinese Government adopts a less than liberal interpretation of the Joint Declaration and the Basic Law.[44]

Chinese Patriotism, Hong Kong Identity and Legitimacy

Already, there are signs of problems in China's efforts at setting up the HKSAR. The PWC, the first official organization created with the specific task of setting up the first HKSAR Government, is described as having done "little to contribute to a smooth transition and much to make the community fearful about life after 1997," because of its ill-advised proposals for reversing the democratic development in Hong Kong, and

---

[43] *SCMP*, 11 July 1996.

[44] In his controversial *Newsweek*, 13 May 1996 interview, Patten made this point crystal clear when he criticized the convergence strategy: "If we'd made the accommodations that some old Sinologists had wanted, we would now have in place less freedom, less democracy, less protection of human rights. All that would have had happened is that we would have had those things before 1997, with Britain's connivance and Britain's imprimatur, Britain's chop. Who do you think the demonstrations [against the Preparatory Committee] would have been against?" See p. 13. The British Prime Minister, John Major, also made it clear in his speech in Hong Kong in March 1996 that Britain would have a duty to pursue every legal and other avenue available to it to rectify any breach of the Joint Declaration after 1997. See *SCMP*, 5 March 1996.

because its thirty-eight Hong Kong appointees "failed to speak out against even the most misguided ideas."[45]

Nor has the successor of the PWC, the Preparatory Committee (PC), fared better, even though 96 of its 150 appointed members are prominent members of the Hong Kong community. In a territory-wide survey published in June 1996, only 1.2% of the respondents had high confidence in the PC, compared with 94.9% with low to no confidence in the same committee.[46] The PC is generally regarded as secretive (because of its confidentiality rule) and unrepresentative and people are sceptical of its ability to defend the interests of Hong Kong. Its level of intolerance was graphically demonstrated by its Secretary General, Mr. Lu Ping's public hostility towards Mr. Fredrick Fung, the only Hong Kong member who dared to vote against the creation of the Provisional Legco at a PC plenary meeting in March 1996.

In spite of this, the Chinese Government, being the lawful government in China, has the ultimate authority to take decisions over the future of the HKSAR. The fact that Beijing holds supreme power over Hong Kong has already proved adequate to induce many Hong Kong elite to offer their allegiance to the future sovereign. Aside from the PWC and the PC, hundreds of community leaders have become appointed advisers to the Chinese Government on Hong Kong affairs. The growth of pro-China elite in Hong Kong is gathering pace.[47]

But as argued above, legal authority will only be secured if its exercise is found compatible with people's central political values. At the moment,

---

[45] See the editorial of *SCMP*, 6 December 1995. PWC's more problematic proposals included the creation of the Provisional Legco which the general public will not have the right to vote for its members; the requirement for civil servants to give prior notice to stay after 1997; the dilution of the Bill of Rights and the reinstatement of the six draconian laws; the cut-off date for returnees to retain the right of abode in Hong Kong; and the requirement to vet school textbooks. Some of these proposals were subsequently watered down or revised. See Chris Yeung, "Players in the Power Game," *SCMP*, 7 December 1995, p. 17.

[46] *SCMP*, 24 June 1996, p. 14.

[47] See Sonny Lo Shiu-hing and Donald H. McMillen, "A Profile of the 'Pro-China Hong Kong Elite': Images and Perception," *Issues and Studies*, Vol. 31, No. 6 (June 1995), pp. 98–127.

it is doubtful whether China has shown adequate sensitivity towards political pluralism, civil liberties, tolerance, and greater participation in governance desired by the people of Hong Kong. The fact that Beijing failed to include any leading Hong Kong democrat,[48] except members of the ambivalent Association for Democracy and People's Livelihood in efforts to set up the HKSAR, may suggest that the legitimacy of the future HKSAR Government is yet to be tested. Indeed, since the Provisional Legco is not explicitly provided for in the Joint Declaration and the Basic Law and its related documents, this not only makes people who take the rule of law seriously feel uneasy, but has reportedly prompted Martin Lee, the leader of the Democratic Party, to prepare to challenge the legality of the Provisional Legco in court once it has been established.

However, one must not forget that British colonial rule in Hong Kong, no matter how benign, is an alien rule which is an affront to the Chinese state and Chinese patriots. Chinese patriotism in Hong Kong is certainly a central political value to be reckoned with, which could easily be exploited by the Chinese state to rally support. Tung Chee-hwa, the first HKSAR Chief Executive designate, proclaims in his political platform that he is proud of being a Chinese.

According to Ming K. Chan, a Hong Kong historian, Chinese patriotism has played important roles in many of the major social disturbances in pre-war Hong Kong.[49] For example, the 1912–1913 Tramway Boycott was triggered off by the colonial administration's ban on the importation and circulation of Chinese currency in Hong Kong which "was regarded by many Chinese in Hong Kong as an unfriendly act and highly disrespectful toward the new republic" just established in China.[50] In May

---

[48] Only one minor member of the Democratic Party breaks rank to apply for nomination to the Provisional Legco elections despite press reports alleging quite intensive lobbying by some Pro-China elite to do so. This indicates the solidarity of the democrats in their opposition against this retrogressive measure in Hong Kong.

[49] Ming K. Chan, "Hong Kong in Sino-British Conflict: Mass Mobilization and the Crisis of Legitimacy, 1912–26," in *Precarious Balance: Hong Kong between China and Britain, 1842–1992*, edited by Ming K. Chan (Hong Kong: Hong Kong University Press, 1994), Chapter 3.

[50] *Ibid.*, p. 29.

1919, as a spillover of the May Fourth Movement in the mainland, a boycott of Japanese goods developed among Chinese merchants in Hong Kong.[51] The 1925–1926 Canton–Hong Kong General Strike-Boycott against British imperialism, which lasted for sixteen months, drawing some 250,000 Hong Kong strikers and their families back to the Pearl River delta, not only paralysed the colony, but was supported and encouraged by the Canton [Guangdong] authorities, and involved prominent Chinese revolutionary leaders like Liao Zhongkai and Zhou Enlai.[52]

Yet for wider strategic or national considerations, we see that Chinese patriotism in Hong Kong, though certainly a potential threat to the British rule, has always given way to greater interests of the Chinese state. The 1925–1926 Strike-Boycott came to an end largely because the Nationalist authorities in Canton thought that in view of the imminent launch of the Northern Expedition, it was expedient to conclude the Strike-Boycott with the British administration in Hong Kong.[53] Similarly, when the Communist Party rose to power in 1949, the party leadership made no attempt to recover Hong Kong because of its economic value to China under British rule. Zhou Enlai, the Chinese Premier, even said that Hong Kong would be a valuable instrument for China to divide the British from the Americans in the Cold War.[54] Even at the height of the Cultural Revolution in 1967 when anti-British riots were rampant in the colony, pro-China factions in Hong Kong never once publicly demanded the repossession of Hong Kong by China.[55]

With the resumption of Chinese sovereignty, one may think that these so-called greater national priorities restraining the growth of Chinese patriotism in Hong Kong would become history. Yet the Diaoyu islands disputes in the summer of 1996 clearly demonstrated that Beijing was more

---

[51] *Ibid.*, pp. 45–52.

[52] *Ibid.*, pp. 47–48.

[53] *Ibid.*, p. 47.

[54] Steve Tsang, "Maximum Flexibility, Rigid Framework: China's Policy towards Hong Kong and Its Implications," *Journal of International Affairs*, Vol. 49, No. 2 (Winter 1996), pp. 419–20.

[55] John D. Young, "The Building Years: Maintaining a China–Hong Kong–Britain Equilibrium, 1950–71," in *Precarious Balance*, p. 142.

afraid of the rise of spontaneous mass patriotism in China and Hong Kong than the territorial threat from Japan. Its lukewarm response to Hong Kong patriots' demand for stronger actions against Japanese occupation of the Diaoyu islands could well be repeated even after Hong Kong reverts to the motherland. Further, Hong Kong's developing pluralism also enables most people to be aware of the distinction between loyalty to the nation *vis-à-vis* loyalty to the government. The fact that the Democratic Party of Hong Kong was at the forefront of this patriotic movement (by sending two members, together with others, to attempt to land on the islands in face of Japan's military blockade) forced the Chinese authorities to admit that even the democrats were patriotic, though many leading members of the Democratic Party have been labelled as subversive by Beijing after the June 4 incident because of their support to the dissident students. In doing so, the democrats have also demonstrated that patriotism is not a state monopoly. It is consistent with demands for greater democracy and political pluralism, values dear to many people in Hong Kong who fear that their rights and liberties may be curtailed under Chinese rule.

Behind these political values, it is possible to discern a distinct Hong Kong identity emerging, an identity which is different from the traditional monistic, harmony conscious, and submissive Chinese identity. To be sure, given the vicissitudes of political life in China and Hong Kong, this emerging pluralist, rights-conscious, and participation-oriented identity will most likely have an uncertain future. Yet when 70% of the people regard themselves as Hongkongers or Hong Kong Chinese rather than as Chinese, it is a significant development,[56] and the political values constituting this identity would play a major role in the legitimation not only of the HKSAR Government, but also of China's policy over Hong Kong.

> By 1989 China had been open for more than ten years, and we knew enough about what was happening there to have no more illusions. We knew that the country was fraught with problems, we knew that corruption was very bad, we knew the people had a lot of resentment towards the bureaucracy ...
>
> [W]here there is conflict, or competition between two systems, the better system always prevails.... You can already see how much Hong Kong has influenced China's development. In many of the major cities in China you can see Hong Kong culture spreading very extensively. I have friends in Hong Kong who

---

[56] Sonny Lo and Donald H. McMillen, "A Profile of the 'Pro-China Hong Kong Elite'," pp. 100–1.

have come here from China over the past ten years or so. Now they tell me they find it very frustrating to do business with their counterparts from across the border. They can see the deficiencies in the systems which operate in China; they have become Hong Kong people.[57]

These are not the words of a Hong Kong democrat. Nor do they come from an ordinary Hong Kong person. These are the words of a Chinese patriot, the Chairman of the Beijing-sponsored political party in the territory, the Democratic Alliance for Betterment of Hong Kong, Mr. Tsang Yuk-shing, whose party commands forty-six votes in the Selection Committee. Tsang is a Hongkonger, as are many of his friends who came from China just a decade ago. By his own admission, the fall of the "Gang of Four" in China in 1976 made him question his pro-China communist ideology.[58] If patriotism is not founded on government ideology and is perhaps even critical of the government system, it certainly would augur well for the emerging pluralist Hong Kong identity. If political values form an indispensable part of the foundation of a state's legitimacy, the HKSAR authorities will probably find that ignoring this emerging identity will not only be extremely unwise, but could also be at their peril.

---

[57] Tsang Yuk-shing, "Coming of Age in 1967," in *Hong Kong Remembers*, edited by Sally Blyth and Ian Wotherspoon (Hong Kong: Oxford University Press, 1996), pp. 100–1.

[58] *Ibid.*, p. 100.

2

A Catalyst for Change? The Hong Kong Special Administrative Region and Chinese Politics

Michael Yahuda

Understandably, most of the concern about the implications of the retrocession of Hong Kong's sovereignty has centred on Hong Kong itself, while the implications for China have been relatively neglected. Given the enormous disparity between tiny Hong Kong and giant China and the vulnerability of the territory's economic system and its way of life to influence and pressure from the north, it may seem strange to suggest that the return of Hong Kong to the Chinese motherland poses very serious issues for the development of politics in China and for the conduct of China's foreign relations in particular. In so far as Hong Kong is thought to exercise influence on China it is generally suggested that it is confined to the economic realm. Indeed it has become customary for business people especially to argue that Hong Kong's survival depends upon upholding their business and commercial operations as these are said to be the principal matters in which the Chinese are interested. Nevertheless I shall argue that the recovery of Hong Kong raises fundamental political issues for the Chinese mainland and in the final analysis it is the political rather than the economic interest that will guide policy.

Various reasons account for this. First of all, the recovery of Hong Kong by agreement and in accordance with the concept of "one country, two systems" is seen as a matter of sovereignty and patriotism. It has been portrayed not only as a major step in reversing historical wrongs, but as a major step towards the recovery of the even greater prize of Taiwan. Secondly, at a time of officially inspired resurgence of nationalism designed to hold together a people no longer inspired by communist ideology, China's new leaders cannot afford to be seen to fail this first test of their leadership. Thirdly, the economic influence of Hong Kong is a major factor in sustaining China's high GNP growth rates that fuel the growing prosperity of the people and which in turn underpins the leaders' claim to legitimacy in the post-Soviet era. Fourthly, Hong Kong has been described by China's leaders as their bridge to the international financial community and to the overseas Chinese communities in particular.

Clearly, if China's leaders were to fail to preside over a smooth transition the consequences would be serious and far-reaching. Were the concept of the "one country, two systems" to be seen to have failed in the relatively favourable circumstances of Hong Kong, Beijing would no longer have a viable policy for the peaceful reunification with Taiwan and it would be left with force as the only conceivable option. That could only lead to the intensification of the defence of Taiwan probably with the open assistance of the United States. Indeed relations with Japan and the United States would suffer. A manifest failure in Hong Kong would also damage relations with the Chinese communities overseas, it would undermine confidence of overseas investors not only in Hong Kong, but probably in the mainland as well. The economy on the mainland would suffer and China's leaders would inevitably draw inwards in a mood of truculent defiance. The consequences would be incalculable as social tensions amid a heightened sense of bruised nationalism could lead at one extreme to a kind of fascism or at the other to the effective fragmentation of the country. It is debatable as to which would be worse for the Chinese people and the world around them.

If, however, the transition on 1 July 1997 were to proceed relatively smoothly leading to the emergence of a Hong Kong Special Administrative Region (HKSAR) that did indeed enjoy a considerable degree of autonomy, the beneficial consequences paradoxically could also prove to be highly challenging to the communist regime. To be sure the adverse circumstances that would arise from failure would be reversed. Thus Beijing would feel even more confident about the viability of its approach to Taiwan; relations with Japan and the United States would be eased and the doubts of Southeast Asian governments would abate. Hong Kong would indeed prove to be a bridge to the Chinese communities overseas and to the international financial community. Doubtless the prospects for China's entry into the World Trade Organization (WTO) would improve as confidence grew in Beijing's capacity to handle such a vulnerable symbol and effective model of the values and practices that underpin the international economic system. Yet by allowing Hong Kong to flourish as a separate system under the umbrella of Chinese sovereignty, Beijing may be tolerating a degree of pluralism that could challenge the fundamentals of Communist Party rule in the mainland itself.

By following the precepts of the Basic Law that was endorsed by its own National People's Congress, Beijing would leave Hong Kong to operate under the rule of law, with its apolitical and clean civil service and with a degree of democracy and basic freedoms that before too long would be desired by many in China. For example, it would surely be only a matter of a relatively short time before people in Shanghai would demand for themselves some of the conditions that applied in Hong Kong so that they too could once again become a truly international financial centre. In short Hong Kong could become the trigger or the catalyst for another movement for political reform in China.

A Peculiar Neglect

Curiously, the larger political significance of Hong Kong has been little discussed in Beijing. In fact little attention has been paid to Hong Kong down the years. As a place administered by the British, but technically claimed by China, it has occupied a kind of bureaucratic no-man's land as it was neither a domestic matter nor an issue for foreign affairs. Various local conventions and practices had evolved pragmatically over the years to manage cross-border affairs and to take advantage of the anomalous condition of the territory, while the big questions concerning Hong Kong were kept under the strict personal control of the supreme leaders. Thus Hong Kong was under the personal charge of Mao Zedong and Zhou Enlai and after them Deng Xiaoping took the key decisions. It was he who controlled the negotiations with Britain leading to the Joint Declaration in 1984 and it was he who supervised the key policy issues of the transition thereafter until he became incapacitated by advanced age towards the end of 1993. Interestingly, the official organizations that deal with Hong Kong are not part of any of the major bureaucratic systems (*xitong*) that are inherent in the Chinese administrative system, with the result that they are not linked with the many organizations that have developed economic interests in the territory. The Ministry of Foreign Affairs, which nominally handles negotiations with the British Foreign Office, like similar ministries elsewhere does not have an obvious domestic constituency. The Hong Kong and Macau Affairs Office which enjoys ministerial status under the State Council is not linked or affiliated with any of the other ministries, and unlike its first head, Liao Chengzhi who died in 1983, Lu Ping has not been a close and trusted colleague of the core leader and he is not even a senior figure in the Party hierarchy. The Xinhua Branch in Hong Kong is also an orphan within the Chinese bureaucracy answerable in part to the Ministry of Foreign Affairs, the formal Xinhua Agency in Beijing and a number of different departments of the Central Committee of the Communist Party. Its head, Zhou Nan, like Lu Ping, does not rank high in the Communist Party.

Moreover, unlike the case of Taiwan, which may also be considered to inhabit a kind of limbo that has placed it outside the conventional domestic or external bureaucratic spheres, Hong Kong has not been the subject of prolonged intense concern by the Chinese military and political elites. Similarly it has not been at the core of China's national security interests or at the centre of Beijing's relations with the world's major superpower. The small part that Hong Kong has occupied in Chinese political consciousness may be seen from the absence of a single institute devoted to Hong Kong under the Chinese Academy of Social Sciences or of any similar centre or society at any of the higher education institutions, except for one in Zhongshan University in Guangzhou that focuses mainly on economics. Indeed over the past few years none of my various academic hosts in Beijing were able to identify a single researcher who with whom I could discuss socio-economic developments within Hong Kong, yet there was never an absence of researchers who claimed to have studied these developments within Taiwan. This void was all the more remarkable in view of the many organizations and people who had economic interests in Hong Kong, some of whom like the Bank of China had a cumulative experience of nearly fifty years.

In the absence of informed opinion, it is hardly surprising that myths and stereotypes about Hong Kong and its people flourish in Beijing and elsewhere in north China in particular. At the popular level and even among intellectuals a common view is that the people of Hong Kong are to some extent tainted by having lived under British capitalist colonial rule. Hence they are regarded as corrupt and to be an especially corrupting in-fluence in the mainland, as they are alleged to bribe officials and to exploit disadvantaged fellow countrymen. As compatriots they are thought to have uniquely benefited from Hong Kong's proximity to the mainland which is said to account for much of their prosperity which northern people typically see as the product of a windfall rather than the result of their industry, entrepreneurialism and professionalism. Much of the prejudice of the northerners against the supposedly excessive commercialism and lack of intellectual interests that allegedly typifies the Cantonese is directed still more strongly against the people of Hong Kong. In short there is considerable resentment and envy that is fuelled by ignorance. Even professionals in Beijing exhibit an alarming lack of understanding of China's officially declared position about the concept of "one country, two systems" and how it is to be applied to Hong Kong. Many appear to believe that after the transition to Chinese sovereignty they will be able to find work in Hong Kong where they too will enjoy salaries some hundred fold more than they can earn on the Chinese mainland. All that they will need is the right connections (*guanxi*) with the appropriate officials.

Since the establishment of the People's Republic of China (P.R.C.) in 1949 China and Hong Kong have evolved in fundamentally different ways with very little institutional contact between them. In the early years there were people close to the senior leaders in Beijing such as Liao Chengzhi who had extensive ties with the leading business families in the Chinese communities overseas and members of Zhou Enlai's entourage who were familiar with conditions in Hong Kong during and after the Japanese occupation. But these personal ties that had served Beijing well in the 1950s and into the 1960s were weakened during the political upheavals in China. By the time the elderly survivors in Beijing tried to pick up the pieces again in the late 1970s conditions had changed and they were simply out of touch with the new middle class of Hong Kong and the modernity that had emerged there.

Although Hong Kong people were able to visit family members resident across the border, these social contacts did not impinge on the conduct of the two separate systems. The people of Hong Kong are largely made up of refugees or the children of refugees who had fled from the regime of mainland China, their life experiences have made them different social and political beings. Their evolution under British rule has accustomed them to the rule of law and to operating in a highly complex and diverse civil society where they have enjoyed all the basic liberties of a Western liberal system save the right to choose their rulers. They have not experienced the tumultuous upheavals of the political history of the P.R.C. with the callous loss of life and suffering inflicted on countless millions. Nor have they been subject to the pervasive and often arbitrary discipline of the ruling Communist Party. Even the Chinese officials who are regularly responsible for managing relations with Hong Kong often exhibit a lack of understanding of key characteristics that underpin the territory's way of life. Xu Jiatun, the former head of the Xinhua Branch in Hong Kong complained in 1988 about his communist colleagues back in China: "They always judge capitalism by old standards. They do not notice its changes. Had I not worked in Hong Kong for four years, I would probably have entertained the same idea as those comrades."[1] Local born senior journalists and officials who have lived and worked for Communist publications in Hong Kong for all or most of their lives complain privately that their colleagues from the mainland have a "totally different mentality" that causes them to misunderstand "even simple things" about Hong Kong.[2]

There are signs that senior leaders in Beijing are aware that something is seriously amiss in their understanding of Hong Kong. In a talk in March 1995, Li Ruihuan, a member of the Standing Committee of the Politburo of the Chinese Communist Party, publicly admitted that the leaders had a dangerously insufficient understanding of Hong Kong. He warned that "taking Hong Kong back is an unusually complicated job" with "many issues and difficulties" and that it is "inevitable that we shall fail to manage some things appropriately and well." He then famously compared Hong Kong to a hundred-year-old Yixing teapot whose value lay in some sediments attached to the inside. The well-meaning but ignorant old lady who owned the pot cleaned away the sediments whereupon her prospective purchaser pronounced the pot valueless. Li drove home his message by concluding, "if you don't understand something, you are unaware of what makes it valuable and it will be difficult to keep it intact."[3]

---

[1] Kevin Rafferty, *City on the Rocks: Hong Kong's Uncertain Future*, revised edition (London: Penguin, 1991), p. 492.

[2] Author's interviews with various journalists and officials attached to the Xinhua News Agency and its related newspapers in Hong Kong.

[3] Li Ruihuan's address to the Hong Kong and Macau representatives on the Chinese People's Political Consultative Conference on 13 March 1995 was carried in full in the Hong Kong communist-controlled newspaper, *Wen Wei Po*, and is available in English translation in BBC, *Summary of World Broadcasts*, FE/2253/F1–4.

Hong Kong between the "Browns" and the "Blues"

Since the larger problems posed by the retrocession of sovereignty over Hong Kong have not been openly addressed within China, the question of their impact on Chinese politics will have to be considered through the perspectives of an outside observer with all the risks that entails of oversight and misdirection. In my judgement the reversion of Hong Kong is taking place at a time of great moment in contemporary Chinese history. The process of economic development and reform has reached the point at which fundamental political change is once again on the agenda. In part this arises from the nature of the reform process itself and in part from the character of the unfolding political succession. Since it was first begun way back in December 1978 the reform process has entailed a series of economic cycles of rapid expansion and restraint that have been mirrored politically by cycles of opening out and tightening up (Deng Liqun has referred to them as recurring patterns of *fang* and *shou*). At present China may be said to have engineered a soft landing after the economic leap induced by Deng Xiaoping's "southern tour" of 1992 and the question is whether China should now follow a neo-conservative strategy or take the economic reforms onto the next stage. This may be a defining moment in political terms as it is linked with the question of succession and both are scheduled to be formalized at the next national congress of the Communist Party due only some three months after the reversion of Hong Kong in July 1997.

It may be useful at this point to try and locate these issues in historical perspective. Within China the reversion of the sovereignty of Hong Kong is presented as a major rectification of a historic wrong. The seizure of Hong Kong by the Treaty of Nanking in 1842 — the first of a series of unequal treaties — in conventional Communist historiography marked the beginning of a hundred years of Chinese national humiliation that was only ended with the establishment of the P.R.C. Indeed the nationalist tone of much of Beijing's rhetoric against the West and especially the United States can only be understood against this backlog of wounded pride. In less avowedly nationalist terms, the impact of the West should be seen in broader terms as the challenge of modernity. Since the 1840s China as both a state and a civilization has been reeling from the impact of the forces of the modern world that began with the challenge of the military power and political character of the European states allied to the restless expansion of capitalism and international trade. Indeed the inherent restlessness of dynamic and uncertain change has continued to confront China's leaders ever since. The challenge has been seen by successive Chinese generations as one of trying to retain a distinctive sense of identity while modernizing so as to enable the country to survive and prosper in a hostile world. Every attempt at significant change to meet that challenge has taken the process of adaptation further, but it has so far foundered in the attempt to reconcile the tensions inherent in the process itself.

In broad brush strokes it is possible to depict a fault line that has run through the different stages of Chinese attempts to modernize. On the one side have been those who have stressed the priority of upholding a distinctively Chinese ideology with a paternalist state taking responsibility for administering the economy for the equitable benefit of the general populace. That has required drawing a sharp barrier against the intrusive and destabilizing capitalist forces of the West. This approach has been consistent with the continentalist traditions of the autocratic imperial state that was pilloried in the famous television series of 1988 called *He Shang (River Elegy)* that so angered the party elders. On the other side have been those who have argued in effect for embracing those forces from the West in the interests of catching up with the prosperity and technological levels of the economically advanced countries. Since the former were associated by the *River Elegy* with that long-standing symbol of eternal China, the muddy Yellow River, I have called them the "Browns"; and as the television series depicted the crystal blue waters of the Pacific Ocean into which the river flows as the symbol of modernity and openness I have called the latter the "Blues." Both sides have professed to desire their country to be once again one of the world's leading states enjoying both strength and prosperity. The trouble has been that both may be seen as ultimately defective. The Browns hold out the promise of upholding a distinctive Chinese identity, but at the risk of falling further behind the technological levels of others until the country should once again be vulnerable to attack as in the 19th century. The Blues promise to ensure the attainment of sufficiently high levels of prosperity and technology, but at the price of a loss of a distinctive identity and the fragmentation of the state.

These views may be seen as latter day versions of the *ti-yong* dilemma according to which the Confucianist reformers of the 19th century sought to retain the essence of Chinese culture and its traditional way of life by just grafting on Western technological know-how for practical purposes. Deng Xiaoping appears to believe that it is possible to retain a socialist political system while integrating the economy into the market-based international economy and he has called the resulting hybrid "Socialism with Chinese characteristics." It is a rather volatile mix of the Browns and the Blues. Lucian Pye has suggested that the Chinese would have done better to have described modernity as the universal essence and then allowed for cultural variations in its application — perhaps as exemplified by the Japanese experience.[4]

Nevertheless Deng has clearly rescued China from the disastrous period of inward-looking convulsions of Mao Zedong's later years and in the process he has once again brought in the Chinese communities beyond the mainland into the mainstream. So far their contribution has been confined ostensibly to economics, but in reality their influence extends far beyond that to include culture and senses of identity.[5] It can be argued that not since the early days Sun Yatsen's republicanism have these external Chinese communities been so influential in helping to shape the development of the mainland. Unlike their mainland cousins, they have been exposed to a whole range of cosmopolitan and capitalistic influences.

None more so than Hong Kong which has been rightly called the "capital of the Overseas Chinese" since many have either emanated from there or passed through *en route* to the outside world, but more fundamentally, because the different varieties of Chinese overseas can feel at home in Hong Kong where more often than not they can find fellow speakers of their dialects and, more significantly, they are free from unwanted challenges in political, cultural or ethnic terms.

For some years there has been discussion in the mainland about the feasibility of taking Singapore as a kind of a model. Different leaders have found its mix of politics and economics appealing as a mix of tight social discipline allied to a capitalism of a highly efficient and open kind. But now they will have under the umbrella of their sovereignty the Special Administrative Region of Hong Kong (HKSAR). Whether the leaders like

---

[4] Lucien W. Pye, "Deng Xiaoping and China's Political Culture," *The China Quarterly*, Voi. 135 (September 1993), p. 442.

[5] See *The China Quarterly*, Vol. 136 (December 1993), Special Issue on "Greater China" and in particular the articles by Harry Harding, "The Concept of 'Greater China': Themes, Variations and Reservations," pp. 660–86 and by Thomas B. Gold, "Go with Your Feelings: Hong Kong and Taiwan Popular Culture in Greater China," pp. 907–25.

it or not, the HKSAR will inevitably serve as a model of a kind. In its own way it may be seen as a relatively acceptable example of a Chinese attempt at modernization. Although it grew up under British colonialism, it is the Hong Kong Chinese who have built up the place and transformed it into one of the world's most successful economies. To be sure they benefited from the British application of the conventions of the Common Law and an apolitical civil service and they have enjoyed the basic civil freedoms despite the absence of democratic representative government. Since the end of the Second World War Hong Kong has developed its own multifaceted identity. The mixture of survivors of the Japanese occupation and the refugees from the different parts of China during the civil war provided a platform on which the people took advantages of the challenges of their unique situation first as a tiny window for the P.R.C. to maintain links with the Western world and the Chinese overseas. It became at first a manufacturing centre and then in the last twenty years it rapidly adapted to become a service centre for China and indeed for the wider region. During this time a middle class developed able and willing to articulate a new cultural identity. In many ways Hong Kong has become a place of intellectual ferment as Chinese debate afresh the nature of their identity. As is well known Hong Kong has long been a centre for its own styles of fashion, music, publishing, etc. Like other Chinese centres on the maritime periphery of the mainland it has shown that modernization does not lead to a loss of identity in as a variant of the United States or Western Europe, but rather to the evolution of a rich and complex society and culture. In other words, if Hong Kong may be taken to symbolize the "Blueish" side of the spectrum, it will be seen that it is not at the cost of lost identity, but rather with the benefit of enriching and developing an identity that must forever adapt to the pressure of rapid change which lies at the core of modernity.

Conclusion

By way of conclusion I shall return to the question of the place of Hong Kong in the politics of China in the late 1990s. As a new leadership seeks to consolidate its position it is unlikely to engage in bold experiments in reform that may challenge powerful interests and threaten the positions of important segments of society. But sooner or later the momentum of the reforms will have to pick up lest the burden of the state-owned enterprises for example should become too onerous and necessary improvements in productivity be held back. That would minimally mean an expansion of the role of law and open regulatory mechanisms at the cost of secretive administrative direction. It would call for a proper banking system and the development of institutions for macro-economic control to better manage the vast sprawling semi-marketized economy. There would be a need for greater professionalism in management and in state administration. The demand for greater accountability would necessarily increase. All of this would inevitably transform the role of the Communist Party as it would have to accommodate itself to greater legality, pluralism, openness and accountability. Already there are signs that with the disappearance of the founding generation of the Party and the state, authority is becoming less personal and more institutional.

These themes of legality, professionalism, accountability and plurality may be said to be central to what has been sometimes called the "Hong Kong way of life." Once the British depart at the end of June in 1997, the colonial and foreign dimensions of Hong Kong will no longer be barriers to mainlanders in approaching Hong Kong. Tiny Hong Kong will be an enclave at the mercy of the giant motherland. Some of the conservative "Browns" may see it as a cancer, but there is little doubt that whatever tactical victories the "Browns" may win in the short term, the reform process will sooner or later take off again. At that point Hong Kong may yet prove to be the catalyst that will enable China to complete its integration into the modern world.

3

Mainland-funded Enterprises and the Hong Kong Economy before and after 1997

Lin Tzong-biau and Kan Chak-yuen

Introduction

Local governments in China have, in the past, set up liaison offices in major cities such as Beijing, Shanghai etc., in order to facilitate communication and promote their respective region's development. These cities are China's political or business centres. After 1979 when China started to open up the country to the outside world and liberalize its economy, Hong Kong quickly became the new centre of activities. Consequently each ministry and commission under the State Council in the central government, each provincial government and its equivalent municipalities, as well as state-owned enterprises have rushed to Hong Kong to establish offices or branches there. Many have created new local companies or collaborated with local companies to form joint ventures. Moreover, the existing Chinese companies in Hong Kong, such as the China Resources, Bank of China, China Travel Agency etc., have greatly expanded their business. As a result, Chinese firms in Hong Kong have mushroomed.

According to a report prepared by the Control Division of the State Council, the Chinese firms in Hong Kong numbered about 3,640 (excluding their subsidiaries, representative offices, and joint-venture companies) by early 1994. Some 420 of them were located in Macau. An estimated 71,400 Chinese workers were employed by the Chinese firms, of which,

5,800 were engaged in Macau.[1] It has been estimated that by 1995 about US$42.5 billion had been invested in Hong Kong by the Chinese firms,[2] surpassing the United States' and Japan's investments, and second only to the United Kingdom. At present, China's business operation has spread to every corner of the Hong Kong economy. Owing to their close network and political mission, the Chinese firms have become one of the most influential forces in Hong Kong. On the other hand, local companies can also make good use of these Chinese firms to expand their business into the mainland. The impact of the Chinese firms is therefore two-fold. They have precipitated the economic integration in south China, especially in the Pearl River Delta.

It is anticipated that after July 1997 the Chinese firms will in due course take over the role which is currently played by the British companies. The objectives of this chapter are to critically review the past development and present situation of the Chinese firms in Hong Kong, as well as analyse and project their role in and likely impact on the Hong Kong economy during the transition period before and after 1 July 1997.

Phases and Development of the Chinese Firms in Hong Kong

Prior to 1949, a number of state-owned enterprises had been operating in Hong Kong. These included the China Travel Service and the China Merchants (Hong Kong). At the same time, some companies under the control of the Communist Party were also active in Hong Kong. A prominent example was the Yeh-Hua Company, which was established in 1938 and has been operating in Hong Kong ever since. After 1949, most of the companies controlled by the Kuomintang (KMT) had hastily left Hong Kong and the remaining ones were handed over to the new government in Beijing. Therefore, right after 1949 the Chinese firms in Hong Kong consisted of two groups, namely the companies originally controlled by the Communist Party and those which were previously controlled by the KMT but were handed over to the People's Republic of China after 1949.

---

[1] Pak Ka Publisher, *Cheng Ming Monthly* (July 1994), p. 21.

[2] *Hong Kong Economic Journal*, 11 September 1995.

As mentioned previously, some of the Chinese firms had been in existence before 1949. China Merchants (1872), Bank of China Hong Kong Branch (1917), China Travel Service (Hong Kong) (1928), Tak Pui Hong (1946), Chi Yu Bank (1947), etc. were only some of the more prominent examples. The main function of the firms was to conduct trade business between Hong Kong and the mainland. More specifically, they exported Chinese products to Hong Kong, and from Hong Kong to other foreign countries, using the latter as an entrepôt. The bulk of their business was carried out by four major groups. Among the four, the Bank of China was and is probably the most important. The Bank has been the leader among the thirteen Chinese banks. It is one of the leading banking groups in the financial sector, handling all the banking and financial matters in relation to mainland China. In the past, the Chinese banks conducted only traditional business, but recently their business has expanded into modern areas. Since this group of banks has extensive network of branch offices throughout the territory, it collects more deposits than it can possibly handle, and as such it is always a net lender in the Hong Kong money market. The Bank of China in Hong Kong is administratively under the Bank of China in Beijing. The second group is the China Resources, which is under the Ministry of Foreign Trade and Economic Cooperation. This group is responsible for all the international trade matters of China. The remaining two groups are China Merchants and the China Travel Service. Both belong to the Ministry of Transport. The former is primarily in charge of shipping Chinese goods to and from China and the latter does all the travel-related business. Generally speaking, before 1979 all commercial business with China was monopolized by the Big Four groups discussed above. The local Hong Kong firms did not have many opportunities to do business with them.

The Thirteenth Session of the Central Committee of the Communist Party held on 11 December 1978 marked a watershed in China's foreign trade and economic policy. At this conference, China decided to open up its economy and liberalize its foreign trade policy. Direct foreign investments were not only welcomed, but incentive measures were proffered to attract them. Joint ventures were set up in a bid to improve international cooperation. Economic decision-making authority was decentralized to provincial levels, and local governments were allowed to negotiate with foreign companies directly. Four special economic zones were created, followed by the opening up of thirteen coastal port cities. Thousands of companies or offices were established by the Chinese authorities, including those of the ministries, state-owned enterprises, provincial governments, and county/municipality authorities, in Hong Kong. This trend began in 1979, but gathered real momentum only after 1984 when the Sino-British Joint Declaration was signed. In the following four years, Chinese firms in Hong Kong mushroomed. This phenomenon was temporarily blunted by the infamous events of June 4, 1989. When China's paramount leader Deng Xiaoping revisited Shenzhen Special Economic Zone (SEZ) in 1992 and reconfirmed China's commitment to the open door policy, the economic relations between Hong Kong and China improved greatly and Chinese firms in Hong Kong entered an era of consolidation. Not only did direct investments from Hong Kong in the Shenzhen and the Pearl River Delta increase, China's investments in Hong Kong also grew tremendously. By 1994, there were about 3,220 (excluding subsidiaries) Chinese firms actively operating in Hong Kong.

The history of the Chinese firms' investments in Hong Kong may be divided into five phases.[3]

Phase 1: The Period of Slow Development (1949–1978)

During this period, there were the Korean War of the early 1950s and the Vietnam War of the 1960s. Owing to China's involvement in these wars, economic sanctions were imposed by the United Nations on China. Towards the end of the 1960s, due to the conflicts between China and the Soviet Union, China was forced to turn to Japan and Western Europe for industrial equipment and machinery. In order to finance these imports, China had to increasingly depend on Hong Kong as the source of foreign exchange income through export of its goods, predominantly from the primary sector, to Hong Kong and via Hong Kong to other countries, mostly in the Southeast Asian region. In this period the traditional Chinese firms in Hong Kong were also discriminated against and were rather isolated. Consequently they were unable to expand their business in Hong Kong. Business was still largely carried out by the Big Four groups. Few new Chinese firms were set up in Hong Kong during this period. Besides

---

[3] T. B. Lin and C. Y. Kan, "The Role of Chinese Enterprises in Hong Kong before and after 1997: Implications for Taiwan," Mainland Affairs Council, December 1995, pp. 12–15.

traditional businesses like shipping, banking, trading, tourism and retailing, etc., the scope of business was very limited. The Chinese Big Four did not have much autonomy in their decision making, and operated strictly under Beijing's control. Their business developed very slowly.

Phase 2: Expansion Period (1979–1984)

Because the British Government took the initiative in the late 1970s to negotiate with China over Hong Kong's political future after 1997, China was forced to decide to regain Hong Kong's sovereignty on 1 July 1997. This decision precipitated China to think positively about Hong Kong's long-term future in respect of its political and economic development. As a result, the Chinese firms started to take root in Hong Kong and make plans for the long term. Since 1979 their status and influence in Hong Kong have been greatly improved. On the one hand, the Big Four group of the Chinese firms in Hong Kong helped China to establish new companies there, and on the other, they used Hong Kong as a platform to launch their development programmes overseas. With the increased decentralization of decision making, each organization, from the central to the town level, and each state-owned enterprise jumped on the Hong Kong bandwagon. The end result was the proliferation of Chinese firms during this period.

Each Special Economic Zone (SEZ) came to Hong Kong to set up a big company, and there were eight companies created by the eight provincial governments neighbouring Hong Kong. Particularly worthy of mention are the two big groups, namely, the China International Trust and Investment Corporation (CITIC) and the Everbright Company, both of which are directly under the State Council. Even provinces in very remote areas such as Inner Mongolia and Tibet rushed to Hong Kong to set up a business office for their products. As the concessions and privileges granted to them varied from case to case, the performance of these newly established firms was far from uniform. As a matter of fact, the performance of most of them was less than satisfactory. To illustrate, the Guangdong Enterprise Holdings from Guangdong province has enjoyed a higher status than the Fujian Enterprise Holdings from Fujian province in Hong Kong. This is mainly because the province of Guangdong is economically much more advanced and liberal in its economic system than the latter. Therefore the equity of Guangdong Enterprise Holdings has been selected as one of the components in the Hang Seng Index of the Hong Kong Stock Exchange.

Phase 3: The Period of Conglomeration (1985–1988)

During this period the Chinese firms started to multiply rapidly. All the big companies engaged in establishing joint ventures and subsidiaries. A natural consequence of this development was the formation of groups, of which the more important are: the China Merchants Group (1985), the China Travel Service (1985), the China Resources Group (1983), the Bank of China Group (1983), the Guangdong Enterprise Holdings (1983), the China Everbright Holdings (1983) and the CITIC Group (1987). In addition to developing their business in Hong Kong, these conglomerates also assisted local companies in doing business in the mainland. During 1987–1988 Beijing introduced a series of economic reforms aimed at liberalizing its economic system and decentralization, and this encouraged the Chinese firms in Hong Kong to diversify their business and to expand their operation into foreign markets, notably to the Southeast Asian region and the United States. The Chinese firms have ever since been very active in Hong Kong's real estate and stock markets, though not all of them have been successful.

Phase 4: The Period of Consolidation (1989–1991)

Mainly triggered by the events of June 4, 1989, Beijing launched a cleansing and consolidation campaign between 1989–1991. A substantial number of the Chinese firms in Hong Kong were illegal and engaged in unscrupulous activities, mostly highly speculative, and irregularities were rampant. Although the Chinese authorities were well aware of this situation even prior to the events of June 4, due to political reasons and inertia as well as simple procrastination, these problems were never dealt with squarely before. The events of June 4 and the ensuing criticism and power struggle provided the political climate for tackling the problems and tightening up the supervision and monitoring of the problems faced by Chinese firms. The consolidation campaign resulted in the closing down of hundreds of the less efficient Chinese firms.

One may ask why did the Hong Kong Association of the Chinese Firms, which was formed under the instruction of the State Council, fail to exert proper and effective control over the Chinese firms before? To answer this question, the following reasons may be advanced:

1. According to the decrees issued by the State Council after 1989, all those firms which were not recognized by the central government

had to be withdrawn from Hong Kong. However, many of these companies had made substantial profits in the past and had retained a large portion of these profits in Hong Kong. For this reason these firms did not care to pay heed to instructions from Beijing.

2. According to the regulations, those firms in which the Chinese capital had a stake of 50% or more were required to report to Beijing. In order to avoid this, many Chinese firms deliberately kept their capital below this threshold.

3. Those companies which were under the purview of the central and provincial governments were subject to Beijing's supervision. But there were a large number of the Chinese firms which were established by the county/township authorities and were basically free from the control of the central government.

4. There were quite a few firms which served as outfits of secretive organizations in China, such as military units and had deliberately chosen not to join the Association.

The consolidation campaign resulted in a drastic reduction in the number of Chinese firms. By 1992 the members of the Association numbered only 952.[4] But if the four reasons mentioned above were taken into consideration the actual number would be considerably higher.

Phase 5: The Period of Steady Development since 1992

The clampdown on the Chinese firms launched in the wake of the events of June 4 had only a very short-term impact. In 1992, Deng revisited the Shenzhen SEZ which immediately caused another wave of China fever. The direct investments from Hong Kong and Taiwan have since revived quickly. At the same time, the Chinese firms have also embarked on large-scale expansion programmes through the buying of shell companies and the take-over of listed companies in Hong Kong. In so doing, they were able to raise capital in Hong Kong and return to the mainland to invest in infrastructure and real estate. But this trend was checked in 1993, when Beijing introduced macro-economic control measures and tightened the credit supply for fear of high inflation.

---

[4] *The Hong Kong Chinese Enterprises Association Annual Report 1991*, p. 12.

At present there are about 3,220 Chinese companies in Hong Kong and Macau. This figure does not include their subsidiaries and joint venture companies. Their tentacles have spread to every corner of the economy. Indeed, Chinese firms have become a formidable force to be reckoned with in Hong Kong. Sixty-eight of them were listed on the Hong Kong Stock Exchange with a total capital of HK$191 billion, accounting for more than 7.14% of the total capitalization on the stock exchange (see Table 6).

Classification and Characteristics of the Chinese Firms

Classification of the Chinese Firms

According to their hierarchical structure, the Chinese firms can be classified into the following five categories:

1. Those which are under purview of various ministries and commissions of the State Council, including the Big Four groups of the traditional Chinese firms, namely Bank of China, China Merchants, China Resources, and China Travel Service, as well as two new groups, the China Everbright and the CITIC (Hong Kong). Table 1 shows the list of the companies, which are representatives of the various branches of the central government in Hong Kong.
2. Those companies which are set up by the provincial or its equivalent institutions such as Guangdong Enterprise Holdings (Guangdong province); Fujian Enterprise Holdings (Fujian province); Shanghai Industrial Investment (Shanghai municipality) and the other companies are listed in Table 2.
3. Those firms which are established by the companies in the two categories mentioned above, as joint ventures or as holding companies.
4. Those firms which are set up by private individuals with the money entering Hong Kong through legal or illegal channels. They are usually local firms, some with foreign participation. Most of them are connected with township enterprises in the Pearl River Delta region. Quite a few of them were set up by the military authorities. The operation of these firms is quite secretive for security reasons.
5. "Illegal and underground" companies which are illegal in the eyes of the Chinese authorities. They came to Hong Kong without

official sanction and support and with questionable sources of funds.

Characteristics of the Chinese Firms

As mentioned above, the development of the Chinese firms in Hong Kong began in the early 1980s. Chinese firms in the post-consolidation period of the late 1980s and early 1990s can be classified into the five categories discussed above with different features and characteristics.

The Firms Belonging to the First Category

These companies were initially set up by the central authorities for specific purposes and are directly under their control. The Big Four groups have a rather clear-cut division of labour in Hong Kong. The Bank of China group specializes in finance and banking, while the China Resources group is confined to trade and retail business. The China Travel Service group focuses on tourism and related business, and the China Merchants Holdings is in charge of shipping Chinese goods abroad. The two new powerful groups, namely the CITIC (Hong Kong) and China Everbright, belong to the State Council. They are involved only in big public works projects, such as the new airport and related infrastructure programmes and technology transfer business.

These companies enjoy virtually unlimited support of the central authority in terms of funding and business opportunities. Most of them have a long history of doing business in Hong Kong. Their presence in Hong Kong has been considered as quite positive for the Hong Kong economy. Whenever the economy was in crisis, these companies on the instructions of the central government had often stepped in to stabilize the market. An example is the crisis in 1989 when the economy was shaken by the Tiananmen incident. These Chinese firms came out in flocks to counter-operate transactions in a bid to stabilize the stock and foreign exchange markets. The results were quite satisfactory. It should be noted that the Bank of China has since 1994 been granted the privilege enjoyed by the British banks — Hong Kong Bank and the Standard Chartered Bank to issue the Hong Kong banknotes.

In recent years these companies have branched out into other nontraditional areas. Diversification has become the trend. Now they are also engaged in finance, insurance, import-exports, shipping, tourism,

Table 1: Representative Companies in Hong Kong of the
Various Institutions of the Central Government

	Units	Representative in Hong Kong
1	The State Science and Technology Commission	China Venturetechno International Co. Ltd.
2	Ministry of Finance	CCAFM E and Y Management Services, Ltd.
3	China State Construction Engineering Corp.	China Overseas Building Development Co. Ltd.
4	Ministry of Energy	China International Water and Electric Corp. (HK)
5	International Railway Ministry	China Railway Services (HK) Ltd.
6	Ministry of Communication	China Merchants Holdings Co. Ltd.
7	Ministry of Machinery and Electronics Industry	China Everbest Machinery Enterprises Co. Ltd.
8	China National Aero-technology Import and Export Corp.	Vastford Company Limited
9	Ministry of Metallurgical Industry	China Metallurgical Construction Corp.
10	Ministry of Light Industry	Shui Hua Development and Enterprises Ltd.
11	Ministry of Textile Industry	Eternal Sky Investment Ltd.
12	Ministry of Posts and Telecommunications	Asia Telesys (HK) Ltd.
13	Ministry of Commerce	Waddy Company Ltd.
14	Ministry of Foreign Trade and Economic Corporation	China Resources (Holdings) Co. Ltd.
15	The People's Bank of China	Bank of China Hong Kong–Macau Regional Office
16	The People's Insurance Company of China	China Insurance Group HK–Macau Regional Office
17	Overseas Affairs Office	China Travel Service (Holdings) HK Ltd.
18	Civil Aviation Administration	China National Aviation Corporation
19	National Travel Administration	China International Travel Service (Holdings) HK Ltd.
20	China National Building Material and Equipment Corp.	Zhong Cheng Building Materials International Ltd.
21	The Chinese Academy of Sciences	Fortune Hand Industries Ltd.
22	China Everbright Co. Ltd.	China Everbright Holdings Co. Ltd.

Table 1 (Cont'd)

	Units	Representative in Hong Kong
23	China International Trust and Investment Corp.	China International Trust and Investment Corp. (HK) Ltd.
24	China Nuclear Energy Industrial Corp.	Yenaut Industrial Co. Ltd.
25	China State Construction Engineering Corp.	China State Construction Engineering Corp. (HK)
26	China State Shipbuilding Corporation	China United Shipbuilding Co. Ltd.
27	China National Tobacco Corp.	Tian Li International Co. Ltd.
28	China Association for International Exchange of Personnel	Beijing–HK Exchange of Personnel Centre Ltd.
29	Register of Shipping	Far East Marine Surveyors Ltd.
30	China Council for the Promotion of International Trade	China Legal Service (HK) Ltd.
31	China National Offshore Oil Corp.	China Ocean Oilfields Services (HK) Ltd.
32	China National Nonferrous Metals Industrial Corp.	Oriental Metals (Holdings) Co. Ltd.

Source: The Hong Kong Chinese Enterprises Association, *Directory of Enterprises with PRC Capital in Hong Kong*, April 1992.

construction, real estate, department stores, advertising, hotel industry etc. They have also ventured into overseas markets and many of them have returned to tap the vast market potential in China, often in joint ventures with local firms. A large number of them have served as middlemen for the indirect trade and investments between Taiwan and mainland China.

Their new strategies are diversification, conglomeration and internationalization. Some of them have been quite successful in raising capital in Hong Kong for their expansion programmes.

Their management style is conservative and their organization is quite sound. Most of their high-ranking managers are assigned directly by Beijing.

The Firms Belonging to the Second Category

These firms share the following features: (1) The top managers are invariably sent to Hong Kong by their home institutions, such as the provincial government, city governments, etc. (2) There exists a rather rigid

Table 2: Companies in Hong Kong Set Up by the Provincial or
Its Equivalent Institutions

Province/Municipality	Representative in Hong Kong
Beijing	Scriven Trading Ltd.
Tianjin	Tsinlien Company Ltd.
Shanghai	Shanghai Industrial Investment Co. Ltd.
Nanjing	Hong Kong Shen Nan Trading Co. Ltd.
Heilongjiang	H.H.K. Consultancy and Development Co. Ltd.
Jilin	Zhong Ji Ltd.
Liaoning	China Liaoning Ltd.
Inner Mongolia	Inner Mongolia Hing Yuen (HK) Co. Ltd.
Henan	Henan Hong Kong Enterprises Ltd.
Hebei	Hebei Enterprises Ltd.
Shandong	China Shandong Co. Ltd.
Shanxi	Hong Kong Heng Shan Co. Ltd.
Shaanxi	Lishan Co. Ltd.
Gansu	Gansu Co. Ltd.
Sichuan	Jialing (HK) Co. Ltd.
Hubei	YI F. Trading Co. Ltd.
Hunan	Hunan Trading Co. Ltd.
Jiangxi	Hua Gan Enterprises Co. Ltd.
Jiangsu	Zhong Shan Co. Ltd.
Zhejiang	Zhejiang Fuchuen Co. Ltd.
Anhui	Can High International Trading Ltd.
Fujian	Fujian Enterprise (Holdings) Co. Ltd.
Guangdong	Guangdong Enterprise (Holdings) Ltd.
Guangxi	Gui Jiang Enterprises Ltd.
Yunnan	Yunnan and Hong Kong Co. Ltd.
Guizhou	Gui Da Co. Ltd.
Ningxia	Kachant Development Ltd.
Qinghai	Qhl Trading Co. Ltd.
Xinjiang	Xinjiang Development Ltd.
Tibet	China Tibet Qomolangma Trade and Travel Ltd.
Shenzhen	Shum Yip Holdings Co. Ltd.
Zhuhai	Zhuhai International Ltd.
Shantou	Longxing Development Co. Ltd.
Xiamen	Xing Xia Co. Ltd.

Table 2 (Cont'd)

Province/Municipality	Representative in Hong Kong
Guangzhou	Yue Xiu Enterprises Ltd.
Hainan	Hua Hai Co. Ltd.
Nanhai	Chiu Hoi Trading Co. Ltd.
Beihai	Jan Hai An Enterprises Ltd.
Fuzhou	Hua Rong Co. Ltd.
Dalian	Dalian International Co. Ltd.
Qinhuangdao	Hai Yue Co. Ltd.
Qingdao	China Qingdao Development Co. Ltd.
Yantai	China Yantai Co. Ltd.
Nantong	Zhennan Development Co. Ltd.
Ningbo	Ning Shing Development Co. Ltd.
Wenzhou	Ngan Tong Co. Ltd.
Shenyang	Shen Gang Ltd.
Xi'an	Grown Smark Ltd.
Wuhan	Ever Eagle Co. Ltd.
Chongqing	Y.F. International Ltd.
Harbin	Kwok Nea Development Ltd.
Jiangmen	Five Towns Development Co. Ltd.
Dongguan	Tong Hing Transportation Co. Ltd.
Foshan	Gold Delta Development Ltd.
Zhaoqing	Winwide Development Ltd.
Wuzhou	Fillpark Ltd.
Sanming	Sing Ming Industries Ltd.
Shunde	Richfirm Industries Ltd.

Source: The Hong Kong Chinese Enterprises Association, *Directory of Enterprises with PRC Capital in Hong Kong*, April 1992.

administrative/managerial control and coordination inside the company. They are held responsible for losses sustained, by virtue of the privilege of autonomous management. (3) Their main functions are to conduct negotiations, coordinate and arrange for local business people to visit and invest in their city or province. In a sense these companies serve as middlemen between the Hong Kong business people and the region which they are supposed to represent. For instance, the Shanghai Industrial Investment Co.

in Hong Kong is to promote and arrange for business people to invest in Putong region, a new developing area to the east of the original Shanghai city.

The Firms Belonging to the Third Category

These firms were formed jointly by the companies belonging to the first two categories mentioned above. They came into being through take-over, break-up, and the purchase of shell companies. Their main goals were to make profits and raise capital for their mother companies. In recent years some of these firms have returned to China as foreign firms to tap its vast market potential. Their businesses concentrate on real estate development and manufacturing. An example is the development project of Changzhou region in Fujian province involving the Bank of China and the China Merchants Holdings. The subsidiaries help the mother companies to diversify, conglomerate and internationalize. For instance, the China Shipping group has broadened the scope of its business from the traditional shipping to trading, finance, insurance, godown, hotel and real estate development.

The Firms Belonging to the Fourth Category (The So-called "Grey" Companies)

These firms came to Hong Kong without any formal approval from the Chinese authorities. They were in the eyes of Chinese authorities illegal. But there are some which are considered too sensitive for national security reasons to expose their true identity to the public. Part of their capital came from the township and village enterprises; and part from some defence-related organizations. Many of these firms also have local participation. The majority of them are not members of the Hong Kong Chinese Enterprises Association.

The Firms Belonging to the Fifth Category (The "Underground" Firms)

Firms in this category are invariably illegal. They do not have official backing and endorsement. Some of these firms were secretively set up by unscrupulous officials with money obtained through dubious sources. The bulk of them were created by individuals from China, who as entrepreneurs had made a lot of money and ventured into Hong Kong to try their luck. In general, they do not join the Hong Kong Chinese Enterprises Association.

The Current Situation and New Developments

The Current Situation

According to a survey conducted by the State Council, the Chinese firms operating in Hong Kong numbered about 3,640 (excluding subsidiaries, and joint venture companies), of which 420 were located in Macau. Some 71,400 people were appointed from China to man these companies, with about 5,800 working in Macau. This is indeed quite a significant number. Secondly, by the end of 1994 there were about 990 members of the Hong Kong Chinese Enterprises Association.[5] Most of them belonged to the Big Four groups mentioned above, or were firms set up by the SEZs, especially under the umbrella of Shum Yip Holdings (Shenzhen municipality SEZ), Zhuhai International Co. (Zhuhai municipality), Xing Xia Co. (Xiamen), Longxing Development Co. (Shantou). In addition, each provincial government has also set up its commercial outfit in Hong Kong. The important ones are listed below:

- Fujian Enterprise Holdings (Fujian province)
- Guangdong Enterprise Holdings (Guangdong province)
- China Liaoning Ltd. (Liaoning province)
- Hebei Enterprise Ltd. (Hebei province)
- China Shandong Co. (Shandong province)
- Zhong Shan Co. (Jiangsu province)
- Zhejiang Fuchuen Co. (Zhejiang province)
- Jialing (HK) Co. (Sichuan province)
- CITIC (State Council)
- China Everbright Co. (State Council)

Table 3 shows the classification by sectors of the Chinese firms currently operating in Hong Kong.

The influence of the Chinese capital has been all pervasive. Its tentacles have reached every corner of the economy. In addition to their traditional business, their presence in department stores, advertising, consulting, packaging, publishing, hotels, specialized services, etc. is also very considerable.

---

[5] The China Resources Holdings Co. Ltd., *Hong Kong Market*, October 1994, p. 62.

Table 3: Classification of the Chinese Firms by Sectors

	Sector	Percentage
1	Import and Export	38.8
2	Transport and Godown	8.5
3	Tourism	3.5
4	Construction and Real Estate	6.9
5	Finance and Insurance	10.4
6	Manufacturing etc.	11.5
7	Others	20.4

Source: The Chinese Resources Holdings Co. Ltd., *Hong Kong Market*, October 1994,
         p. 62.

In general, their operation takes the following forms:

1. In the last few years the big groups have been trying to diversify their business and go international. Their operations have expanded into mainland Chinese markets and abroad.

2. Many big companies including some well-known state enterprises in China tried to get themselves listed on the Hong Kong Stock Exchange in order to tap the local capital market through merging, take-over, and break-up. The shares of these companies are called "H" shares. By July 1996, sixty-eight Chinese companies had been successfully listed on the Hong Kong Stock Exchange, of which twenty-one were "H" shares. Their total value of capitalization amounted to about of 7.14% of the Hong Kong stock market as a whole.

3. Many Chinese firms have joined hands with local companies and have returned to do business in China. In so doing they enjoy the status of a foreign company. Many of their investments were concentrated on infrastructure projects, like port facilities, power generation, hotels, etc.

4. Since 1987, a large number of the Chinese firms have been involved in real estate. Their businesses involving billions of dollars include development of large-scale housing projects, hotels, and luxurious residential buildings. Some of them were quite speculative and caused destabilization in the market. But since 1993, as a consequence of China's macro-economic consolidation campaign,

the unscrupulous activities of such Chinese companies have been largely curbed.

5. Some Chinese firms have been actively participating in large-scale public works projects including container terminals, airport and their related infrastructure projects. The Chinese banks have also been actively involved in syndicated loans.

By 1995 the accumulated amount of Chinese investments in Hong Kong had reached US$42.5 billion, surpassing those of the U.S. and Japan. China is now the biggest investor in Hong Kong after the United Kingdom and if the current trend continues China will replace Britain in due course.

In the following sections the Chinese investments in each sector of the Hong Kong economy are discussed in more details.

Manufacturing Sector

According to the survey "External Investment in Hong Kong Manufacturing Industries 1995" conducted by the Hong Kong Government Industry Department, China's investments in Hong Kong's manufacturing sector ranked third, after Japan and the U.S. Its direct investments accounted for about 10% of the total foreign direct investments (FDI) in this sector. Thirty-seven Chinese firms were engaged in manufacturing, and their combined investments amounted to HK$4.2 billion. Seventeen of them were solely owned and 20 of them were joint ventures.[6] These Chinese investments were heavily concentrated on electronics, textiles and clothing, and the bulk of them were made after 1987.

The Chinese investments in the manufacturing industries started with the take-over of the then renowned electronic Conic Group. This company was established in 1965 and specialized in electronic products. In 1993, the China Aviation Industry Co. acquired its ownership and subsequently changed its name to Aviation Technology International Co. It is listed on the Hong Kong Stock Exchange. Also worthy of mention is the case of Shougang Corporation, an important company in Beijing, which in its first

---

[6] Hong Kong Government Industry Department, *1995 Survey of External Investment in Hong Kong Manufacturing Industries*, December 1995, pp. 20 and 25.

foray into the manufacturing industry in Hong Kong took control of the Tong Wing Steel Co.

Chinese capital has also been very active in the mass media business, with many publishing firms under Chinese control.

Import and Export

The majority of the Chinese firms dealing with trade are directly under the control of the central and provincial governments. The main items of trade are chemicals, machinery, equipment, metals, textiles, clothing and food. The bulk of imports and exports were handled by such big firms as China Resources, CITIC (Hong Kong), Guangdong Enterprise Holdings and their myriad subsidiaries.

The companies which were set up by the provincial and municipal authorities are into transport, shipping, trade, consulting services, as well as public works projects.

Since 1985, China has become Hong Kong's number one trading partner. This indicates how important trade is for the Chinese firms in Hong Kong.

Tourism and Transport

The China Travel Service (Holdings) HK Co. Ltd. is the dominant force in this sector. It was established in 1928 under the name of the Hong Kong China Travel Service. The Guangdong Provincial Government has also set up a travel company in Hong Kong, as the majority of Hong Kong residents originated there. Therefore this province received the bulk of the tourists from Hong Kong. In addition to the main tourist services, these firms are also engaged in related businesses, such as hotels, local tour services, and hotel management. There are 400 firms under the China Shipping Group providing all sorts of transporting and shipping services.

In the airline business, the CITIC (Hong Kong) group has been very aggressive. It has held 28.5% of the Hong Kong Dragon Airlines, and 25% (May 1996) of the Cathay Pacific and 10% of the Hong Kong Air Terminal Services. The Chinese firms are also equally strong in land transport business.

Construction and Real Estate

In the last decade the government of Hong Kong has launched several large-scale public works projects. The most prominent one was the construction of the new airport and its related highway, bridge, and railway projects. In order to have a slice of this big pie and to cash on the booming construction and real estate sector, China set up many construction companies in Hong Kong. Although their skills and technology still lag behind those of the Japanese and Western companies, they are good enough for basic infrastructure projects, such as land reclamation, roads and highways, ordinary high-rise buildings, port facilities, etc. As a rule, the construction companies under the control of the central and provincial governments have stronger financial backing and technical capability. Partly because of their close connections with the authorities in China, these Chinese construction companies are assured of the required construction materials often at much lower prices. Some of them have also cooperated with foreign firms and formed consortiums to handle big projects. They have also engaged foreign consulting firms to provide technical and managerial support. In the process these Chinese firms have benefited from precious technology transfer. As many Chinese firms are engaged in property development/speculation, it is only natural that they set up their own construction companies as their subsidiaries to internalize their business benefits.

Finance and Insurance

Chinese investments in the financial and banking sector have a long history. The thirteen Chinese banks led by the Bank of China have branches spreading throughout the territory and have collected enormous deposits. On the Hong Kong overnight money market the Chinese banks are always net lenders. By the end of 1994 the Chinese banks had some HK$450 billion in deposits, accounting for about 23.1% of the total deposits in the Hong Kong banking system. In the same period their combined loans amounted to HK$260 billion, representing a 17.6% growth over the previous year.[7] The bulk of their lending went to industries, commerce, and infrastructure projects. On 1 May 1994 the Bank of China was officially granted the privilege of issuing the Hong Kong dollar banknotes. Although to date its share is only about 5% of the total issuance, it is expected that after 1997 when Hong Kong reverts to Chinese rule, the Bank of China will play an ever-increasing role in the financial sector.

---

[7] *Hong Kong Monetary Authority Annual Report 1994*, June 1995.

The group owns about 350 branches and 300 automatic teller machines. It is by far the biggest, even surpassing the Hong Kong Bank group. The Chinese banks have been very active in the last decade in financing large-scale projects, such as mass transit systems, cross-harbour tunnels, power stations, airport and its related transport systems. In these projects the Chinese banks have a stake of more than HK$2 billion. In 1995 alone, about 20 new branches of the Chinese banks were added.[8]

China's stake in the insurance business has also been very strong. By 1992 there were fifteen insurance companies controlled by Chinese capital. All of them are members of the Hong Kong Chinese Firms Association. By 1993 their investments in this sector alone were estimated at HK$15 billion.[9] No figures are available for 1995, but it is assumed that the amount has in the meantime increased substantially.

Property and Real Estate

The first major Chinese building of China was the old Bank of China building situated on Queen's Road Central in Hong Kong adjacent the Hong Kong Bank building. Since then the Chinese firms have built numerous large buildings locating in every corner of the territory. The most magnificent of them is unquestionably the new Bank of China building, which was designed by the renowned Americans Chinese architect I. M. Pei. This pristine structure was the tallest building when it was finished. It is one of the most visible landmarks of Hong Kong, dominating the beautiful skyline of Hong Kong. China's massive investments in this sector began in the 1980s. During this period the Big Four groups started to erect huge buildings for their own use as office space and for leasing for profit.

Many Chinese firms entered Hong Kong to engage in its prosperous property and real estate market. Many unscrupulous firms, belonging to the fourth and fifth categories mentioned above, indulged in speculation in this highly volatile sector. And for this reason, this gave rise to corruption. A clampdown campaign was launched in early 1990 and consequently many

---

[8] *Hong Kong Express Daily News*, 4 January 1995, p. 11.

[9] George Shen, "China's Investment in Hong Kong," in *The Other Hong Kong Report 1993*, edited by Choi Po-king and Ho Lok-sang (Hong Kong: The Chinese University Press, 1993), p. 436.

illegal small Chinese firms were ordered to close down. The activities of these firms have often been blamed for the fluctuating and skyrocketing property prices. It has been estimated that by 1991 some HK$7.4 billion had been poured into this sector by Chinese firms. In 1992 alone about HK$850 million was invested by Chinese firms in this sector. Their projects covered practically every sub-sector, including residential, industrial and commercial complexes. Their investments in this sector generally take the following three forms:

1. Acquisition of new lands through public auction by the government or purchasing them from private owners and developing them for sale or in partnership with other developers.
2. Purchasing existing buildings and reselling them.
3. Buying completed buildings and holding on to them for a long time. These buildings are primarily for their own use or as long-term investments.

New Developments and Trends

Since 1992 one of the most significant phenomena has been the attempt of many Chinese companies to get themselves listed on the Hong Kong Stock Exchange. Their methods involved buying shell companies, acquiring controlling interest in the existing listed companies, and etc. Besides, since 1993 many state enterprises in China have also entered Hong Kong to raise capital in the local market. Because these companies have close ties with the authorities in mainland China and many local business people are eager to penetrate the vast Chinese market, their shares sold like hot cakes initially. The fact that Hong Kong would revert to Chinese rule on 1 July 1977 also helped.

In fact, since the early 1980s the Chinese had started to buy shell companies as an avenue to enter the local capital market. The most famous example was the acquisition of the Conic group by the consortium of the Bank of China and the China Resources. Since then, hundreds of Chinese companies have followed suit and have acquired many local listed corporations. Particularly worthy mentioning is the case of the Cathay Pacific and Hong Kong Telecom groups. Both companies were formally controlled by British capital. But in the last few years more than 12% each of these two companies have been held by Chinese firms, notably, the CITIC (Hong Kong). As a result, 35% of Cathay Pacific has been controlled by the

Chinese capital. In 1992, the China Shipping Group and the China Resources broke up their companies and had some their subsidiaries listed on the stock exchange. Every time high-quality shares of a Chinese firm goes public, they are oversubscribed heavily, some times by more than 400 times. This phenomenon fully indicates the interest of the general public and business people in Hong Kong in Chinese companies. To date, forty-seven Hong Kong Chinese companies are listed on the Hong Kong Stock Exchange. A full list of such companies is given in Table 4.

Table 4: Hong Kong Chinese Companies Listed on the Hong Kong Stock Exchange

	Company	Shareholder
1	China Aerospace International Holdings Ltd.	China National Aero-tech Import and Export Corporation
2	Seaunion Holdings Ltd.	Fujian Enterprise (Holdings) Co. Ltd.
3	Eastern Century Holdings Ltd.	Shougang Concord International Enterprises Ltd.
4	Continental Mariner Investment Co. Ltd.	China International Trust and Investment Corp.
5	Guangzhou Investment Co. Ltd.	Guangzhou Enterprises Ltd.
6	CNPC (HK) Ltd.	Sun World Ltd.
7	China Treasure Telecom Holding Ltd.	China Treasure Investment Co. Ltd.
8	China Merchants Hai Hong Holdings Co. Ltd.	China Merchants (Holdings) Co. Ltd.
9	Shenzhen International Holding Ltd.	Shenzhen Construction and Materials Co. Ltd.
10	Beijing Development (HK) Ltd.	Beijing Trust & Investment Corp.
11	IHD Holding Ltd., China	Everbright Corp.
12	China Assets (Holdings) Ltd.	Beijing Trust & Investment Corp.
13	Silver Grant International industries Ltd.	Silver Grant International Industries Ltd.
14	The Ka Wah Bank Ltd.	China International Trust and Investment (HK) Corp.
15	Denway Investment Ltd.	Guangzhou Denway Co. Ltd.
16	Shanghai International (HK) Ltd.	Shanghai International (HK) Ltd.
17	Min Xin Holdings Ltd.	Fujian Enterprises (Holdings) Co. Ltd.
18	First Shanghai Investment Ltd.	Shanghai International (HK) Ltd.

Table 4 (Cont'd)

	Company	Shareholder
19	ONFEM Holdings Ltd.	China National Nonferrous Metals Industry Corp.
20	China Everbright Technology Ltd.	China Everbright Holdings Co. Ltd
21	China Everbright International Ltd.	China Everbright Holdings Co. Ltd.
22	Poly Investment Holdings Ltd.	Continental Mariner Investment Co. Ltd.
23	CITIC Pacific Ltd.	China International Trust and Investment (HK) Corp.
24	Top Glory International Holdings Ltd.	Top Glory Development Corp.
25	Guangdong Investment Ltd.	Guangdong Enterprise (Holdings) Ltd.
26	China Resources Enterprises Ltd.	China Resources (Holdings) Co. Ltd.
27	China Travel International Investment Hong Kong Ltd.	China Travel Service (Holdings) HK Ltd.
28	Union Bank of Hong Kong Ltd.	China Merchants Holdings Co. Ltd.
29	Hoi Sing Holdings Ltd.	Dragon Light Ltd.
30	Hualing Holdings Ltd.	Hua Qing
31	Stone Electronic Technology Ltd.	Stone Group
32	China Foods Holdings Ltd	Top Glory International Holdings Ltd.
33	San Tai Manufacturing Ltd.	Shougang Concord International Enterprises Co. Ltd.
34	Suwa International Holdings Ltd.	Dong Hui Investment Holdings Ltd.
35	China Overseas Land and Investment Ltd.	China Overseas Group
36	Shougang Concord International Enterprises Co. Ltd.	Beijing Shougang Corp.
37	Shougang Concord Grand (Group) Ltd.	Beijing Shougang Corp.
38	Shanghai Growth Investment Ltd.	Shanghai International Trust Co. Ltd.
39	ING Beijing Investment Co. Ltd.	Beijing International Trust and Investment Corp.
40	Guangnan Holdings Ltd.	Guangdong Enterprises (Holdings) Ltd.
41	China Merchants — China Fund	China Merchants Holdings Co. Ltd.
42	Allied Group Ltd.	Allied Group
43	Hong Kong Macau (Holdings) Ltd.	Carbery Co. Ltd.
44	Ng Fung Hong Ltd.	China Resources
45	Pudong Development Holdings Ltd.	Shanghai Municipality

Table 4 (Cont'd)

	Company	Shareholder
46	Oriental Metal Holdings Co. Ltd.	China National Nonferrous Metals Industry Corporation
47	Shanghai Industrial Enterprises Ltd.	Shanghai Municipality

Sources: From various newspapers.

Since 1993 the Hong Kong stock market has entered a new era. The world-renowned beer company the Tsingtao Brewery from China has been successfully listed on the local stock exchange. Five more state enterprise companies were also listed in the same year. The shares of these companies were called "H" shares in Hong Kong. In 1994 nine additional companies of China were listed. Up to July 1996, a total of twenty-one companies from China were listed in Hong Kong. Together, these companies raised over HK$23 billion in the local capital market. A full list of these companies is provided in Table 5.

Table 5: China's State Enterprises Listed in Hong Kong

	Company	Province	Fund raised (HK$100m)
1	Tsingtao Brewery	Shandong	8.89
2	Shanghai Petrochemical	Shanghai	26.54
3	Beiren Print Machinery	Beijing	2.08
4	Guangzhou Shipyard	Guangdong	3.01
5	Maanshan Iron and Steel	Anhui	39.34
6	Kunming Machine Tool	Yunnan	1.29
7	Yizheng Chemical Fibre	Jiangsu	26.80
8	Tianjin Bohai Chemical Industry	Tianjin	4.08
9	Dongfang Electrical Machinery	Sichuan	4.81
10	Luoyang Glass	Henan	9.13
11	Qingling Motors	Chongqing	10.35
12	Zhenhai Refining	Zhejiang	14.28
13	Shanghai Haix	Shanghai	15.76
14	Harbin Power	Harbin	11.22
15	Chengdu Telecommunication	Sichuan	4.48

Table 5 (Cont'd)

	Company	Province	Fund raised (HK$100m)
16	Jilin Chemical	Jilin	8.99
17	Northwest Electronics	Liaoning	2.57
18	Jingwei Textile Machinery	Tianjin	1.60
19	Nanjing Panda	Jiangsu	2.42
20	Guangdong Kelon	Guangdong	3.82
21	Guangshen Rail	Guangdong	14.31
	Total		215.77

Sources: From various newspapers.

Altogether, up to July 1996 sixty-eight Chinese companies were listed on the Hong Kong Stock Exchange, of which twenty-one are state enterprises. Their combined total capitalization amounted to HK$191 billion, equivalent to about 7.14% of the entire Hong Kong Stock Exchange's capitalization. Table 6 lists the names of these companies. Besides the names, the number of shares issued, their prices, and respective value of capitalization are also displayed for easy reference.

Table 6: Mainland-funded Listed Companies in Hong Kong

		Issued shares (in thousand)	HK$	Capitalization (in thousand)
1	China Aerospace Int. Holdings Ltd.	1,116,306	1.23	1,373,056.38
2	Seaunion Holdings Ltd.	2,984,896	0.139	414,900.544
3	Eastern Century Holdings Ltd.	643,948	0.7	450,763.6
4	Continental Mariner Investment Co. Ltd.	436,214	1.23	536,543.22
5	Guangzhou Investment Co. Ltd	2,501,387	2.125	5,315,447.3
6	CNPC (HK) Ltd.	2,714,756	0.285	773,705.46
7	China Treasure Telecom Holding Ltd.	511,359	0.31	158,521.29
8	China Merchants Hai Hong Holdings Co. Ltd.	706,134	2.2	1,553,494.8
9	Shenzhen Int. Holding Ltd.	1,042,436	0.183	190,765.788
10	Beijing Development (HK) Ltd.	100,000	1.11	111,000

Table 6 (Cont'd)

		Issued shares (in thousand)	HK$	Capitalization (in thousand)
11	IHD Holding Ltd., China	664,947	1.62	1,077,214.14
12	China Assets (Holdings) Ltd.	74,383	3	223,149
13	Silver Grant Int. Industries Ltd.	181,874	1.84	334,648.16
14	The Ka Wah Bank Ltd.	1,107,472	2.625	2,907,114
15	Denway Investment Ltd.	1,320,005	0.395	521,401.975
16	Shanghai Int. (HK) Ltd.	333,182	0.68	226,563.76
17	Min Xin Holdings Ltd.	295,702	1.25	369,627.5
18	First Shanghai Investment Ltd.	432,469	0.55	237,857.95
19	ONFEM Holdings Ltd.	284,282	3.675	1,044,736.35
20	China Everbright Technology Ltd.	976,722	0.182	177,763.404
21	China Everbright Int. Ltd.	1,327,305	0.58	769,836.9
22	Poly Investment Holdings Ltd.	1,213,515	0.29	351,919.35
23	CITIC Pacific Ltd.	2,133,186	31.3	66,768,721.8
24	Top Glory Int. Holdings Ltd.	1,830,834	0.93	1,702,675.62
25	Guangdong Investment Ltd.	2,147,426	4.8	10,307,644
26	China Resources Enterprises Ltd.	1,204,726	6.2	7,469,301.2
27	China Travel Int. Investment Hong Kong Ltd.	1,896,568	1.82	3,451,753.76
28	Union Bank of Hong Kong Ltd.	237,065	8.2	1,943,933
29	Hoi Sing Holdings Ltd.	223,605	0.88	196,772.4
30	Hualing Holdings Ltd.	600,000	0.8	480,000
31	Stone Electronic Technology Ltd.	605,907	0.66	399,898.62
32	China Foods Holdings Ltd.	590,371	1.17	690,734.07
33	San Tai Manufacturing Ltd.	415,035	0.48	199,216.8
34	Suwa Int. Holdings Ltd.	463,713	0.24	111,291.12
35	China Overseas Land and Investment Ltd.	3,922,478	2.125	8,335,265.75
36	Shougang Concord Int. Enterprises Co. Ltd.	1,511,583	1.23	1,859,247.09
37	Shougang Concord Grand (Group) Ltd.	668,994	0.7	468,295.8
38	Shanghai Growth Investment Ltd.	9,635	5.95	57,328.25
39	ING Beijing Investment Co. Ltd.	500,000	0.79	395,000
40	Guangnan Holdings Ltd.	543,524	4.475	24,322,699
41	China Merchants — China Fund	95,240	4.188	398,865.12

Table 6 (Cont'd)

		Issued shares (in thousand)	HK$	Capitalization (in thousand)
42	Allied Group Ltd.	3,066,284	0.66	2,023,747.44
43	Hong Kong Macau (Holdings) Ltd.	158,739	3.25	515,901.75
44	Ng Fung Hong Ltd.	1,003,640	3.775	3,788,741
45	Pudong Development Holdings Ltd.	1,011,139	1.82	1,840,272.9
46	Oriental Metal Holdings Co. Ltd.	543,700	1.3	706,810
47	Shanghai Industrial Holdings Ltd.	516,000	11.40	5,882,400
	Subtotal			172,086,000
	State-owned Enterprises "H" shares			
48	Tsingtao Brewery	346,850	2.625	910,481.25
49	Shanghai Petrochemical	100,000	1.6	160,000
50	Beiren Print Machinery	100,000	0.95	95,000
51	Guangzhou Shipyard	157,398	1.86	292,760.28
52	Maanshan Iron and Steel	1,732,930	1.31	2,270,138.3
53	Kunming Machine Tool	65,000	2.025	131,625
54	Yizheng Chemical Fibre	1,400,000	1.63	2,282,000
55	Tianjin Bohai Chemical Industry	340,000	0.63	214,200
56	Dongfang Electrical Machinery	170,000	2	340,000
57	Luoyang Glass	250,000	1.37	342,500
58	Qingling Motors	980,000	2.6	2,548,000
59	Zhenhai Refining	600,000	2.125	1,275,000
60	Shanghai Haix	1,080,000	0.55	594,000
61	Harbin Power	469,151	1.31	614,587.81
62	Chengdu Telecommunication	160,000	1	160,000
63	Jilin Chemical	964,778	1.07	1,032,312.46
64	Northwest Electronics	257,950	1.41	363,709.5
65	Jingwei Textile Machinery	180,800	1.04	188,032
66	Nanjing Panda	242,000	1.26	304,920
67	Guangdong Kelon	382,991	3.15	1,206,421
68	Guangshen Rail	1,431,300	2.75	3,936,075
	Subtotal			19,256,421
	Total			191,342,421
	Hong Kong Market Capitalization			2,678,366,000
	Share			7.14%

Note: Market capitalization as on 30 July 1996.
Sources: Stock Exchange of Hong Kong, *The Securities Journal*, July 1996; *Hong Kong Economic Journal*, 31 July 1996.

In summary, since 1992 the Chinese companies have used four approaches to gain access to the Hong Kong capital market: (1) take-over, (2) buying shell companies, (3) breaking up of the group and getting some of their subsidiaries listed, and (4) floating "H" shares by the state enterprises. Through these methods, the Chinese companies have expanded their business horizon, learnt the working of the capitalist system, and raised much needed capital overseas. This development is beneficial to Hong Kong as well, because it has offered the Hong Kong business people opportunities to cooperate with the Chinese bureaucrat-turned business people and has, at the same time, created new opportunities for the local investors. This development also signifies the mutual interdependence between Hong Kong and China.

The Role and the Impact of the Chinese Firms in the Hong Kong Economy

From the preceding sections one can gauge how pervasive and important the Chinese firms are to the Hong Kong economy. Their presence is visible in every economic sector. But banking and property sectors are by far the most significant ones as far as their influence is concerned. It is therefore befitting to look at these two sectors in more details.

The Bank of China Group

By 1993 this group had thirteen licensed banks with 378 branches throughout the territory. They employed about 18,000 people[10] and their combined asset value was HK$588 billion, equivalent to 9.6% of the total asset value in the banking system. This group has a share of 23% of the total deposits in the entire banking system in Hong Kong. In 1994 their deposits amounted to HK$450 billion and their loans at HK$260 billion.[11] In recent years the growth rate of their deposits has always been above the Hong Kong average, mainly because the economies of China and Hong Kong have become more closely integrated and the Chinese economy has expanded at a very rapid pace. The burgeoning indirect trade between

---

[10] *Economic Reporter*, 2 May 1994, p. 12.

[11] T. B. Lin and C. Y. Kan, "The Role of Chinese Enterprises in Hong Kong before and after 1997: Implications for Taiwan," p. 80.

Taiwan and China is also a favourable factor. Lastly, the large number of branch offices made it convenient for the residents to deposit their money. All these factors have contributed to the high growth of the deposits for the Chinese banking group.

To date, the Chinese bankers have occupied several important positions in the financial sector of Hong Kong. First, since 1993, the general manager of the Bank of China has been made a member of the Foreign Exchange Reserve Advisory Committee. The Bank of China is an executive member of the Hong Kong Banking Association. And since 1994, the Bank of China has joined the Hong Kong Bank and the Standard Chartered Bank, both of British capital, to issue Hong Kong banknotes. Besides, an official of the Bank of China has been on the Council of the Hong Kong Stock Exchange. In view of the fact that all these organizations deal with monetary and financial policies in Hong Kong, the Bank of China has already exerted its influence in the policy-making process through its presence in these important organizations.

Real Estate and Property Sector

It is said that if one has money, the easiest way for him to make more (if luck favours) will be to start with the stock and property markets. This is exactly what has happened with Chinese capital. Since 1987, the Chinese capital started to flow into Hong Kong, much of which was first invested in stocks and real estate. By mid-1993, some HK$13.2 billion[12] had been sunk into this sector, pushing the property prices to very high levels. After July 1993 Beijing started to tighten the money supply and credit expansion through more effective macro-economic management. As a result, the speculative activities of Chinese firms in this sector were temporarily curbed. However, in 1995 they became active again in this sector, con-centrating on commercial buildings this time. Many choice buildings were bought by the Big Four groups and other lesser known Chinese companies. Though nobody knows the exact quantum of their investments in this sector, it is generally held to be staggering.

Moreover, the Chinese banks have in this period been actively involved

---

[12] George Shen, "China's Investment in Hong Kong," in *The Other Hong Kong Report 1993*, p. 437.

in syndicated loans for financing large-scale development projects. This will, of course, have very significant long-term implications. Through their lending policy the Chinese banks can influence property and real estate markets. And because of this link, the fortunes of the Chinese banks will be affected by fluctuations in the property market, which is quite volatile. Any over-exposure to this market will inevitably put the banks in a vulnerable situation.

The Chinese Firms during the Transition Period

Generally speaking, the Chinese firms have played a positive role in the development of the Hong Kong economy. But their rise to prominence in the local scene began in earnest in the second half of the 1980s. During the transition period the Chinese firms have contributed greatly to the development of the economy. Their major contributions may be summarized as follows.

Help to Promote Trade and Investments between Hong Kong and China

After the Chinese economy was opened up, China's trade with the outside world increased dramatically. Hong Kong has played the role of a middle-man in addition to being the biggest investor in China's FDI. Many local firms have conducted business with the Chinese firms. Many Chinese firms in Hong Kong have camouflaged themselves as foreign firms and returned to China to transact business. These Chinese firms have indeed played a very active and catalyst role in the entrepôt trade, transhipment, indirect bilateral trade and investments between the two sides of the Taiwan Strait and in doing so have brought a lot of business to Hong Kong.

Introduce the So-called "China Factor" and Help to Expand the Economic Horizon of Hong Kong

Through daily contacts with these Chinese firms, Hong Kong and foreign business people come to learn the way in which the Chinese do their business. This helps them in redefining and reformulating their business strategy towards China. Secondly, through their investments in Hong Kong the Chinese firms also contribute to its economic development and some-times help stabilize it when a crisis hits Hong Kong. The Chinese firms are also useful for those manufacturing firms in Hong Kong which want to move their production operation to mainland China. The creation of the four SEZs and the opening up of a dozen coastal port cities effectively give the sunset industries of Hong Kong a place to extend their life span and flourish. This has facilitated the much needed restructuring and transformation of the Hong Kong economy. Hong Kong's economic sphere has expanded and its economic boundary has been pushed into the Pearl River Delta area.

Help to Promote Hong Kong as an Important Financial Centre in the Asia-Pacific Region

In addition to the fact that the Bank of China has become a note-issuing bank and the Bank of China group has become the second most important banking group in Hong Kong, many specialized banks in China have come to Hong Kong to set up their offices. This has boosted the general confidence in Hong Kong, and as a result, has attracted many more top overseas banks to Hong Kong as their base for regional operation. There are 180 banks in Hong Kong and 85 of world's top 100 banks have set up branch offices or representative offices there. Despite the fact that China is trying to promote Shanghai as a financial centre, the massive investments by China in the banking sector in Hong Kong strongly indicate China's intention of keeping Hong Kong as a financial centre after 1997.

Help Local Business People to Penetrate New Overseas Markets

Before 1979 China's closest ally was the Soviet Union. For this reason, China always maintained close ties with Russia and the east European countries. Since the economies of these countries have now been liberalized and started to move forward, the market potential of these virgin lands is substantial. The Hong Kong business people can take advantage of the Chinese firms' connections with these countries and expand their business to this region, thereby creating fresh business opportunities for Hong Kong.

Create Job Opportunities

The Chinese firms employ a large number of people. Although top management positions are manned by officials from China, local people are hired as middle echelon managers and general clerks. Currently there are about

100,000 people working in Chinese firms and this figure is expected to increase as the number of Chinese firms increases. At a time when the unemployment rate has started to climb up, this contribution of the Chinese firms is of increasing significance to Hong Kong.

In contrast to the positive contributions of the Chinese firms, there are also negative aspects associated with their operation in Hong Kong. Firstly, the Chinese firms are in general unfamiliar with the concept of fair competition and the rule of law. Their *modus operandi* is quite different from those of the local firms in Hong Kong. They are generally considered more corrupt than the latter, especially those which are run by the children of high-ranking officials (the so-called "Prince Gang"). These companies normally enjoy special privileges and conduct business through back-doors in order to get special contracts. After the establishment of the Independent Commission Against Corruption (ICAC) in the early 1970s, Hong Kong bureaucracy has become relatively efficient and clean. It remains to be seen whether this would continue after Hong Kong reverts to China's rule in 1997. It is hoped that the ICAC will continue to conduct impartial investigations into allegations of corruption and bring those people who violate laws to justice. Hong Kong should, according to the Basic Law, continue to function as a capitalist society, but a clean and efficient government machinery is a *sine qua non* for the success of Hong Kong in the post-1997 era.

The impact of Chinese firms on the Hong Kong economy is varied and depends upon the category in which they fall. Among the five categories, those of the first and second categories normally conduct their business in a way not much different from that of the normal local companies. Because they are under central and provincial authorities, they are also charged with the responsibility of maintaining Hong Kong's stability. So at time of crisis, such as in the Tiananmen Square events and during the 1983–1984 sensitive period of negotiations between Britain and China over Hong Kong's political future, these Chinese firms, especially the Big Four, invested heavily in Hong Kong in a bid to stabilize its economy. The firms of the third category behave more or less in the same way as their parent companies, and as such have positive impacts on the Hong Kong economy. However, this is not the case with the fourth and the fifth categories of the firms. Since their sources of funds are generally dubious, and they are not recognized by Beijing, they do not follow instructions from China. As these firms do not have any official backing and lack stable business volume, their operations are often speculative in nature. Consequently, they may represent a destabilizing force in the Hong Kong economy. However, this does not mean that all the firms in these categories are bad. As a matter of fact, most of them do business by the rules. It expected that as the time goes by, these firms will learn to do business in the conventional Hong Kong way and refrain from clandestine operations. Once that happens, these firms will also make substantial positive contribution to the further development of the Hong Kong economy in the post-1997 era.

Summary and Conclusions

The Chinese firms have a long history in Hong Kong. Before 1979, the Chinese firms were largely represented by four major groups, namely the Bank of China, the China Travel Service, the China Resources and the China Merchants. After 1979, a massive amount of money entered Hong Kong as a result of the newly adopted open door economic policy of Beijing. By 1989, during which the infamous "June 4 incident" occurred, there were about 3,000 Chinese firms operating in Hong Kong. After the incident Beijing's supervision and control of these Chinese firms tightened and a period of consolidation began. Hundreds of illegal firms were dismantled, and the number of the Chinese firms drastically decreased. At the behest of the Xinhua News Agency, the "Hong Kong Chinese Enterprises Association" was established, which claimed to have a membership of some 990. Before long, the Chinese operation in Hong Kong had expanded further and by 1994, the number increased to 3,640 (not including their subsidiaries), of which 420 were operating in Macau. Out of an estimated 71,400 people dispatched from China to run these companies, 5,800 of them were in Macau.

Five Major Categories

The Chinese firms can be roughly classified into five categories as follows:

1. Those under the direct control of the State Council, ministries or commissions.
2. Those which were set up by the provincial or its equivalent authorities.
3. Those which were jointly established by the companies mentioned in the preceding two categories.
4. The so-called "grey" companies, which were created either by

secretive organizations such as defence and military authorities, or by county/township municipalities.

5. The "underground" companies, which were not sanctioned by the Chinese authorities and as such were considered illegal.

The first three categories of the companies are mostly financially rather strong and have played a significant and positive role in the Hong Kong economy, while the last two categories of the firms are mostly small in size and are often engaged in speculative activities. Therefore, their role is sometimes counterproductive and destabilizing for the local economy.

Recent Trends and New Developments

1. Through purchases of the so-called "shell companies" or take-over of the existing companies, the Chinese firms have gained easy access to the local capital markets, thus enabling them to raise funds.
2. The state-owned enterprises have normally strong and solid financial foundation. It is not difficult for them to obtain listing on the Hong Kong Stock Exchange.
3. The Chinese firms which have strong financial backing and good reputation try to forge joint ventures with local companies or foreign companies. These newly formed companies are treated by the Chinese authorities as foreign companies and as such will be entitled to the incentives and privileges accorded to foreign companies when they operate in the mainland.

To date, the tentacles of the Chinese firms have extended to every corner of the economy. But they are most influential in such sectors as banking and finance, trade, construction, tourism, transport, shipping, etc., where they have been playing an increasingly important role.

Until recent years the paramount factor in the decision making of the Chinese firms was political. They operated under the direction from Beijing in order to make the "one country, two systems" model a success. They pursued the goal of profit maximization under the constraint of the preset political goal, maintaining the twin objectives of stability and prosperity during the transition period. A concrete example was the "June 4 incident." At the height of the crisis, the Chinese firms were ordered to actively intervene in the stock and the foreign exchange markets in a bid to stabilize the prices. But in recent years, owing to the fact that the political stability in both China and Hong Kong has been restored, the Chinese firms have in a large measure shaken off the burden of political mission, and concentrated their energies on business.

The Positive Impact of the Chinese Firms

They may be summarized as follows:

1. They have contributed greatly to the growth of trade volume and their mutual FDI between Hong Kong and China.
2. They have introduced the "China Factor" and effectively enlarged the economic sphere of Hong Kong.
3. They have served as useful conduits for Hong Kong companies to establish business ties with Chinese authorities at all levels, including central, provincial, county and township governments.
4. They have strengthened Hong Kong's role as a regional operation centre in the Asia-Pacific region.
5. The Chinese firms have their own business connections especially with the former East European countries and have helped Hong Kong in penetrating these markets.
6. They also provided considerable employment opportunities for the local people.
7. Their massive investments in Hong Kong have improved and enhanced the people's confidence in Hong Kong's future.

On the other hand, their negative impact may be summarized as follows: The Chinese firms have brought in bad business practices, such as back-door operations and corruption, etc., into Hong Kong. The case of Zhou Beifang of the Shougang Corporation is a case in point. Another example in this regard is that of the CNPC (Hong Kong) Ltd., formerly known as Paragon Ltd. This company was alleged to be involved in irregular dealings in Hong Kong stocks.

The ultimate conclusion of this chapter is that the Chinese firms in Hong Kong will continue to work to the advantage of the economy during and after the transition period, simply because they are charged with the political responsibility of maintaining the declared twin goal of stability and prosperity of Hong Kong. But there are concerns among the people that the Chinese firms will bring with them bad and undesirable business practices, which would tarnish the Hong Kong's image as a progressive and efficient commercial centre.

Bibliography

Choi Po-king and Ho Lok-sang, eds. *The Other Hong Kong Report 1993*. Hong Kong: The Chinese University Press, 1993.

Economic Information and Agency Holdings Ltd. *Economic Report*. Hong Kong: May 1994.

Hang Seng Bank Ltd. *Hang Seng Economic Monthly*. Hong Kong: October 1993.

Hong Kong Economic Journal, 11 September 1995.

Hong Kong Foundation Ltd. *China–Hong Kong Economic Monthly*. Hong Kong: March 1993.

Hong Kong Government Industry Department. *1995 Survey of External Investment in Hong Kong Manufacturing Industries*. Hong Kong: Government Printer, 1995.

Hong Kong Monetary Authority. *Hong Kong Monetary Authority Annual Report 1994*. Hong Kong: 1995.

Hong Kong Stock News, Hong Kong. "State-Owned Enterprises, Red Chips" (in Chinese), September 1994.

Kan Chak-yuen. *Mainland-Funded Enterprises and the Hong Kong Economy*. Newsletter of the Department of Economic and Finance, City University of Hong Kong, Vol. 5, No. 2 (November 1995).

————. *The Emergence of the Golden Economic Triangle—Mainland China, Hong Kong and Taiwan*. Taiwan: Lifework Press, 1994.

Lin Tzong-biau and Kan Chak-yuen. *The Role of Chinese Enterprises in Hong Kong before and after 1997: Implications for Taiwan*. Taiwan: Mainland Affairs Council, 1995.

Pak Ka Publisher. *Cheng Ming Monthly*. Hong Kong: July 1994.

The American Chamber of Commerce in Hong Kong. *PRC Business Firms in Hong Kong and Macau*. Hong Kong: 1988.

The China Resources Holdings Co. Ltd. *Hong Kong Market*. Hong Kong: October and November 1994.

The Hong Kong Chinese Enterprises Association. *Directory of Enterprises with PRC Capital in Hong Kong*. Hong Kong: April 1992.

The Hong Kong Chinese Enterprises Association. *The Hong Kong Chinese Enterprises Association Annual Report 1991*. Hong Kong: 1992.

The Stock Exchange of Hong Kong. *Securities Journal*. Hong Kong: July 1996.

4

Marginalization Crisis of Hong Kong Labour: The Impact of Economic Reunification of China and Hong Kong

Wong Hung

Introduction: Marginalization of the World Labour Force

Restructuring of the labour force is a significant and widespread phenomenon in Western capitalist countries. The numbers and ratios of women workers, part-time workers, casual workers, self-employed workers and home-workers in the workforce have continuously and significantly increased since the 1980s. One important signal of the end of Fordism and the rise of flexible accumulation of capital is the marginalization of workers and their movements.

In the Third World and newly industrialized economies (NIEs), persistence of the "informal sector" coincides with the growth of export processing industrialization. Enormous numbers of migrant workers have been working in the export processing zones. However, the majority of this workforce is in the "informal sector." Most of them are self-employed manual or service workers, workers in small establishments, family workers, agricultural workers and peasants.[1] All these workers are undergoing

---

[1] Jacques Charmes, "A Critical Review of Concepts, Definitions and Studies in the Informal Sector," in *The Informal Sector Revisited*, edited by D. Turham, B. Salome and A. Schwarz (Paris: Development Centre of the OECD, 1990).

similar marginalization process as their counterparts in the Western capitalist countries.

Using a different term to describe a similar phenomenon, Harrod estimates that "unprotected workers" represent more than 50% of the total world labour force.[2] He also suggests that unprotected workers may constitute as much as 85% to 90% of a country's workforce in some Third World countries.

"Marginal" and "marginality" have been widely used both in common usage and academic research. Perlman states that the common use of "marginal" and "marginality" loosely refers to the poor in general, the jobless, migrants, members of other subcultures, racial and ethnic minorities, and deviants of any sort.[3] Marginalization can be seen as the process of identification and separation of the marginal groups from the mainstream society. It is the subordination of labour through its gender, ethnical, occupational, and international division by capital, usually with assistance from the state. Under such division of labour, the wage levels, working conditions and job security of the marginal workers have deteriorated enormously. Marginalization of labour also increases the authority of capital, which under the label of "flexible management" cuts back the collective power of workers and their movements.

Marginalization of labour is a worldwide phenomenon. Hong Kong has followed the trend of flexible accumulation of capital in other industrialized capitalist countries. However, Hong Kong is unique. It will become a Special Administrative Region (SAR) with a capitalistic system under the sovereignty of China after 30 June 1997. Although, logically, the socialist China would have to provide more protection for Hong Kong workers after that date, I would argue that the economic reunification of Hong Kong and China is an accelerating factor in the marginalization crisis of Hong Kong labour.

---

[2] J. Harrod, *Power, Production and the Unprotected Worker* (New York: Columbia University Press, 1987).

[3] J. E. Perlman, *The Myth of Marginality: Urban Poverty and Politics in Rio de Janeiro* (Berkeley: University of California Press, 1976).

Marginalization Crisis of Hong Kong Labour

Restructuring of the Economy

The first characteristic of the marginalization crisis of Hong Kong labour is the rapid restructuring of the economy after the 1980s. Hong Kong has completed its transformation from a fishing village to a world city since 1842. Hong Kong is the focal point of entry for world mercantile and transnational capital into China. Before the Second World War, Hong Kong was basically a trading port. Only after the export-oriented industrialization during the1950s and 1960s did Hong Kong become one of the NIEs.

With the advent of economic reforms in China in 1979, Hong Kong's economy has been gradually integrated with the economy of southern China, especially the Zhujiang Delta Region (ZJDR). Most of the manufacturing industries relocated their production to China to avail of the cheap labour and rent. Deindustrialization in Hong Kong became significant and rapid after the early 1980s. Employment in the manufacturing sector as a percentage of total employment decreased from 47% in 1971 to 41.3% in 1981 and further to 35.8% in 1986. At the time, the number of workers employed in the manufacturing industry was 946,653. It was still the largest industry of Hong Kong in terms of workers employed. Owing to the continuous outflow of production capital, employees in manufacturing industry decreased to 570,200 at the end of 1994, which represented only about 20% of the total employed persons in Hong Kong.[4]

In line with other industrialized countries, employment growth in Hong Kong after the 1980s has been mainly in the service sector. For example, employment in wholesale and retail trades, restaurants and hotels increased from 16.2% in 1971 to 19.2% in 1981, and thereafter significantly to 28.8% in 1994. Employment in finance, insurance, real estate and business services increased from 2.7% in 1971 to 4.8% in 1991, and thereafter to 11.4% in 1994.[5]

At the same time, there has also been a concomitant change in the

---

[4] Census and Statistics Department, *Hong Kong Annual Statistical Digest of Statistics*, 1995 edition (Hong Kong: Hong Kong Government Printer, 1995), and Census and Statistics Department, *Hong Kong 1991 Population Census, Main Report* (Hong Kong: Hong Kong Government Printer, 1993).

[5] *Ibid.*

internal employment structure of the manufacturing industries. From 1981 to 1991, the number of operatives fell 43% while non-production staff increased 11%.[6] Manual workers in manufacturing industries have been doubly affected by this coincidental transformation of deindustrialization and white-collarization. Many workers were forced to leave the manufacturing industries for other industries. Owing to their poor education, most of them could only shift to low-paid, unskilled and insecure jobs in service industries.

More and more manual workers, especially women, middle-aged and elderly workers, are facing the impact of economic restructuring.[7] The displaced workers, who earlier worked in manufacturing industries, encounter difficulties in securing jobs because their skills hold little market value. Some of them feel humiliated when their new employers demand that they do unskilled work. Their weakened bargaining power in manufacturing industries and their lack of suitable training and experience in service industries force them to become marginal workers, both in manufacturing and service industries.

Those who remain in manufacturing industries often experience underemployment and receive lower incomes. Among different industries, the situation in the garment industry is the worst, where the workers face slow increase in wages and deteriorating living standards.[8]

Production workers in manufacturing industries who can retain their jobs or can find low-paid jobs in the service industries are fortunate, although they have much lower incomes. Many laid-off workers cannot re-enter the labour market and secure employment. The problem of this structural unemployment and underemployment will be discussed in the next section.

---

[6] Census and Statistics Department, "Structural Changes in Manufacturing Industries 1981–1991," in *Hong Kong Monthly Digest of Statistics*, September 1993 (Hong Kong: Hong Kong Government Printer), p. 119.

[7] Relevant local research includes Chan Kit-wa, *et al.*, "Women Workers under Industrial Restructuring in Hong Kong," mimeo., 1994; Stephen Chiu and David Levin, "Labour under Industrial Restructuring in Hong Kong: A Comparison of Textiles and Garments," *Occasional Paper No. 21* (Hong Kong: Hong Kong Institute of Asia-Pacific Studies, The Chinese University of Hong Kong, 1993).

[8] See Industry Department, *Hong Kong's Manufacturing Industries* (Hong Kong: Hong Kong Government Printer, 1994), p. 28.

Rise of Structural Unemployment

The second feature of the marginalization crisis of Hong Kong labour is the rise of structural unemployment. During the late 1980s and the first half of 1990s, the unemployment rate of Hong Kong stayed below 2%,[9] which is extremely low when compared with the current situation in Western industrialized countries. However, the unemployment scenario has deteriorated since 1995. The official unemployment rate was over 3% for the first time in the last ten years. The level, and the causes for the rise of unemployment, which are similar to those in Western capitalist countries after the mid-1970s, make Hong Kong's current unemployment problem a structural and long-term one. Since 1995, unemployment has become the social problem that arouses the greatest concern in Hong Kong. The problem of unemployment in Hong Kong has changed from periodical to persistent at high levels, from temporary to permanent, and from sectional to territory-wide.[10]

The unemployment problem in Hong Kong was periodical during the 1970s and 1980s. The rise of unemployment followed the economic cycle, in which the downturn lasted only for two to three years. Over the last seven years, it has exhibited an increasing trend. Hong Kong appears to follow other Western capitalist countries, where unemployment becomes stagnant at a high level.

The nature of the unemployment problem has been altered from the temporary to the permanent. In the first quarter of 1994, the number of persons unemployed for over three months was 21,000, constituting 26.2% of the total unemployed. During the first quarter of 1995, the number increased to 31,000, being 31% of the total unemployed. Furthermore, the present statistics tend to classify the elderly, housewives, disabled persons, and those permanently unemployed persons as "economically inactive

---

[9] Census and Statistics Department, *Hong Kong Social and Economic Trends* (Hong Kong: Hong Kong Government Printer, 1995), p. 17.

[10] Further discussion can be found in Wong Hung, "Essence of the Current Unemployment Problem in Hong Kong," *Hong Kong Economic Journal*, 10 August 1995 (in Chinese).

population." Therefore, the situation of the long-term unemployed cannot be reflected in the official statistics.[11]

In the past, unemployment in Hong Kong mostly affected manufacturing, construction and handicraft industries, especially small and medium-sized establishments. But now, unemployment has spread to retailing, catering, hotel, restaurant and transport industries. Moreover, under keen competition, many large-scale and well-established companies have implemented flexible management. The main objective is to reduce staff cost by cutting staff number and wage level. Two recent examples are the Hong Kong Telecom Company and China Light and Power Company. Despite huge profits, they still retrench staff from the lower to middle ranks through "voluntary" early retirement and involuntary redundancy. Job security enjoyed by the staff of these public utilities for many years has been destroyed by this flexible management method. The shadows of unemployment have thus spread from small and medium-sized enterprises to large enterprises. Unemployment has now become a territory-wide problem, affecting businesses of every scale and industry.

The first cause of structural unemployment in Hong Kong is the restructuring of the economy, which has been dwelt upon in the previous section. Another cause of unemployment is the inadequate protection of workers. Upholding its "positive non-intervention" philosophy, the Hong Kong Government believes that the unemployment problem should be solved by market forces, not by its intervention. In Hong Kong, there is no protection against unfair dismissal. Workers can be fired without any reason. Fortunately, in accordance with labour legislation, they are entitled to dismissal compensation. However, loopholes exist in the legislation concerning severance and long service payments. Workers must work for a minimum of two to five years with the same employer in order to successfully claim the compensation. Many employers retrench workers before they complete their minimum period to avoid paying the compensation, thereby circumventing the regulation and contributing to the rise in unemployment.

The lack of job security, inadequate legal protection, stress, and loss of self-respect have increased the vulnerability of the workers to exploitation by their employers.

---

[11] For detail discussion, please refer to Wong Hung, "Does Government Deliberately Underestimate the Unemployment Rate?" *Hong Kong Economics Times*, 9 November 1995 (in Chinese).

The third cause for the current structural unemployment is the institutional discrimination against certain marginal groups in a segmented labour market. The segmented labour market provides employers with greater profit and control over labour, through the divide and rule strategy.

There exists institutional discrimination based on age, sex and ethnicity. For example, women and new immigrants, despite good qualifications and experience, usually find themselves trapped in unskilled and low-paid jobs. These institutional discriminations have intensified further by the importation of foreign labour. Employers can easily find cheap foreign labour to perform jobs that could be taken up by the marginal groups. The authority to hire and fire employees has increased. The labour importation scheme amplifies the existing discrimination against the aged, female, new immigrants and the disabled. Members of these marginal groups are usually the first to be laid off. Furthermore, they face barriers while re-entering the labour market and rarely find a new job after being dismissed. That is why most of the long-term unemployed belong to these vulnerable groups.[12]

Changing Labour Market and Employment Relation

The third symptom of the marginalization crisis of Hong Kong labour is the changing labour market and employment relations in both public and private sectors. The *de jure* employment relationship has been withered away by employers in order to lower labour cost.

The first significant change in the labour market is the "privatization" in the government and public sectors. Being the largest employer in Hong Kong, the Hong Kong Government has set the example by contracting out peripheral services to reduce labour cost. Consequently, many services provided by workers of the rank of civil servants are now provided by temporary and contract staff employed by the contractors and agencies. Besides, tenders minimize the cost borne by the government. However, lower wages, longer working hours and diminished job security are the basic terms of employment of companies providing privatized services.[13]

---

[12] Wong Hung, *"Labour and Poverty: Round Table Discussion Paper"* (presented in Poverty and Social Development Summit organized by The Hong Kong Council of Social Service, 3 February 1996).

[13] *Ibid.*

For example, all car park services of the Housing Authority are contracted to various private companies. In 1995, a dispute arose when one of these car park companies changed the shift system. It prolonged the staff's working hours from eight to twelve hours a day. However, the pay rise failed to match the increase in working time.

Another significant change in the labour market is the termination of the *de jure* employment relation between employers and employees in the private sector. Various methods like contracting-out, renting-out, occasional termination of contract are used by the employers. In Hong Kong, most ironing sections of the garment factories are now run under the contract-out system, in which the foreman or the head of the section becomes the contractor who bears the liabilities under Hong Kong's labour legislation. Ironing workers are now legally employed by the contractor and not the original employer. The production process, nevertheless, which is the same as before, is controlled by the ex-employer.

Examples can also be found in other handicraft industries like tailoring and jewellery. Tailors who were paid by piece-rate are now required by the employers to "rent" their working tables. Legally, the relationship between the tailors and the employer has changed from employer-employee to business partners. Under this new relationship, ex-employers merely supply orders to the tailors at a rate slightly higher than before. However, the tailors have to pay back rent, and forgo all the protection under labour legislation.[14] In the jewellery industry, elegant craft works for high-value-added jewellery are now being distributed as out-contract work to individual experienced ex-employees.

All in all, the main objective of these arrangements is to terminate the *de jure* employer-employee relation and to avoid conceding the minimum standard of welfare and benefits required by labour legislation. Without any employer-employee relationship, employers do not even need to lay off workers when they face a downturn in business. They just stop doing "business" with the ex-employees. However, the labour process does not undergo any significant changes. It is still the same person, the ex-employer who decides what to produce and how to produce. Employers still enjoy the *de facto* control of the labour process.

---

[14] The information of these examples came from interviews with full-time officials of the Garment Workers' and Tailors' Union.

Increasing Poverty and Inequality

Marginalization of workers can also be proved by the widening gap between the poor and the rich. Owing to the rise in unemployment and underemployment of marginal workers and stagnant real wages, poverty and inequality in Hong Kong have increased.

The number of cases under the Comprehensive Social Security Assistance (CSSA) Scheme, the only government-financed income support scheme in Hong Kong, rose sharply from 66,675 in 1990–1991 to 165,000 in 1996–1997. The rate of increase in the number of CSSA cases was 15% in 1993–1994 and 21% in 1996–1997. Unemployment cases rose to 31% in 1993–1994 and to 54% in 1994–1995. The figures show that an increasing number of marginal workers' households have been living below the official poverty line.[15]

This is only the tip of the iceberg. Unless faced with a critical crisis, few workers would like to apply for the CSSA. Most of the workers prefer to reduce their expenditure, or borrow from relatives and friends rather than apply for assistance from the government. Households receiving CSSA also live in hardship, having to survive with the small amount of money provided. Under the stress of long-term poverty, most workers are forced to accept any job that can be found in the labour market.

Using secondary data of the Household Expenditure Survey, Wong and Chua estimated that in 1994–1995 over 60,000 persons or 25,000 households in Hong Kong lived in absolute poverty.[16] The gap between household incomes during 1981 and 1991 has been widening. The Gini Coefficient rose from 0.451 in 1981 to 0.476 in 1991. This shows the growing discrepancy in incomes.

During the same period, households with the lowest incomes have shown no sign of improvement, but there is a sign of decrease in the actual income of the low-income households. In fact, 20% of the households with the lowest income earned only 4.6% of total household incomes. The figure increased slightly in 1986 to 5.0%. But in the period from the 1986 to 1991,

---

[15] Census and Statistics Department, *Hong Kong Annual Statistical Digest of Statistics*, 1995 edition.

[16] Wong Hung and Chua Hoi-wai, *Report of the Research on Expenditure Pattern of Low Expenditure Household* (Hong Kong: Hong Kong Council of Social Service and Oxfam Hong Kong, 1996).

the figure fell to 4.3%.[17] We can see that the income gap is widening and the situation of low-income households has worsened.[18]

In short, the marginalization of workers of Hong Kong can be exemplified by three trends in recent years: the rise of structural unemployment, the changing labour market and employment relation, and the increasing poverty and inequality.

Causes of the Marginalization Crisis

Causes of the marginalization crisis of Hong Kong workers can be identified at three levels: global, regional and local. At the global level, flexible accumulation of capital becomes a worldwide trend as a post-Fordist capitalistic mode of production. Economic reunification of the regional political economy of China and Hong Kong, and the unlimited supply of surplus workers in China are two important factors at the regional level. At the Hong Kong local level, importation of workers and the increasing authority of capital also contribute to the marginalization crisis of Hong Kong labour.

Flexible Accumulation of Capital: A Worldwide Trend

Flexible accumulation of capital is a worldwide trend in both Western industrialized countries and the NIEs. The trend can be understood at two levels: first, at the macro level, the capitalist world system intends to solve the rigidity problem of the Fordist model of accumulation. Second, at the micro level, the plant managers want to achieve functional and numerical flexibility to meet the demands of an ever-changing market.

Harvey claims that the transformation of Fordism to flexible accumulation is inevitable.[19] According to him, flexible accumulation involves a

---

[17] Census and Statistics Department, *Hong Kong 1991 Population Census, Main Report*, pp. 66–67.

[18] For detail discussion of poverty among different deprived groups, see Lui Tai-lok and Wong Hung, *Disempowerment and Empowerment — An Exploratory Study on Low-Income Households in Hong Kong* (Hong Kong: Oxfam Hong Kong, 1995).

[19] D. Harvey, *The Condition of Postmodernity* (Oxford: Basil Blackwell, 1989) pp. 147–50.

direct confrontation with the rigidities of Fordism. It rests on flexibility in the labour processes, labour market, products and patterns of consumption. The "time-space compression," which has enhanced powers of flexibility and mobility, has allowed employers to exert stronger pressures of labour control on account of high unemployment. Thus, Harvey suggests that "Flexible accumulation appears to imply relatively high levels of 'structural' unemployment, rapid destruction and reconstruction of skills, modest (if any) gains in the real wage, and the roll-back of trade union power."

Atkinson describes the model of a "flexible firm."[20] He makes a distinction between functionally and numerically flexible workers. Functionally flexible workers, according to Atkinson, are those workers who are able to change their skills and tasks in line with changing market conditions and are at the core, whereas numerically flexible workers are those at the periphery, whose numbers can be adjusted as market conditions fluctuate.

Although the marginalization crisis should be understood in this worldwide context, regional political economy should also be examined. The political force which regulates labour and their movement is important in creating the uniqueness of a particular case over the ideal type of the model.

An Accelerating Factor: The Economic Reunification of Hong Kong and China

Sassen correlates the migration of labour and capital to the restructuring of capital in the world system.[21] The labour flows are associated with worldwide trends in the recomposition of capital. Sassen argues that the restructuring of the world economy assumes specific forms in locations ceding manufacturing and in those receiving it. The new labour migrations to the core and those within the periphery are articulated with different movements of the capital migration circuit. The former is articulated with the recomposition of the economic structure of the world economy's old

---

[20] See J. Atkinson, "The Changing Corporation," in *New Patterns of Work*, edited by D. Clutterbuck (Aldershot: Gower, 1985), or J. Atkinson and N. Meager, *Changing Working Patterns: How Companies Achieve Flexibility to Meet New Needs* (London: NEDO, 1986).

[21] S. Sassen, "Issues of Core and Periphery: Labour Migration and Global Restructuring," in *Global Restructuring and Territorial Development*, edited by J. Henderson and M. Castells (London: Sage, 1987).

centres that are now in decline; and the latter with the relocation of manufacturing and clerical activities to selected peripheral areas. Regional concentration of these activities and their labour intensive character maximize the impact on people, promoting internal migration to the new industrial zones. This provides the basic theoretical explanation for the huge migration of labour and capital between Hong Kong and the ZJDR.

The regional political economy between China and Hong Kong has long been in existence. The economy of Hong Kong has been integrating intensely with the economy of southern China, especially the ZJDR. The role of Hong Kong in the regional political economy should be understood from the trend of regional capital recomposition and the role of Hong Kong acting as a "Secondary World City" in the region.

It was the rise of Hong Kong after the Opium War in 1842 which saw the imperial capital's use of gunboat to destroy resistance from the domestic mode of production. Hong Kong became the theatre of the accumulation of regional and foreign capital and acted as a focal point to identify the surplus market of China. After the 1949 Revolution, the main focus of the Chinese Communist Party (CCP) was to eliminate the imperial power from China and to gain independence and autonomy. Therefore, a closed door policy, which separated the development of Hong Kong and Macau from the rest of ZJDR, was implemented.[22]

However, owing to the economic reforms and the open door policy since 1979 and also to the changing international division of labour (CIDL) of the world system,[23] the intensive flow of labour, capital and commodity between Hong Kong, Macau and the ZJDR reintegrated the three parts into a regional political economy.

In 1979, the central Chinese Government approved the request by the Guangdong and Fujian governments to set up export processing zones

---

[22] For economic relationship between Hong Kong and China, see A. J. Youngson (ed.), *China and Hong Kong: The Economic Nexus* (Hong Kong: Oxford University Press, 1983).

[23] About the difference between new international division of labour (NIDL) and changing international division of labour (CIDL), see F. Frobel *et al.*, *The New International Division of Labour* (Cambridge; New York: Cambridge University Press, 1980), and R. Cohen, *The New Helots: Migrants in the International Division of Labour* (Aldershot: Gower, 1987).

(EPZs), which were officially named special economic zones (SEZs). Two of the SEZs, Shenzhen and Zhuhai, are located in the ZJDR. As a follow-up to the setting up of the SEZs, the central government in 1984 approved a list of fourteen coastal cities as "open cities," which enjoyed the special policy concessions of the SEZs. In 1985, the central authority set up an open zone for the remaining areas of ZJDR and named it the Zhujiang Delta Open Zone (ZJDOZ). The zone was to enjoy similar policy concessions similar to the coastal cities, which in fact made the zone the largest EPZ in China.[24]

Sassen argues that EPZs represent the institutionalization of key patterns underlying the new industrialization in selected areas of the periphery. The relocation of manufacturing, the associated intra-periphery migrations and the new migrations to the core can be shown to be interdependent occurrences when we introduce a set of explanatory variables that can be summarized under the notion of class struggles.[25]

Owing to the struggles of the labour movement in Hong Kong in the 1970s, labour gained certain improvements in working and living conditions by improving labour legislation and social services. However, Hong Kong capital responded to the labour's gains by relocating the production process to the periphery, i.e. the SEZs and the ZJDOZ, where low wage, unorganized and highly controllable labour, most of them migrants from the rural areas, could be easily employed. The capital could thus make use of these migrant labour to suppress the demand and struggle of labour in Hong Kong by threatening to move their production to the periphery.

Another feature of the current CIDL is the integration of the world capital system under the hierarchic control of "World Cities." The dispersion of industrial capital has also generated new forms of concentration of managerial and specialized services in major urban centres. Besides generating a large volume of high-income professional jobs, this new economic core also offers a wide array of low-wage jobs. Immigration has

---

[24] For development of ZJDOZ, see T. M. H. Chan, *The Development and Prospects of the Zhujiang Delta Open Zone* (Shanghai: Friedrich Ebert Foundation, 1988).

[25] S. Sassen-Koob, "The New Labour Demand in Global Cities," in *Cities in Transformation*, edited by M. P. Smith (Beverly Hill, CA: Sage, 1984).

become the supplier of low-wage and typically powerless workers, facilitating these strategic centres to control and manage the world economy.[26]

Following these arguments is the theoretical tradition of the World City Hypothesis developed by Friedmann (1986) and Sassen (1984) linking urbanization processes to global economic forces. The World City Hypothesis is about the spatial organization of the CIDL. It concerns the contradictory relations between production in the era of global management and the political determination of territorial interests.

The recent development experience of Hong Kong and its new role in the region support the projections of the above World City Hypothesis. Hong Kong is now the managerial, information and financial centre of the ZJDR's regional political economy. Employment and capital in Hong Kong are being restructured, shifting from export-oriented manufacturing production to trading and financial businesses which control the production process of the whole of ZJDR.

In the external world system, world capital seeks to enter the huge market and identify the source of surplus value in China. Its traditional, prosperous trading activities provide Hong Kong with an excellent transportation and communication network with other countries. With its advantageous geographic location and educated workforce, Hong Kong is used by world capital as a "basing point," creating a continuous inflow of financial and production capital into the territory. In turn, Hong Kong acts as a capital wholesaler to fuel rapid industrialization and urbanization in the ZJDR. Hong Kong thus performs the functions of a "world city" by facilitating the whole region's integration into the world system and by controlling the capital accumulation process of the whole region.[27]

In conclusion, we should understand the economic restructuring of Hong Kong in the context of the economic reunification of Hong Kong and China. The relocation of different circuits of migration of capital and labour in ZJDR and Hong Kong is the result of the economic reforms in China,

---

[26] *Ibid.*, and J. Friedmann, "The World City Hypothesis," *Development and Change*, Vol. 17 (1986), pp. 69–83.

[27] For information about migration of labour and capital in ZJDR, see Wong Hung, "The Changing International Division of Labour: Migration of Labour and Capital in the Zhujiang Delta Region" (M.A. dissertation, Department of Sociology, University of Warwick, 1989).

the CIDL and Hong Kong's status as a "world city." This, in turn, is a factor accelerating the marginalization crisis of Hong Kong labour.

Unlimited Supply of Surplus Workers in China and ZJDR

The migration of Hong Kong production to ZJDR and the transformation of production capital to financial capital are the underlying causes of the marginalization of Hong Kong labour. The precondition for the migration of Hong Kong capital is the unlimited supply of cheap labour in China and ZJDR. The following paragraphs will outline some different opinions on the causes for these "surplus workers."

Before the economic reforms, the condition of agricultural and industrial labour in China was stagnant. Since 1959, every citizen in China has had a designated place of residence. A social control system coordinated the housing, food supply, employment, social welfare and even marriages of the citizens. Local authorities were thus able to control population movements by administrative means. Requests for change of residence registration status from rural to urban areas were usually denied, preventing peasants from migrating to the cities, a common phenomenon in other third world countries.

Until the 1980s, all China's urban citizens, after completing their schooling, waited for the local officials to allocate them a job. Once assigned to a job, their residence registration or *hukou*, was fixed to their work unit, the *danwei*,[28] and they were attached to that work unit and assured of life-long employment. The work unit looked after their wages, housing, living subsidies, medical benefits, political activities, marriage and other family affairs.[29]

In 1979, under the economic reform policies, a new "contract labour system" was introduced to reform the fixed employment system. A fixed-term contract between employer and employee was adopted and the guarantee of a permanent job for the worker was no longer provided. The reformers believed that by introducing fixed-term, renewable working contracts to state employees, productivity would improve. The system would

---

[28] W. Y. Leung, *Smashing the Iron Rice Pot, Workers and Unions in China's Market Socialism* (Hong Kong: Asia Monitor Resource Centre, 1988).

[29] *Ibid.*, and L. Sklair, "Shenzhen: A Chinese 'Development Zone' in Global Perspective," *Development and Change*, Vol. 16 (1985), pp. 571–602.

also offer greater freedom to individuals to change jobs and to managers to expand or reduce their workforce according to production needs.

The "iron rice bowl" was adversely affected by the introduction of "temporary labour." These temporary workers, usually young migrants from rural areas, represented the most marginalized sector of the workforce. They had even less job security and welfare protection than the contract labour. At the end of 1986, the Chinese Government estimated that over 10 million rural population were working in China's cities.[30] Most of them were employed on short-term contracts — one to three years — in the construction, textile and machinery industries, with the lowest pay and the worst working conditions.

Reform of the labour employment system in the ZJDR is easier and more successful than in other regions of China. This is because most of the establishments in the SEZs and the ZJDOZ are new. Unlike other big industrial cities, for instance Shanghai and Wuhan, the ZJDR has no burden of a vast number of aged and retired workers in the state enterprises. The newly established enterprises could easily attract the rural population in ZJDR and other provinces to accept the new labour system. Consequently, most of the migrant workers in the ZJDR are under the two new forms of labour system, that is, contract labour and temporary labour.

Other related reforms in ZJDR are the household registration system and the food-grain purchase and supply system. The migrants are allowed to reside temporarily on condition that they would bring with themselves the necessary food-grains or could afford to buy food-grains in the market. The municipal government would not supply them with any food-grains at the official price. They are known as the "self-managed food-grain household."

In most of the Chinese literature on the mobility of labour,[31] the focal point of debates rests on "the mobility of the rural surplus population."

---

[30] *China Daily*, 5 March 1988.

[31] Meng Kei and Bai Nansheng, *Jiegou Biandong: Zhongguo Nongye Laodongli di Zhuanyi* (Structural Transformation: The Migration of Rural Labour Force in China) (Zhejiang: Zhejiang Renmin Chubanshe (Zhejiang People's Publisher), 1988), and Xu Xueqiang, Liu Qi and Zeng Xiang, *Zhujiang Sanjiaozhou di Fazhan yu Chengshihua* (The Development and Urbanization of Zhujiang Delta Region) (Guangzhou: Zhongshan Daxue Chubanshe (Zhongshan University Publisher), 1988).

This is considered to be the fundamental factor in the huge migration of labour taking place in recent years in China. Meng and Bai identify three historical factors to account for the particularly large rural surplus population in China.[32] First, owing to the shortage of cultivated land and the rapid growth in population, per capita cultivated land in China is scarce when compared with other countries. Second, the traditional monopolistic product based on food-grain and the self-sustained economy have formed a vicious cycle, making agriculture unable to absorb its own surplus labour. Third, the urban areas where the enterprises have already borne heavy social benefits cannot absorb any surplus population. These arguments echo those of the "push and pull" theory.

In accounting for the continuous use of migrant workers in different phases of capitalism, a "push and pull" theory was developed by demographers and geographers. The theory considered overpopulation, poverty, traditional value and economic stagnation of the homeland as the "push factors." The diplomatic, demographic and economic needs, modern values and economic opportunities in the receiving countries were regarded as the "pull factors." However, this school has been heavily criticized for its individualistic, domestic and ahistorical view.[33]

Marx argues that overpopulation in rural areas, that is, rural surplus population, is in fact a historical product of the capitalist mode of production. He suggests that as soon as capitalist production methods intrude into the rural world, agricultural employment sharply decreases, such that part of the agricultural population is at any time at the point of passing over into the urban or manufacturing proletariat.[34] The rural population thus becomes the source of relative surplus population.

The History Task Force sums up the Marxist view on the law of population in the capitalist mode of production as follows: under capitalism, population becomes population for capital.[35] The capitalist

---

[32] *Ibid.*

[33] See History Task Force, Centro de Estudios Puertorriquenos, *Labour Migration under Capitalism: The Puerto Rican Experience* (New York: Monthly Review Press, 1979), and also refer to Note 21 and Note 23.

[34] K. Marx, *Capital: A Critique of Political Economy*, Vol. 1 (Harmondsworth: Penguin Books, 1976).

[35] History Task Force, *Labour Migration under Capitalism: The Puerto Rican Experience*.

mode has as its fundamental premise the dispossession of the majority of the population of their instruments and means of production. This majority is transformed into waged labour, that is, a human mass defined not by its need for subsistence but by its production of capital, which involves both the accumulation and increasing concentration of social wealth and the reproduction of capitalist relations as such. But systematic expropriation and the demand for labourers are not matched by a capacity to absorb ever larger numbers of workers into the productive apparatus. In augmenting its numbers, the working class reproduces its own superfluity within the society. In contrast to other modes of production, it is the very mechanism of capitalist development in its explosive revolutionary expansion that generates ever larger relative overpopulation.

Under the Marxist's critique, "rural surplus population" in vast rural areas of China should not be an abstract idea with respect to their "productivity" but should be analysed in its relation to production.

Importation of Labour to Hong Kong

The "rural surplus population" in China not only provides unlimited supply of cheap migrant workers in the ZJDR, but also becomes the source of migrant workers in Hong Kong. Most Hong Kong workers arrived from mainland China during the three migration waves: the Second World War, 1960–1963, and 1978–1981. Most of these Chinese immigrants stayed behind and gained Hong Kong citizenship. These successive waves of new immigrants provided unlimited supply of "surplus population" to meet the huge demand for unskilled and semi-skilled workers in the rapid accumulation of capital in Hong Kong. However, owing to the huge number of immigrants who arrived during the late 1970s, the Hong Kong Government decided to terminate the "touch base" immigration policy in 1981. It became illegal for mainland Chinese to enter Hong Kong without legal documents. All such illegal immigrants arrested have been sent back to China since then.[36]

In the early 1990s, it was claimed that Hong Kong had a serious shortage of labour. Responding to this demand of capital, the Hong Kong Government introduced several schemes for the importation of foreign

---

[36] A. J. Youngson (ed.), *China and Hong Kong: The Economic Nexus.*

workers, most of them from China. In 1992, for the first time the Hong Kong Government set up a guest worker system. Migrant workers were permitted to work in Hong Kong on condition that they would return to China on completion of their contracts. Their contracts were fixed at two years, which could only be extended two times.

A general scheme for the importation of labour was first announced in 1992. It proposed that a maximum of 25,000 workers at the supervisory, technician and craftsman level would be allowed to work in Hong Kong. The minimum wage of the imported workers was linked to the median wage of corresponding local workers in the same trade. However, this protection for both foreign and local workers could not be enforced. On the one hand, many foreign workers reported that they were badly treated by their employers and received much lower wages than the legal minimum. On the other hand, local workers complained that the influx of foreign workers had smashed their "rice bowl." The wage level and job opportunity of local workers have been deteriorating tremendously since the introduction of this scheme. Not only workers in manufacturing industries, but also those in service industries, like catering, transport and retailing have been adversely affected.

Another special scheme was set up to import workers for the construction of the new airport. The initial quota was 2,000 in 1990, and this was increased to 17,000 in 1994 and further to 27,000 in 1996. This scheme has had a tremendous impact on the labour market of the construction industry since 1994. Many local construction workers suddenly found themselves unemployed and underemployed. The imported construction workers would only be given around 40% to 50% of the wages of the local workers. The situation changed only after several Chinese guest workers complained against their contractors for illegally denying their basic and overtime pay. Owing to resistance from the imported workers, there was little advantage for the contractors to employ them. The latter thus began to re-employ local workers for the construction work of the new airport. As a result, the unemployment rate in the construction industry has been decreasing since the second quarter of 1996.[37]

In 1994, the Hong Kong Government introduced another scheme of

---

[37] Information extracted from interview with unionists of the Construction Worker's General Union.

importing professionals from mainland China. One thousand graduates from thirty-six major universities in China were permitted to work in Hong Kong. This scheme was not successful as only a few quotas were used. This may be due to the fact that graduates with working experience could find better job opportunities in the mainland than in Hong Kong. This also confirms the fact that there is not really a labour shortage problem as the employers have claimed.

Cohen states four positive benefits of employing migrant labour.[38] First, rooted in classical economic theory, more hands means more production. Second, there is the benefit of savings in the reproduction cost of labour power of migrant labour. Third, migrant labour is cheaper, less well-organized, easier to hire and fire, and has lower economic and social expectations. Fourth, it segregates the working class and fractures the class composition. All these benefits are available to the capital in Hong Kong.

The fundamental impact of importation of workers on local workers is not the actual job loss caused, but the psychological impact. Many workers are afraid of losing jobs, and have to accept whatever pay and conditions offered by the employers. This multiplies the actual job loss effect, and increases the authority of capital in the labour market and the labour process.

Increasing Authority of Capital

Importation of Chinese workers is only one of the reasons for the enlarging gap between the power of capital and labour. The other reason is some Chinese officials, who repeatedly assure the capitalists that Hong Kong would continue to be a paradise for investors.

According to the Sino-British Joint Declaration and the Basic Law, Hong Kong will continue its capitalist system under the framework of "one country, two systems" after 1997 for fifty years. Maintaining the stability and prosperity of Hong Kong is the top agenda of the Chinese Government. Faced with the threat of the retreat of capital before and after 1997, the main strategy of the Chinese officials is to maintain the confidence of the capitalists in Hong Kong. Not only have verbal assurances been given by

---

[38] R. Cohen, *The New Helots.*

the top leaders of China time and again, but the allocation of political power in the future SAR Government also favours capital.

Capitalists continue to complain about Hong Kong's increasing social welfare budget and mounting labour legislation. The reason is that these would destroy the cornerstones of the success of Hong Kong: minimal government intervention and low tax rates. The recent increasing expenditure on social welfare and new labour legislation, according to them, are a conspiracy of the British to destroy the financial tradition of Hong Kong, leaving the mess for the future SAR Government to handle.

Some Chinese officials seem to have accepted the arguments of the capitalists and publicly assert that the rapid increase of social welfare budget will bring disaster to Hong Kong. In the various advisory bodies of Hong Kong affairs within the Chinese Government, most of the appointed representatives are from commercial and business background. Only a few of them possess a grassroots or labour background. Thus the attitude of the Chinese officials reinforces the imbalance of power between capital and labour in Hong Kong.

Political and Economic Impacts of the Marginalization Crisis of Hong Kong Labour

We have just identified the causes of marginalization of Hong Kong workers at different levels. There is a worldwide trend of flexible accumulation of capital at the global level. The economic reunification of Hong Kong and China, and the unlimited supply of rural migrant workers in China are the structural causes at the regional level. At the local level, it is the importation of foreign workers and the increasing authority of Hong Kong capital that induce the marginalization of Hong Kong workers.

Such marginalization crisis of workers has both short-term and long-term political impact on Hong Kong. In the short term, the crisis may arouse discontentment among marginal workers, who may be a threat to the stability of Hong Kong. Previous riots in Hong Kong, for example, the 1966 Star Ferry Riot, the 1982 New Year Riot and the 1984 Taxi Riot, were all unforeseen. Reflecting on the experience of these riots, we discover that anger and frustration of the masses was the root cause of the riots, which were ignited by mob collective behaviour in a crisis situation.

In the short term, the marginalization crisis may also induce new waves of discontentment and critical awareness among workers. In the long term, it may increase the political aspiration and awareness of the marginal workers. As a long-term political impact, the marginalization crisis may reactivate class politics. Class interest may become the new political division line.

We may find some supporting evidence for the increasing importance of class politics. In 1995, several candidates with capitalist background were defeated by the candidates with labour background in the direct election to the Legislative Council, especially among the nine seats of new functional constituencies. Owing to the success of grassroots and labour candidates, various labour laws have been successfully passed in the new Legislative Council.

There were just a few issues on which Legislative Councillors from different union background see eye to eye — fighting the importation of workers and improving labour legislation. Nevertheless, these issues are important in that they represent a breakthrough in the relationship between the pro-China camp and the anti-China camp in Hong Kong and may also signify the possibility of revitalizing of class politics in Hong Kong after 1997.

Marginalization of workers in Hong Kong may provide limits as well as possibilities for the trade union movement and the political development of Hong Kong. It depends on the response from the workers, unions, employers and the government.

In the light of the experience of Western capitalist countries, the persistence of high unemployment rate will strongly hit union participation rate. Furthermore, the basic intent of flexible accumulation of capital is to limit and destroy the power of the unions as well as the bargaining power of individual workers.

In the case of Hong Kong, unions have fewer powers and the unionization rate is much lower than in Western capitalist countries. Workers in Hong Kong join unions not because of the collective bargaining power of the unions, but mainly for protection of employment rights and the welfare and services provided by unions. It is argued that the marginalization of workers may induce two contradicting effects. Owing to the drop in real income, marginal workers may regard the services and welfare provided by the unions as dispensable and stop paying membership fees. On the other hand, workers may participate more actively in unions as their awareness and consciousness increase. If Hong Kong unions demonstrate their ability to safeguard workers' rights and benefits, and not just as welfare and service providers, they may succeed in tackling the marginalization crisis of workers. Otherwise, their influence may probably fade, and their organizing role be replaced by political parties representing different classes.

The marginalization crisis of workers, like other social issues, has been overshadowed by the political conflict between the British and the Chinese Governments. The two governments may be aware of such crisis, but they give it a low priority in their tight agenda on the transfer of the sovereignty of Hong Kong.

The increase in social welfare budget and in the amount of CSSA, the withdrawal of the labour importation scheme, and the implementation of the Mandatory Provident Fund, all signify the present Hong Kong Government's reaction to the marginalization crisis. However, all these "policy fine-tuning" actions are limited by the basic "positive non-intervention" philosophy of the Hong Kong Government. The government requires the employers to be the main providers of workers' welfare and benefits. Moreover, the present Government has limited authority and legitimacy to implement long-term policy, like the Mandatory Provident Fund, which has long-term implications after 1997. The basic strategy of the present Hong Kong Government is to increase social welfare budget temporarily, and to prevent the outbreak of turmoil or disturbance before 30 June 1997.

The future SAR Government, which will have the legitimacy and authority to implement long-term policy to alleviate the impending marginalization crisis, may undertake more definite efforts to solve the problem, so as to maintain social stability after 1997. Although the four well-known candidates for the SAR Chief Executive election are from business and legal backgrounds, they still need popular support from the grassroots by addressing reforms in social welfare, housing, education and health policy, which is the method of the Fordist mode of production in solving the marginalization crisis of labour.

Marginalization of workers will produce social factors that Marx predicted would result in the "povertization" and "socialization" of the proletariat. Flexible accumulation of capital aims to destroy the "rigidity" within the Fordist mode of production. However it will also destroy the welfare state, the cooperatism, and the "safety valve" mechanism linked with the Fordist mode of production.

Faced with an enlarging population of marginal workers, flexible accumulation of capital cannot solve the crisis of under-consumption and over-production. This fundamental economic crisis of capitalism provided the base of class awareness and class politics for workers in the nineteenth century Europe as also for those in the twenty-first century Hong Kong.

The need for stability in the post-war Western capitalist countries induced the Fordist mode of production, which corresponds to the need for stability of the post-1997 Hong Kong. Therefore the future SAR Government may reintroduce some of the features of Fordist mode of production to solve the marginalization crisis of Hong Kong labour.

5

The Uneasy Balance: The Sino-Vatican-Hong Kong Relations after 1997

Beatrice Leung

The Political Nature of Catholic Church

World religions with their organizational structures have been an important social force within national politics. And Christianity in general, and Catholicism in particular have exercised their own impact on the world order in the history of Europe, because of their distinctive world views and attitudes to socio-political and economic issues.[1] In general, with very few exceptions, church-state relations have ranged from "tension" in Western democracies to problems of "conflicting authority" in Communist authoritarian regimes.[2] Because of its political influence and its peculiar

---

[1] There are numerous works on how Christianity has been steering the path of European history. Some of the recent works are: Timothy Fuller (ed.), *Michael Oakeshott: Religion, Politics and Moral Life* (New Haven and London: Yale University Press, 1993); Wade Clark Roof (ed.), *World Order and Religion* (New York: State University of New York Press 1991); George Moyer (ed.), *Politics and Religion in the Modern World* (London and New York: Routledge, 1991); Eric Hanson, *Catholic Church and World Politics* (Princeton, N.J.: Princeton University Press, 1987).

[2] For the "tension" between church and state in the West, see T. Robins and R. Robertson (ed.), *Church-State Relations: Tension and Transitions* (New Brunswick and Oxford: Transaction Books, 1987); George Moyer, *Politics and Religion in the Modern World*. For the conflicting authority between church and state in China and the former Soviet Union and Eastern Europe, see H. Stehle, *Eastern Politics of the Vatican 1917–1979*, translated by S. Smith (Ohio: Ohio

organizational structure, the Roman Catholic church has been defined by some political scientists as a transnational actor in international politics.[3] Catholic belief, with its anti-Communist nature (atheism versus deism) together with the anti-Communist strategies of Polish Pope John Paul II made a major contribution to the collapse of Communism in Eastern Europe.[4] The Pope has even openly denounced Communism in the Papal encyclical *Centesimus Annus*,[5] and has remarked that Marxism does not rid the world of injustice and oppression, which Marxism itself exploited.[6]

Ideological and political conflicts have marked the relationship between the government and the Catholic church in China from 1949 until today.[7] Tension peaked when the Pope unilaterally appointed Dominic Deng Yiming as the Archbishop of Guangzhou in 1981. China was furious, regarding this appointment as "an interference in the internal affairs of China," and condemnation of the Vatican and the Pope appeared at every level of government.[8] Amidst this condemnation, China ordered all possible formal interactions between China and the Vatican to be halted, yet the Pope requested the overseas Chinese Catholics to be the bridge between

---

University Press, 1987); and Beatrice Leung, *The Sino-Vatican Relations: Problems of Conflicting Authority* (Cambridge: Cambridge University Press, 1992).

[3] Ivan Vallier, "The Roman Catholic Church: A Transnational Actor," *International Organization*, Vol. 3 (1971), pp. 479–95.

[4] George Weigel, *The Final Revolution: The Resistance Church and the Collapse of Communism* (New York: Oxford University Press, 1992).

[5] John Paul II, *Centesimus Annus* (Vatican: Vatican Polyglot Press, 1991). The tone of the encyclical is to denounce Communism, see Chapter 2, pp. 43–57.

[6] *Ibid.*, p. 51.

[7] Beatrice Leung, *The Sino-Vatican Relations*.

[8] Within the Chinese Catholic church, the church magazine *Catholic Church in China* devoted the whole issue (October 1981) to condemn the appointment. Clergy and laity from many parts of the whole nation contributed articles to echo the government's condemnation. Newspapers in major cities reported the issue and the condemnation made by government officials; see *Wenhui Bao* (Shanghai), 18 June 1981; *Nanfeng Ribao* (Guangzhou), 14 June 1981; *Beijing Ribao*, 17 June 1981.

the Chinese Catholics and the universal church with informal interactions substituting formal communication.[9]

Hong Kong as the largest Chinese diocese in the world with its geographical affinity to China, has been an important part of this bridge. The revival of the Catholic church in China in Deng's era of modernization with the open door policy and the material and spiritual support given by overseas Catholics in general and Hong Kong Catholics in particular, had contributed to the process of religious revival in China. As a bridge, the Hong Kong Catholics, before the signing of the Sino-British Agreement on the future of Hong Kong, had a golden opportunity to learn how to deal with the Chinese Government in religious matters, and difficult bilateral problems between China and the Vatican had been eased by the working of the triangular relations of China, the Vatican and Hong Kong. Hong Kong could play this role because it has been in a political environment embedded in the British tradition which not only allowed religious freedom but also promoted a very warm church-state relations. As a rule, questions related to Catholicism are complicated because they can be categorized as international affairs and domestic issues as well. In terms of the triangular relationship between China, Vatican and Hong Kong after 1997, I suggest that the balance of this relation will tilt away from Hong Kong when the latter becomes a part of China. In consequence, Hong Kong will have to leave the triangle, and look for a new role more acceptable to Beijing.

The Hong Kong Catholic Church in Transition

Owing to cultural affinity, Christian churches (including the Catholic church) have, since the "establishment" of Hong Kong in 1841, enjoyed a smooth church-state relationship. Although the Hong Kong colonial government is not a democratic government, Hong Kong citizens have been enjoying a good measure of freedom, and have been protected by the rule of law under the British tradition. As a result, Hong Kong Christians including Catholics have been enjoying the maximum degree of religious freedom as their counterparts in the Western democracies. Based on the

---

[9] Pope John Paul II in February 1984 made this request when he received the Taiwan bishops who made their *"ad liminia"* visit to the Holy See; see Beatrice Leung, *The Sino-Vatican Relations*, Chapter 7.

harmonious church-state relations, the Hong Kong Catholic church has been playing the role of the "contractor," by sharing a large portion of the government's responsibility for providing many social services, educational and medical care.[10] Through the social services provided, the social gap between the rich and the poor has been slightly narrowed. The church has thus helped the Hong Kong Government to dilute the possible class conflict while reciprocally it has been dependent on government subventions to finance church service. In the one hundred and more years of the colonial rule, the Catholic church and other Christian denominations have rendered important services to British rule in Hong Kong.

However, in the past two decades, the church-society relations have changed. In the 1970s, new trends in theological teaching have advocated the integration of Catholic faith in the secular world. The setting up of the Commission of Justice and Peace at the diocesan level was an indication of the Church's concern in socio-political affairs.[11] Also, the opening up of China in Deng's era has been giving Hong Kong Catholics firsthand understanding of the restrictions on religious life imposed by the Chinese Communist Party (CCP).[12]

By adopting a rather conservative approach to Beijing in the past two decades, the top Catholic leaders in Hong Kong were basically distancing themselves from China and Xinhua News Agency, the Hong Kong

---

[10] Ambrose King suggested the term of administrative absorption of politics in Hong Kong. See Ambrose Y. C. King, "Administrative Absorption of Politics in Hong Kong: Emphasis on the Grass Roots Level," in *Social Life and Development in Hong Kong*, edited by Ambrose Y. C. King and Rance P. L. Lee (Hong Kong: The Chinese University Press, 1988), pp. 127–46.

[11] This commission is a pontifical commission with headquarters at the Vatican, and aims at promoting justice and peace, two main themes of the Catholic social teaching. Under the wish of the Pope, the Commission of Justice and Peace of diocesan level have been established to promote Catholic social teaching at the grassroots level.

[12] Owing to the theory of "conflicting authority," CCP retains the authority of teaching within the Party itself, disregarding the teachings of all major religions such as Buddhism, Islam and Christianity. Catholicism with the Vatican as the administrative centre, and with its strict hierarchical structure, clashes with China on the question of the cutting relation with the Holy See and Chinese Catholic Church. See Beatrice Leung, *The Sino-Vatican Relations*, Chapter 5.

communist agent. This was the result of their pro-Vatican stance, and of the unsettled dispute between China and the Vatican. As a matter of fact, all religions have problems in adjusting to the atheist rule of the CCP, yet the administrative nature of the Vatican poses extra difficulty on the Catholic and China relations.[13] However, within the Catholic circle there is a limited degree of pluralism, which offers enough scope for China's agents in Hong Kong to exercise the united front strategy by organizing visits and exchanges with some sympathetic and peripheral Catholics to facilitate the "bridge" function.

The combination of efforts to implement Christian social teachings in the local context; support for human rights and social justice together with political support for pro-democracy elements, all suggest a difficult church-state relationship after 1997.

Although the Sino-British Agreement on the future of Hong Kong promised "one country, two systems" and the Basic Law of the Hong Kong Special Administrative Region (SAR) pronounces that religious freedom will continue as before, Hong Kong Catholics feel that the present type of religious freedom they are enjoying under the British rule will evolve into the type of "religious freedom" which will be defined by the CCP.[14] This is because, in the central bureaucracy in Beijing, very few senior officials are involved in Hong Kong affairs. The final decision on Hong Kong matters rest with the supreme leaders such as Deng Xiaoping and Chen Yun who are orthodox Marxists and the last batch of revolutionary Chinese

---

[13] There are numerous reports on the restrictions imposed by China on Chinese Catholic believers. The major works are: L. Ladany, *The Catholic Church in China* (New York: Freedom House, 1987); Asia Watch Committee (U.S.), *Freedom of Religion in China* (New York: Human Rights Watch, 1992); Beatrice Leung, *The Sino-Vatican Relations*.

[14] In every version of the Chinese Constitution "religious freedom" has been included, yet for non-religious reasons, religious believers are arrested even now. Chinese leaders have their own interpretation of "religious freedom," and religious activities are circumscribed by regulations issued by the CCP; see "Document 19," in *Xinshiqi Zongjiao Gongzuo Wenxian Xuanbian* (Selected Document on Religious Work of New Age), edited by Documentation Centre of Party Central and Policy Section of Religious Affair Bureau (Beijing: Zongjiao Wenhua Press, 1995), pp. 55–76.

Communists.[15] Given their experience and world-view, they can be liberal in economic matters, but conservative in ideological and political matters. In the transition period, in economic matters, China never imposed the Chinese socialist system on Hong Kong's capitalist system. However, in the political system, the Chinese interference was increasingly felt, when China denounced the 1995 Legislative Council (Legco) election and declared that it would not allow the elected Councillors to retain their seats after 1 July 1997. Against the provisions of the Basic Law, Beijing decided to set up a temporary legislative body even before the transfer.

As a result, Hong Kong people began to doubt whether China will honour its pledge as recorded in the Sino-British Agreement and the Basic Law to allow Hong Kong to maintain its rule of law and basic freedoms that have been responsible for its remarkable success, from which China has greatly benefited.[16] Religious freedom is an important indicator of social freedom, and it is closely linked with the degree of ideological and political freedom. Thus, when political democracy is being curbed and freedom of press is under threat, and when "one country, two systems" policy is unlikely to be honoured in socio-political fields, Hong Kong Catholics, based on their knowledge on the Catholic church in China, have reasons to believe that after 1997, Hong Kong's church-state relations will change from the "contractor" model to the "political absorption of religion" model.[17] This is because, in China, religion is under the control of the CCP and religious organizations are absorbed into the political orbit. The fear

---

[15] See Michael Yahuda's chapter "A Catalyst for Change? The Hong Kong Special Administrative Region and Chinese Politics" in this book.

[16] Many foreign scholars hold this opinion. Most recently Professor Michael Leifer of London School of Economics and Political Science echoed the same doubt in his "Foreword" to Michael Yahuda, *Hong Kong: China's Challenge* (London and New York: Routledge, 1996).

[17] Chan Shun-hang borrowed the term of administrative absorption of politics in Hong Kong from Ambrose King in the discussion of church-state relations of Hong Kong after 1997; see Chan Shun-hang, "Xianggang Zhengjiao Guanxi Fazhen de Qianzhan" (The Future of the Development of The Hong Kong's Church-state Relations), in *Christian Faith and the Development of Hong Kong Society*, edited by Agatha M. Y. Wong (Hong Kong: Hong Kong Christian Institute), pp. 139–48.

of the possibility of a drastic change of church-state relations in the near future led directly to the announcement of a pastoral policy for the future. In 1989, the Hong Kong prelate, Cardinal Wu issued a pastoral exhortation — "March into the Bright Decade."[18] However, in this pastoral letter he suggested a multi-front strategy comprising seven strategies to respond to the political change in Hong Kong beyond 1997. One of these is to have more participation in socio-political affairs with Christian principles and to strengthen the Christian community through internalization of religious belief and faith. The role of being a bridge was retained as the seventh theme of the document.[19] In other words, the pastoral letter spelt out guidelines for the Catholic presence in Hong Kong after 1997. Although social involvement was not the main theme of this document, it did suggest that the church play a prophetic role by paying "serious attention to human rights, justice, labour, the poor in an affluent society and other problems, and discover the underlying reasons for them; besides, we should study government policies on labour, housing, health, etc., and respond in a responsible way."[20] How prophetic will it be? How is this to be implemented? Whatever the answers, this statement foreshadowed the involvement of the Church in socio-political issues in the transition period.

After five years of implementing Cardinal Wu's "March into the Bright Decade," except in the matter of the formation of the laity, the interim evaluation did not reveal any prominent progress in the carrying out of the pastoral policy by the clergy, religious men and women.[21] Only the fruit of the formation of the laity was reflected in their socio-political participation, e.g., high Catholic voting rate in the Legco 1991 and 1995 elections, and their independent voice on the Selection Committee and their

---

[18] Cardinal John B. Wu, "March into the Bright Decade: Pastoral Exhortation of Cardinal John B. Wu on the Pastoral Commitment of the Catholic Diocese of Hong Kong," n/p., 1989.

[19] *Ibid.*, p. 8 on Chapter 7.

[20] Ironically the pastoral letter was issued in July 1989, after the June 4th incident at the Tiananmen Square in 1989 while the whole of Hong Kong was in a state of utter instability. John B. Wu, "March into the Bright Decade," section VI.

[21] John B. Wu, *Proclaim the Gospel of the Lord Spread the Kingdom of God*, n/p., 1995.

non-acceptance of the Provisional Legislative Council.[22] In the matter of sending representatives to the Selection Committee, opinions were divided within the Hong Kong Catholic church especially from the laity. After going through the training in Catholic social teaching, some Catholic lay leaders advised the church authority to play a prophetic role to go against the current by not accepting the Provisional Legislative Council. Although some "patriotic" priests held a contrary view, the Hong Kong Catholic authority eventually adopted a policy on this matter incorporating much of the laity's attitude.[23] On this issue the Catholic church of Hong Kong learned from its Protestant brothers by soliciting views of the laity on this thorny question.[24] The effects of grassroots consultation is twofold: it won the support of the laity and avoided a split within the church on the controversy which occurred among Hong Kong Protestants.[25]

The formation of the Catholic Institute of Society and Religion in 1984 aimed at harmonizing Christian theology with teachings on socio-political issues, in order to satisfy the needs of Catholics to implement their faith in daily life. This led to training programmes to achieve this goal. The June 4th incident at Tiananmen Square in 1989 stimulated the creation of another organization, the Catholic Support for the Pro-Democratic Movement in China. Indeed, a leading priest of this movement became the key figure in

---

[22] This author witnessed some Catholic laity leaders in a meeting with the church hierarchy openly advising the Cardinal not to send any Catholic representative to the Selection Committee because of the Committee's support for the establishment of the provisional legislative council which is widely believed to be against the Basic Law.

[23] See the notice sent by the Catholic Chancery Office on 19 August 1996 on the "Guideline on Participating the Selection Committee." Unlike the Hong Kong Catholics, the Hong Kong Protestants did not have a system of open consultative process. Since the decision on this issue was arrived at without resorting to consultation, opinions were divided among the Hong Kong Protestants.

[24] The Catholic Chancery Office issued a notice to launch a consultation on the parish level in May 1996. The Hong Kong Protestants did not have open consultations like the Hong Kong Catholics. For want of a consultative process, opinions of the Hong Kong Protestants were divided on the decision of the Protestant leaders on this issue.

[25] *Sing Tao Daily*, 24 and 30 May 1996; *Hong Kong Economic News*, 7 and 25 June 1996.

the Steering Committee of the Hong Kong Citizens Supporting the Pro-Democratic Movement in China.

Catholic political activity has also been visible in the Legco elections. As early as in the 1988 Legco election, the diocese issued guidelines to encourage Catholics to cast their votes to fulfil the duty of citizens. In 1990–1991, when the Hong Kong Catholic diocese celebrated its one hundred and fiftieth anniversary, its motto was "to walk with the people" and actions were taken to promote the 1991 Legco election. Not only were sermons delivered to encourage Catholics to participate in the election, but assistance was also given to Catholics to help them register as voters in some parishes. As a result, the voting rate among Catholics was much higher than that of the general public (86% versus 39%).[26] In 1992, the Committee of Catholic Supervision of Legislative Councillors was established and occasional reports on the performance of Legislative councillors as well as on their attitudes to social issues debated in the Legco were published. A few months before the 1995 Legco election, the Diocesan Commission of Justice and Peace published booklets to guide Catholics in their choice of candidates.[27] When the 1995 Legco election took place amid the dispute between China and the British over political reform in Hong Kong, the Catholics revealed their voting behaviour in two ways: first by a higher voting rate than that of the general public (81.5% versus 35.8%) and secondly, by opting for the Democratic Party (DP) although the future

---

[26] Beatrice Leung, "The Catholic voters," in *Votes without Power: The Hong Kong Legislative Council Election 1991*, edited by R. Kwok *et al.* (Hong Kong: Hong Kong University Press, 1992), pp. 151–84.

[27] Commission of Justice and Peace of Catholic Diocese, *Dao Zai Zhenggang Zhong* (The Word in the Political Platform: A Social Analysis and Suggestion for Improvement) (Hong Kong: Commission of Justice and Peace of Catholic Diocese, July 1995). An abridged version of this book together with the original text was distributed to Catholics in all the parishes of the Hong Kong dioceses to lead Catholics to choose candidates according to their merits and performance. Another booklet titled *Xuanju yu Nin* (Election and You) (Hong Kong: Commission of Justice and Peace of Catholic Diocese, July 1995), provided materials for discussion in the meeting of basic Christian communities groups throughout Hong Kong. This booklet aimed at guiding Catholics on election based on Christian social teaching.

of the DP in the future Hong Kong SAR political system seemed doubtful. In contrast, the pro-China Democratic Alliance for Betterment of Hong Kong (DABHK) received less Catholics support than average.[28]

Hong Kong Catholics and the Bridge

The Hong Kong Catholics together with the overseas Chinese church communities were invited by Pope John Paul II in 1982 to be the bridge between the church in China and the universal church and the means of bonding the Chinese church to the Holy See.[29] While Hong Kong Catholics have actively played their role as a bridge, they are aware of China's religious policy and its restrictive record of treating Chinese Catholics.[30] The Sino-British negotiations on Hong Kong began in 1980, and the signing of the Sino-British Agreement in 1984 shocked the Hong Kong Catholics. They suddenly realized that after 1997 they could face the same treatment which their fellow Catholics in China received from the CCP.

In 1978, Hong Kong Catholics began to take the initiative in contacting Catholics in China. Hong Kong Catholics touring China made grassroots contacts. This was the first "bridge" established prior to the request of the church authority. After 1978, not only did local Hong Kong Catholics stream in to visit China, because of their sense of patriotism and feeling of national identity, they also formed a small group of young clergy and laity with ulterior apostolic interests in China. In addition to conducting visits, they held discussions and reflections on China's policy of religious freedom, arising out of what they had seen of the religious revival and re-opening of churches in China. Furthermore, their progressive political outlook, the consciousness of their own national identity and their romantic

---

[28] C. P. Chan and Beatrice Leung, "The Voting Behaviour of Hong Kong Catholics in the 1995 Legislative Council Election," in *The 1995 Hong Kong Legislative Council Election*, edited by H. C. Kuan (Hong Kong: Hong Kong Institute of Asia-Pacific Studies, The Chinese University of Hong Kong, 1995), pp. 275–314.

[29] Beatrice Leung, *The Sino-Vatican Relations*, Chapter 7.

[30] *Ibid.*, Chapters 4 and 5.

patriotism, led them to sympathize with the Catholic Patriotic Association (CPA) in so many ways that they gave it strong support and agreed with the CPA on almost every stand that it took. They therefore formed very warm relations with the CPA which desperately needed overseas supporters to make itself acceptable to the universal church. The group played the role of a messenger or a bridge to make the CPA known to Hong Kong Catholics as well as to the overseas Catholics.

In 1980, a second bridge was formed when the Hong Kong diocese was asked by the Vatican to establish research and personal contacts with China. A church study centre (the Holy Spirit Study Centre) was formed and it became the official point of liaison between China, the Hong Kong Catholic church and the Vatican. Triangular interactions were found on this second bridge through senior staff of this centre, because it is an official liaison body between China and the Vatican.

A third type of bridge was built by missionary societies, which still had their own religious priests and nuns in China. The lack of contact from the 1950s to the 1970s between these foreign missionary societies (the Jesuits for example) and their Chinese members led to fact-finding missions and investigations on some controversial issues, including the marital status of priests and bishops, the motivation of priests in joining the CPA and their willingness to be ordained as bishops and so on. Through the contacts of this type of bridge, the situation of the unofficial church became known.[31] Usually these visits were made quietly. They had a completely different orientation and approach, arising out of previous history and experience in China. This type of bridge was resented by the Chinese Government and those making it were regarded as "hostile religious forces from the outside designed to set up underground churches and other illegal organizations."[32] However, reports were made to high-ranking

---

[31] The unofficial church refers to those Chinese Catholics who refuse to follow the state's demand to be independent from the Holy See. Subsequently they refused to participate in religious activities organized by government-sponsored Catholic Patriotic Association, and have religious activities held privately without official sanctions. Thus, this sector of Chinese Catholics are called the underground or unofficial church.

[32] "Document 19," para. 11, in *Xinshiqi Zongjiao Gongzuo Wenxian Xuan-bian, pp. 55–76.*

officials of responsible religious societies and to the Vatican to supplement the picture painted by the CPA and the official Chinese Catholic church.

The fourth type of bridge (like the third) was built by foreign missionary societies who had carried out mission work in China before 1949, but, unlike the previous type had no Chinese religious members of their own in China. They initiated a new type of mission not by directly sending their missionaries to China as they had done before, but by trying to work for Chinese Catholics in the spirit of reconciliation which they felt the Chinese church needed the most. In their own way, they played the role of a bridge in contacting CPA with a very sympathetic attitude and approach. Informally they invited the CPA to send its members for visits aimed at softening the antagonistic attitude of the CPA to the Vatican and at breaking the isolation of CPA by giving it a chance to come out of its shell and see for itself that the local churches in Hong Kong, Germany, the United Kingdom and the United States operated with a great amount of freedom and autonomy while keeping their essential spiritual union with the Holy See. At the same time, this group, through their international connections, was able to offer material assistance to the CPA in the form of donations of books to seminaries, and scholarships and grants for Chinese students to study abroad, as well as financial assistance in many other ways.

The fifth type of bridge has been built by overseas Catholic intellectuals and professionals who responded to the needs of social service institutions and tertiary education sector in China. They went to China as professionals. In Hong Kong, an agent called Association of International Technological, Educational and Cultural Exchange (AITECE) was set up to provide service and assistance to Catholic professionals for China's modernization programmes. Also, Catholic international social service institutes such as Caritas International, Miserior and Missio (Germany), as well as Caritas in European countries through Caritas Hong Kong and through Hong Kong Catholics, offered social service projects especially in rural areas to improve their living standard. Up to now, no foreign missionaries have been allowed a direct preaching and pastoral role. Thus, foreign missionaries, both clergy and lay get into China only as experts in language, science and technology through AITECE, as a Christian presence in an atheistic society, whose values and attitudes are different from those of the Catholics. According to regulations laid down by the CCP and the State Council, the Chinese Catholic church is not free to preach and evangelize, but Catholic-funded projects are welcome to penetrate into the interior even as far as Tibet.[33]

Thus, through these bridges various kinds of assistance were provided to the Chinese church (official and unofficial sectors), in the form of the training of church personnel, provision of religious literature, and financial aid to church-related enterprises in rural and urban areas. Even after the June 4th incident at Tiananmen Square, when many international NGOs' social assistance pulled out from China, Catholic social assistance continued. Most of this assistance, funded by foreign Catholic resources with the blessing of the Vatican, was kept as low-key as possible. An annual coordination meeting was held in Hong Kong, for planning as well as evaluating previous projects but the exact cost of all this assistance was not released.[34] Nonetheless, we know the expenses from the German Miserior and Missio, two major donors, in 1994 was approximately DM 3–4 million.[35] Researchers can use this tip of the iceberg figure as a basis for estimating the whole iceberg.

The impact of this assistance from the overseas Catholics through Hong Kong has been a major factor in the revival of the Chinese Catholic church to such a degree that it caused alarm in the government as is revealed by a crucial document issued by the Party Central with regulations (Document No. 3, 1989) aimed at curbing the revival of religion through foreign assistance.[36] The revival of religion in general and of the Catholic church in particular has taken place at a time when the Communist Party has been

---

[33] See "Document 19," and "Regulation No. 145 of Council of the State, On Managing Places of Religious Activities," in *Xinshiqi Zongjiao Gongzuo Wenxian Xuanbian*, pp. 55–76; 275–77.

[34] Since 1990 the papal representative in Hong Kong has been chairing this coordinating meeting every year. Participants are selected from those who are themselves or representatives of the religious associations engaged in helping China in various ways.

[35] A private and reliable source of information obtained from the top administration of German Miserior and Missio.

[36] Circular on "Stepping up Control over the Catholic Church to Meet the New Situation," Central Office Document, No. 3, (The Central Office of the Communist Party and of the State Council Transmitted to the Central Government's United Front and the Religious Affairs Bureau of the State Council, 1989), in Beatrice Leung, *The Sino-Vatican Relations*, pp. 376–83.

suffering from its own crisis and Communism as an ideology has been vanishing into the thin air.[37] Recently, even under intensified "supervision" the continued spread of religion had drawn the attention of the late Chen Yun, the paramount leader next to Deng Xiaoping, who ordered Jiang Zemin, the Party's General Secretary, to do something to curb it. A translation of Chen's letter revealed the deep-seated fear of CCP leaders in the face of the spread of religion, especially among the Chinese youth:[38]

> Comrade Zemin,
>   I am deeply troubled after reading reports on the ever-increasing of infiltration of religion, especially on those materials about anti-revolutionary activities under the cloak of religion in the new situation. It has been the customary techniques employed by our class enemies, both within and outside the country to make use of religion to snatch away our youth. This is also a painful lesson to learn from some Communist Party states where the Party lost political power. Now is the right time for the Party Central to grasp this important issue firmly. It is important not to allow this issue to become a new element contributing to social instability. You may have read all these documents and reports, yet I wish you to send them back to you for a second reading.
>
>   Chen Yun
>   4 April 1990

    This response of the Chinese authorities to the revival of the Catholic church through the "bridge" has caused considerable concern. This concern was particularly reflected in Jiang Zemin's statement of 1 July 1996 (anniversary of the CCP), reiterating the need for ideological control.[39] At a time when China was relaxing economic control but tightening political and ideological control, the achievements of the Hong Kong church were welcomed by Chinese Catholics but not by the Chinese Government. In some areas, competitions between Catholicism and the CCP for "teaching authority" especially in the youth sector are real.

---

[37] After the 1989 Tiananmen incident China perceived that foreign enemies were launching "peaceful evolution" to topple Communism. CCP leaders on many occasions reiterated this point. See the speech of Jiang Zemin in the Seminar on the Party Theory on 20 November 1989; Li Zonglin *et al.* (ed.), *Dang Wei Gongzuo Daquan* (A Comprehension on the Work of Party Members) (Beijing: Chinese Broadcasting Press, 1992), p. 1.

[38] *Xinshiqi Zongjiao Gongzuo Wenxian Xuanbian*, p. 177.

[39] *Qiushi* (Seeking the Truth), 1 July 1996, p. 1.

Conflict of Interest: Local Church and Bridge Church of Hong Kong

The key to the Sino-Vatican-Hong Kong triangular relationship is the fact that normal bilateral diplomatic relations between China and Vatican are not possible, due to the severance of Sino-Vatican diplomatic relationship in 1952. As long as Sino-Vatican negotiation is still in process, Hong Kong has the role of a diplomatic bridge between the Vatican and China, and the supplier of aid to China from overseas. Thus, in the first half of the transition period, given the uncertainty Hong Kong Catholics are facing after 1997, they do not reserve resources for themselves because they continue to render help to their fellow Catholics in China in response to Cardinal Wu's call in his pastoral letter "March into the Bright Decade," to develop "the relations of the diocese with China and with the church in China."[40]

Hong Kong Catholics make certain gains by acting as a bridge. It offers them the opportunity for contact with the Chinese Government and Chinese Catholics and enhances their understanding of church-state relations, before the real transfer takes place. Yet, from the perspective of a local church, there is a price for being a bridge. First, the local church's limited resources have to be shared with China. Take the training of church personnel for example, the students of the local Hong Kong Catholic seminary (the Holy Spirit Seminary College) complained that their studies were affected when many of their professors and teaching staff spent long periods of time in China and their attention was focused on seminaries in the mainland, so much so that the quality of teaching and learning in Hong Kong was neglected.[41]

The second conflict of interest appears in the area of the church's social involvement and political participation. In spite of the guideline in Cardinal Wu's pastoral letter, and in spite of the deep Catholic involvement in supporting pro-democratic movements in China, the priest most deeply involved in this movement and local politics was suddenly removed from

---

[40] John B. Wu, "March into the Bright Decade."

[41] The author came to know about this issue when she read a notice of the seminary to call a meeting of students to discuss this matter in October 1995.

a public post and was asked to do further studies.[42] This action was inter-
preted as reflecting Chinese pressure in the process of negotiation with the
Vatican. This removal weakened the political activities of Hong Kong
Catholics.

Hong Kong Catholic Church after 1997

Most Catholics believe that after 1997, church-state relations in Hong
Kong will shift from the "contractor model" to the "political absorption of
religion" model under the Hong Kong SAR.[43] Recent research has revealed
that Hong Kong Catholics are not happy with China's interference in the
political reform of Hong Kong since 1992. Because Hong Kong Catholics
observed the restrictions Beijing imposes on religious believers, they feel
more vulnerable to the uncertainties involved in the political transition after
1997. Thus, Catholics participated in large numbers in the 1995 Legco
election and demonstrated a stronger tendency to choose pro-democratic
instead of pro-China parties and candidates to promote Hong Kong's great
autonomy.[44] This anti-Chinese sentiment and sense of uncertainty that
also stem from the experience of being a bridge have been increasing as
the take-over approaches. The more anti-Chinese sentiment and sense of
uncertainty they have, the more it would jeopardize their effectiveness as
a bridge. Until 1997, the Hong Kong Catholics can function effectively as
a bridge; but after 1997 in a quite different political environment under the
Hong Kong SAR, new church-state relations will be established which will
very much affect the role of the bridge in the days to come. On the other
hand, the religious revival and penetration caused by the bridge in the
mainland will also affect future church-state relations between the Hong
Kong Catholic Church and the Hong Kong SAR Government.

Hong Kong's role as a bridge has been effective in the last fifteen
years, partly because of its geopolitical affinity. Hong Kong has been far

---

[42] This priest was a committee member of the Hong Kong Citizens Supporting
Pro-Democratic Movement in China, and had been contemplating to campaign for
a seat in the Legco in 1991. But he was removed from his post as the director of
Catholic Social Communication Centre and was asked to do a doctoral programme
on church history.

[43] Chan Shun-hang, "Xianggang Zhengjiao Guanxi Fazhen de Qianzhan."

[44] C. P. Chan and B. Leung, "The Voting Behaviour of Hong Kong Catholics."

from China's jurisdiction, and its Catholics could work to promote religious revival, while it was close enough to China to get firsthand information on the real situation there. After 1997, Hong Kong will become a part of the People's Republic of China. Even now many Catholics suspect that their role of a bridge will undergo changes after the transfer of sovereignty. In his visit to Hong Kong in June 1996, Ye Xiaowen, the director of China's Religious Affairs Bureau of the Council of State told Hong Kong Catholics indirectly that the work of a bridge might not be permitted. Ye reiterated that the relationship between Hong Kong religious adherents and their counterparts in China should be based on non-subordination, non-interference and mutual respect as laid down in the Basic Law. Ye also emphasized that mainland people should not try to make Hong Kong people conform to mainland ideas and vice versa.[45] If one reads between the lines, it is not difficult to see this is as a warning from China to Hong Kong Catholics against participating in efforts to support the Chinese Catholic revival, that had led to pro-papal sentiments undermining the Party's effort on religion for over forty years. In January 1997, this author got a clear and confirmed message from the Hong Kong and Macau Affairs Office of the Council of State in Beijing when she paid an official visit. Party Central's Document No. 3 of 1989 and Chen Yun's letter to Zhang Zemin were signs from CCP that religious revival in general and the Catholic revival in particular were the result of foreign "interference in Chinese religious affairs," and which should be curbed.[46] Since Hong Kong, the fortress of foreign help for the revival, will be under the Chinese sover-eignty in less than a year, it appears to be the time for China to give its first warning, then a clearer message.

On the other hand, quite a number of Catholic agents engaged in the work of the bridge, and who have a prophetic view on China's move on strait-jacketing religion in Hong Kong, have moved away from the colony before 1997. The Catholic publication house in Hong Kong which mainly published religious literature for mainland China since 1984, decided to liquidate its publication work after it had just finished a big project of translating a set of six volumes of textbooks on Dogmatic Theology this year. The director of this project simply invited Chinese Catholic dioceses

---

[45] *Sunday Examiner*, 5 July 1996.

[46] Document No. 3, and Chen Yun's Letter.

with printing facilities to pirate the Catholic religious literature of this house. The Jesuit office dealing with China affairs has also moved away from Hong Kong, with its research and documentation sections going to Taiwan, and administration to Manila. A number of Religious Orders also moved their China-related documentation away from Hong Kong. The Hong Kong-based Union of Catholic Asian News (UCAN) which used to issue a great deal of news on the Catholic church in China (including the unofficial sector and official sector of the church) moved their headquarters to Bangkok three years ago. Consequently, both in terms of quantity and quality, the Catholic news on China has declined drastically. The senior staff from the diocesan research centre, the Holy Spirit Study Centre, recently remarked that once the Centre had accomplished its mission as a bridge, it had no need to exist. Whether the mission of a bridge played by the Hong Kong Catholic church has been completed is debatable. Yet the remark from this senior staff hinted that this Vatican-related research centre which is one of the earliest bridges between China and Hong Kong Catholics is preparing itself to terminate its mission should the need arise. Above all, from the side of the Vatican, Pope John Paul II remarked in 1995 that the bridge relationship between the Chinese Catholic Church and the overseas Chinese Catholics was no longer required, as they are now "sister Churches." Although there was no official explanation of the switch over from the bridge relationship to sister relationship from the Vatican or from the Hong Kong Catholic Diocese, one thing that is certain is that the idea of the "bridge" has given way to the "sister church."[47]

Implications

From the Catholic perspective, the anti-Communist feelings of Hong Kong Catholics will pose a difficulty to the Catholic church after 1997 on how to cooperate with the future Hong Kong SAR Government.[48] Church-state cooperation will not be possible without a considerable degree of trust. In the course of the development of church-state relations, it seems that there is a lack of trust between Vatican and China. The Hong Kong Catholic

---

[47] *Tripod*, Vol. 15, No. 8 (August 1995), p. 1.

[48] Refer to the research findings of C. P. Chan and B. Leung, "The Voting Behaviour of Hong Kong Catholics."

Church is headed by a Cardinal of the Vatican and has warm relations with the colonial government. It will take time to establish mutual trust and switch from the "contractor" model to the "political absorption of religion" model of church-state relations after 1997. For the survival of the Hong Kong Catholic church, it has a great need to eliminate the Chinese perceived "unwelcome" enterprise of the bridge and enhance the church-state cooperation in days to come.

Also the political environment of Hong Kong after 1997 will be disadvantageous to the conventional function of a bridge. The gradual moving away of some religious agents of the bridge from Hong Kong speaks for itself. Thus, Hong Kong will have to consider very seriously the subtle request from the director of the Religious Affairs Bureau to eliminate the activities of the bridge. For the interests of the church, Hong Kong Catholics have to devise a new model of the bridge acceptable to China on the one hand, and for the interests of the religious sector of Hong Kong on the other.

From the Hong Kong SAR's perspective, although "'progressive" Catholic groups in Hong Kong have sometimes been an irritant to the colonial government and to Hong Kong business, they have never posed a serious threat to the government or to the fundamental interests of the society in general and the business sector in particular. Overall, there has been a good working relationship between the Catholic church and the Hong Kong Government and society. Anything the Beijing leaders may do to change this after 1997 is likely make things worse rather than better. Theoretically, under "one country, two systems," Catholic life in Hong Kong has no need for alteration. But Chinese interference has been prominent in socio-political affairs, and the hints provided by the head of Religious Affairs Bureau would be a sign for Catholics to review the current policy of the "bridge" as well as to engage in systematic planning after 1997 on the Catholic service. It is true that the Catholics through education have a genuine intention of serving the people, while preserving the church identity. Nevertheless, given the present political mood of Beijing, the hidden agenda in religion is to curb the influence of religion in general and of Christianity in particular.[49] Unless the "one country, two

---

[49] In an internally circulated document, Ye Xiaowen, Director, Religious Affairs Bureau expressed this view of the CCP to the trainees of the Party School; see Ye Xiaowen, "Dangqian Woguo de Zongjiao Wenti" (The Contemporary

systems" policy is honestly implemented and religious freedom of the present type is allowed to be practised, Beijing's style of religious control will leave little room for the preservation of Catholic social service, not to mention the activities of the church. Yet this control and the consequent withering of the Catholic church in Hong Kong will offer an indication to foreign investors who are constantly aware of Hong Kong's environment of investment in which religious freedom constitutes an important indicator of the socio-economic health of this city.

Conclusion

Since 1982, called upon by the Pope, overseas Chinese Catholics have been taking up the role of bridges of various types in narrowing the rift between Catholics in China and the universal church. The Hong Kong Catholics have put up a remarkable performance in building up this bridge. The five types of bridges after functioning for more than ten years have reaped visible fruits. Because of the work of these bridges, the revival of the Chinese church was possible, causing worries to top leaders of Beijing on ideological grounds. On the other hand, the present status of the bilateral relationship between China and the Vatican requires Hong Kong as a vehicle to transmit some messages. Thus, it adds different shades of colour in the triangular relationship between China, the Vatican and Hong Kong. However, in Hong Kong, the role of bridges can be sustained and supported only by the political environment as under the British rule.

However, our research reveals that due to the changing political environment in Hong Kong after 1997, its role as a bridge has been undergoing a gradual change, which includes switching the bridge enterprise away from Hong Kong. This suggests that the Catholic church in Hong Kong is being forced to move away from the triangular relation. In other words, whether Hong Kong likes it or not, the triangular relationship between China, the Vatican and Hong Kong is disappearing. At this stage of development, is a bilateral relationship enough for communication between China and the Vatican? If the answer is negative, the next question will be: what can Hong Kong do to establish a new relationship with their

---

Religious Questions of the Motherland) in *Zhonggong Zhongyang Dangxiao Baogao Xuan* (Selected Reports of the Central Party School), Vol. 101, No. 5 (1996), pp. 9–23.

fellow Chinese Catholics which will be acceptable to Beijing and in the interest of Catholics in China? This will become an important topic for further research for those who are interested in the church-state relations in Hong Kong and China.

Acknowledgements

The author is grateful to Professor Christopher Howe of the School of Oriental and African Studies, University of London and Professor Michael Yahuda of London School of Economics and Political Science for their suggestions and comments on an earlier draft.

6

NGOs in Hong Kong: The Present and the Future[1]

Ren Yue

Hong Kong as an international financial centre, a free port and a gateway to China has been attractive to many international non-governmental organizations (NGOs) as a place either to establish offices or to hold conventions. Besides close to one hundred NGOs having secretariats in the territory, Hong Kong itself is also a member of well over one thousand such organizations. However, despite a worldwide increase in the influence of NGOs, to date there has been little systematic study of the role of the NGOs in Hong Kong's political, societal and economic life. As the transfer of sovereignty approaches, some of the NGOs in Hong Kong, especially those which have a political nature or are associated with Taiwan, are likely to face new challenges under China's Special Administrative Region (SAR) government after July 1997.

This chapter aims to address three questions concerning the NGOs in Hong Kong. First, what are their major roles and how effectively can they play the roles in society? Second, how active are these organizations in their respective fields? Lastly, how confident are the leaders of these NGOs about the future of their organizations? The chapter begins with a discussion on the general roles of NGOs in international society as well as in Hong Kong. Then, based on some aggregate data collected from a telephone survey in August 1996, it analyses the activeness of the

[1] This paper has been originally published in *Journal of Contemporary China*, Vol. 6, No. 16 (1997), pp. 449–60. The Author wishes to thank the journal's editors and its publishers, Carfax Publishing Ltd., PO Box 25, Abingdon, Oxfordshire OX14 3UE, United Kingdom, for their permission to reproduce it.

territory's NGOs, using some descriptive statistics. In addition, the confidence level of the NGO leaders on their organizations' prospects under China's sovereignty is measured by a set of indices included in the survey. The focus is on those organizations like Amnesty International and other human rights or environmental groups, the main functions of which are likely to be in conflict either with the Basic Law of the Hong Kong SAR or with current Chinese polity. The survey results reveal that despite Beijing's explicit guarantee of the freedom of NGO activities laid down in the Basic Law, a clear majority of the NGO leaders expressed their doubts or responded negatively with regard to their organizations' future.

A Typology of NGOs in Hong Kong

In contemporary international relations, international organizations (IOs) can be classified as intergovernmental organizations (IGOs) and non-governmental organizations (NGOs).[2] While IGOs, especially the United Nations (UN) and its affiliated organizations, may look more prominent in the international arena, the overwhelming majority of IOs are actually NGOs (95% of the total IOs). According to the statistics given by the Union of International Associations, which has been publishing the *Yearbook of International Organizations* since the 1950s, over 20,000 NGOs have been included in its 1995/96 edition. The number of conventional NGOs has increased by more than four times since the late 1950s.[3] In the case of Hong Kong, almost every IO is an NGO. This is not surprising, since the forming principle of most of the IGOs is associated with the concept of sovereignty, and Hong Kong is not a sovereign state.[4]

---

[2] Sometimes the term NGOs is used to mean both international and domestic non-governmental organizations. However, NGOs in this chapter refer only to international non-governmental organizations.

[3] Peter Willetts (ed.), *The Conscience of the World: The Influence of Non-Governmental Organisations in the UN System* (Washington, D.C.: Brookings, 1996), p. 9.

[4] The Hong Kong Government may send representatives to those IGOs that accept regional government delegations or participate as part of the British delegation in such organizations where only sovereign nations are allowed to become members.

The classical definition of NGO is given by a UN Resolution 288 (X) of 27 February 1950: "Any international organization which is not established by intergovernmental agreement shall be considered as a non-governmental organization for the purpose of these arrangements." Later, in Resolution 1296 (XLIV) of 25 June 1968, the United Nations Economic and Social Council (UNESCO) further held the view that the NGOs that are on the UNESCO's consultative status list may include "... organizations which accept members designated by government authorities, provided that such membership does not interfere with the free expression of views of the organizations."[5] Though there are different views from time to time on how to define NGOs, it is beyond the scope of this chapter to discuss this point in detail. Suffice it to say that in the past several decades the world witnessed a proliferation of international NGOs which have increasingly influenced international as well as domestic affairs.

The *Yearbook of International Organizations, 1995/96* listed ninety-four NGOs as having secretarial offices in Hong Kong, in addition to around 1,450 NGOs in which Hong Kong is a member. Linked with so many NGOs, this territory has in a way enhanced its cosmopolitan status. At the same time, it offers a good opportunity to observe the activities of NGOs.

Without going into details on their activities, the bare figures themselves indicate that NGOs in Hong Kong are both comprehensive in range and huge in number.

The first four types of NGOs in Table 1 are generally regarded as "conventional international bodies." Despite its small size and the fact that it is not a sovereign nation, Hong Kong, nevertheless, has joined eighteen of the world's existing thirty-eight federations of NGOs and is also a member of over 70% of the world's universal membership NGOs. Similar to the composition of the world's NGOs in general, most of such organizations in Hong Kong are single-issue/agenda or specialized/professional organizations covering almost every stratum of society. Some organizations may have very few members, but some have a sizeable membership.

The majority of Hong Kong's NGOs have developed since the 1970s when the territory emerged rapidly as one of the major international centres

---

[5] See Union of International Associations (ed.), *Yearbook of International Organizations, 1995/96*, 32nd ed., Vol. 1 (Munich, Germany: K. G. Saur, 1995), p. 1662.

Table 1: Hong Kong's NGOs, by Type

Classification	Secretariats (Main and secondary)		Membership (Excluding secretariats)	
Federations of international organizations	1	(1.06%)	17	(1.17%)
Universal membership	4	(4.26%)	337	(23.23%)
Intercontinental membership	1	(1.06%)	353	(24.33%)
Regional membership	24	(25.53%)	249	(17.16%)
Other types	64	(68.09%)	495	(34.11%)
Total	94	(100%)	1,451	(100%)

Source: Compiled from Union of International Associations (ed.), *Yearbook of International Organizations, 1995/96*, 32nd ed., Vol. 2 (Munich, Germany: K. G. Saur, 1995), pp. 638–48.

in trade, finance, shipping and the service industry. Its economic growth helped Hong Kong to establish more ties with the international community and, as part of this transition, the number of international NGOs mushroomed. This is indeed a mutually reinforcing process. As will be discussed in the next section, the multiple links of Hong Kong NGOs with the world have in turn expedited the territory's political, economic and social development.

The Roles of NGOs in Hong Kong

Since the post-World War II period, the widespread diffusion of NGOs has closely corresponded with the scientific and technological progress of mankind. With NGOs' ever-growing influence, some of the roles traditionally within the domain of national governments have been either replaced or supplemented by these organizations. A political scientist explains the phenomenon this way: "The economic, informational and intellectual resources of NGOs have garnered them enough expertise and influence to assume authority in matters that, traditionally, have been solely within the purview of state administration and responsibility."[6] Hong Kong as a

---

[6] Ann Marie Clark, "Non-Governmental Organizations and Their Influence on International Society," *Journal of International Affairs*, Vol. 48, No. 2 (Winter 1995), p. 508.

rapidly growing, newly industrialized economy is certainly no exception to this trend. NGOs, with their enormous information resources, their expertise in various fields, and in some cases their popular support from the grassroots of the society, have become actively involved in almost every aspect of life in Hong Kong. It goes without saying that they are most influential in those areas to which the government cannot or does not want to give priority.

The highly diversified nature of the Hong Kong NGOs in terms of their objectives, structure, sizes, financial resources and influence makes it very difficult to include in this chapter all the roles they play in the territory. Our discussion, therefore, would only be limited to some of the major roles NGOs play, namely, creating norms; disseminating information; interacting with IGOs; and influencing domestic policy outcomes.

Norm Creation

In discussing the roles of IOs in changing the international human rights regimes, Jack Donnelly noticed how these institutions had created norms and principles that eventually shifted human rights from the traditional domain of the states to the international arena.[7] Over the years, NGOs have created new norms that have supplemented or even replaced the old ones in the related societies. In Hong Kong, one obvious case is that NGOs like the Red Cross and Oxfam had brought new elements into Chinese society's traditional concepts of helping those in need. The Saturday morning donation drives sponsored by many NGOs have become a prominent feature of life in the territory.

NGOs also contribute to the promotion of regional and international regimes. They can play very important roles in regime creation and maintenance. Lawrence Woods's study on the lessons drawn from some Asia-Pacific NGOs' effort to promote regional cooperation has made some

---

[7] Jack Donnelly, "Human Rights and International Organizations: State, Sovereignty, and the International Community," in *International Organization*, edited by Friedrich Kratochwil and Edward Mansfield (New York: Harper Collins, 1994), pp. 202–19.

convincing arguments on this point.[8] It is well accepted that regime building itself is a process of norm creation.[9] Though different NGOs may have different sets of norms and principles to govern their activities, as in the case of the human rights regime, the environmental protection regime, etc., yet taking them as a whole, the norm-creating function may profoundly change a society's philosophy of life.

With regard to the issue of human rights, NGOs have brought about obvious changes in Hong Kong. In the traditional Chinese society and during the long-time British colonial rule, human rights, especially political rights, had by and large been considered an official business by ordinary people, and were usually given a low priority by governments. Thanks partly to the efforts of NGOs such as Amnesty International, Human Rights Watch, and some women and children's rights organizations, the human rights record in Hong Kong has improved substantially in recent years. Vigorous efforts of some NGOs against the prejudices and discrimination against women, the disabled and the disadvantaged ethnic or regional groups have also been recognized by more and more people in Hong Kong.

Information Dissemination

One of the factors that enables NGOs to play an important role at the local level is their ability to exchange information through their own networks. The "sharing of information is a key aspect in the growth of NGO influence, for NGO activity increasingly takes place outside of formal inter-governmental channels."[10] The NGOs, because of their single-issue orientation and their expertise in their respective fields, have made Hong Kong residents aware of many issues that have been traditionally neglected or ignored by the government. The NGOs often mobilize people's awareness of a particular issue by disseminating relevant information and educating them on the importance of the issue. Modern means of communication,

---

[8] See Lawrence T. Woods, "Learning from NGO Proponents of Asia-Pacific Regionalism," *Asia Survey*, Vol. 35 (September 1995), pp. 812–27.

[9] For a detailed discussion of regimes, see Stephen D. Krasner (ed.), *International Regimes* (Ithaca, N.Y.: Cornell University Press, 1983).

[10] Ann Marie Clark, "Non-Governmental Organizations and Their Influence on International Society," p. 518.

such as televisions, newspapers and radio, have helped the NGOs to publicize their views. With the popularization of computer networks, many NGOs have made use of their Internet home pages to bring certain issues to public attention.

The exchange of information between the local branches and their headquarters or other branches may just be part of their routine work, yet it may have tremendous influence on local events. During the 1989 Tiananmen turmoil and afterward, the human rights organizations in Hong Kong played a very important role in terms of information collection and dissemination both to and from mainland China and the world. The recent Defend Diaoyu Island movement has further confirmed this point.

Interaction with International Governmental Organizations

Many NGOs have acquired UNESCO's consultative status, thus establishing links with the world's largest IGO, the UN and its affiliated organizations. Such links usually suggest more NGO influence on their member states. For obvious reasons, the consultative status is a kind of recognition, which many NGOs need to help their operations at the local or domestic level. This is especially important for NGOs in Hong Kong. Through these NGO connections, the people of Hong Kong may have gained more channels to let their voices be heard. Otherwise, it would be very difficult for them to do so, given the fact that Hong Kong is not a sovereign state and has no representatives in the UN. The NGO linkage may also give Hong Kong a kind of independent status in its dealings with the international community. On the other side of the coin, the UN and other IGOs have also benefited from their NGO counterparts. The NGOs' informational, intellectual, and sometimes financial resources can help the UN to accomplish its declared goals of promoting peace, stability and prosperity everywhere in the world.

When the Commonwealth countries held their summit in New Zealand in November 1995, three Hong Kong legislators, Christine Loh, Elizabeth Wong and Margaret Ng, representing an NGO called the Commonwealth Association of Universities, presented a letter to the Heads of Commonwealth nations demanding that Hong Kong be mentioned in their communiqué. They expressed their hope that after the sovereignty transfer, Hong Kong would still "be able to participate in some capacity among the many Commonwealth non-governmental organizations as [it] has done for many years." They also urged Commonwealth nations to recognize the

British National (Overseas) and the Special Administrative Region Passports, and grant visa-exempt status to such passport holders.[11] Here, their capacity as NGO representatives helped them to address Hong Kong issues at an international summit, which would otherwise not have happened. Beside political influence, NGOs also have leverage in economic and other matters. Their connections with IGOs like Asia Pacific Economic Cooperation Forum and the Asia Development Bank prove to be very important for the economic development of Hong Kong.

Influence over Domestic Policy Outcomes

Within a state, the government interacts with various political parties, interest groups and other social organizations. These groups function like watchdogs, the government needs to pay close attention to their support or criticism. In an international arena, NGOs may perform the same function as their domestic counterparts. Through their branches or affiliates, the NGOs can put pressure on the national governments to make policies in favour of their interests.

NGO activities in the political field are most likely concentrated on those areas which the government regards either as of secondary importance or as "hot potatoes," i.e. where government policies clash with popular interests. Take human rights and environmental protection as examples. In these areas, the interests of the government are likely to be in conflict with those of the NGO activists. This is very obvious; human rights and environmental NGOs are usually quite critical of government policies. This is generally true even in a democracy. Governments usually have other priorities such as foreign relations and economic growth. Some industrial development may endanger the environment, but if the damage is less severe or overshadowed by the benefits, policy makers may well give such development a green light. Yet the environmental NGOs, because of their single issue focus and because of the expertise they usually possess, may conclude that the government has ignored our ecosystem in order to acquire political capital.

Another example which shows NGO influence on local politics is seen from the fact that, after the Fourth United Nations World Conference on

---

[11] *South China Morning Post* (Hong Kong), 7 November 1995, p. 2.

Women in 1995 passed an international blueprint for women's rights, the Hong Kong Government admitted that before its passage by Hong Kong, views of NGOs had been sought after the Conference.[12]

Of course, the influence of NGOs on government policies varies. The effectiveness with which NGOs can exert their influence depends on many factors. Some of the most important ones include their financial resources, their structure, the degree to which they can mobilize international as well as domestic support, and the tension between their goals and those of the government.

In addition to the above general roles NGOs play, in Hong Kong they also have special roles. First, these NGOs can be bridges between mainland China and Taiwan. The fact that nearly half the NGOs in Hong Kong have business or professional connections with Taiwan, and about the same number with China could be very important for the policy makers and people on both sides of the Taiwan Strait. "People-to-people diplomacy" has proved to be an effective means to solve difficult political problems. With the transfer of sovereignty, Hong Kong could be a very important place to host NGO conferences, where both sides may feel relaxed about participation and may explore possibilities for cooperation. Furthermore, NGOs in Hong Kong may also serve as a bridge between the East and the West. Very few places can compete with Hong Kong in this regard. With its bilingual environment and mixed cultures, the territory can allow people from different parts of the world to feel at home. Quite a number of NGOs, especially those with an Asia-Pacific focus, have their headquarters set up in Hong Kong. Many international conferences sponsored by NGOs choose the territory as their ideal meeting site.

The Activeness of NGOs in Hong Kong

Having discussed the roles the NGOs in Hong Kong have played or may play, naturally it raises the question of whether they are actively involved in carrying out their missions or not. In order to examine how active Hong Kong's NGOs are and how confident these NGOs are about the transfer of sovereignty in July 1997, a telephone survey was conducted in August 1996 with all the NGOs that have either main or secondary secretarial offices in

---

[12] *South China Morning Post* (Hong Kong), 19 December 1995, p. 5.

Hong Kong. The response ratio was about 40%.[13] Of the thirty-eight NGOs that responded, seven are universal membership organizations, two are intercontinental organizations, nine are regional membership organizations and twenty are other types of NGOs. The percentage of each NGO type in this survey is fairly close to the population.

The survey examines NGO's activeness by using two questions, one on its international operations and the other on its publicity. The results are summarized in Table 2.

Table 2: Activeness of NGOs in Hong Kong

Value label	Internal activeness	Public activeness
No activities	6 (15.8%)	12 (31.6%)
Once or less a year	5 (13.2%)	0 (0%)
2–4 times a year	8 (21.1%)	6 (15.8%)
Over 5 times a year	19 (50%)	20 (52.6%)

Valid cases = 38   Missing cases = 0

Half of the organizations surveyed have frequent internal activities.[14] Approximately the same ratio are active publicly. Depending on their different professions, these NGOs hold conferences, concerts, exhibitions, rallies and promotional drives in Hong Kong. They also participate in various social and public events. All these activities have undoubtedly made a notable impact on society.

In addition to the internal and external activities of these organizations, we also surveyed their links with their headquarters or local branches. This

---

[13] The response ratio is calculated by dividing the total NGOs responded by the total number of NGOs that have secretarial offices. The individuals responded to my questionnaire were either the organizations' top administrators or those who were in charge of public relations. The responses therefore could at least reflect the views of the top NGO leadership, if not that of the organizations as a whole.

[14] Internal activeness is measured by how often these organizations have their all-member, representative, or board of directors meetings in a year over the last three years. Public activeness is a measure of how often they either sponsor or participate in public events in the name of their organizations.

is based on the assumption that since all these organizations are international/regional in nature, they should have regular overseas connections. The results confirmed this assumption convincingly: over 76% of the respondents have frequent contacts more than once a month with their headquarters or their subordinate branches. Another 13% have such contacts fairly regularly (between two to twelve times a year).

To sum up, the survey showed that, in general, the NGOs in Hong Kong are fairly active in their respective fields. Over the years, they have functioned as liaisons between the territory and the world. Statistical tests also reveal that their activeness has little to do with the specialization, financial resources and geographical focus of their organizations.[15]

The Confidence Level for NGOs' Future Activities

Whether they like it or not, Hong Kong's return to China is an important factor affecting the lives of individuals, companies and institutions in the territory. For a long time, this coming event has been welcomed by some, resented by others and been perplexing to many. From a psychological point of view, even those who claim to be indifferent indicate some kind of attitude towards this sovereignty transfer. The rest of this chapter will discuss the attitudes of the NGO leaders and explore the possible explanations behind their responses to our survey.

In our survey, three questions serve the purpose of measuring Hong Kong NGO leaders' confidence level about the change of sovereignty in 1997. One question asks if they think Hong Kong's return to China will help their organizations' activities in the future; another focuses on how much they can count on the future SAR Government to guarantee the independent status of their organizations. A third question asks those organizations whether currently they have professional or other contacts with Taiwan and whether they intend to continue such relations or not.

It is obvious that more than half of the respondents expressed their doubts about the post-1997 perspective. Though only a small portion answered negatively, the "don't know/not sure" answers also indicated

---

[15] Cross tabulations showed no significant relationships between organizational activities, both internal and public, and their geographical focus, budget sources and political orientation.

Table 3: Response to "Do You Think Hong Kong's Return to China Will Help Your Organization's Activities in the Future?"

Help	7	18.4%
No effect	8	21.1%
Not help/Hinder	4	10.5%
Don't know/Not sure	19	50%

Valid cases = 38   Missing cases = 0

Table 4: Response to "Can You Count on the Future SAR Government to Guarantee the Independent Status of Your Organization?"

Yes	13	34.2%
No	3	7.9%
Don't know/Not sure	22	57.9%

Valid cases = 38   Missing cases = 0

some kind of pessimistic feelings. On several occasions, the respondents chose not to answer the questions directly or implied that there was nothing they could do to control their organizations' fate. In that case, even though they said they didn't know or were not sure, the true response would be a negative one.

The attitudes of those NGO leaders who responded doubtfully or even negatively to our survey cannot be attributed to the lack of legal protection for their activities in the future, nor can they be attributed to whether their organizational goals are in conflict with current Chinese policies. Many whose organizations have nothing to do with politics also expressed doubts about their future. The Basic Law of the Hong Kong SAR indeed stipulates in a very clear way the rights and duties of the NGOs in Hong Kong. Chapter Six of the Basic Law in general gives the green light to Hong Kong NGOs in the fields of education, science, technology, culture, art, sports, the professions, medicine and health, labour, social welfare and social work, and also to religious organizations. Their relationship with their mainland counterparts "shall be based on the principles of non-subordination, non-interference and mutual respect" (Article 148) and they "may maintain and develop relations with their counterparts in foreign countries and regions and with relevant international organizations" (Article 149). In addition, the Basic Law also makes clear the SAR Government's relations with various international IGOs (Articles 150–152).

The Culture Panel of the Preliminary Working Committee of the Preparatory Committee of the Hong Kong SAR held a working conference in October 1995 in which the issue of the participation in IOs and conferences by NGOs in Hong Kong after 1997 was discussed. Three prerequisites would become the guidelines to regulate future activities of Hong Kong NGOs: the first is to abide by the Basic Law; the second is to reassure these NGOs that they may count on the SAR Government's assistance in maintaining the status quo and joining new IOs as stipulated in the Basic Law; and the third is to reiterate the obligation for Hong Kong's NGOs to uphold the "one China" principle in its contacts with Taiwan.[16]

These Chinese policies are well known to the public. As long as the NGOs observe the Basic Law and other legal regulations, it seems that they should have little to worry about. The question then is why so many of them are still in doubt. One of the possible reasons for these NGO leaders' lack of confidence with the future might be that they do not fully trust what is written in the Basic Law. They are not so sure whether Beijing will keep its word. Even if they have no intention of being provocative to the Chinese authority, they are not sure if the future SAR Government would share the same understanding with them. After all, the Chinese Government had reportedly been denying certain Hong Kong NGO representatives permission to attend the World Conference on Women held in Beijing in September 1995.[17]

Another reason to explain this lack of confidence is less politically biased. It emanates from technical considerations. A typical case would be that in some NGOs Hong Kong is a member while China is not. Such a situation may give rise to a conflict of interest. Though the Basic Law

---

[16] BBC Monitoring Service — Far East, 12 October 1995. For a detailed report, see Xinhua News Agency, Beijing, 24 September 1995. Both materials can be found on *Dialog*, File 799.

[17] See Central News Agency, Taiwan, 31 March and 7 April 1995, *Dialog*, File 728.

already guarantees their continued operation, some NGOs are nevertheless taking steps to ensure that their activities will not be interrupted by the sovereignty transfer.[18] Needless to say, those organizations which political nature is known to be at odds with Beijing have more reason to worry about their future activities. One responsible individual from a human rights NGO told us in the telephone interview that it would be very difficult to solve the dilemma the organization would have to face in the future: how to accomplish its organizational goals within the restrictions of current Chinese policies.

Though some hybrid NGOs, i.e. those with government members, such as the International Labour Organization and the Red Cross, may expect the government's support and sometimes even active participation, most of the NGOs are not so fortunate. Certainly, some of the politically active NGOs may have reasons for worrying about their future (see Table 5).[19]

The statistical test suggests a significant relationship between the political activeness of NGOs and their leaders' confidence with the future. Politically active NGOs significantly outnumbered the non-political NGOs

Table 5: Political Activeness and NGOs' Belief in Their Post-1997 Perspective

Believe in SAR Government's guarantee of independent status (by number of organizations)	Political activeness		Total
	Not active	Active	
Negative/Not sure/Don't know	8	15	23
No effect	7	1	8
Positive	5	2	7
Total	20	18	38

---

[18] For example, the World Medical Association has amended its constitution so that its Hong Kong branch can retain independent membership after 1997. See *South China Morning Post*, 11 September 1995, p. 4.

[19] Whether an NGO is politically active is determined by either its organizational goals (e.g. to promote human rights), or its membership composition (e.g. student organizations). Their confidence on the future is measured by their answers to the question: "Can you count on the future SAR government to guarantee the independent status of your organization?"

in giving negative and "don't know/not sure" answers. Non-political organizations are more optimistic about the future. Even though the sample size is small and one should be cautious not to exaggerate this finding, it is quite obvious that the different political systems between China and Hong Kong have influenced these NGO respondents' answers.

Conclusion

In conclusion, this study finds that Hong Kong NGOs have been quite active, making their mark on almost every aspect of public affairs and getting involved in almost every stratum of the society. However, a majority of these NGO leaders still have doubts about how their organizations are going to fare under the Chinese SAR Government. Such doubts will inevitably influence their current operations and future plans. For example, it remains doubtful whether China will submit the Hong Kong human rights report to the UN. Britain, as a signatory nation to the International Covenant on Civil and Political Rights, has been submitting such a report on Hong Kong's behalf, but China is not covered by the Covenant. This would be a great challenge for human rights NGOs in Hong Kong.

In spite of some uncertainties, the NGOs are expected to continue to exert influence in Hong Kong. This prediction can be attributed to several factors. First, the rapid development of modern society has already made irreversible the trend for more and more traditional governmental functions to be replaced or supplemented by the NGOs, given the latter's advantages in information resources, expertise and, in many cases, popular support. Second, the future SAR Government may also like to see most of the Hong Kong NGOs continue their daily operations uninterrupted, especially those in the non-political fields. This would enhance the "one country, two systems" image, something Beijing would like the world to see. Also, Hong Kong's special ties with Taiwan may actually provide the Chinese Government with more avenues to contact the alienated island. Hong Kong NGOs would certainly be able to make their contributions to this purpose. Third, NGO activities in Hong Kong will probably benefit from the territory's status as an international free port, one of the world's financial centres, and a newly industrialized economy. A large proportion of Hong Kong NGOs is of commercial and professional nature. Their activities, such as holding conferences and exhibitions, exchanging scientific, technological and industrial information will, in general, have a positive impact on the territory's economy. Fourth, since most of the NGOs have independent financial sources, as long as their activities are permitted by the Basic Law, there is little reason to believe that the government would change the status quo. Lastly, most of the current NGOs in Hong Kong would still be able to exert their influences for the sake of stability in the SAR, due mainly to the fact that over the years they have already created certain norms in Hong Kong society and that many of them have achieved either grassroots support or close relationships with local organizations. This is a force no government can afford to ignore.

7

Hong Kong and the Continuation of International Obligations Relating to Human Rights after 1997[1]

Andrew Byrnes

Introduction

The 1984 Sino-British Joint Declaration, under which the British and Chinese Governments agreed that Hong Kong be returned to the People's Republic of China in 1997, raised the question of whether and how Hong Kong's existing international bilateral and multilateral treaty relationships should be continued or renewed after 1997, and the level of autonomy to be accorded to the Hong Kong Special Administrative Region (SAR) in international affairs. While some of these issues were addressed in general terms in the Joint Declaration and subsequently in the Basic Law, and the decision taken to preserve in large measure Hong Kong's existing web of international relationships, the detailed work of identifying the treaties to be continued and the manner in which this could be achieved politically and legally has been a major undertaking since the signing of the Joint Declaration. The successful management of what is largely the continuation of Hong Kong's existing international relationships has been important from the point of view of generating confidence that Hong Kong would

[1] This chapter draws on material that has been collected by the Hong Kong Treaty Project of the Centre for Comparative and Public Law, The University of Hong Kong. This project is supported by a generous grant from the Hong Kong Research Grants Council.

remain basically the same after 1997 and would continue to benefit from existing international treaties applicable to it.

The continuation of the human rights guarantees contained in international treaties applicable to Hong Kong has been an important and contentious issue, with the continuation of the guarantees themselves and the acceptance of international supervision in the form of reporting to the United Nations (UN) assuming considerable symbolic importance. The attempt by the United Kingdom to ensure the continuation of reporting under the International Covenant on Civil and Political Rights (ICCPR) and the International Covenant on Economic, Social and Cultural Rights (ICESCR), and the refusal by the Chinese Government to accept the obligation to report to the UN in respect of these two treaties has both contributed to a sense of crisis so far as these guarantees are concerned and obscured the continuity of reporting under other human rights treaties which will continue to apply to Hong Kong after 1997.

This chapter will argue that the general goal of maintaining the international status quo of Hong Kong so far as international obligations and participation in international regimes are concerned strongly favours China's undertaking to submit reports under the two Covenants in a manner similar to Britain before 1997, whatever the merits of China's argument that is not obliged to do so.

The Nature of the Settlement

In managing the return of Hong Kong to China, the two governments have had to deal with hundreds of existing treaties in the web of relationships between Hong Kong and the rest of the world. While the rule applicable to in the case of Hong Kong is unclear,[2] my own view is that, if the matter

---

[2] Roda Mushkat originally argued that the "moving treaty frontiers" rule was the applicable rule in: "Hong Kong as an International Legal Person," *Emory International Law Review*, Vol. 6, No. 1 (1992), pp. 146–51. However, more recently, in the light of her evolving analysis of the nature of Hong Kong's international personality, she argues that the "moving treaty frontier principle" is inapposite, and that Hong Kong's situation "def[ies] easy categorization," noting that it is not surprising that the two governments have adopted a pragmatic solution. See Roda Mushkat, *One Country, Two International Legal Personalities? The Case of Hong Kong* (Hong Kong: Hong Kong University Press, 1997), p. 28. See

were left to general international law, the default rule for Hong Kong, as a dependent territory becoming part of another State, would be the so-called "moving treaty frontiers rule." Under this approach the treaty regime of the

---

also Roda Mushkat, "Managing the Transfer of Sovereignty over Hong Kong: The Case for Continuity of Treaties," Chapter 8 of this book. However, Mushkat also considers it arguable that there may be a presumption in favour of continued application of multilateral treaties on human rights matters, referring to the developments which followed the dissolution of former Yugoslavia and the break-up of the Soviet Union, *ibid.* at pp. 29–30. She does not clearly state what she considers the result would be in a case (such as the one under discussion) if agreement were not reached between the parties, though her argument would appear to support continuity. Mushkat argues that:

> Clearly, the traditional (and to an extent, discredited) theory of "clean slate" — vesting a "newly independent State" with power to decide which bilateral and multilateral treaties will remain in force — has no direct relevance. Given the highly autonomous status of Hong Kong (distinguished from total absorption/integration with another state), the "moving treaty frontiers" rule, which postulates that a territory automatically passes out of the treaty regime of a former sovereign into the treaty regime of the successor sovereign, also becomes inapplicable. Specifically, whereas substitution of treaty regimes may be rationalized on the basis of loss of identity and ensuing inability to perform international obligations, the HKSAR, contrastingly, is set to enjoy a wide latitude in the management of external affairs, including a capacity to establish and maintain treaty relationships.
>
> Indeed, it may be contended that the HKSAR, displaying the "international legal personality" as it does, should appropriately be designated the "successor." (Mushkat, Chapter 8 of this book [footnotes omitted])

Yet it is by no means clear that the moving treaty frontiers rule only applies where there is "total absorption or integration," but is inapplicable where the territorial unit joining the State continues to possess a considerable degree of autonomy in a number of fields. See, for example, the case of the union of Newfoundland with Canada in 1949, where the Canadian government took the view that agreements binding upon Newfoundland prior to the union lapsed and Newfoundland became bound by treaty obligations of general application to Canada. However, an exception was made "for those obligations arising from agreements locally connected which had established proprietary or quasi-proprietary rights": see *Yearbook of the International Law Commission*, Vol. II, Part 2 (1971), p. 133.

new State is substituted for that of the former State, with some exceptions.[3] This is, however, by no means an invariable rule and the States concerned may make other arrangements *inter se* and in relation to third States.

In the case of Hong Kong the basic approach adopted by the two governments was to try to preserve existing multilateral treaties entered into by the United Kingdom in so far as they related to Hong Kong and if they had continued relevance to Hong Kong activities, and the recreation of many bilateral links that would not survive the resumption of sovereignty by China.[4]

So far as multilateral agreements are concerned, the first step taken by the two governments was to agree on those treaties that they considered important for Hong Kong in the future and should therefore continue in force, with China taking over international responsibility from Britain. However, as a matter of general principle such an agreement between Britain and China, entered into without reference to the other States which

---

[3] See Eckart Klein, "Treaties, Effect of Territorial Changes," in *Encyclopedia of Public International Law* (Max Planck Institute for Comparative Public Law and International Law) (Amsterdam: North-Holland Pub. Co., 1984), Vol. 7, pp. 473–76; Wilfred Fiedler, "State Succession," in *Encyclopedia of Public International Law* (Max Planck Institute for Comparative Public Law and International Law) (Amsterdam: North-Holland Pub. Co., 1987), Vol. 10, pp. 446–56. Article 15 of the Vienna Convention on Succession of States in Respect of Treaties 1978 is generally taken to represent customary international law in this regard, although that law can be modified by States. Article 15 provides:

"When part of the territory of a State, or when any territory for the international relations of which a State is responsible, not being part of the territory of that State, becomes part of the territory of another State:

(a) treaties of the predecessor State cease to be in force in respect of the territory to which the succession of States relates from the date of the succession of States; and

(b) treaties of the successor State are in force in respect of the territory to which the succession of States relates from the date of the succession of States, unless it appears from the treaty or is otherwise established that the application of the treaty would be incompatible with the object and purpose of the treaty or would radically change the conditions for its operation."

[4] See R. Mushkat, "Hong Kong as an International Legal Person." See also "Hired Gun" [Interview with Mr. David Edwards, Law Officer (International Law) with the Hong Kong Government], *The New Gazette* (August 1993), pp. 16–21.

are parties to the agreements, cannot of itself simply substitute China for Britain in each and every multilateral context. In order to do this, the bilateral arrangement has to be taken in some form to the other treaty partners for their agreement or acquiescence.[5] Whether Hong Kong can continue its pre-July 1997 participation under Chinese sovereignty therefore depends on the terms of the relevant treaty and the response of the States parties or other authoritative body with competence to interpret the treaty.

The approach that was taken in relation to Hong Kong in the multilateral area was a two-stage one. The first stage dealt with the various international organizations in which Hong Kong participated in some capacity or other.[6] These were the subject of early agreement between the two governments. Following this the two governments sent notes to the respective secretariats of a number of these organizations informing them that the United Kingdom was relinquishing sovereignty over Hong Kong from 30 June 1997, that China would therefore be responsible for the international relations of Hong Kong, and also that Hong Kong would continue to participate in the activities of the relevant organization in the same capacity as previously or in an analogous one.[7]

However, for other multilateral treaties, including a number of UN human rights treaties, the two governments compiled a complete list of treaties which they wished to continue in force after 1997. That list was

---

[5] This may in some cases arguably involve either the interpretation by reference to the subsequent practice of the parties to the treaty (under article 31(3) of the Vienna Convention on the Law of Treaties) or, in effect, amendment: see I. Sinclair, *The Vienna Convention on the Law of Treaties*, 2nd ed. (Manchester: Manchester University Press, 1984), pp. 135–38.

[6] See *Achievements of the Joint Liaison Group and its Sub-Group on International Rights and Obligations, 1985–May 1990.*

[7] See, for example, the notes sent to the International Labour Organization "Participation of Hong Kong in the Activities of the International Labour Organization: Communications from the Governments of the United Kingdom of Great Britain and Northern Ireland and of the People's Republic of China," *ILO Official Bulletin*, Vol. LXXIII, Series A, No. 1 (1990), p. 25, reproduced in A. Byrnes and J. Chan, *Public Law and Human Rights: A Hong Kong Sourcebook* (Singapore: Butterworths, 1993), pp. 524–26. See also Shin-ichi Ago, "Application of ILO Conventions to Hong Kong after 1997," *Dalhousie Law Journal*, Vol. 17 (1994), p. 612.

not finalized until early 1997, and in June 1997 similar steps were taken to those taken in relation to Hong Kong's participation in the activities of international organizations, with notifications to the UN Secretary-General and other treaty depositaries.[8]

So far as bilateral treaties are concerned, it was not possible simply to substitute China as a party in place of the United Kingdom. As a result, existing bilateral treaties in areas such as extradition, air services, and visa abolition agreements have had to be renegotiated. Progress has been slow, and the coverage in these areas was less extensive immediately after 30 June 1997 than it was before then, although that may be remedied over time.

The UN Human Rights Treaties

The lead-up to change of sovereignty in 1997 has brought with it many uncertainties about the future, including to those who are optimistic about Hong Kong under Chinese rule and those for whom "human rights issues" are matters of little or no concern in their everyday lives. Nevertheless, there are many in Hong Kong's international and local business community who are concerned about the erosion of existing rights and freedoms, especially those which they consider to be of importance to sustain the rule of law and the exercise of rights essential to the conduct of commerce in a relatively free society (such as freedom of expression and the media, freedom of movement, freedom from arbitrary action at the hands of government). This is a destabilizing factor in planning for the future.

For business groups, as indeed for the broader community, it is the perceived threat of inroads being made on the enjoyment of existing rights and freedoms that is of central importance. The question of continued reporting under UN human rights treaties (about which many members of the community know little or nothing) is a minor one, its significance lying in the symbolic importance of China being seen to accept (or to refuse) continuing international supervision, as an indicium of its general attitude.

Of course, there are a number of groups in Hong Kong which have

---

[8] For details, see the Note of 20 June 1997 from the Permanent Representative of China to the United Nations addressed to the Secretary-General of the United Nations.

been actively engaged in the discussion of the issue of continued reporting which they see as an important part of the overall structure for the continued protection of human rights in Hong Kong. They see a willingness on China's part to continue to submit reports under the two Covenants as an important symbolic statement of its commitment to ensure the guarantees of the two Covenants. In addition, they believe that, if the rights guaranteed by those instruments are restricted or violated after 1997, recourse to UN bodies may be of some assistance in remedying the situation.

The British Government itself strongly supports the continuation of reporting (as did the Hong Kong Government before 1997), arguing not merely that this is something desirable but that China is under an *obligation* to report.[9] From the British Government's point of view, the issue was important in itself, besides constituting evidence of the approach China takes to fulfilling this and other obligations which, in the British view, it has assumed under the Joint Declaration. The government was in agreement with the many human rights groups in Hong Kong on this issue, if not on others.

A range of articulate and active "human rights groups" and other non-governmental organizations,[10] as well as a solid core of members of the former Legislative Council, share the view that continued reporting is critical and that China or the Hong Kong SAR should submit reports under the two Covenants after 1997. In written submissions and oral briefings in Geneva, New York, and Hong Kong, these human rights groups raised the issue internationally with the two treaty bodies concerned in the context of the hearings on Hong Kong that have been held since 1994. Similarly, in addition to its practice of holding regular hearings on government reports, the former Legislative Council, starting in November 1994, sent a

---

[9] The British Government has consistently stated its view that by agreeing in the Joint Declaration that the two Covenants shall remain in force in respect of Hong Kong, China has thereby accepted an obligation to report under them.

[10] Groups which have supported continued reporting under the two Covenants, and in many cases have submitted material to the UN treaty bodies on the issue include the Hong Kong Bar Association, JUSTICE, the Hong Kong Human Rights Monitor, the Society for Community Organization, the (non-governmental) Human Rights Commission, as well as others.

delegation to attend each treaty body meeting at which Hong Kong's case was considered.[11] On each occasion the delegation supported continued reporting and urged the relevant committee to ensure this. However, there was some dissent within the Council, and it was plainly not the view of all members that continued reporting was a matter that should be pursued in this way.[12] It is far from clear that there is a unified view among the new political elite (in particular the Chief Executive and the members of the provisional legislature), it seems likely that they will not openly seek to pressure China to accept its obligation to report, though they may consider reporting to be desirable.[13]

---

[11] In November 1994, a delegation from the Constitutional Affairs Panel attended the meeting of the Committee on Economic, Social and Cultural Rights, following a divided vote in the House Committee which meant that a delegation representing the whole Council could not be sent. A number of Councillors sent a letter to the Committee stating that the delegation's views on this matter did not represent their own views. In October 1995 (following the September 1995 elections) the House Committee decided to send a delegation to the Human Rights Committee, which also argued for continued reporting: *South China Morning Post*, 14 October 1995, p. 4; Emily Lau, "United Front on Human Rights," *South China Morning Post*, 16 October 1995, p. 18. Delegations from the Council were also sent to the October 1996 hearings of the Human Rights Committee and the November 1996 hearings of the Committee on Economic, Social and Cultural Rights, to make similar submissions.

[12] Some members of the former Legislative Council (including a number who are now members of the Provisional Legislative Council) appear to be of the view that the matter of reporting is essentially one within China's sovereignty and the responsibility of the Central People's Government. This does not necessarily indicate an opposition to continued reporting, but a sensitivity to the Central Government's concerns about sovereignty and the "internationalization" of the issue of Hong Kong. For example, Tsang Yok-sing, the leader of the pro-Beijing Democratic Alliance for Betterment of Hong Kong, has stated that the best way to address the issue would be for China itself to ratify the Covenants, though he has resisted any suggestion that the Hong Kong SAR Government itself could submit a report: *South China Morning Post*, 3 May 1994, p. 5.

[13] In the week before his selection, the Chief Executive failed to respond to a list of questions submitted to him and other candidates for the position by the Hong Kong Human Rights Monitor. The list included a question as to whether he intended to ensure that his government prepared reports for submission under the two Covenants.

China's Attitude to International Treaty Obligations and Other Procedures Relating to Human Rights

The controversy over whether or not reporting under the ICCPR and the ICESCR is to continue after 1997 is somewhat curious in view of China's record under other human rights treaties to which it has been a party since the early 1980s, as well as its response in relation to a number of other UN human rights mechanisms which have subjected it to inquiry.

China has ratified four of the six major UN human rights treaties which are under supervision by a body of independent experts,[14] as well as other human rights treaties. Despite indications that it might ratify the two Covenants, it has yet to do so.[15]

Under each of these four treaties, though, China has accepted an obligation to report regularly to the body of independent experts established under the individual treaties. China has performed its reporting obligations reasonably conscientiously by submitting regular reports and any additional reports requested by the various committees, though it has been criticized for the content of some of these. China has also regularly appeared before the various treaty committees and has on most of the occasions been subject to relatively close scrutiny, with the treaty committees being quite critical of some aspects of Chinese law and practice in the areas covered by the relevant treaty. In a number of cases, China has been requested to submit additional or supplementary reports because the committee considered its original submission inadequate and this has been done. Furthermore, the Chinese Government has consistently provided responses to the inquiries of UN thematic Special Rapporteurs, although the latter have frequently been far from happy with the substantive content of those responses or the underlying acts and practices they relate to.

While China's record in the realization of the guarantees contained in these treaties still falls well short of the applicable international standards, in relation to the formal and reporting aspects of these treaties its record has been relatively good and compares well with many other countries. This is consistent with both the considerable rhetorical emphasis China has

---

[14] These are the Racial Discrimination Convention, the Women's Discrimination Convention, the Convention against Torture, and the Children's Convention.

[15] In late October 1997, China signed, though it did not ratify, the Economic Covenant.

placed on its adherence to these treaties and its participation in other human rights activities of the UN, as well as a reasonably good (though mixed) record in relation to performance of obligations under other treaties.[16]

The reasons for the apparent refusal so far by the Chinese authorities to undertake to submit reports under the ICCPR and ICESCR after 1997 does not seem, therefore, to lie in any deep-seated or principled objection to the international supervision of national law and practice by independent expert bodies such as those established under the ICCPR and ICESCR. The answer must be sought elsewhere.

There are a number of factors which may underlie China's stance on this question to date. These include concern that the scope of the two Covenants would permit a much wider-ranging and potentially more critical review of the enjoyment of human rights in Hong Kong than under the other treaties to which China is already a party, and that reporting in respect of Hong Kong might have the effect of permitting an indirect review of the situation in the rest of China or be used to put pressure on the Chinese Government to accede to the Covenants. Also important may be the feeling that during the negotiations on the Joint Declaration the United Kingdom misled the Chinese Government as to the extent of implementation of the ICCPR in Hong Kong (and perhaps also as to the existence of a post-1997 obligation to report). It may also be that the Chinese authorities are of the view that China is under no legal obligation to report and does not wish to be pressured into doing so; or that China considers that there are significant or insurmountable legal obstacles to submitting reports under the two Covenants in respect of Hong Kong only (or permitting the SAR government to do so).

The most likely explanation appears to lie in a feeling on the part of the Chinese Government that they have been the victims of British deception, perhaps in conjunction with a perception that this issue is part of an attempt by various Western powers (the United Kingdom and United States in particular) to use human rights as a means of attacking and containing China. The controversy surrounding the Bill of Rights Ordinance — the domestic enactment of the ICCPR — also appears to have soured the Chinese response on reporting under the ICCPR. One of the major

---

[16] See James V. Feinerman, "Chinese Participation in the International Legal Order: Rogue Elephant or Team Player," *The China Quarterly*, Vol. 141 (March 1995), p. 186.

Chinese objections to the passage of the Bill of Rights Ordinance in 1991 was that, when the Joint Declaration was being negotiated in the early 1980s the British Government told China that the provisions of the Covenant were implemented in Hong Kong through existing legislation and the common law.[17] While the sweeping statement that the Covenants were fully implemented in Hong Kong in 1984 was somewhat disingenuous and was challenged internationally and domestically at the time, this position has consistently been the official British view before the Human Rights Committee. Although the Chinese Government should perhaps not have taken such asseverations completely at face value, one can understand the feeling that the British Government was hypocritical to claim shortly before 1997 that a Bill of Rights is required in Hong Kong to further implement the Covenants after having maintained for so long that it was not.[18]

The Two International Covenants

A great deal of attention has been devoted to the question of the continued applicability of the two International Covenants to Hong Kong, and in particular to the question of continued reporting after 1997.[19] Both

---

[17] Wu Jianfan, "The Bill of Rights: China Responds to Criticism of the PWC's Legal Proposals," *Window*, 10 November 1995, p. 10 (referring to the initial report of the United Kingdom in respect of Hong Kong submitted in 1978). See *Initial Report of the United Kingdom of Great Britain and Northern Ireland in Respect of Its Dependent Territories*, UN Doc CCPR/C/1/Add.57 (1978), reprinted in *Yearbook of the Human Rights Committee 1979–1980*, Volume II (New York: United Nations, 1989), UN Document CCPR/C/2/Add.1, pp. 169–81.

[18] The reason for the change in view lies, of course, in the Beijing massacre of 1989, but direct reference to this was hardly likely to persuade the Chinese Government of the necessity of the Bill of Rights.

[19] A. Byrnes, "Hong Kong and the International Covenant on Economic, Social and Cultural Rights — Past and Future," in *Proceedings of the Seminar on Hong Kong and the Implementation of the International Covenant on Economic, Social and Cultural Rights* (University of Hong Kong, 15 October 1994); N. Jayawickrama, "Human Rights in Hong Kong — The Continued Applicability of the International Covenants," *HKLJ*, Vol. 25 (1995), p. 171; J. Chan, "State Succession to Human Rights Treaties: Continued Application of the Covenant on Civil and Political Rights to Hong Kong after 1997," *International and Comparative Law Quarterly* , Vol. 45 (1996), p. 928.

governments agreed in the 1984 Joint Declaration that the two Covenants "as applied to Hong Kong" "shall remain in force," a guarantee reiterated and expanded upon in Article 39 of the Basic Law. There has been vigorous discussion about the exact mode of domestic implementation of the two Covenants that was envisaged by and permissible under those documents, arising especially in relation to the Hong Kong Bill of Rights and its consistency with the Basic Law.[20] Similarly, in relation to implementation at the international level the question of the continuation of reporting after 1997 has given rise to conflicting views of the extent of China's legal obligations and the international legal barriers that might stand in the way of the consideration of reports on Hong Kong, were China to submit them (whether voluntarily or pursuant to an obligation under the Joint Declaration).

The positions held by the two governments are clear, at least so far as the consequences are concerned. Britain maintains that China's acceptance in the Joint Declaration of the continued application of the Covenants was an acceptance not only of an obligation to ensure that the rights guaranteed in the Covenants were implemented in Hong Kong, but also of the obligation to report under the two Covenants after 1997.[21] Interestingly, the British Government has not elucidated how such a bilateral obligation

---

[20] For a discussion of the issues see Y. Ghai, "The Hong Kong Bill of Rights Ordinance and the Basic Law of the Hong Kong Special Administrative Region," *Journal of Chinese and Comparative Law*, Vol. 1 (1995), p. 30. See also *Window* magazine, 10 November 1995, pp. 10–14.

[21] For a recent reiteration see the *Supplementary Report of the United Kingdom in Respect of Hong Kong*, UN Document CCPR/C/117, paras 3–7 (1996) and the statement of the Representative of the United Kingdom Government, CCPR/C/SR.1535 (1996), as well as the statements to similar effect made to the Committee on Economic, Social and Cultural Rights in November 1996: E/C.12./SR.39 (1996). In 1994 the Foreign Affairs Committee of the United Kingdom Parliament, following its hearings on relations between the United Kingdom and China, recognized that there was some controversy on this issue and recommended that the United Kingdom Government "seek the opinion of the UN Human Rights Committee on the interpretation of [JD156] about the application to Hong Kong of the International Covenants on Human Rights": *Foreign Affairs Committee, First Report: Relations Between the United Kingdom and China in the Period up to and beyond 1997, Volume I*, HC Session 1993–94 (London: HMSO, 1994), para 202, p. lvii.

under the Joint Declaration would bind China, as a non-State party to either of the Covenants, to report under them or in other words, how the terms of a bilateral agreement to this effect could bring about this position under the multilateral treaty regimes of the two Covenants.

China, on the other hand, maintains that it is not under any obligation to report under the Covenants.[22] In public statements China maintains that as it is not a "State party" to the Covenants, it is not required to report, since the Covenants impose such obligation only on "States parties," though it is not clear whether this stance rules out the possibility that China might nonetheless choose to report voluntarily.[23] China also seems to maintain that the international bilateral agreement guaranteeing that the Covenants shall "remain in force" is a matter between the United Kingdom and China, and relates to the domestic implementation of the rights guaranteed in those two treaties. The Chinese statements, however, do not address the implications of a situation in which both the United Kingdom and China notified the States parties to the two Covenants of China's proposal to assume the reporting obligations of the United Kingdom in respect of Hong Kong, and in which the States parties acquiesced in this arrangement.

Since late 1994, the Human Rights Committee and the Committee on Economic, Social and Cultural Rights have given detailed consideration to the issue on two occasions. The Human Rights Committee has taken a firm and explicit stance that China is under an obligation to submit reports, finding the source of that obligation either in the Joint Declaration or in the asserted customary international law rule that human rights treaties devolve with territory. The Economic Committee has come to a similar conclusion. Both committees have indicated that they are prepared to be flexible in arranging for the submission of these reports.

The Economic Committee was the first to address the issue in detail. In November 1994, the Committee, in its first consideration of the issue, commented in the following terms.[24]

> 20. The Committee welcomes the terms in the Sino-British Joint Declaration and the Basic Law which affirm that the provisions of the Covenant will remain

---

[22] See CCPR/C/SR.1535 (statement by Mr. Henry Steel describing the Chinese position).

[23] See J. Chan, "State Succession to Human Rights Treaties."

[24] *Concluding Observations*, UN Document E/C.12/1994/19, at paras 20 and 32.

in force and continue to apply to Hong Kong after 1997. The Committee also welcomes the incorporation of the Covenant as a justiciable constitutional guarantee in article 39 of the Basic Law. While the Committee realizes that the continuation of reporting in respect of Hong Kong after 1997 may pose some legal and technical problems, it emphasizes the very important role played by reporting in relation to the protection of economic, social and cultural rights. The Committee is aware that there are various options by which these problems may be overcome. On this basis the Committee affirms its willingness and indeed, its strong wish to receive reports on Hong Kong from the People's Republic of China or, if the authorities so decide, directly from the Hong Kong Special Administrative Region. In the meantime, especially in view of the commitments entered into in the Joint Declaration, the Committee hopes that the People's Republic of China will accede to the Covenant.

...

32. The Committee urges the Government of the United Kingdom to inform the Committee as soon as possible of the modalities arrived at in agreement with the Government of China by which the reporting obligations under the Covenant will continue after 1997.

The Committee seemed to assume that China had accepted an obligation under the Joint Declaration to report (although the Committee does not say so in terms). While the Committee recognized that the existence of any such bilateral obligation did not resolve the issue of China's standing as a non-State party, its comments were a clear indication that, if China were prepared to report, then ways and means would be found by the Committee to facilitate this.

When the matter came before the Human Rights Committee almost a year later, in October 1995, that body took an even firmer stance, with the Chairperson of the Committee issuing a statement on its behalf in the following terms.[25]

The Human Rights Committee — dealing with cases of dismemberment of States parties to the International Covenant on Civil and Political Rights — has taken the view that human rights treaties devolve with territory, and that States continue to be bound by the obligations under the Covenant entered by the predecessor State.

---

[25] Statement made by the Chairperson on behalf of the Human Rights Committee relating to the consideration of the part of the fourth periodic report of the United Kingdom relating to Hong Kong, read out by the Chairman at the Committee's 1453rd meeting on 20 October 1995: UN Document CCPR/C/79/Add.57 (1995).

Once the people living in a territory find themselves under the protection of the International Covenant on Civil and Political Rights, such protection cannot be denied to them by virtue of the mere dismemberment of that territory or its coming within the jurisdiction of another State or of more than one State.

However, the existence and contents of the Joint Declaration of the Government of the United Kingdom of Great Britain and Northern Ireland and the Government of the People's Republic of China on the Question of Hong Kong make it unnecessary for the Committee to rely solely on the foregoing jurisprudence as far as Hong Kong is concerned. In this regard, the Committee points out that the parties to the Joint Declaration have agreed that all provisions of the Covenant as applied to Hong Kong shall remain in force after 1 July 1997. These provisions include reporting procedures under article 40. As the reporting requirements under article 40 of the International Covenant on Civil and Political Rights will continue to apply, the Human Rights Committee considers that it is competent to receive and review reports that must be submitted in relation to Hong Kong.

Accordingly, the Committee is ready to give effect to the intention of the parties to the Joint Declaration as far as Hong Kong is concerned, and to cooperate fully with the parties to the Joint Declaration to work out the necessary modalities to achieve these objectives. (footnotes omitted)

As can be seen, the Committee considered that the provisions of the Joint Declaration obliged China to submit reports under the ICCPR, bolstering the argument with reference to its view on the "territorial" nature of human rights treaties and, drawing upon its recent experience in relation to the States that emerged from the Former Yugoslavia.[26] As was the case with the Economic Committee, this conclusion was, however, reached after having heard directly from only one of the parties to the Joint Declaration. While the outcome is surely desirable as a matter of policy and the Committee may on its own initiative have considered the range of arguments for and against such an interpretation of the Joint Declaration, the procedure the Committee followed illustrates the dilemma faced by the various treaty

---

[26] While some writers have maintained that it has now become a rule of customary international law that human rights treaties run with the land, others maintain that the practice supporting the existence of such a rule is inconsistent and does not support the claim that such a rule has become part of customary international law. See N. Jayawickrama, "Human Rights in Hong Kong," and J. Chan, "State Succession to Human Rights Treaties," for differing views of the status of the law.

bodies in considering this issue in the absence of the Chinese Government, the party which is to fulfil these obligations.[27]

Each of the Committees reviewed a report from Hong Kong in late 1996, at which stage the Human Rights Committee firmly reiterated its earlier view in these terms:[28]

> 4. At its 1453rd meeting, on 20 October 1995, the Committee envisaged issues in connection with reporting obligations on the part of Hong Kong after the transfer of sovereignty to the People's Republic of China on 1 July 1997. It recalled that, in dealing with cases of dismemberment of States parties to the International Covenant on Civil and Political Rights, it had taken the view that human rights treaties devolve with territory, and that States continue to be bound by the obligations under the Covenant entered into by the predecessor State. Once the people living in a territory enjoy the protection of the rights under the International Covenant on Civil and Political Rights, such protection cannot be denied to them merely by virtue of dismemberment of that territory or its coming under the sovereignty of another State or of more than one State.
>
> 5. The Committee reiterates that the existence and contents of the Joint Declaration of the Government of the United Kingdom of Great Britain and Northern Ireland and the Government of the People's Republic of China make it unnecessary for the Committee to rely solely on the foregoing jurisprudence as far as Hong Kong is concerned. In this regard, the Committee pointed out that the parties to the Joint Declaration have agreed that all provisions of the Covenant as applied to Hong Kong shall remain in force after 1 July 1997. These provisions include reporting procedures under article 40: since the reporting requirements under article 40 will continue to apply, the Human Rights Committee expects that it will continue to receive and review reports submitted in relation to Hong Kong.
>
> 6. Accordingly, the Committee is ready to give effect to the intention of the parties to the Joint Declaration as far as Hong Kong is concerned, and to cooperate fully with the parties to the Joint Declaration to work out the necessary modalities to achieve these objectives. (footnotes omitted)

---

[27] Attempts were made for the 1996 hearings before the Human Rights Committee to involve China in the process by inviting it to participate in some informal way in the hearings. However, these efforts were unsuccessful, partly it seems because of the considerable amount of publicity the invitation received prior to the meeting: see *South China Morning Post*, 13 October 1996, p. 1 (quoting the Chairperson of the Human Rights Committee as saying that China had agreed to send observers to the meeting). As matters transpired, the Chinese Government did not send any representatives to the meeting.

[28] *Concluding Observations of the Human Rights Committee*, CCPR/C/79/Add.69 (1996), adopted on 6 November 1996.

By the time the Economic Committee considered the issue once again in November 1996, it too was prepared to formulate its observations more strongly, this time speaking of an "obligation" on China to report:[29]

> 32. In the light of the terms of the Sino-British Joint Declaration and of the recent practice of UN human rights treaty bodies, the Committee is of the firm view that, following the resumption of sovereignty over Hong Kong by the People's Republic of China, the People's Republic of China is under an obligation not only to ensure the enjoyment in the Hong Kong Special Administrative Region of the rights guaranteed by the Covenant but also to submit reports pursuant to Article 16 of the Covenant. The Committee therefore considers that it is competent to examine the implementation of the Covenant after 1 July 1997, on the basis of reports or such other material as will be before the Committee, and reiterates its willingness to receive reports in respect of the Hong Kong Special Administrative Region from the People's Republic of China or, if the authorities so decide, directly from the Hong Kong Special Administrative Region. The Committee encourages all parties concerned to work out as soon as possible the modalities of submitting such reports and to inform the Committee of these modalities. The Committee is convinced, however, that the best way to resolve this particular issue would be for the People's Republic of China herself to become a party to the International Covenant on Economic, Social and Cultural Rights.

Thus, it appears that the British Government, the two treaty bodies, many human rights organizations and a number of academics are of the view that China is under an obligation to submit reports, whether arising out of the terms of the Joint Declaration or the asserted rule that human rights treaties devolve with the territory, or a combination of both. Yet China continues to maintain that it is under no such obligation. The next section argues that China is under an obligation, but that the nature of that obligation and the manner in which it is to be performed is different from and more complex than the analyses advanced to date suggest.[30]

---

[29] *Concluding Observations of the Committee on Economic, Social and Cultural Rights*, E/C.12/1996/Add.10, adopted on 6 December 1996.

[30] One member of the Committee on Economic, Social and Cultural Rights, Professor Bruno Simma, made reference to the argument advanced in the original version of this chapter in discussions with the United Kingdom delegation and asked for their response. However, no direct response was given at the meeting.

The Law of Treaties, the Joint Declaration and the Covenants

As a matter of international legal analysis, the question should initially be approached through the accepted rules relating to the interpretation of treaties under international law. It is generally accepted that Articles 31 and 32 of the Vienna Convention on the Law of Treaties embody customary international law. When one attempts to apply these to the question, at least on the basis of the material available publicly, the position does not appear to be as clear-cut as either of the governments maintains.

As a start, one must give the provisions of the Joint Declaration providing for continued applicability of the two Covenants their ordinary meaning in their context and in the light of the object and purpose of the Joint Declaration. The first issue is whether the provision involves more than an obligation to ensure that the provisions of the Covenants are fully implemented under *Hong Kong* law and practice, that is, does China simply accept a bilateral obligation to implement the guarantees in Hong Kong, rather than seeking to step into Britain's shoes and to take over its existing international obligations *vis-à-vis* other States parties. The former interpretation has been advanced, based in part on the argument that the phrase "as applied to Hong Kong" means "as implemented in Hong Kong" by the laws of Hong Kong. While this view has received support from various quarters including tentative support from a member of the Hong Kong Court of Appeal,[31] it is not one that can be convincingly maintained since "application to Hong Kong" surely means application as a matter of international law.

If this is so, the question arises whether intention of the provision is to put China in Britain's shoes under the Covenants so far as Hong Kong is concerned. *Prima facie*, the reference to the Covenants would be a reference to all the provisions of the Covenant, including the reporting obligations. The reporting procedure is clearly a critically important feature of the scheme of the two Covenants, as has recently been recognized by the Human Rights Committee in its *General comment 24(52)* on reservations to the ICCPR.[32] Accordingly, the argument can reasonably be made that taking over the obligations of Britain included taking over the reporting obligations.

---

[31] *Tam Hing-yee v Wu Tai-wai* (1991) 1 HKPLR 261 at 267, per Cons VP.
[32] UN Document CCPR/C/21/Rev.1/Add.6 (1994)

If this were accepted, then the British view that the Joint Declaration obliges China to report would prevail, at least as a bilateral matter.

If one accepts that this is so, it is not the end of the interpretive process. Article 32 of the Vienna Convention permits reference both to the circumstances of the conclusion of the treaty and the preparatory work "in order to confirm the meaning resulting from the application of Article 31, or to determine the meaning when the interpretation according to Article 31:

(a) leaves the meaning ambiguous or obscure; or
(b) leads to a result which is manifestly absurd or unreasonable.

From the Chinese Government's point of view, it could reasonably be argued that this interpretation leads to a manifestly absurd or unreasonable result. Since China had no entitlement or obligation under the Covenants to submit a report and have it considered, it would be an absurd interpretation to require it to do so. That China was not a party to either of the Covenants at the time of the Joint Declaration and was under no obligation to accede to them is part of the relevant circumstances of the conclusion of the treaty. Presumably the parties were aware of the legal difficulties that followed from this and knew that merely entering into a bilateral agreement to transfer all Britain's obligations under the Covenants to China would not be effective within the framework of the multilateral framework of the Covenants. Accordingly, one could maintain that the parties could not have intended China to accept an obligation to report under the Covenants, if that possibility was simply not open to it as a non-State party. If this argument were accepted, then the Chinese position that the Joint Declaration did not oblige China to submit reports under the Covenants would have some force.

Recourse might also be made to the preparatory work of the treaty. The content of the negotiations between the British and Chinese Governments may contain statements or assurances that would resolve the issue one way or the other (if, for example, the matter was explicitly discussed and an understanding reached that there was no obligation to report or vice versa). As neither government has produced evidence either way which shows that the issue was addressed explicitly, it seems likely that the *travaux préparatoires* are inconclusive or silent on this issue.[33]

---

[33] Although it does appear that the British side explained the existing reporting obligations and how they were carried out (showing the Chinese side the initial

At this stage an observer might say that, in the absence of further evidence, neither side's argument is particularly compelling. But there may be another interpretation of the treaty, which accommodates both Britain's view that reporting was accepted as a fundamental aspect of the Covenant scheme that China was agreeing to continue, and the Chinese view that a bilateral agreement could hardly be construed to involve the acceptance of obligations under a multilateral treaty without reference to the other parties to that multilateral treaty. This interpretation would be that there is an obligation on both parties to the Joint Declaration to exercise their best efforts to bring about a situation which would enable China to submit reports to the two treaty committees and to have those reports considered in the normal way.

This interpretation would not oblige China to do what was futile — to report to a committee which refused to accept a report on the ground that it had no competence to do so or over the opposition of States parties to the treaties in question — but would require both Britain and China to take whatever reasonable steps were within their power to bring about a situation in which a report would be submitted by China and would be considered. Such an interpretation would give effect to the terms of the Joint Declaration, maintain the status quo in relation to Hong Kong in this respect (presumably a purpose of the Joint Declaration), and ensure the continued international supervision of human rights in Hong Kong. It would also mean that the fact that China was not a State party to the Covenants could not be taken as the end of the matter, since China would be obliged to explore ways in which the two regimes might nonetheless permit it to participate, including submitting a report voluntarily if the committees were prepared to accept it.

The implications of adopting this interpretation would be to accept that both China and Britain should work together to encourage the States parties

---

report under the ICCPR), this in itself may not be conclusive of an understanding that China, as a non-State party, would be expected to report. The Chinese Government would have been well aware of the nature of a reporting procedure, having itself submitted a report in May 1983 under the similar procedure established by the Convention on the Elimination of All Forms of Discrimination against Women, which entered into force for China in September 1981: see UN Document CEDAW/C/5/Add.14 (considered by the Committee on the Elimination of Discrimination against Women in 1984).

to the Covenants and the two supervisory committees to permit China to submit reports in respect of Hong Kong and to have the two committees examine them in the usual manner. This would mean, in the first instance, both the British and Chinese Governments notifying the States parties to each of the Covenants that China proposed to assume the obligations, including reporting obligations, of Britain under the ICCPR and ICESCR in respect of Hong Kong. This was done in June 1997, though without any specific mention of reporting obligations. If no State party objects, then it would be open to China to submit reports in respect of Hong Kong or to permit the SAR Government to do so.

In sum, without it being necessary to endorse fully either of the positions taken by the British and Chinese Governments in relation to the existence under the Joint Declaration of an obligation on China to submit reports, the agreement is reasonably open to an interpretation which would oblige both States to use their best efforts to explore ways in which the reporting in respect of Hong Kong under the two Covenants can continue. In view of the apparent acquiescence so far by States parties in the expressed willingness of the Committee on Economic, Social and Cultural Rights and the Human Rights Committee to receive and consider reports submitted in respect of Hong Kong, it seems unlikely that there would be objection taken by States parties if the two governments were to notify them that China proposed to assume Britain's reporting obligation in respect of Hong Kong. In the short term, however, it is up to China, which can earn the glory for being seen to report voluntarily. If it does not do so, it seems inevitable that one or other of the treaty bodies will endeavour to consider the situation in Hong Kong without an official report, a development which would be far less desirable.

If one accepts that the interpretation proposed in this chapter is a plausible one, then it opens the way for both parties to work together towards a situation in which reporting under the Covenant can continue. While this reading of the treaty offers less in formal terms than the United Kingdom's interpretation, it achieves the same practical result, deals with the issue of the relationship between a bilateral treaty and multilateral arrangements, and still permits the United Kingdom to rely on the provisions of the Joint Declaration (seen in the context of the practice under the multilateral regimes by both the treaty bodies and the other States parties). From the Chinese point of view, this reading preserves what appears to be the underlying Chinese position that a non-party to a multilateral treaty cannot be subjected to an obligation to report under it by a bilateral treaty unless that bilateral agreement somehow engages the multi-lateral regime. At the same time it gives effect to the principle of good faith in treaty interpretation and the accepted importance of the reporting procedures to each of the treaties. Finally, this interpretation is not inconsistent with the position taken by the two committees (although it may not go as far as they do).

If this is the case, then the practical question arises of what steps need to be taken. Essentially, however, it is up to China, since all other interested parties have agreed that reporting can and should continue. As a formal matter, no step needs to be taken. This was done in June 1997, when China circulated to other States parties a notification that the two Covenants as applied to Hong Kong remain in force, though without any specific mention of reporting.[34] Any report submitted by China would be welcomed; the challenge is how to persuade China that reporting in respect of Hong Kong is the best way forward, short of ratifying the Covenants themselves.

Other Human Rights Treaties

So much attention has been given to the issue of continued reporting under the two Covenants that it is often forgotten that China is party to other UN human rights treaties which also apply to Hong Kong: these are the Racial Discrimination Convention, the Convention against Torture, the Children's Convention and the Women's Discrimination Convention. Since China is a party to these, it will have then an obligation to report, whether as a consequence of the "moving treaty frontiers principle" as the default rule (Hong Kong as part of the territory covered by the original Chinese ratification) or as a result of bilateral agreement between the two governments leading to the creation of a special status for Hong Kong by modification of existing multilateral treaty arrangements.

Despite the general agreement to continue these treaties in force after 1 July 1997, the terms on which this has been done involve a lessening of international scrutiny. Although the reservations entered to each of these treaties by China in respect of the mainland differ from those the United Kingdom entered when it extended them to Hong Kong, in some cases significantly, there is also the question of the applicability of the complaints

---

[34] See Note 8 above.

procedures which applied to Hong Kong before 1 July 1997 under the Convention against Torture and the Racial Discrimination Convention. When the United Kingdom ratified the Convention against Torture, it accepted the jurisdiction of the Committee against Torture under Article 21 to receive inter-State complaints and did not opt out of the jurisdiction of the Committee under Article 20. China accepted neither the individual nor the inter-State complaint procedures and opted out of the Article 20 procedure. Thus the procedures applicable to Hong Kong by virtue of Britain's ratification were more extensive than those applicable to (mainland) China.

Procedure	*Britain*	*Hong Kong* *Before 1997 [After 1997]*	*China*
Article 19 (reporting)	Yes	Yes *[Yes]*	Yes
Article 20 (inquiry)	Yes	Yes *[No]*	No
Article 21 (inter-State)	Yes	Yes *[No]*	No
Article 22 (individual)	No	No *[No]*	No

Until June 1997 the exact extent of the obligations that would be assumed by China in respect of Hong Kong was unclear in so far as the implementation procedures under Articles 20 and 21 of the Convention were concerned. The initial report under the Convention in respect of Hong Kong[35] did not clarify the issue, nor was it clarified at the hearing before the Committee against Torture in November 1995.[36]

On 10 June 1997, however, China notified the UN Secretary-General that the two conventions would continue to apply to Hong Kong with similar reservations. However, China refused to accept the Article 20 inquiry procedure under the Convention against Torture (applicable to Hong Kong under British rule), and the inter-State procedures under both the Racial Discrimination Convention and the Convention against Torture. We come once again to the issue of whether and how this action by China in pursuance of an agreement with the United Kingdom can affect the relationships between them and other parties to the treaty, and the competence of the supervisory body created by the treaty.

---

[35] UN Document CAT/C/25/Add.6, paras 320–449 (1995)

[36] See CAT/C/SR.234 and 235 (1995) and *Concluding Observations of the Committee against Torture*, UN Document A/51/44, pp. 12–14 (1995).

Conclusion

The issue of the continued applicability of human rights obligations, especially the issue of continued reporting in respect of Hong Kong under the Covenants, has attracted a great deal of attention. What is often given less emphasis is the fact that reporting under four (out of six) other UN human rights treaties in respect of Hong Kong will continue. So far as the Covenants are concerned, it seems unfortunate that the matter seems to have led to something of a stand-off between the two governments, each insisting on its own interpretation of the Joint Declaration (neither of which is without its problems). It is clear that those legal difficulties that do exist (and are not merely imagined) can probably be overcome in the light of the explicit views expressed by the two treaty bodies concerned and the apparent acquiescence of States parties. But the onus lies on the two parties to the Joint Declaration to make this happen, and the heavier onus lies on China, as the undisputed sovereign power from 1 July 1997.

For China there is a good deal to be gained at this stage by agreeing to submit reports under the Covenants. While it may feel that it has been pressured into doing so by the United Kingdom (and other countries), the treaty bodies and non-governmental organizations, adopting the interpretation proposed in this chapter would enable China to maintain much of its position. If China fails to follow this course (or to accede to the Covenants themselves), this will have an impact on confidence in Hong Kong in the short term. Additionally, even if China does not submit a report according to schedule, it seems likely that the two committees concerned will review the human rights situation in Hong Kong nonetheless. This is a procedure that has been adopted by various committees in relation to "rogue" governments, among whose company China might not wish to see itself classified. Undertaking to report will not only bolster confidence in Hong Kong, but additionally will help China to further build its image as a responsible and significant member of the world community.

Note: On 22 November 1997, after the completion of this chapter, the Chinese Government announced that it would submit reports in respect of Hong Kong. *Sunday Morning Post*, 23 November 1997, p. 1.

Part 2
International Order

8

Managing the Transfer of Sovereignty over Hong Kong: The Case for Continuity of Treaties[1]

Roda Mushkat

Hong Kong is moving inexorably towards the point of transition from British to Chinese rule with all the institutional challenges that it entails. One of the critical issues confronting the territory is the continuity of the existing arrangements for sustaining external interactions embedded in international treaty law. Needless to say, this issue has far-reaching implications for Hong Kong as a leading financial centre and a highly autonomous player in the global economic arena. The purpose of this chapter is to demonstrate that within the context of prevailing international legal norms, the multilateral treaties currently applicable to Hong Kong should remain intact through the transition and beyond.

The Relevant International Legal Framework

It is a truism that the Hong Kong case defies easy categorization. Not only is the "creation" of the Hong Kong Special Administrative Region (HKSAR) — as a unit in the "one country, two systems" configuration — an original mode of political transformation, even the locating of the instant discourse within the subject known as "State succession" has been

---

[1] This chapter is an abbreviated and modified version of my article on "Hong Kong and Succession of Treaties," *International and Comparative Law Quarterly* (January 1997).

questioned.[2] Yet there is little doubt that the "transition" on 1 July 1997 largely comports with the definition of "State succession"[3] — as "the replacement of one state by another in the responsibility for the international relations of territory"[4] — and that the issues raised as a result of this event are generally covered within the branch of international law which "deals with the legal consequences of change of sovereignty over territory."[5] While the assistance to be derived from the international legal framework falls short of "bright-line answers," basic guiding principles are nonetheless offered. Coupled with the flexibility and practical wisdom advocated by

---

[2] It is China's contention that no transfer of sovereignty is taking place since it merely "resumes" the exercise of sovereignty over Hong Kong. At the other extreme, it has been suggested that "since the Joint Declaration does not provide for complete responsibility by China for the international relations of Hong Kong, but rather provides for a transfer of sovereignty over Hong Kong without a complete transfer of autonomy, what will occur is a limited incorporation of the sovereign powers of the territory of Hong Kong into China. Such incorporation should more properly be characterized as 'accession,' rather than 'succession,' because China will come into possession of only some of the sovereign rights of the incorporated state." See Shawn B. Jensen, "International Agreements between the United States and Hong Kong under the United States — Hong Kong Policy Act," *Temple International and Comparative Law Journal*, Vol. 7 (1993), p. 180, Note 76.

[3] See Article 2(1)(b), 1978 Vienna Convention on Succession in Respect of Treaties. Although the "codificatory" nature of the Convention is limited (only 14 States have ratified the Convention; inadequate correspondence between its provisions and political reality), its definition of State succession is "widely accepted by commentators as the best available." See Michael John Volkovitch, "Righting Wrongs: Towards a New Theory of State Succession to Responsibility for International Delicts," *Colombia Law Review*, Vol. 92 (1992), p. 2164, Note 1.

[4] See Section 4, "Explanatory Notes," *A Draft Agreement between the Government of the United Kingdom of Great Britain and Northern Ireland and the Government of the People's Republic of China* (26 September 1984), at p. 35 ("… in relation to foreign and defence affairs, *which are now the overall responsibility of Her Majesty's Government, and will with effect from 1 July 1997 become the overall responsibility of the Central People's Government of the People's Republic of China…*" [emphasis added]).

[5] Michael Akehurst, *A Modern Introduction to International Law* (London: Allen and Unwin, 1987), p. 159.

experts, these principles might contribute to an orderly and equitable adjustment of related problems.

Clearly, the traditional (and to an extent, discredited[6]) theory of "clean slate" — vesting a "newly independent State" with power to decide which bilateral and multilateral treaties will remain in force — has no direct relevance. Given the highly autonomous status of Hong Kong (distinguished from total absorption/integration with another state), the "moving treaty frontiers"[7] rule, which postulates that a territory automatically passes out of the treaty regime of a former sovereign into the treaty regime of the successor sovereign, also becomes inapplicable. Specifically, whereas substitution of treaty regimes may be rationalized on the basis of loss of identity and ensuing inability to perform international obligations, the HKSAR, contrastingly, is set to enjoy a wide latitude in the management of external affairs, including a capacity to establish and maintain treaty relationships.[8]

---

[6] Or, at least, considerably qualified; see Robert Jennings and Arthur Watts (eds.), *Oppenheim's International Law*, 9th ed. (Harlow, Essex: Longman, 1992), pp. 228–30 (listing several exceptions — e.g. "locally connected" treaties; treaties "specifically made for/specifically extended to [the territory] by the former parent state" — and emphasizing extensive state practice of continuity and devolution agreements).

[7] See Succession Convention, *supra* Note 3, Article 15: "When part of the territory of a State ... becomes part of the territory of another State ... (a) treaties of the predecessor State cease to be in force in respect of the territory to which the succession of States relates from the date of the succession of States; and (b) treaties of the successor State are in force in respect of the territory to which the succession of States relates from the date of the succession of States, unless it appears from the treaty or is otherwise established that the application of the treaty to that territory would be incompatible with the object and purpose of the treaty or would radically change the conditions for its operation." For a discussion of the theory of "moving treaty boundaries," see Daniel P. O'Connell, *State Succession in Municipal Law and International Law* (Cambridge: Cambridge University Press, 1967), Vol. I, p. 25.

[8] See *Agreement between the Government of the United Kingdom of Great Britain and Northern Ireland and the Government of the People's Republic of China on the Future of Hong Kong* (26 September 1984), reprinted in *International Legal Materials*, Vol. 23 (1984), p. 1366 [hereafter: Joint Declaration], Annex I, Section XI.

Indeed, it may be contended that the HKSAR, displaying the "international legal personality"[9] as it does, should appropriately be designated the "successor." In particular, being endowed with both jurisdictional competence and effective control over territory, the local government may be held internationally responsible for commitments assumed under treaties. Arguably, the territory's admission as a party to international agreements or as a member of international organizations has been implicitly predicated in its possession of the necessary authority (to enter into international agreements and join international organizations) as well as its acceptance of contingent liabilities.

The "Hong Kong Formula"

To a certain extent, the parties to the Sino-British Joint Declaration have been cognizant of Hong Kong's special predicament (including the fact that the replacing sovereign, the People's Republic of China (P.R.C.), is not a party to many of the international agreements presently extending to the territory and is not a member of all the international organizations of which Hong Kong is a member), opting for a pragmatic formula of succession. Accordingly, international agreements "implemented in Hong Kong"[10] remain in force, even if the P.R.C. is not a party to the agreement,

---

[9] For a detailed discussion, see Roda Mushkat, *One Country, Two International Legal Personalities: The Case of Hong Kong* (Hong Kong: Hong Kong University Press, 1997). [Hong Kong's case for international legal personality is founded on its factual "stately" attributes (permanent population, distinct territory and effective government); the international recognition extended to it as an autonomous entity; a substantiated claim to "international legitimacy" (by virtue of adherence to international norms — rule of law, democratic principles, protection of universally recognized human rights and fundamental freedoms); an international legal entitlement (right to self-determination); membership in the "international civil society" (international organizations and associations); as well as *sui generis* qualities.]

[10] It is submitted that the term "implemented" ought to be given a broad construction in light of the Joint Declaration's overall object and purpose (i.e. the "maintenance of the prosperity and stability of Hong Kong" — Preamble) and in accordance with the "presumption of continuity" (as elaborated in the first part of this Article). The term may nonetheless indicate an intention that existing reservations made (by Britain) in respect of the territory would be maintained.

while international agreements to which the P.R.C. is a party (but not Hong Kong) would apply to the territory by the Central People's Government only after seeking the views of the HKSAR Government.[11] In addition, the Chinese Government "shall, as necessary, authorize or assist the government of the Region to make appropriate arrangements for the application to the Region of other relevant international agreements."[12]

In the Joint Declaration particular attention is accorded to agreements regarding Hong Kong's international air transport relations, in order to ensure the maintenance of the territory's status as "a centre of international and regional aviation."[13] Thus, the HKSAR, acting under authorization from China, may "renew or amend Air Service Agreements and arrangements previously in force ..."[14] Also specifically identified among treaties to be succeeded to by the HKSAR, are the International Covenant on Civil and Political Rights and the International Covenant on Economic, Social and Cultural Rights whose continuance has been expressly guaranteed by the Joint Declaration.[15]

Notwithstanding the reasonableness of the Hong Kong formula or the "devolutionary" function of the Sino-British Joint Declaration, questions may be posed in relation to the binding effect on third parties.[16] Yet, while a devolution agreement does not by itself create a legal nexus between the

---

[11] Joint Declaration, Annex I, Section XI.

[12] *Loc. cit.*

[13] Joint Declaration, Annex I, Section IX.

[14] *Loc. cit.* In fact, not only will the HKSAR succeed to aviation-related rights currently enjoyed by Hong Kong, but it may also assume additional international responsibilities with respect to the management of civil aviation. These responsibilities include the negotiation and conclusion of new Air Services Agreements (ASAs).

[15] Joint Declaration, Annex I, Section XIII.

[16] As a general rule (reflected in Article 34, Convention on the Law of Treaties), a treaty does not create obligations or rights for a third state without its consent (*pacta tertiis nec nocent nec prosunt*). Note, however, that where a treaty codifies customary international law, third states would be bound by that law. Third party's interests (or rather the interests of the whole community of states) are also recognized in the rule (incorporated in Article 53, Convention on the Law of Treaties) that a treaty is void if, at the time of its conclusion, it conflicts with a peremptory norm of general international law (*jus cogens*).

successor State and third parties,[17] States have tended to regard such agreements as giving rise to a presumption of the continuance in force of the
respective treaties.[18] Combined with the general presumption of continuity,[19] it may be surmised that third parties are inclined to accept a "nova-
tion."[20] More radically, it is arguable that the Sino-British Joint Declaration
has erected an "objective regime" of *erga omnes* applicability.[21]

Again, the parties to the Joint Declaration have proceeded in a pragmatic manner to procure third party acceptances of the arrangements pos-
tulated[22] and endorsements from the members of the relevant international
organizations for the succession of the territory's membership in these

---

[17] See Succession Convention, *supra* Note 3, Article 8: "The obligations or
rights of a predecessor State under treaties in force in respect of a territory at the
date of a succession of States do not become the obligations or rights of the
successor State towards other States parties to those treaties *by reason only of
the fact that the predecessor State and the successor State have concluded an
agreement providing that such obligations or rights shall devolve upon the successor State*" [emphasis supplied].

[18] See *Oppenheim's International Law*, *supra* Note 6, p. 231, Note 20 (citing
the International Law Commission's review of state practice).

[19] See most recently, International Law Association Helsinki Conference
(1996), "*Rapport Preliminaire sur la Succession D'etats en Matiere de Traites.*"
See also Christine Chinkin, *Third Parties in International Law* (Oxford: Clarendon
Press, 1993), p. 2 (putting forward the thesis that "bilateralism is no longer appropriate as the paradigm model for the regulation of activities in the international
arena").

[20] It may be interesting to note the formal acceptance to the Hong Kong
succession formula as expressed in the United States — Hong Kong Policy Act
1992, reprinted in *International Legal Materials*, Vol. 32 (1993), p. 545 (providing
that the U.S. should continue to fulfil its obligations to Hong Kong under international agreements, whether or not China is also a party to those agreements).

[21] See Martin Dixon, *Textbook on International Law*, 3rd edition (London:
Blackstone Press, 1996), p. 67 (suggesting as an example that "it will not be open
to any state to claim that the United Kingdom is still the legitimate sovereign of
Hong Kong after the treaty of cession with China takes effect in 1997").

[22] Instrumentally, "notes" from the British and Chinese Governments, enclos-
ing a "list of agreed multilateral treaties" are to be communicated to the UN
Secretary-General. Concurrently, the depositories of the respective treaties will be
informed of the continued application beyond 1997 and allowed a reasonable
period for objection.

organizations.[23] Such a task has been assigned to the Joint Liaison Group (JLG), which lists among its "achievements" the securing of Hong Kong's continued participation in thirty international organizations[24] (including notably retention of Hong Kong's own membership in the GATT/WTO[25])

---

[23] This is commonly expected given the peculiarities of membership in international organizations. A case in point (involving, in fact, both membership in an international organization as well as continued application of the organization's conventions) is Hong Kong's affiliation with the International Labour Organization (ILO). Specifically, account had to be taken of the fact that the operation of the ILO conventions in Hong Kong had been by virtue of its status as a "Non-Metropolitan Territory" (NMT) of the United Kingdom and that after 1997 HKSAR would not be deemed to be a NMT. The "solution" adopted took the form of a "Communication" from the British Government and a "Declaration" by the Government of the P.R.C., addressed to the General Secretary of the ILO to the effect that for the purpose of enabling the HKSAR to continue its participation in ILO activities and to continue to have ILO conventions applied to it, the relevant articles of the ILO Constitution will be applied "by analogy" to the HKSAR. See International Labour Office, "Communications from the Government of the United Kingdom of Great Britain and Northern Ireland and the People's Republic of China to the Director-General of the ILO," *Official Bulletin*, Vol. 73 (1990), p. 25. The ILO "analogous format" is expected to be used in relation to other international organizations. See, however, the reservations expressed in Shin-ichi Ago, "Application of ILO Conventions to Hong Kong after 1997," *Dalhousie Law Journal*, Vol. 17 (1994), p. 612.

[24] See *Achievements of the Joint Liaison Group and Its Sub-Group on International Rights and Obligations, 1985–May 1990* (Hong Kong: Government Printer, 1990); agreement for continued participation in three additional organizations was secured since 1990. For the position in respect of specific organizations as of 31 March 1996, see *United States–Hong Kong Policy Act Report* (1 April 1996), pp. 24–26.

[25] Hong Kong became a separate contracting party to GATT in 1986. See Accession of Hong Kong, Succession, GATT Doc. L/5976 (21 April 1986), reprinted in *GATT: Basic Instruments and Selected Documents*, Vol. 4, 34th Suppl. (1988), p. 27. GATT has been "transformed" into the World Trade Organization (WTO) on 1 January 1995. It may be noted that the significance of "succession" as distinct from application for a new membership of the WTO is well illustrated in respect of the P.R.C.'s claim to "resuming" membership once held by China under Kuomintang leadership. See Detlev F. Vagts, "State Succession: The Codifiers' View," *Virginia Journal of International Law*, Vol. 33 (1993), pp. 293–94.

as well as the preserving of the application to the territory of most of the multilateral agreements currently in force in Hong Kong.[26]

The Case for Continuity of Applicable Treaties

Adopting as a legitimate point of departure the established "presumption of continuity," it may be possible to garner additional reinforcement for a continuing applicability of Hong Kong's treaties from the particular exigencies of the territory's "social life." More specifically, there is little doubt that the preservation of Hong Kong's prosperity and its status as a major international commercial centre hinges on the continuation of its external ties and international agreements.[27] That both the British and Chinese Governments were fully apprised of such a fundamental desideratum to the "future of Hong Kong" is clearly reflected in the detailed provisions of their Joint Declaration, the sustained efforts at implementation as well as the issuing by the parties of relevant reassurances directed at the international community.

On the other hand, there seem to exist no special considerations which might operate to rebut the continuity presumption. While the transition from British to Chinese rule would inevitably affect the territory's domestic socio-political order, its international legal identity/personality remains essentially the same.[28] Indeed, given the extent to which the local law and administrative practices already incorporate germane international treaties,

---

[26] See Constitutional Affairs Branch, *List of Agreed Multilateral Treaties* (10 October 1996). See also Joint Liaison Group, *Joint Communique*, 35th Meeting (6, 7, 9 February 1996), announcing that the parties "reached an agreement in principle on the mechanism for giving legal form to all the agreements on international rights and obligations reached so far by the IRO [International Rights and Obligations] Sub-Group." Both documents are on File, "Treaty Project Archives" (Centre for Comparative and Public Law, Faculty of Law, University of Hong Kong).

[27] Including agreements that create international organizations in whose activities Hong Kong participates.

[28] Factors relevant to such a determination include the retaining of land mass, population, resources and, notably, the legal order.

the maintenance of the "laws currently in force in Hong Kong"[29] would envelop a *de facto* succession of treaties.[30] In a similar vein, the transfer of sovereignty over Hong Kong cannot be deemed a "fundamental change" that "radically transforms" the nature of the territory, allowing claims of *rebus sic stantibus*[31] to refute continuity of the applicable treaty regime. In fact, as proclaimed under the Joint Declaration, the "history of Hong Kong and its realities ..."[32] have been taken into account in the establishment of the HKSAR.

It is particularly evident that no change in circumstances arising out of the succession of Hong Kong may act to deflect the application of treaties codifying customary international law. As aptly observed,[33] not only is the implementation of "codificatory treaties" unlikely to be made incompatible or more onerous as a result of a political transformation, but abandoning them could also place the successor in a position of an "outlaw."[34] It may be further emphasized that an enduring commitment to be bound by such treaties is coterminous with the established principle that all subjects of international law are presumed to have accepted the obligations and rights under customary international law.[35]

---

[29] See Joint Declaration, Article 3(3): "... The laws currently in force in Hong Kong will remain basically unchanged." Annex I, Section II: "After the establishment of the Hong Kong Special Administrative Region, the laws previously in force in Hong Kong (i.e. the common law, rules of equity, ordinances, subordinate legislation and customary law) shall be maintained ..."

[30] See O'Connell, *supra* Note 7, p. 190 (discussing the "factor of inertia in state succession practice").

[31] The principle is incorporated in Article 62 of the 1969 Convention on the Law of Treaties. In the context of succession, the principle would mandate the validity of predecessor's treaties so long as there is no material change in relevant facts and circumstances that would make performance of the agreement inequitable responsibility.

[32] Joint Declaration, Article 3(1).

[33] See Vagts, *supra* Note 25, p. 290.

[34] *Loc. cit.* (suggesting as an example that "a new state repudiating its predecessor's adherence to the Genocide Convention would raise questions about its intentions to violate the prohibitions against mass murder").

[35] See Karol Wolfke, *Custom in Present International Law* (Dordrecht: M. Nijhoff, 1993), p. 162.

Specific Contexts

Diplomatic Relations

Clearly identifiable among the codificatory treaties applicable to Hong Kong are the conventions pertaining to diplomatic and consular relations, which are generally perceived as foundation to international order and cooperation. It is not surprising, therefore, that arrangements[36] have been made for post-1997 application of the 1961 Convention on Diplomatic Relations, the 1963 Convention on Consular Relations, the 1946 Convention on the Privileges and Immunities of the United Nations, and the 1947 Convention (with annexes) on the Privileges and Immunities of the Specialized Agencies of the United Nations[37] as well as the 1973 Convention on the Prevention and Punishment of Crimes against Internationally Protected Persons (and more generally, the Charter of the United Nations and the Statute of the International Court of Justice). Though perhaps not fully qualified as "customary international law," it is nonetheless regrettable that the Optional Protocols [to the 1961 & 1963 Diplomatic/Consular Conventions] on Compulsory Settlement of Disputes (and for that matter the 1899 and 1907 Hague Conventions on the Pacific Settlement of International Disputes, and the 1928 General Act for the Pacific Settlement of International Disputes) have been omitted.[38]

Equally unfortunate is the relinquishing of the codificatory 1969 Convention on the Law of Treaties (to which the P.R.C. is not a party), although international treaty law — like other customary international laws — will continue to have effect in the territory through the common law.[39] In this

---

[36] See generally *List of Agreed Multilateral Treaties, supra* Note 26.

[37] It may be noted, however, that diplomatic status extended to certain international bodies (e.g., the International Committee of the Red Cross and the United Nations High Commissioner for Refugees) is governed by bilateral treaties with Britain which expire on 30 June 1997.

[38] Note in this connection the P.R.C.'s general reluctance to submit to third party adjudication in the settlement of international disputes.

[39] It is an "established rule" that customary international law is incorporated into English law automatically and constitutes part of the law of the land (unless in conflict with an Act of Parliament). See *Oppenheim's International Law, supra* Note 6, pp. 56–57. The common law applicable in Hong Kong (and for that matter local legislation incorporating international law) will remain in force in accordance with Article 3(3) of the Joint Declaration, *supra* Note 29.

vein, it is expected that the Law of War and the relevant humanitarian rules applicable in armed conflict — which have acquired the status of customary international law — will retain their binding force in the HKSAR, notwithstanding the omission from the *List of Agreed Multilateral Treaties*[40] of certain specific accords previously applied to Hong Kong.[41]

Refugees

Reliance on customary international law may also be dictated in respect of international refugee law, given that the main codificatory treaty — the 1951 Convention on the Status of Refugees (and its 1967 Protocol) — has not been extended to Hong Kong by Britain, and that no agreement has been reached on the maintenance of the conventions on the status of stateless persons beyond 1997.[42] Nor is it likely that the P.R.C. (which has acceded to the Convention and Protocol Relating to the Status of Refugees) will take the necessary steps to facilitate their application in the HKSAR, although, regardless of Chinese demands, the resolution of the territory's

---

[40] *Supra* Note 26. Contained in the list are: the four 1949 Geneva Conventions (i.e. Convention for the Amelioration of the Condition of Wounded and Sick in Armies in the Field; Convention for the Amelioration of the Condition of Wounded, Sick and Ship-wrecked Members of Armed Forces at Sea; Convention on the Treatment of Prisoners of War; and the Convention on the Protection of Civilian Persons in Time of War. Also included are: the 1968 Treaty on the Non-Proliferation of Nuclear Weapons; and the 1972 Convention on the Prohibition of the Development, Production and Stockpiling of Bacteriological (Biological) and Toxin Weapons and for their Destruction.

[41] The 1925 Protocol on the Prohibition of Use in War of Asphyxiating, Poisonous or Other Gases and of Bacteriological Methods of Warfare; 1930 Treaty for the Limitation and Reduction of Naval Armament; and the 1977 Convention on the Prohibition of Military or Any Other Hostile Use of Environmental Modification Techniques.

[42] Currently extended to Hong Kong are: the 1954 Convention on the Status of Stateless Persons and the 1961 Convention on the Reduction of Statelessness as well as the 1930 Protocol on Certain Cases of Statelessness and 1930 Special Protocol Concerning Statelessness. The P.R.C. is not a party to the above treaties. The pertinence of the "Stateless Conventions" in the local refugee context has recently been highlighted in relation to difficulties of repatriating asylum-seekers considered "non-nationals" by Vietnam.

"refugee problem" before July 1997 does not appear feasible. On the other hand, the body of relevant human rights norms should be enhanced by continued application of the 1984 UN Convention against Torture and Other Cruel, Inhuman or Degrading Treatment or Punishment[43] as well as, more generally, the 1966 International Covenant on Civil and Political Rights and International Covenant on Economic, Social and Cultural Rights.

Environmental Protection

Consistent with the strong presumption in favour of continuity of conventions of a "universal" nature (in the sense of being "open to ratification by all States" and "expressing norms adopted at international assemblies by near-unanimity on the part of States from all regions of the world"),[44] environmental conventions have been guaranteed to continue to be applicable in the HKSAR. Included are agreements pertaining to the prevention and control of marine pollution,[45] curtailment of ozone-depleting

---

[43] The Convention incorporates, *inter alia*, one of the fundamental principles of refugee law, namely *non refoulement*, or the obligation not to expel or return (*refouler*) a refugee in any manner whatsoever to the frontier of territories where his/her life or freedom would be threatened on account of his/her race, religion, nationality, membership of a particular social group or political opinion; not to expel, return (*refouler*) or extradite a person to another state where there are substantial grounds for believing that he/she will be in danger of being subjected to torture; and not to expel a stateless person lawfully staying in the territory except on grounds of national security or public order.

[44] See Oscar Schachter, "State Succession: The Once and Future Law," *Virginia Journal of International Law*, Vol. 33 (1993), p. 259.

[45] The 1969 Convention on Civil Liability for Oil Pollution Damage (and its 1976 Protocol); 1969 Convention Relating to Intervention on the High Seas in Cases of Oil Pollution Casualties (and its 1973 Protocol); 1971 International Convention for the Establishment of the International Fund for Compensation for Oil Pollution Damage (and its 1976 Protocol); 1972 Convention on the Prevention of Marine Pollution by Dumping of Wastes and Other Matters (and 1978 Amendments and 1980 Protocol Amending the 1972 Convention); 1973 Convention for the Protection of Pollution from Ships (and its 1978 Protocol). Note, however, that the 1958 Law of the Sea Conventions [Convention on the High Seas; Convention on the Territorial Sea and Contiguous Zone; Convention on Fishing and Conservation of the Living Resources of the High Seas; Convention on the Continental

substances,[46] protection of endangered plant and animal species,[47] preservation of natural habitat,[48] control of transboundary movements of hazardous wastes and their disposal,[49] as well as the regulation of activities in outer space[50] and liability in the field of nuclear energy.[51] The territory, however, is not yet subject to international agreements monitoring climate change (greenhouse gas emissions) and the preservation of biological diversity. Although the essential principles of international environmental law[52] are applicable either as customary international law, or under highly

---

Shelf] has not been included in the *List of Agreed Multilateral Treaties, supra* Note 26. Note also that the P.R.C. has signed and ratified the 1982 United Nations Convention on the Law of the Sea (UNCLOS) which offers a significantly more comprehensive regime of marine environment protection.

[46] The 1985 Convention for the Protection of the Ozone Layer; 1987 Protocol on Substances that Deplete the Ozone Layer (and its 1990 and 1992 Amendments).

[47] The 1956 Plant Protection Agreement for the South East Asia and Pacific Region (and 1967 Amendment); 1973 Convention on International Trade in Endangered Species of Wild Fauna and Flora (and its 1979 Amendment); 1979 Convention on the Conservation of Migratory Species of Wild Animals; 1946 International Convention for the Regulation of Whaling (and its 1956 Protocol).

[48] [Ramsar] Convention on Wetlands of International Importance Especially as Waterfowl Habitat; 1972 Convention for the Protection of the World Cultural and Natural Heritage; 1988 Convention on the Regulation of Antarctic Mineral Resource Activities.

[49] The 1989 Convention on the Control of Transboundary Movements of Hazardous Wastes and Their Disposal.

[50] The 1967 Treaty on the Principles Governing Activities of States in the Exploration and Use of Outer Space, including the Moon and Other Celestial Bodies; 1968 Agreement on the Rescue of Astronauts, the Return of Astronauts and the Return of Objects Launched into Outer Space; 1972 Convention on International Liability for Damage Caused by Space Objects; 1974 Convention on Registration of Objects Launched into Outer Space.

[51] The 1960 Convention on Third Party Liability in the Field of Nuclear Energy (and its 1964 Protocol).

[52] The rule pertaining to the responsibility of states to ensure that activities within their jurisdiction or control do not cause damage to the environment of other states or of areas beyond the limits of national jurisdiction; the "precautionary principle" which aims at ensuring that activities posing a threat to the environment will be prevented, even if there is no conclusive scientific proof linking them to

authoritative "soft law,"[53] it is nonetheless desirable for the relevant conventions to be extended to the HKSAR by the P.R.C.[54]

As a final observation, since the general bilateral treaties (unless of a "dispositive"[55] type) are expected to lapse "when the predecessor State is no longer party to the original agreement,"[56] the consideration of proposals for negotiation and conclusion of bilateral agreements have been prominent on the JLG's agenda, and are regarded as essential to the sound administration of justice and cooperation with third countries.[57] Particular attention has been paid to agreements on the Surrender of Fugitive Offenders, Mutual

---

environmental damage; the "polluter pays principle," whereby those who burden or harm the environment are required to bear the costs of avoiding, eliminating or compensating for these injuries; the undertaking of environmental impact assessments for proposed activities that are likely to have a significant adverse impact on the environment.

[53] Notable "soft" international environmental instruments are the three major documents adopted unanimously at the 1992 "Earth Summit" (the Rio Declaration on Environment and Development, Agenda 21, and the Non-Legally Binding Authoritative Statement of Principles for a Global Consensus in the Management, Conservation and Sustainable Development of All Types of Forests).

[54] China signed and ratified the 1992 Framework Convention on Climate Change; and the 1992 Convention on Biological Diversity.

[55] Treaties which transfer or create real (*in rem*) rights are regarded as permanent and independent of the personality of the State exercising sovereignty over the territory [See Note, "Taking Reichs Seriously: German Unification and the Law of State Succession," *Harvard Law Review*, Vol. 104 (1990), p. 597 (and references therein)]. As such, they "run with the land," survive changes in sovereignty and remain attached to the successor's territory [see Daniel P. O'Connell, "Recent Problems of State Succession in Relation to New States," *Recueil des Cours d'Academie de Droit International*, Vol. 130 (1970-II), pp. 193–94].

[56] See O'Connell, *supra* Note 7, p. 212.

[57] See Constitutional Affairs Branch, *Joint Liaison Group: Achievements in the Past Ten Years* (November 1995) [on File, "Treaty Project Archives," *supra* Note 26]. Note also the agreement reached in the JLG on the conclusion of a network of bilateral Investment Promotion and Protection agreements (as part of "strengthening the economic infrastructure and institutions") as well as the arrangements made for "separating air services agreements from those signed by the United Kingdom which also cover Hong Kong, and concluding agreements with new aviation partners"). *Loc. cit.*

Legal Assistance in Criminal Matters, the Transfer of Sentenced Persons and the Reciprocal Enforcement of Judgement. Arguably, a "renegotiated succession" of bilateral treaties in such fields need not be affected by the territory's transition, given the assumption that "states entered into these treaties without regard to the size, wealth, or other qualities of the treaty partners, with the exception perhaps of the level of civilization which their judicial systems are deemed to have attained."[58] On the other hand, the peculiarity of the Hong Kong case (its distinct "one country, two systems" configuration) has given rise to special needs involving bilateral agreements with the mainland on issues of "conflict of laws" (including extradition, recognition and enforcement of judgements[59]).

Conclusion

Although the law of State succession may not succeed in providing "watertight" solutions to Hong Kong's predicament, it offers a useful "management" tool. Reflecting global interests (such as minimizing disruption in international legal relations; avoiding the creation of an international legal void; safeguarding legitimate expectations), responding to political vicissitudes and the demands of pragmatism, and inspired by the decision to ensure Hong Kong's continued stability and prosperity, contemporary international law lends normative support to the route chartered by the parties to the Sino-British Joint Declaration in respect of the territory's network of treaties. The legal framework needed to render the potentially difficult transition from the predictable past to the uncertain future is largely in place and, provided an enlightened attitude is adopted regarding the limits of sovereignty, the 1997 challenge may be effectively addressed.

The evidence so far suggests that the two parties will proceed to handle the transition in a constructive manner. There is recognition on both sides that the benefits of sustaining the politico-economic status quo beyond 1997 are substantial. This is a matter of honour as well as strategic advantage. The post-transition applicability of the long list of treaties which seems to have been ensured through the timely initiatives of the British

---

[58] See Vagts, *supra* Note 25, p. 291.

[59] Note the inapplicability to legal cases between Hong Kong and China of the 1958 Convention on the Recognition and Enforcement of *Foreign* Arbitral Awards [emphasis supplied].

Government and the generally favourable responses of its Chinese counter-part attests to the importance that the parties accord to maintaining international legal continuity.

The considerable success achieved in the particular domain of "treaty succession" reflects the great priority that China attaches to preserving Hong Kong's position as a dynamic economic entity. The dynamism of the local economy, in turn, is due to a flexible economic structure and a high degree of integration into the international capitalist economy. The accommodative attitude with respect to legal continuity may be viewed as an acknowledgement of the causal relationship between this factor and such key economic attributes. In areas where the connection is absent, the Chinese attitude may prove less elastic.

Acknowledgements

To the extent that material relied upon in this chapter has been collected by the Hong Kong Treaty Project of the Centre of Comparative and Public Law, University of Hong Kong, the author wishes to thank the Hong Kong Research Grants Council which has generously supported this project.

9

Hong Kong's Changing International Relations Strategy

Jane C. Y. Lee and Gerald Chan

Introduction

Hong Kong has never enjoyed the status of an independent sovereign state. As a British colony since 1842, it has had limited scope of freedom in developing its external relations until very recently.

Article 13 of the Basic Law states that the Central People's Government (CPG) shall be responsible for the foreign affairs relating to the Hong Kong Special Administrative Region (SAR). Within this framework, the Hong Kong SAR will be granted a high degree of autonomy in external affairs as guaranteed in the Sino-British Joint Declaration of 1984. Article 10 of the Declaration states that "the Hong Kong SAR may on its own maintain and develop economic and cultural relations and conclude relevant agreements with states, regions and relevant international organizations." This has been further elaborated in various sections of the Chinese Annexes of the Declaration as well as Chapter VII (Articles 150–157) of the Basic Law, which identify specific aspects of the maintenance of Hong Kong's external relations.

A Sino-British Joint Liaison Group (JLG) responsible for the transitional arrangements was set up in 1986 to enable the Hong Kong SAR to maintain its bilateral economic relations, as well as continued adherence to international agreements and application of international rights and obligations affecting Hong Kong.[1] In the ten years between 1986 and 1996,

---

[1] *Joint Declaration of the Government of the United Kingdom of Great Britain and Northern Ireland and the Government of the People's Republic of China on*

substantial arrangements have been agreed upon through the JLG, largely pragmatic, to provide for Hong Kong's continued participation in a number of international organizations after 1997. Hong Kong's external relations have become increasingly independent of Britain. By 1996 the degree of autonomy in Hong Kong's external relations had become greater than that in the pre-1986 period. The work of the JLG has not only maintained, but also virtually strengthened, Hong Kong's international presence in the ten years since 1986.

A lot of good groundwork has been prepared by the JLG in the transition period. This was largely achieved by China's pragmatic attitude towards Hong Kong. Even so, the Hong Kong SAR will have to conform to China's foreign policy principles in the post-1997 period. It is and will remain controversial as to what makes a proper balance between pragmatic practices and sovereign principles. The extent to which the concept of "one country, two systems" is applied in matters of external relations and foreign affairs is an area not fully explored in academic circles. This chapter investigates into the strategy adopted by the Hong Kong Government which enables it to achieve the greatest possible extent of autonomy. We shall explain what is Hong Kong's international relations strategy and the problems and challenges facing Hong Kong in its transition to 1997 and beyond. Special attention will be paid to the impact of China's influence on this strategy. Three specific issues, namely Hong Kong's relations with international organizations, the United States, and Taiwan will be analysed to illustrate potential dilemma. First of all, let us review some theoretical and policy issues relating to the reversion of Hong Kong to Chinese rule.

Some Theoretical and Policy Discussions: Realism Meets Liberalism

When we discuss Hong Kong's international relations here, we refer to international relations in an inclusive, liberal sense. Apart from state-to-state diplomatic relations in the realist perception of the world, international relations include political, economic and social interactions among states and non-state actors. It is self-evident that Hong Kong has never been

---

the Question of Hong Kong, 1984 Annex II, terms of reference of Sino-British Joint Liaison Group, Article 4.

accorded the status of a nation-state in the international legal system before and is unlikely to acquire one in the foreseeable future. In this regard we sometimes use the term external relations to refer to Hong Kong's international relations.

The tying together of two different systems, a socialist one in mainland China and a capitalist one in Hong Kong, to form a single entity under the diplomatic umbrella of the People's Republic of China (P.R.C.) carries interesting implications for the development of Hong Kong's international relations. From a theoretical perspective, China is regarded as a classic realist.[2] Its main concern in international politics is the protection of its state sovereignty. Although China is in a process of change from a hardcore communist state to a socialist country with Chinese characteristics, as a result of reform and opening up to the outside world, its political ideology is still very much a collective, controlled and power-oriented one. Hong Kong, on the other hand, is a free, if not democratic, society. Personal freedoms of various kinds are well-developed, with a successful *laissez-faire* market that is the envy of many countries, developed as well as developing. Short of democratic general elections, Hong Kong is a shining example of liberalism at work.

The meeting of realism and liberalism generates interesting outcomes for Hong Kong's international relations. Being a minor player in its own transition from British to Chinese rule, Hong Kong does have some bargaining power in shaping its own international relations.

A number of factors facilitate the growth of Hong Kong's autonomy in external economic and certain semi-official relations. Hong Kong's economic success is of primary importance. By the end of 1995, Hong Kong had experienced thirty-five years of uninterrupted growth, building some of the world's largest infrastructure projects like the new airport and container ports. Hong Kong's foreign reserves of US$55.4 billion is among the world's largest. Moreover, it is the world's fourth largest exporter and fifth largest importer, with an overall ranking at fourth place in two-way trade.[3]

---

[2] See Gerald Chan, "Towards an International Relations Theory with Chinese Characteristics" (paper presented at the International Studies Association and Japanese Association of International Relations joint convention in Makuhari, Japan, on 20–22 September 1996); and Thomas F. Christensen, "Chinese Realpolitik," *Foreign Affairs*, Vol. 75, No. 5 (September/October 1996), p. 37.

[3] Hong Kong Trade Development Council Statistics, August 1996.

China's foreign policy priority in maintaining a peaceful international relations for effective modernization and development is another factor facilitating Hong Kong's achievement. In addition, the global environment which favours peace, stability and increasing economic interdependence provides a congenial framework for Hong Kong's continued success and participation in various spheres of international activity. Initiatives taken by the major powers, the United States in particular, to treat Hong Kong as a separate entity within China and their continued enthusiasm to invest in Hong Kong and China have helped to sustain, and indeed enhance, Hong Kong's international position.

China's attitude is the most crucial factor affecting Hong Kong's international status after 1997. In general, Hong Kong's existing international status is beneficial to China both economically and politically. China's attitude is largely pragmatic (or functional) but fundamentally ambiguous. Its baseline is that its political supremacy should not be threatened by the practice of "one country, two systems." In principle, China accepts the importance of maintaining Hong Kong's international economic position. On the other hand, its leaders remain extremely sensitive to the process of "internationalization" of the Hong Kong issues, especially in the political arena.[4] China is often conscious that over-emphasizing Hong Kong's international position and autonomy has the danger of encouraging independent sentiments in the territory. Moreover, the internationalization of the Hong Kong issue is a potential challenge to China's foreign policy. The concept of "state sovereignty" is a core foreign policy principle of the P.R.C. which calls for Western respect for the national government's power over its own territory. Such interpretation of sovereignty explains why China resists the Western concept of popular sovereignty and thus often reacts strongly against Western, especially the U.S., pressures on what it considers to be domestic issues relating to human rights, self-determination of its ethnic minorities, and national reunification with Taiwan.[5]

The foreign policy principle of state sovereignty certainly has important implications for Hong Kong's domestic policy and the development

---

[4] See *Wen Wei Po*, 11 April 1992.

[5] Ren Yue, "Sovereignty in Chinese Foreign Policy: Principle and Practice," in *China Review 1996*, edited by Maurice Brosseau, Suzanne Pepper and Tsang Shu-ki (Hong Kong: The Chinese University Press, 1996), pp. 145–74.

of its external relations. China, Tibet and Taiwan have long been treated as external powers during the 150 years of colonial rule. As part of the "Western world," Hong Kong represents the British presence in the Far East, but the latter's influence has become increasingly weak. Hong Kong has a relatively good record of human rights. Media in Hong Kong is free to report and discuss issues of human rights in China. The political situation in Hong Kong even allows some Hong Kong democrats to support political dissidents in China and overseas. Moreover, Hong Kong has been developing much closer cultural and economic ties with Taiwan than with other parts of the Chinese territory in the mainland. After 1997 China will regard issues of political reform and democracy in Hong Kong as part of its state sovereignty. The decade-long debates on democratic and constitutional reform in Hong Kong have earned the sympathy of most liberal democracies, and since 1992 Hong Kong Governor Christopher Patten has further mobilized greater international concern. China, being apprehensive about the Western conspiracy to split and weaken its global influence, will not only be confined to its resistance to Western pressures on domestic issues, but may also be extended to the questions of democratic reform, human rights, and media freedoms in Hong Kong.[6] This would have significant impact on Hong Kong's external relations, especially with major players in East Asia, namely the United States, Taiwan, and even Japan.

China has long been exercising a pervasive influence over Hong Kong. The Hong Kong Government has been accustomed to taking into subtle consideration the China factor when handling its external relations (including non-political matters) under colonial rule. Until 1997 the Hong Kong Government has to follow the British policy direction. Examples are the embargoes against South Africa and Argentina. Even so, the Hong Kong Government has often been careful not to provoke China's possible criticism or even interference, especially on sensitive subjects. The strategy of the Hong Kong Government can be described as trying to achieve the greatest possible extent of autonomy within limits. First, the Hong Kong Government's participation in international organizations is often justified

---

[6] *Hong Kong Economic Times*, 8 August 1996. In a report about a meeting between Lu Ping, the Director of Hong Kong and Macau Affairs Office, and a group of Hong Kong journalist representatives in Beijing in August 1996, Lu explained that Hong Kong SAR would not be allowed to advocate separatist movements in Tibet and Taiwan.

on the ground of economic and cultural needs, emphasizing its apolitical geographical identity. Second, the Hong Kong Government is always sensitive to issues affecting China's sovereign interests. Thus the Hong Kong Government is aware that the territory should not be a base for counter-revolutionary activities or a centre of international movement for political independence. Beyond these critically sensitive areas, the Hong Kong Government attempts to strike a delicate balance between maintaining its freedom and provoking China's veto. As Norman Miners has argued, the Hong Kong Government has always been conscious of protecting its own freedom of action,[7] while persuading Beijing (as well as other foreign governments) to treat Hong Kong as a separate territorial entity.

The strategy outlined above is likely to continue after 1997, but Hong Kong will face new challenges. First, the Hong Kong Government has greater freedom in manoeuvring the degree of autonomy before 1997, taking advantage of the British umbrella. After 1997 it will have less freedom in handling sensitive issues like Chinese dissidents going overseas through Hong Kong. Second, a stronger sense of patriotism will emerge in the SAR legislature and non-governmental organizations, which may either take the form of criticizing the foreign policy practices of the central government or the SAR Government. The public protests in Hong Kong in September and October 1996 over the occupation of the Diaoyu islands by some right-wing Japanese is an example. The tremendous gap between the policy of the central government and local sentiments foreshadows potential tensions in Sino-Hong Kong relations after 1997. More importantly, these sensitive issues will no longer remain as matters relating to "diplomatic" or "external" relations under British administration, but will become "domestic" policy issues having implications for Hong Kong's international presence. What has worked before 1997 may not be so after the change of the sovereign master. Relations with international organizations and, more critically, with the United States and Taiwan will be significant testing grounds for the practice of "one country, two systems."

Hong Kong's Relations with International Organizations

Hong Kong's autonomy in conducting its external relations has increased

---

[7] Norman J. Miners, *The Government and Politics of Hong Kong*, 5th edition (Hong Kong: Oxford University Press, 1991), p. 230.

significantly in the last decade of colonial rule and the territory has assumed in many ways the functions of a "state" in terms of international presence and internal governance.[8] After Britain joined the European Community in 1971, Hong Kong has become autonomous in entering into multilateral agreements. Soon after the formation of the JLG in 1986, China agreed to allow Hong Kong to become a contracting party of the General Agreement on Tariffs and Trade (GATT). In 1991 Hong Kong became an independent member of Asia-Pacific Economic Cooperation Forum (APEC). By the end of 1995 the JLG had agreed upon the continued participation of the Hong Kong SAR in thirty international organizations. The Hong Kong SAR will be a full member in six of these organizations, including GATT, the Asian Development Bank (ADB), and the World Trade Organization (WTO). In others, Hong Kong will either participate as part of the P.R.C. delegation or as an associate member. Agreements have also been reached on the continued application of 193 multilateral agreements to Hong Kong after 1997[9] as well as bilateral agreements relating to investment promotion and protection, surrender of fugitive offenders, and air services agreements. (For details, see Appendix 1.)

The *Yearbook of International Organizations*[10] shows that Hong Kong is a member of fifty-three intergovernmental organizations (IGOs) as of 1995. (They are listed in Appendix 2.) Of these, China is a member of thirty-three. According to the Basic Law, Hong Kong's participation in IGOs must be registered under the name "Hong Kong, China" and its participating member or members should join a government delegation led by China. In principle, it is highly unlikely that this stipulation will be violated, since after 1997 Hong Kong will come under Chinese rule. In practice and probably for a long time to come, Hong Kong's status in these organizations is unlikely to change, for several reasons. First, China can no doubt put enough political pressure to bear on the Hong Kong SAR Government to force it to toe the Chinese line in considering policy issues in these organizations. Second, China will probably allow Hong Kong to

---

[8] James T. H. Tang, "Hong Kong's International Status," *The Pacific Review*, Vol. 6, No. 3 (1993), p. 205.

[9] *Hong Kong 1996* (Hong Kong: Hong Kong Government, 1996), Appendix 5A.

[10] *Yearbook of International Organizations 1995/96* (Munich: K. G. Saur, 1995), Vol. 2.

retain its status in these organizations, since China can count on Hong Kong to vote in its favour should circumstances require decisions in these organizations be made through the ballot. Third, most, if not all, international organizations would not worry too much about any possible bickering between China and Hong Kong in their organizations if China does not make too much fuss about Hong Kong's status. As to the change of name from Hong Kong to "Hong Kong, China," it depends on whether China reinforces the same. Otherwise, the other parties involved, that is, Hong Kong and the international organizations concerned, may not take the trouble to initiate such changes.

Of the other twenty IGOs of which Hong Kong is a member but China is not, the most controversial ones are those that belong to the British Commonwealth, and there are six of them. As a matter of principle, China is likely to demand or even direct Hong Kong, if it has not already done so, overtly or privately, to terminate its membership in them for the reason that Hong Kong by mid-1997 will be part of China, not part of the United Kingdom, and hence all its colonial ties must be severed, including those with the British Commonwealth.

The net result likely after the take-over of Hong Kong by China is that Hong Kong's membership in IGOs will shrink. In the short term, Hong Kong's total membership of IGOs will be small and is likely to remain so until China takes the initiative to encourage Hong Kong to increase its participation in IGOs. This possible Chinese move depends on several conditions: first, that China gradually becomes more liberal, thus allowing Hong Kong greater freedom to take part in IGO activities; second, that China sees the political benefits of Hong Kong's support in addressing global problems; and third, that China is confident of Hong Kong's allegiance in international politics. For these conditions to be met, it might require more time on the part of China to learn more about the diverse functions of various international organizations.

Hong Kong's Relations with the United States

Among the major powers in the world, the United States' treatment of Hong Kong as a separate entity of mainland China is important. While recognizing that Hong Kong will become a part of the P.R.C., the United States has taken initiatives to accord Hong Kong a special status in its China policy. This is evident in the passing of the U.S.–Hong Kong Policy Act of 1992 and the issuing of a separate human rights report on Hong Kong. From the

U.S. point of view, the proper handling of its relations with Hong Kong is conducive to improving Sino-U.S. relations and vice versa.

The United States has been rather pragmatic in handling Sino-U.S. relations and hence relations with Hong Kong. For example, the United States continues to link bilateral trade issues with human rights, arms sales, intellectual property protection, and U.S.–China trade deficit. The United States also pushes China to further liberalize its market. The ultimate objective of the United States is to fully integrate China into the global market-based economic and trading system. Such pressures are not applied on Hong Kong, mainly because Hong Kong is already the world's most liberal trading economy.[11] Support for the maintenance of Hong Kong's free market economy is an important part of the United States' China policy. Hong Kong is seen as a catalyst in China's economic modernization and development. Thus the United States has often taken careful consideration of the Hong Kong factor in Sino-U.S. economic relations. The U.S. support for Hong Kong's separate participation in WTO is an example. Debates in the United States on the renewal of China's most-favoured-nation status in the past few years is another. A cautious approach in maintaining the Hong Kong's separate economic status is certainly an important part of the United States' broader China policy strategy.

Economically, Hong Kong is the thirteenth largest trading partner of the United States. In 1995 two-way merchandise trade surpassed US$24 billion. The United States' exports to Hong Kong reached US$14.2 billion, while the value of U.S. imports of Hong Kong products amounted to US$10.3 billion. Principal Hong Kong imports from the United States included computers, telecommunications equipment and foodstuff. Major Hong Kong exports to the United States included clothing apparel, office machines and electrical machinery.[12]

In 1995 there were 1,000 American businesses in Hong Kong, including 198 regional headquarters and 228 regional offices, employing 250,000 Hong Kong workers (which was about 10% of the workforce in Hong Kong). According to a confidence survey conducted by the American

---

[11] Bryan T. Johnson and Thomas P. Sheehy, *Report on The Index of Economic Freedom* (Washington: Heritage Foundation, 1995).

[12] *U.S.–Hong Kong Policy Act Report*, 31 March 1996.

Chamber of Commerce in mid-1995,[13] American companies held a favourable view on Hong Kong's business environment.

The U.S.–Hong Kong Policy Act requires the Department of State to report to Congress annually on the status of Hong Kong and the process of reversion of sovereignty. The March 1996 Report shows that efforts to maintain bilateral ties with Hong Kong are fairly comprehensive and include the conclusion of bilateral agreements, the promotion of trade and investment, the arrangement of high-level visits, the broadening of law enforcement cooperation, and the bolstering of educational, academic and cultural links.

Political development in Hong Kong is also of great importance in the United States' China policy. Critical issues include human rights, freedom of the press and democratic reform after 1997. From the U.S. point of view, it is strategically important to maintain Hong Kong as a liberal society within the broader authoritarian non-democratic environment in China. There are two major views in the United States regarding the Hong Kong issue. The sceptics favour a close monitoring of Hong Kong's democratic and human rights issues. They urge U.S. policy makers to apply continued pressure on China (and the future SAR Government as well) to uphold the promises of the Sino-British Joint Declaration. Another view argues that handling Hong Kong's transitional policy issues with sensitivity is crucial to improving U.S.–China relations. The latter requires efforts of the policy makers in Washington and Beijing to communicate positively and enter into rational dialogues frequently.

Tensions in bilateral relations often exist on issues concerning human rights, individual freedoms and democratic reform, which are regarded by China as matters within its area of state sovereignty. After 1997 these issues may become the most sensitive areas affecting Sino-U.S. and Hong Kong–U.S. relations. Any attempts by local democratic and human right lobbyists to seek U.S. support will cause embarrassment to the Hong Kong SAR Government. Such activities may be seen by the Chinese Government as infringing on China's sovereignty, hence provoking intervention of the central government. The current strategy of the Hong Kong Government is to avoid making comments and curbing local attempts to lobby U.S. support for the development of democratic institutions in the territory.

---

[13] *Ibid.*

Hong Kong's Relations with Taiwan

Hong Kong's relations with Taiwan is part of the British foreign diplomacy until 1997. Since the British Government established formal diplomatic relations with the People's Republic of China (P.R.C.) in 1972, Taiwan's representation in Hong Kong has been primarily semi-official and economic in nature.

After 1997 Hong Kong–Taiwan relations will be dominated by political considerations. Taipei will regard the Hong Kong SAR as part of the communist regime. Similarly the Hong Kong SAR can no longer regard relations with Taiwan as "external," but rather "regional" or "provincial." The SAR's relations with Taiwan will become a part of China's policy towards Taiwan, and will hence be affected directly by relations across the Taiwan Strait from time to time. Proper treatment of pragmatic economic activities in Hong Kong by Taiwan businesses remains important, requiring careful, subtle, but flexible attitude of the three governments in Beijing, Taipei and Hong Kong.

Unlike other transitional issues, Hong Kong–Taiwan relations are regarded as China's internal policy. Therefore, they have never been discussed in any of the meetings of the JLG. An exception was the Taiwan–Hong Kong inter-airline arrangement of June 1996.[14] Until 1996 the Hong Kong Government did not have a proper channel for negotiations concerning its future relations with Taiwan. Since this remains a diplomatic issue in the pre-1997 period, there are no specific authorities within the Hong Kong Government to prepare for transitional issues affecting Hong Kong–Taiwan relations.

In China, the management of Hong Kong–Taiwan relations involves offices at various levels, including the Central Committee's Leading Group of Taiwan Affairs, the State Council's Taiwan Affairs Office, Xinhua Agency (Hong Kong Branch), and the Association for Relations Across the Taiwan Strait. This differs significantly from other transitional issues which are mainly coordinated and managed by the State Council's Hong Kong and Macau Affairs Office and the Ministry of Foreign Affairs.

---

[14] The arrangement was agreed to in London in a meeting held on 5–7 June 1996. It was regarded as part of the JLG's terms of reference relating to international rights and obligations. See Legislative Council Constitutional Affairs Panel (Hong Kong: Hong Kong Government, June 1996).

So far, the preparation for the Hong Kong SAR's relations with Taiwan is controlled centrally by Beijing. The seven points elaborated by Foreign Minister Qian Qichen in June 1995 were the only official version clarifying China's policy principles in Hong Kong–Taiwan relations after 1997.[15] Qian emphasized that the CPG would be responsible for whatever issues affecting national sovereignty and relations across the Strait. The CPG would delegate to the SAR Government in the handling of official contacts with Taiwan including commercial negotiations, representative offices and entry visa.

Qian's seven points were announced at a time when China–Taiwan relations were at a low ebb. In the nine months leading to Taiwan's presidential elections in March 1996, schedules arranged between the two unofficial bodies, the Straits Exchange Foundation (Taiwan) and the Association for Relations Across the Taiwan Strait (P.R.C.), to discuss matters of Hong Kong–Taiwan relations were dropped. Even after the presidential elections, China–Taiwan relations did not improve significantly. Qian's seven-point principles allowed Hong Kong's continued exchange of economic and cultural relations with Taiwan and guaranteed Taiwan's continued investment in the SAR. Yet until the second half of 1996, no details were provided. On 19 August 1996 Beijing announced that, subject to individual situations, thirteen consulates stationed in Hong Kong but having diplomatic relations with Taiwan would be allowed to remain in Hong Kong in principle (in a semi-official capacity).[16] Some practical issues, such as the rights and visa status of Taiwan people staying in the Hong Kong SAR, trade and commercial relations, as well as cultural and academic exchanges remained unresolved.

In August 1996, reports from various informal sources suggested that Beijing remained sceptical of the basic attitude of President Lee Teng-hui towards national reunification. China refused to conduct negotiations on Hong Kong–Taiwan affairs before basic differences on the "one China" policy principle between Beijing and Taipei were settled.[17] Beijing was also said to be concerned with Taiwan's intention to interfere with the successful implementation of the "one country, two systems," and hence

---

[15] See *Sing Tao Daily*, 23 June 1995.

[16] These consulates are mainly representing countries in central and south Africa, Central America, and the South Pacific. *Ming Pao*, 20 August 1996.

[17] See *Hong Kong Economic Times*, 8 August 1996.

set strict conditions for Taiwan's semi-official representatives stationed in the Hong Kong SAR. China strictly prohibited Taiwan representatives to use either official or unofficial capacity to conduct political activity in Hong Kong and forbade any attempt to advocate "two Chinas" or "Taiwan's independence" in the territory.[18]

Qian guaranteed Taiwan's continued economic investment and trade in Hong Kong. In any case, Hong Kong's economic relations with Taiwan are fairly strong. Hong Kong is Taiwan's second largest trade partner. In 1995 Taiwan's investment in Hong Kong amounted to US$99.6 million. The value of imports from Taiwan to Hong Kong was US$27,949 million, accounting for 13% of Taiwan's total trade.[19] Without proper protective arrangements after 1997, Taiwan may suffer significant economic loss.

Hong Kong–Taiwan economic relations will continue to be affected by volatile relations across the Strait. An example is the negotiation on direct navigation across the Strait. Although both Beijing and Taipei have made unilateral suggestions, no concrete agreement has been reached. Naturally navigation issues between Hong Kong and Taiwan are also affected. Another example is the call made by Lee Teng-hui for slowing growth in China-bound investments in August 1996. This warning reflected the president's concern for Taiwan's over-reliance on the economy of the mainland. By the first quarter of 1996, 31.7% of Taiwan's overseas

---

[18] According to an informal journalist report, China would not allow activities of Taiwan representatives in Hong Kong to carry the name of Republic of China; to advocate "two Chinas," "one China, one Taiwan" and "Taiwan's independence"; to use official capacity to get involved in political activity; to use unofficial capacity to support anti-China and anti-Communist subversive behaviour; to make use of the capacity of registered limited companies to conduct any political activities inconsistent with the nature of the company; and to conduct any functions or political propaganda by Taiwanese political parties. *Hong Kong Economic Journal*, 12 July 1996.

[19] Taiwan's Ministry of Economic Affairs (updated as at 17 October 1996), the value of export from Taiwan to Hong Kong was US$26,106 million and the import from Hong Kong to Taiwan was US$1,843 million in 1995. The information provided by the Hong Kong Trade Development Council (TDC) is slightly different. According to the TDC, the value of import from Taiwan to Hong Kong was HK$130,000 million in 1995 (updated as at August 1996).

investment was in mainland China.[20] Hong Kong has been playing an important role in facilitating investment and trade between China and Taiwan.

The Hong Kong Government seems to enjoy the least autonomy, among all other issues, in its relations with Taiwan. Maintenance of the relations between the Hong Kong SAR and Taiwan within the pre-1997 framework would be difficult. Full preparation cannot be arranged because of escalated tensions across the Taiwan Strait in the last two years prior to the 1997 hand-over. This is clearly an area in which the SAR's pragmatic economic interests will be subordinated to the political principles of national sovereignty.

Hong Kong has been playing an important role in bridging the relations between China and Taiwan. Taiwan will monitor closely the working of "one country, two systems" in Hong Kong and Macau. The Hong Kong SAR will remain an important entrepôt for Sino-Taiwanese trade. Subject to whatever breakdowns or breakthroughs in negotiations between Beijing and Taipei, Hong Kong will remain an important stepping stone for Taiwan's investment in the mainland as well as a centre of information exchange across the Strait.

Conclusion

The above discussions suggest that China's attitude towards the maintenance of Hong Kong's external relations is largely pragmatic. By 1996, Hong Kong had obtained the support of the major powers in attaining separate international status, especially in the areas of economic and cultural exchanges. Hong Kong's participation in international organizations has remained largely intact, and shall continue so except that it may have to sever intergovernmental links with the British Commonwealth for obvious political reasons.

Owing to its special political status in the past, Hong Kong has never had its own independent foreign policy. The special status of Hong Kong has allowed the territory to survive well and, at the same time, successfully

---

[20] See Taiwan's Ministry of Economic Affairs (updated as at 17 October 1996).

avoid getting involved in complicated political troubles in East Asia and beyond. The emphasis on practical economic and cultural relations is likely to continue after 1997.

The SAR Government will face new challenges. The Chief Executive will have to take into subtle consideration the foreign policy principles of Beijing and adapt to them. Some issues, which allow the existing Hong Kong Government a greater degree of flexibility under British rule, will require subtle adjustments by the SAR Government. Diplomatic issues such as the internationalization of Hong Kong's democratization and human rights issues and its relations with Taiwan will become domestic concerns of the P.R.C.

Some problems are likely to result from the SAR's insensitiveness towards the changing political environment and China's foreign policy direction, as well as overemphasis on economic pragmatism in handling its external relations. To achieve the greatest possible extent of autonomy in external relations will require good cooperation and communication between the Chief Executive of the SAR, the central government in Beijing, and the Hong Kong representatives of the Ministry of Foreign Affairs. Furthermore, internal pressures on the SAR Government to retain autonomy in sensitive and controversial areas will be strong. Pressure from a few radicals criticizing democratization and human rights issues will challenge the SAR Government and test its skills in trying to maintain freedom of action and yet to be able to avoid China's veto. A careful distinction between the area of CPG's foreign policy and the area of SAR's internal policy will determine the degree of autonomy that the SAR Government will enjoy. Astute persuasion, skilful communication, and goodwill between the SAR Government and CPG will be fundamental to the practice of "one country, two systems" after 1997.

Appendix 1: The Nature and Extent of Hong Kong's Participation in International Organizations and Multilateral Agreements after 1997

Progress of Sino-British Joint Liaison Group (JLG)
October 1996

I.   JLG progress on Hong Kong's participation in international organizations
   1. International organizations in which Hong Kong's continued participation has been agreed to in the JLG until October 1996:
       *   Asian Development Bank (ADB)
       *   Asian and Pacific Development Centre (APDC)
       *   Asia-Pacific Postal Union (APPU)
       *   Asia-Pacific Telecommunity (APT)
       *   Customs Cooperation Council (CCC)/World Customs Organization (WCO)
       *   Economic and Social Commission for Asia and the Pacific (ESCAP)
       *   Food and Agriculture Organization (FAO)
       *   General Agreement on Tariffs and Trade (GATT) /World Trade Organization (WTO)
       *   Intergovernmental Typhoon Committee (ITC)
       *   International Atomic Energy Agency (IAEA)
       *   International Bank for Reconstruction and Development (IBRD)
       *   International Civil Aviation Organization (ICAO)
       *   International Criminal Police Organization (INTERPOL)
       *   International Development Association (IDA)
       *   International Finance Corporation (IFC)
       *   International Hydrographic Organization (IHO)
       *   International Labour Organization (ILO)
       *   International Maritime Organization (IMO)
       *   International Maritime Satellite Organization (INMARSAT)
       *   International Monetary Fund (IMF)
       *   International Telecommunications Satellite Organization (INTELSAT)
       *   International Telecommunication Union (ITU)
       *   International Textiles and Clothing Bureau (ITCB)
       *   Multilateral Investment Guarantee Agency (MIGA)

- Network of Aquaculture Centres in Asia and the Pacific (NACA)
- Statistical Institute for Asia and the Pacific (SIAP)
- United Nations Commission on Narcotic Drugs (UNCND)
- United Nations Conference on Trade and Development (UNCTAD)
- Universal Postal Union (UPU)
- World Health Organization (WHO)
- World Intellectual Property Organization (WIPO)
- International Textiles and Clothing Bureau (ITCB)
- World Meteorological Organization (WMO)

2. International organizations in which Hong Kong currently participates, but JLG approval for Post-1997 participation remains pending:
   - Asian Productivity Organization (APO)

3. Other organizations in which Hong Kong currently participates, and which JLG agreement is not required for Hong Kong's continued participation:
   - Asia-Pacific Economic Cooperation Forum (APEC)
   - Asia-Pacific Metrology Program
   - International Association of Lighthouse Authorities
   - International Association of Ports and Harbours
   - International Organization for Standardization
   - National Conference of Standards Laboratories
   - United Nations Development Program
   - United Nations Environment Program
   - United National Fund for Drug Abuse Control
   - United Nations Fund for Population Activities

4. Organizations in which the Hong Kong SAR will be a full member:
   - Asian Development Bank (ADB)
   - Asian Productivity Organization (APO)
   - Customs Cooperation Council (CCC)/World Customs Organization (WCO)
   - General Agreement on Tariffs and Trade (GATT)/World Trade Organization (WTO)
   - International Textiles and Clothing Bureau (ITCB)
   - Network of Aquaculture Centres in Asia and the Pacific (NACA)
   - World Meteorological Organization (WMO)

5. Organizations in which the Hong Kong SAR will participate as part of the P.R.C. delegation:

- Asia-Pacific Postal Union (APPU)
- Food and Agriculture Organization (FAO)
- International Atomic Energy Agency (IAEA)
- International Bank for Reconstruction and Development (IBRD)
- International Civil Aviation Organization (ICAO)
- International Criminal Police Organization (INTERPOL)
- International Development Association (IDA)
- International Finance Corporation (IFC)
- International Hydrographic Organization (IHO)
- International Labour Organization (ILO)
- International Maritime Satellite Organization (INMARSAT)
- International Monetary Fund (IMF)
- International Telecommunications Satellite Organization (INTELSAT)
- International Telecommunication Union (ITU)
- United Nations Commission on Narcotic Drugs (UNCND)
- United Nations Conference on Trade and Development (UNCTAD)
- Universal Postal Union (UPU)
- World Intellectual Property Organization (WIPO)

6. Organizations in which the Hong Kong SAR will be an associate member:
   - Asian and Pacific Development Centre (APDC)
   - Asia-Pacific Telecommunity (APT)
   - Economic and Social Commission for Asia and the Pacific (ESCAP)
   - Intergovernmental Typhoon Committee (ITC)
   - International Maritime Organization (IMO)
   - Statistical Institute for Asia and the Pacific (SIAP)
   - World Health Organization (WHO)

7. List of JLG agreed multilateral treaties
   By the end of 1995 the JLG has approved Hong Kong's participation in 173 multilateral agreements. Up to October 1996, a total of 193 multilateral agreements have been approved. For details, see *Hong Kong 1996* (Government Information Services Department, 1996), Appendix 5A, pp. 427–31; and Note for the Legislative Council Constitutional Affairs Panel, *Progress of the Joint Liaison Group* (Constitutional Affairs Branch, Hong Kong Government, October 1996).

II. JLG progress on bilateral agreements
   1. Investment Promotion and Protection (IPP):
     • 18 negotiating partners have been agreed by the JLG, namely:

Australia	South Korea
Austria	Netherlands
Belgium	New Zealand
Canada	Singapore
Denmark	Sweden
France	Switzerland
Germany	Thailand
Italy	The United States
Japan	Vietnam

     • Hong Kong has signed agreements with 9 countries:
        Netherlands
        Australia
        Denmark
        Sweden
        Switzerland
        Germany
        Italy
        France
        New Zealand

   2. Surrender of Fugitive Offenders (SFO):
     • Hong Kong has SFO arrangements with 94 countries based on multilateral/bilateral treaties which the United Kingdom has extended to Hong Kong, and on arrangements between the Commonwealth countries which are given effect by means of reciprocal domestic legislation. These arrangements will lapse on 1 July 1997.
     • 18 negotiating partners have been approved by the JLG, namely:

Australia	Malaysia
Belgium	Netherlands
Canada	New Zealand
France	The Philippines
Germany	Singapore
India	South Korea
Indonesia	Switzerland
Italy	Thailand
Japan	The United States

- Hong Kong has signed agreements with 5 countries:
  Netherlands
  Canada
  Australia
  Malaysia
  The Philippines

3. Mutual Legal Assistance (MLA) in criminal matters:
   - A 1994 JLG agreement enabled Hong Kong to negotiate arrangements on criminal MLA with other jurisdictions which could straddle 1997, but this agreement did not cover MLA between Hong Kong and China.[21]
   - Criminal MLA between Hong Kong and China had not yet been brought to the JLG for discussions.[22]
   - 18 negotiating partners have been approved by October 1996, namely:

Australia	Malaysia
Belgium	Netherlands
Canada	New Zealand
France	The Philippines
Germany	Singapore
India	South Korea
Indonesia	Switzerland
Italy	Thailand
Japan	The United States

   - Hong Kong has reached agreements with Australia and the Philippines.

4. Transfer of Sentenced Persons (TSP):
   - Hong Kong currently has arrangements with 24 countries for TSP to their home countries, based on the Council of Europe Convention on TSP and the U.K.–Thailand Agreement. These arrangements will lapse on 1 July 1997.

---

[21] Minutes of the Joint Meeting of the Hong Kong Legislative Council Panel on Administration of Justice and Legal Service and Hong Kong Legislative Council Panel on Security held on 22 April 1996.

[22] *Ibid.*

- 5 negotiating partners have been approved in the JLG XXXV meeting:
  - Australia
  - The Philippines
  - Singapore
  - Thailand
  - The United States
5. Reciprocal Enforcement of Judgements (REJ) in civil and commercial matters
  - Hong Kong Government is in the process of discussing with the Chinese side a model agreement for negotiating new bilateral agreements which will continue to apply after 1997.

III. JLG Progress on the air service agreements

From 1986 to October 1996, a total of 16 air service agreements have been reached between Hong Kong and other countries, namely:

Australia	Malaysia
Brazil	Netherlands
Brunei	New Zealand
Canada	Singapore
France	South Korea
Germany	Sri Lanka
India	Switzerland
Italy	Taiwan[23]

In September 1996, agreements in the JLG have been reached for Hong Kong to commence negotiation on air service agreements with Myanma and Thailand.[24]

Sources:

1. The U.S.–Hong Kong Policy Act Report submitted by the Department of State to the United States Congress on 31 March 1996.

---

[23] In the JLG XXXVI Meeting of June 1996, the Chinese side confirmed to have no objection to the Hong Kong/Taiwan inter-airline arrangements; the relevant commercial agreement was signed in Taipei on 13 June 1996.

[24] Note for the Legislative Council Constitutional Affairs Panel, *Progress of the Joint Liaison Group* (Constitutional Affairs Branch, Hong Kong Government, October 1996).

2. *Hong Kong 1996* (Government Information Services Department, 1996).
3. Note for the Legislative Council Constitutional Affairs Panel, *Bilateral Agreement* (Constitutional Affairs Branch, Hong Kong Government, 11 March 1996).
4. Note for the Legislative Council Constitutional Affairs Panel, *JLG XXXVI: Achievements* (Constitutional Affairs Branch, Hong Kong Government, June 1996).
5. Note for the Legislative Council Constitutional Affairs Panel, *Progress of the Joint Liaison Group* (Constitutional Affairs Branch, Hong Kong Government, October 1996).

Appendix 2: Hong Kong's Membership of Intergovernmental Organizations, 1995

1. International Organization of Migration, secretariat based in Hong Kong
2. *United Nations High Commissioner for Refugees, regional office in Hong Kong
3. Arab Banking Corporation
4. *Asia and Far East Institute for the Prevention of Crime and the Treatment of Offenders
5. *Asia-Pacific Economic Cooperation
6. *Asia-Pacific Telecommunity
7. *Asian Development Bank
8. Asian Development Fund
9. *Asian and Pacific Development Centre
10. *Asian-Pacific Postal Training Centre
11. Asian and Pacific Skill Development Information Network
12. Asian Productivity Organization
13. CAB International
14. Commonwealth Commercial Crime Unit
15. Commonwealth Consultative Group on Technology Management
16. Commonwealth Legal Advisory Service
17. Commonwealth Scholarship and Fellowship Plan
18. Commonwealth Secretariat
19. Commonwealth Youth Programme
20. *COSPAS-SARSAT
21. Current Agricultural Research Information System
22. *ESCAP/WMO Typhoon Committee
23. *European Foundation for the Improvement of Living and Working Conditions
24. Financial Action Task Force on Money Laundering
25. General Agreement on Tariffs and Trade
26. *Global Environment Information Exchange Network
27. International Association of Crime Victim Compensation Boards
28. International Centre for Scientific and Technical Information
29. *International Centre for the Study of the Preservation and the Restoration of Cultural Property
30. *International Centre for Theoretical Physics

31. *International Commission for Scientific Exploration of the Mediterranean Sea
32. *International Criminal Police Organization
33. *International Geological Correlation Programme
34. *International Information System for the Agricultural Sciences and Technology
35. *International Institute of Refrigeration
36. *International Maritime Organization
37. *International Occupational Safety and Health Information Centre
38. *International Organization of Legal Metrology
39. *International Textiles and Clothing Bureau
40. Latin American Information Centre on Migration
41. *Network of Aquaculture Centres in Asia and the Pacific
42. *Regional Network for the Chemistry of Natural Products in Southeast Asia
43. *Regional Network for Microbiology in Southeast Asia
44. *Regional Trade Information Network
45. Southern African Regional Tourism Council
46. *Statistical Institute for Asia and the Pacific
47. *TCDC-INRES, UNDP
48. *United Nations Children's Fund
49. *United Nations Development Programme
50. *United Nations Economic and Social Commission for Asia and the Pacific
51. WHO Regional Office for the Western Pacific
52. *World Customs Organization
53. *World Meteorological Organization

* Indicates that the P.R.C. is also a member (of 33 organizations).

Source: Compiled from the *Yearbook of International Organizations 1995/96* (Munich: K. G. Saur, 1995), Vol. 2, Hong Kong and China entries.

10

Evolution of the State in Taiwan and Uncertainty across the Taiwan Strait

Timothy Ka-ying Wong

Introduction

After Beijing introduced economic reforms and the open door policy in 1979, and Taipei lifted martial law in 1987 and allowed Taiwan people to visit and invest in mainland China, and with the mitigation of the East-West Cold War under the Soviet Union's political and economic restructuring in the mid-1980s, the relations across the Taiwan Strait have changed significantly. Cross-strait ideological and military confrontation has temporarily toned down, while economic and people-to-people interactions have been rampant. In 1984, the estimated amount of cross-strait trade was only US$553 million, but it jumped sharply to US$20.9 billion in 1995.[1] Though Taiwan still does not allow investment from mainland China, its indirect investment in mainland China has been rising since the late 1980s. Up to 1995, the estimated investment capital accumulation was between US$10 billion and US$30 billion;[2] the number of passengers from Taiwan to mainland China was over 8 million, while the number of those from mainland China to Taiwan was over 80,000.[3]

---

[1] *The Republic of China Statistical Yearbook 1995* (Taipei: Directorate-General of Budget, Accounting and Statistics, Executive Yuan, 1996).

[2] Chan Man-hung and Chu Man-hui, "Economic Integration of Mainland China, Taiwan and Hong Kong before and after 1997," *Wide Angle*, No. 285 (June 1996), p. 48.

[3] The number of passengers from Taiwan to mainland China comes from the recorded figure of Taiwan compatriot Certificates released by the China Travel

Yet, the bustling economic and civilian exchanges have not actually dwindled the political conflicts between Beijing and Taipei; a genuine, normalized cross-strait relationship is still far away. The cross-strait political relationship did turn assuasive for several years after Taipei lifted martial law in 1987. Semi-official coordination organizations were set up to deal with the improving cross-strait non-political exchanges. In 1990, Taipei took the initiative to set up the Straits Exchange Foundation (SEF). Beijing reciprocated by establishing the Association for Relations Across the Taiwan Strait (ARATS) in 1991. Both organizations then opened a series of negotiations on economic and civilian exchange affairs. The cross-strait *détente* did not last, however, after Taipei spoke out its desire to return to the United Nations (UN). Beijing thought that it had to thwart Taipei's attempt because the ulterior motive of Taipei was to eternalize the cross-strait split, i.e. to make the independence of Taiwan an objective fact. Taipei, on the other hand, believed that its return to the international community, and to the UN in particular, was a precondition for its survival and reunification with mainland China, and that Beijing's intransigence will only deepen Taiwan people's alienation and confrontation. The "Incident of Lake Qiandao"[4] in March 1994 caused the cross-strait relationship to reach its nadir, which continued to the end of that year[5] due to the September "Asian Games Incident."[6] As both Beijing and Taipei did not

---

Service. The number of passengers from mainland China to Taiwan comes from *Cross-Straits Cultural Exchange 1995* (Taipei: Straits Foundation Fund, 1996).

[4] The "Incident of Lake Qiandao" occurred in late March 1994. In the incident, all 32 people, of whom 24 were Taiwanese, on board a vessel touring Lake Qiandao were found dead after a fire. For more than a week, mainland authorities insisted that it was an accident. Unauthorized autopsies were performed and relatives were compelled to accept the cremation of the victims. The Taiwan people and government were very dissatisfied with the way Beijing handled the incident, and President Lee Teng-hui even openly criticized Beijing as a bandit regime. The cross-strait relations worsened quickly.

[5] Timothy Wong, "From Confrontation to Compromise: A Historical-Structural Account of the Rapid Deterioration of Cross-Straits Relations in 1994," in *China Review 1995*, edited by Lo Chi-kin, Suzanne Pepper and Tsui Kai-yuen (Hong Kong: The Chinese University Press, 1995), pp. 4.16–4.22.

[6] In September 1994, Lee Teng-hui was invited by the Olympics Committee to attend the opening ceremony of the Asian Game to be held in Japan. But the invitation was opposed by Beijing and finally Lee did not go to the ceremony.

want to see their relationship exacerbating, each made attempts to soothe the cross-strait tension. Only then did a better cross-strait relationship dawn in early 1995. In late January 1995, the Chinese President Jiang Zemin gave an eight-point address on cross-strait peaceful unification, which was regarded by Taipei as "quite friendly." The eight points were reciprocated by Taiwan's President Lee Teng-hui with a six-point response in April. Yet, two months later, the cross-strait relationship rapidly deteriorated again after Lee's swift visit to the United States. In retaliation, Beijing unilaterally discontinued all negotiations with the SEF. In July, it even launched a series of intimidating military exercises near Taiwan, posing a war crisis for Taiwan and mainland China unseen over the last two decades. Beijing stopped the military exercises after Taiwan's first democratic presidential election held on 23 March 1996. Nevertheless, it refuses to resume negotiation between SEF and ARATS and the cross-strait relations continue to be in the doldrums.

Why did Beijing and Taipei develop such an unprecedented political and military conflict in the past year, despite the exuberant economic and civilian interactions? As Hong Kong is the main conduit for cross-strait exchanges, and in 1995 enjoyed a total trade value of over US$2.7 billion with Taiwan (of which about 70% constituted indirect cross-strait trade through Hong Kong), how would the conflict affect Hong Kong? This chapter attempts to provide part of the answer to these questions through explicating the evolution of the state in Taiwan. It argues that since the mid-1980s, Taiwan has been experiencing rapid political democratization, which has profoundly transformed the state structure of Taiwan. A libertarian-civic state, driven by indigenous Taiwanese popular support, has been formed quickly. The new state structure is different from the Kuomintang's (KMT) former concept of the Chinese state which emphasizes a unified China. Such a change has ushered in a series of new state behaviours, including the fight for cross-strait mutual recognition on equal terms, the abandonment of the zero-sum struggle against Beijing over the issue of sovereignty, and the quest for a peaceful coexistence with Beijing through dual recognition in the international community, i.e. the recognition of the *de facto* sovereignty of the Republic of China on Taiwan. These new state behaviours, however, were seen by Beijing as a plot by Taipei to divide China peacefully. Hence Beijing reacted to them with threats of violence, thereby resulting in the current cross-strait tension. This tension, in turn, created some temporary disruption in Taiwan's and Hong Kong's economies.

Despite the fact that the tension may remain indefinitely, this chapter argues that several structural constraints are at work to prevent it from easily developing into an all-out confrontation. Firstly, Beijing's stringent military threats will create heavy pressure on any recalcitrant and venturous approach that Taipei may possibly take; secondly, Taiwan's short-cycled, periodic elections will render the state policies incrementalized; thirdly, Taiwan's pluralized society will mediate radical political developments; fourthly, Taiwan's increasing economic dependency upon mainland China will push Taipei to be more pragmatic in handling cross-strait relations; fifthly, the huge economic interests of Taiwan in Hong Kong will limit Taipei from further agitating Beijing; and sixthly, Beijing's rise in the international community will make it difficult for Taipei's pragmatic diplomacy to take effect.

The KMT Authoritarian State

In political science, state is a rather contentious concept.[7] To avoid ambiguity, state here means a political entity with a territory, population and governing capacity, and its nexus is an authoritative central government which has the functions of allocating values in society and establishing diplomatic ties with foreign countries.[8] As such, the Republic of China (R.O.C.), which was defeated by the Chinese Communist Party (CCP) in 1949 and then retreated to Taiwan, can be definitely called a state, though it has always competed against the People's Republic of China (P.R.C.) for the national sovereignty over China, and was ousted from the UN in 1971, and increasingly suffered from international isolation.[9] To date, Taiwan still has diplomatic ties with 30 countries;[10] the KMT central

---

[7] T. Skocpol, "Bringing the State Back In: Strategies of Analysis in Current Research," in *Bringing the State Back In*, edited by P. B. Evans, D. Rueschemeyer and T. Skocpol (Cambridge: Cambridge University Press, 1985), pp. 3–37.

[8] Samuel S. Kim and Lowell Dittmer, "Whither China's Quest for National Identity?" in *China's Quest for National Identity*, edited by Lowell Dittmer and Samuel S. Kim (Ithaca: Cornell University Press, 1993), pp. 242–45.

[9] Byron S. J. Weng, "Sovereignty Split: Towards a Theory of Divided Nation," *Chinese University Bulletin*, Supplement 32 (1995), pp. 21–37.

[10] The number was counted as of 1 September 1996.

government is still the most authoritative governing body, which is independent and legally rules Taiwan and other peripheral islands.

Before lifting martial law in 1987, the KMT-dominated Taiwan basically preserved an authoritarian state system.[11] By authoritarianism, the reference is to any political system that "emphasizes the centralization of power, the flow of decisions from the top down rather than of demands from the bottom up, deference to authority, limited pluralism, and the use of violent repression when other methods of co-optation and control fail."[12] Using this definition as a yardstick, Taiwan's political system before the mid-1980s can surely be described as authoritarian, as it displayed the following features.

First, the KMT exercised one-party rule, which strictly prohibited any organized political opposition activities. Though the Democratic Socialist Party and the Young China Party, both established in mainland China, could legally exist, they were all seen as the KMT's "companions," serving only the window-dressing purpose. Moreover, their leaders were all old mainlanders who never challenged the KMT rule.[13] Except these two companion parties, the KMT banned the establishment of all other parties, so as to obstruct the alliance of opposition forces against the KMT.[14]

Second, since 1949, Taiwan had been ruled under martial law, which was not abolished until 1987. The KMT strictly controlled the media and communication, as well as the freedoms of press, speech, association and other political rights.[15]

---

[11] Edwin Winckler, "Institutionalization and Participation on Taiwan: From Hard to Soft Authoritarianism?" *The China Quarterly*, Vol. 3 (September 1987), pp. 482–99.

[12] Susan Kaufman Purcell and John F. H. Kaufman, "State and Society in Mexico: Must a Stable Polity Be Institutionalized?" *World Politics*, Vol. 32, No. 2 (1980), p. 204.

[13] Tien Hung-mao, *The Great Transition: Political and Social Change in The Republic of China* (Stanford: Hoover Institution Press, 1989), p. 116.

[14] For example, in 1960, a liberalist from mainland China, Lei Zhen was jailed for 10 years because of his attempt to organize the Chinese Democratic Party. In the 1970s, the directors of the *Formosa* magazine wanted to set up a political group to promote political reforms, but they were also suppressed.

[15] From 1950 to 1986, it is estimated that over 10,000 cases related to Taiwan citizens were subjected to military trial. See Tien Hung-mao, *The Great Transition*, p. 111.

Third, since the KMT has always claimed that the R.O.C. is the only legitimate government in China and Taiwan is only a Chinese province, Taiwan still preserves a two-level, central and local, political structure. The central state policy-making bodies were dominated by mainland Chinese political elites. In Taiwan, ethnic mainlanders (migrants from mainland China after 1945 and their descendants) constitute less than 15% of the total Taiwan population. The rest of them are ethnic Taiwanese (migrants from mainland China before 1945 and their descendants) and some hundred thousand aborigines. The mainlanders' monopolization of central power was made possible by suspending indefinitely elections at the central level, including the National Assembly and the Legislative Yuan.[16] The major functions of the National Assembly are to elect the R.O.C. President and Vice-President,[17] and amend the constitution. The Legislative Yuan is to make laws. On the other hand, though local regimes were derived from general elections and were largely controlled by ethnic Taiwanese, their powers and functions were quite limited. In other words, through dominating the central government, ethnic mainlander political elites guaranteed their authoritarianism in Taiwan.

Fourth, under the one-party state structure, the KMT also tightly controlled the military (before the 1990s, the military forces continuously comprised some half a million people) as its ruling backbone. Under martial law, the military not only shielded Taiwan from external threats, but also had special powers to maintain security. These special powers were above the local regimes. Article 9 of the martial law stipulated: "During the enforcement of martial law, the local administrative and judicial matters of the combat areas shall be placed under the jurisdiction of the commander in chief in the said area, and the local administrative officials and judges shall be subject to the direction of the said commander in chief."[18] A Taiwan Garrison Command headquarters was set up in 1950 to take charge of all matters concerning the implementation of martial law. Its powers involved authorizing citizens to travel abroad, monitoring all entries into

---

[16] Since 1972, the KMT had begun to introduce supplementary elections into the Legislative Yuan and National Assembly, but their electoral seats only accounted for a small proportion of the total seats.

[17] In July 1994, the National Assembly amended the R.O.C. constitution, changing the presidential election from indirect to direct.

[18] Tien Hung-mao, *The Great Transition*, p. 110.

Taiwan, approving meetings and rallies, reviewing and sanctioning books and periodicals, and maintaining social order. As such, the Taiwan under martial law was seen as a militarized society.[19]

Taiwan's Democratization and the Formation of the Libertarian-Civic State

The KMT-controlled authoritarian state could no longer last when it entered the 1980s. During the rapid democratization since the mid-1980s, it has quickly transformed into a libertarian-civic state backed by popular support. A libertarian-civic state is said to exist when the political system of a country is based upon liberal democracy in which the state's sovereignty is the sovereignty actually by the citizens of the country. The cardinal organizational principle of the libertarian-civic state, therefore, is liberal democracy, whose power structure is open and institutionalized (e.g. through regular elections). Liberal-democratic politics makes state and society mutually permeative and reinforced, and thus nurtures a stable, self-adjusting social-political system.[20] To put it differently, libertarian-civic state is a social-political collectivity constituted by independent, autonomous citizens through institutionalized democratic participation.[21] In the modern world, the transition from the authoritarian state to the libertarian-civic state symbolizes mainly the state-building process. Once this process is completed, new state behaviours will appear to correspond with the structural necessity of the new libertarian-civic state system. Especially on foreign affairs, state sovereignty and autonomy are always closely linked with the internal structure of the state.[22]

As is widely known, Taiwan's rapid democratization started during the late R.O.C. President Chiang Ching-kuo's last years, a period during which

---

[19] Jon Halliday, "Capitalism and Socialism in East Asia," *New Left Review*, Vol. 124 (1980), p. 7.

[20] Liah Greenfeld, *Nationalism: Five Roads to Modernity* (Cambridge, Mass.: Harvard University Press, 1990).

[21] Jurgen Habermas, "Citizenship and National Identity," in *The Condition of Citizenship*, edited by Bart Van Steenbergen (London: Sage Publications, 1994), pp. 23–28.

[22] J. P. Nettl, "The State as a Conceptual Variable," *World Politics*, Vol. 20 (1968), pp. 563–64.

the Taiwan society and economy became mature and prosperous. Yet, nowadays, very few scholars would see the democratization in the past decade as the result of the ruling KMT's, and in particular, Chiang's reform initiatives, or just a natural product of social and economic development. The consensus is that Taiwan's democratization involves at least five interactive structural forces. The first one is the withering of the first-generation mainlanders, which weakens the Chinese identity and unification awareness. On the other hand, the Taiwan-oriented awareness is on the rise, which ultimately promotes the rise of the indigenous movement against the mainlander domination and the unquestioned acceptance of reunification with mainland China. The second one is the booming of political opposition forces and the rising call for political democracy. The third one is the determination on the part of the ruling KMT elites to launch political reforms. The fourth one is the maturity and pluralization of the civil society due to the rapid economic development, and subsequently the challenge against the KMT party-state authoritarianism. The fifth one is the influence of the then unfolding worldwide democratic wave and the pressure of the international democratic community (especially the United States).[23]

Owing to the interactive effect of these five structural factors, Chiang's sudden death in January 1988 did not alter Taiwan's democratization process. His successor, President Lee Teng-hui, continued the process and then accelerated it after his power was consolidated in the 1990 indirect presidential election in which he was proclaimed the eighth R.O.C. President by the National Assembly.[24] Under favourable subjective and objective conditions during the presidencies of Chiang and Lee, Taiwan has

---

[23] Evan A. Feigenbaum, *Change in Taiwan and Potential Adversity in the Strait* (Santa Monica: RAND, 1995), p. 8; Parris H. Chang, "The Changing Nature of Taiwan's Politics," in *Taiwan: Beyond the Economic Miracle*, edited by Denis Fred Simon and Michael Y. M. Kau (Armonk: M. E. Sharpe, 1992), pp. 27–34; Hsiao Hsin-huang, "The Reorganization of the State-Society Relationship amid Pluralization," in *A New Stage of Taiwan Experience: Continuity and Innovation*, edited by Kau Ying-mao (Taipei: Twenty First Century Fund, 1991), p. 375.

[24] Timothy Wong, "From Confrontation to Compromise," p. 4.3. Some arguments say that a major reason for Lee to speed up political democratic reforms is to make use of social forces outside the KMT to check and eliminate the ailing influence of the mainlander faction in the party. See Chen Ming-tong, *Factional*

managed to remove or alter many of the authoritarian structures of the past, including the lifting of martial law, broadening freedoms of press and expression, legalizing opposition political parties, releasing political prisoners and reducing the use of the judicial system to stifle dissent, and last but not least, introducing for the first time in forty years full elections for the National Assembly in 1991, the Legislative Yuan in 1992, the Governor of the Taiwan Province in 1994, and the direct election of the President of the R.O.C. in 1996.[25]

Among these political structural changes, the most important one should be the legalization of opposition parties. In August 1986, the first opposition party, the Democratic Progressive Party (DPP) was formed. Since the formation of this new party, the KMT authorities have taken no repressive actions. With the lifting of martial law in July 1987, Taiwan has obviously moved into a new political era in which competitive multi-party politics and representative parliamentary democracy have become the most important impetus for political development. Under the new rules of the game, though the DPP was still subjected to various institutional and resource constraints, it has rapidly emerged as a significant opposition party by gathering strength in elections. In the 1989 Legislative Yuan supplementary elections, it captured 29.9% of the popular vote; in the 1991 National Assembly full elections, 23.6%; in the 1992 Legislative Yuan full elections, 31.4%; in the 1993 Mayors and County Magistrates elections, 41.2%; in the 1994 Mayors of Taipei and Kaohsiung and Governor of Taiwan elections, 32%; in the 1995 Legislative Yuan elections, 33.2%, and in the 1996 National Assembly elections, 29.9%.[26] At the same time, the KMT's popular support has been declining; it even failed to get the majority votes in the Mayors and County Magistrates elections, the Taipei City Assembly elections, the National Assembly elections and the Legislative Yuan elections between 1993 and 1996. Besides, in 1993, splitting from the KMT, the New Party was set up and it has been growing stronger with every election. It now appears to be the third biggest political party, and renders

---

Politics and Taiwan's Political Change (Taipei: Yue Dan Publishing Company Ltd., 1995), pp. 197–215.

[25] Timothy Wong, "From Confrontation to Compromise," p. 4.3.

[26] These figures are gathered from the election reports by the major newspapers in Taiwan.

party politics in Taiwan even more competitive.[27] Furthermore, during the election of Governor of Taiwan in December 1994 and the presidential election of the R.O.C. in March 1996, the KMT's Shong Chu-yu and Lee Teng-hui won a majority and retained their seats. After the presidential direct election, Taiwan's central and local regimes have been fully democratized. Though many of the constitutional structures (e.g. the conflicts between the presidential system and cabinet system and between the central and local regimes, and the huge discrepancy between *de jure* sovereignty and *de facto* sovereignty) will continue to remain highly controversial in Taiwan's politics for a long time to come, a democratic, parliamentary, multi-party system built merely upon Taiwan's popular support has begun to dominate forcefully Taiwan's political development. Although the KMT still maintains its ruling status, it is seriously constrained by the existing party politics. Especially after the 1995 Legislative Yuan elections, in which the KMT only captured a thin majority of the total seats (85 out of 164), if the KMT wants to maintain political stability, to compromise and cooperate with the opposition forces has become inevitable. From the perspective of state development, Taiwan's democratization has indeed completely separated the R.O.C. from mainland China. The R.O.C. is no longer the one claimed by the KMT as representing the whole China, and is just the R.O.C. on Taiwan. It is the Taiwan society which is the existing R.O.C.'s base of legitimacy. Reunification or one China is therefore not a must, but an option. Such a structural change is deemed to produce a profound impact on cross-strait relations.

Consequences of the Development of the Taiwan Libertarian-Civic State

Under Taiwan's democratization, i.e. the development of the libertarian-civic state, there are two interrelated results which are quite significant as well as inevitable. The first one is the rise of separatism and the other is the policy change of the state.

---

[27] In the 1994 elections of Mayors of Taipei and Kaohsiung and Governor of Taiwan, the New Party only captured 6.2% of the popular vote. But in the 1995 Legislative Yuan elections and the 1996 National Assembly elections, its popular vote rose to 13% and 13.7% respectively.

The Rise of Separatism

In the international political system constituted by nation-states, the development of multi-party politics and representative democracy also means the development of popular sovereignty.[28] Had Taiwan been an independent nation-state, it would have certainly consolidated the cohesiveness of its people and strengthen the legitimacy of the ruling state. In fact, as democratization deepens, Taiwan increasingly looks more like a popular nation-state with its own sovereignty than a regional government under a higher sovereign state. Paralleling the popular sovereignty is the natural desire for participating in the international community. Nevertheless, due to its unique historical relationship with China, i.e. being one of the two competing states of a divided nation,[29] the ruling KMT still insists on the ideal of "one China," and claims that the R.O.C. on Taiwan is still representative of the whole of China. As a result, the R.O.C.'s *de facto* sovereignty over Taiwan and its *de jure* sovereignty defined in the R.O.C. constitution inevitably appear in sharp contradiction. Worse, most parts of the world do not recognize Chinese sovereignty even in a limited sense. The P.R.C. on mainland China even claims that Taiwan is only a province of China. It also threatens that it may resort to force to bring it back into China under the P.R.C. sovereignty if it considers this necessary, especially should Taiwan opt for *de jure* independence.

Owing to the above specific historical characteristics, along with the long-time cross-strait separation and the institutional and social differences between mainland China and Taiwan, there has appeared a demand in Taiwan for political separation from mainland China. This demand tends to be stronger and more salient amid the deepening democratization, with the withering influence of old mainlanders.[30] This development has seriously challenged the Chinese awareness of the R.O.C. Hence the unfolding of

---

[28] Liah Greenfeld, *Nationalism*, p. 10.

[29] Byron S. J. Weng, "Sovereignty Split," pp. 30–33.

[30] A survey in 1987 showed that the people who were born in mainland China before 1950 account for less than 5% of the total population. As more old mainlanders have died naturally since 1987, the percentage of mainland-born mainlanders should be smaller today. See *Tien Sha* (Taiwan), Vol. 70, 1 March 1987.

the crisis of national culture.[31] Taiwan's separatism is a crisis of national culture because it directly interrogates or even negates the national identity of the R.O.C. during the search for or reconstruction of the new national identity.[32] Taiwan's separatism is not entirely equivalent to Taiwanese nationalism[33] which has a specific cultural-political meaning, as most of the Taiwan people still regard themselves as ethnically Chinese in a broad sense.[34] Many of the advocates of the Taiwan independence do not deny that most of the Taiwan people are Chinese in an anthropological sense. What they object to is the political interpretation of the anthropologically Chinese. They generally believe that "people who share the same language and ethnicity do not necessarily mean that they must belong to the same country."[35] To a large extent, the current national identity problem in Taiwan is caused by the completion of the state-building process brought about by democratization. When the legitimacy of the R.O.C. state retreats from the whole China to the people of Taiwan, the heightened tension between the Chinese nation and the new R.O.C. state in the modern concept of nation-state is obviously unavoidable.

Yet, separatism is not necessarily equivalent to searching for an independent Taiwan, though to make Taiwan an independent country may be

---

[31] Timothy Wong and Sun Tung-wen, "Dissolution and Reconstruction of National Identity: The Experience of Subjectivity in Taiwan," *Political Science Review*, Vol. 7 (May 1995), pp. 321–54.

[32] Wu Nei-de, "Ethnic Awareness, Political Support and National Identity: A Preliminary Study of the Theory of Taiwan Ethnic Politics," in *Ethnic Relations and National Identity*, edited by Zhang Mao-gui (Taipei: Ye Qiang Publishing Company, 1993), pp. 27–52.

[33] Eric Hobsbawm, *Nations and Nationalism since 1780* (Cambridge: Cambridge University Press, 1990); Anthony D. Smith, *The Ethnic Origins of Nations* (New York: Basil Blackwell, 1986). According to Hobsbawm and Smith, nationalism must contain certain primordial sentiments and specific cultural elements (e.g. language, religion, customs, values, etc.) which can bind ethnic group members together, though it also emphasizes the need to construct a modern nation-state.

[34] Lynn White and Cheng Li, "China Coast Identities: Regional, National and Global," in *China's Quest for National Identity*, edited by Lowell Dittmer and Samuel S. Kim, p. 176.

[35] *Taidu Jikan* (Taiwan Independence Quarterly) (New York), Vol. 1 (1981), pp. 113–14.

a choice for separatism. For example, Taiwan can preserve its *de facto* separation from mainland China, without claiming a *de jure* independence. In general, Taiwan's separatism embodies at least six forms of ideas or feelings which are interrelated and are drawn upon by the separatists, with different degrees, to support their identities and actions. They are as follows:

1. The existing territory of Taiwan, especially the Taiwan island, is the place the Taiwan people identify with. Those people outside the territory belong to other ethnic groups, though they may be Chinese in a broad sense.
2. Though the people of Taiwan arrived in Taiwan at different times, they have formed their own ethnic group, and share a common history, culture and destiny.
3. Taiwan should maintain enough military forces to protect itself and the freedom of its people.
4. The future of Taiwan, be it independent or unified with mainland China, should be decided by its citizens' free will, and should not be dominated by the P.R.C. or the international community.
5. Taiwan should enjoy an international status corresponding to its economic power.
6. No matter whether it is recognized diplomatically, Taiwan has an international personality different from the P.R.C.'s, and thus, like other countries, it should have the right to fully, equally and autonomously participate in international affairs.[36]

According to Wong and Sun's Q methodological study, which combined both qualitative and quantitative research, there are at least five distinctive yet interrelated discourses on national identity in Taiwan: Chinese nationalism, status quoism, Taiwan prioritism, Taiwanese nationalism and confused identity. The most interesting discourse is Chinese nationalism. It embodies a tendency of separatism to a certain

---

[36] Timothy Wong, *Democratization and Separatism: Taiwan's Political Development in Recent Years and ROC–PRC Relations*, Occasional Report No. 37 (Hong Kong: Hong Kong Institute of Asia-Pacific Studies, The Chinese University of Hong Kong), p. 6.

extent, emphasizing the independent sovereign status of the R.O.C. on Taiwan *vis-à-vis* the P.R.C. on mainland China.[37]

The problem of separatism in Taiwan is not simply a product of cross-strait separation nor directly provoked by democratic politics. It is instead traceable to the history of the fifty years of Japanese colonial rule and the subsequent KMT-mainlander domination, in which a special kind of Taiwan-oriented awareness developed.[38] What the continuing cross-straits separation has done is to help deepen this Taiwan-oriented awareness and enrich its experience. Furthermore, the main function of democratic politics is that on the one hand, it provides a space for the free discussion about separatism, and on the other, its own institutions can accommodate different political choices. An example is the DPP's call for the building of a libertarian-civic state independent of mainland China. In the early 1990s, the DPP even included using referendum to determine Taiwan's future relationship with mainland China in its constitution, indirectly strengthening the libertarian foundation of the current separatist development.[39] Moreover, even though the KMT still identifies with "China," it also increasingly emphasizes the Taiwan-oriented awareness, along with the rapid indigenization under democratization. It also allows open discussion on the issue of indigenization and makes relevant policies. In the authoritarian era, the discussion about this matter was either prohibited or fully controlled; there was little scope for free discussion in society, not to mention free political choices and the encouragement from the ruling government. With the deepening cross-strait social and economic

---

[37] Wong and Sun, "The Dissolution and Reconstruction of National Identity," p. 338.

[38] Thomas Gold, *State and Society in the Taiwan Miracle* (Armonk: M. E. Sharpe, 1986); Thomas W. Robinson, "Beijing–Taipei Relations Approaching the Year 2000," in *Taiwan: Beyond the Economic Miracle*, edited by Denis Fred Simon and Michael Y. M. Kau, pp. 369–86; Allen Chun, "From Nationalism to Nationalizing: Cultural Imagination and State Formation in Postwar Taiwan," *The Australian Journal of Chinese Affairs*, No. 31 (1994), pp. 49–69.

[39] Timothy Wong, "From Colonial Rule to Divided Nation," in *The Interaction and Integration of Mainland China, Taiwan, Hong Kong and Macau*, edited by Timothy Wong, Sun Tung-wen and K. S. Liao (Hong Kong: Hong Kong Institute of Asia-Pacific Studies, The Chinese University of Hong Kong, 1996), p. 283.

exchanges since the mid-1980s, the myths of overthrowing the CCP, of resuming the R.O.C. in mainland China and of establishing one China have disappeared. The CCP-controlled mainland China has become Taiwan's important trading partner. It is no longer a fatal opponent of Taiwan but a place of huge potential benefit, and the R.O.C. on Taiwan also no longer represents the whole China.

As a developing movement, Taiwan's separatism has attracted more and more people. According to the opinion polls conducted by the "Twenty-First Century Survey Fund" in recent years, the supporters of an independent Taiwan (including those of "make Taiwan independent as soon as possible" and "preserve the status quo and then move towards an independent Taiwan") have been on the rise, from 14% in 1993 to 16.1% in 1995, while the supporters of unification ("unify with mainland China as soon as possible" and "preserve the status quo and then move towards unification") have been declining, from 34.7% to 22.2%. Meanwhile, the supporters of "preserve the status quo forever" and "preserve the status quo and decide Taiwan's future later" also rose from 10.1% to 17.2% and 22% to 34.1% respectively.[40] These figures show that the ideal of unification has been moving away from Taiwan.

Taiwan's New State Policy

Under the combined pressure of both democratization and separatism, Taipei's policies based on the development of the libertarian-civic state tend to be more and more independent and Taiwan-oriented. The KMT's initiative in the past has been subjected to more and more constraints derived from the party politics. As Andrew Nathan succinctly pointed out in 1990, "Political reform in Taiwan has changed the fundamental assumption on which China's Taiwan policy has hitherto been based, that the

---

[40] Gao Lang, Chui Fo-yim, Chen Yi-yim and Hwang De-fok, *An Analytical Report on the Political Satisfaction in the Taiwan Region 1995* (Taipei: Twenty-First Century Survey Fund, 1996), p. 98. In the report, the authors provided eight answer choices for the respondents: make Taiwan independent as soon as possible, preserve the status quo and then move towards an independent Taiwan, preserve the status quo forever, preserve the status quo and decide Taiwan's future later, preserve the status quo and move towards unification, unify with mainland China as soon as possible, no comments, and do not know.

Kuomintang has the power single-handedly to negotiate the future of the island with the CCP. Democratization has so complicated the internal politics of Taiwan that it is now impossible for any deal to be struck with the mainland that does not command popular support in the island. Given the enormous risks that unification would pose for the people of Taiwan, this new political reality bodes ill for reunification on anything like the terms that have hitherto been offered by Peking."[41] Andrew Nathan's observation was supported by the former DPP President Shi Ming-de, who openly admitted in 1994 that the KMT's views on national defence and foreign affairs had been converging with the DPP's.[42] National defence and foreign affairs are the two principal areas in which a state demonstrates itself as a sovereign actor. When the KMT and DPP converge their views on these matters, the convergence to a large extent signals the formation of a broad consensus between the ruling and the opposition parties on the role of the new Taiwan state. Many scholars believe that under the pressure of democratic politics, the KMT has to absorb the DPP's political ideas and policies so as to keep its ruling position. Hence the inevitability of the KMT's tendency to share with the DPP over the status of Taiwan.[43]

Yet, it should be noted that the DPP has also been gradually giving up its radical call for an independent Taiwan, and has begun to actively formulate the kind of cross-strait policies that the Taiwan people can feel comfortable and acceptable. For example, during the presidential election in 1996, the DPP leaders had repeatedly explicated that what they called an independent Taiwan was simply the R.O.C. on Taiwan as an independent sovereign state, and that even if the DPP candidate won the presidency, there was no need for the DPP to hastily change the R.O.C.'s name. Such an explication more or less represents the DPP's gradual adjustment of its state policies. Thus, if the KMT has been subjected to the influence of the DPP, the DPP has also been influenced by the KMT in the process of party interaction. Not only do the KMT and DPP mutually affect each other, the New Party, which has been seen as more obsessed with the

---

[41] Andrew Nathan, *China's Crisis: Dilemmas of Reform and Prospects for Democracy* (New York: Columbia University Press, 1990), p. 153.

[42] *Far Eastern Economic Review*, 23 June 1994, p. 23.

[43] Tsai Zheng-wen, *The ROC's Foreign Policies and Action Orientation* (Taipei: Ye Qiang Publishing Company, 1993).

unification with mainland China, has also tried to forge an alliance with the DPP after the Legislative Yuan elections at the end of last year. Under such circumstances, for the first time, the unification-independence struggle has been marginalized in Taiwan. Only under this political integration promoted by the party interaction can the KMT-led R.O.C. unfold such state behaviours like the search for autonomy and independence. It is therefore not difficult to understand that the change of KMT's state policies is largely a reflection of the transformation of the R.O.C. on Taiwan into a libertarian-civic state, having a strong objective necessity.

To cope with the emerging democratic reality driven by popular support, as well as the rapid unfolding of the cross-strait economic and civilian exchanges, the KMT has abandoned its past, dogmatic mainland China and international policies, and replaced them with a more active approach. The most distinctive feature of this new approach is to abandon the false ideology of claiming representation of the whole China by handling the existing cross-strait and international problems more flexibly and pragmatically. More specifically, Taipei no longer wants to continue the zero-sum struggle against Beijing anymore; it attempts to reverse the trend of international isolation brought about by derecognition of the R.O.C. by the UN in 1971. To achieve this objective, it launches a two-fold strategy: towards the mainland on the one hand and the international community on the other.

Taipei's new mainland policy is to urge the P.R.C. to normalize cross-strait relations by making the P.R.C. recognize Taiwan as a political equal. According to Taipei's agenda, it must first normalize the cross-strait separation, and then on the basis of normalization negotiates with Beijing over the unification matter. Towards this end, Taipei unilaterally went ahead and relaxed its historically antagonistic relationship with Beijing. In May 1989, Shirley Kuo, Taiwan's Minister of Finance led a delegation to attend the annual meeting of the Asian Development Bank in Beijing, the first time ever in forty years that high-ranking KMT government officials made their appearance on the mainland. In October 1990, President Lee set up the National Unification Council to delineate Taiwan's new policies towards China. In the same month, the cabinet-level Mainland Affairs Council (MAC) was established, and in November, the semi-official SEF was founded under the MAC to carry out "unofficial" contacts with the P.R.C. authorities and deal with "non-governmental" matters.

In February 1991, the National Unification Council announced its *National Unification Guidelines* in which short-, intermediate- and long-term policies towards China were clearly spelt out. The *Guidelines* particularly underlines that equal recognition is the most important objective of the short-term policy, without which any transition to the intermediate term would be impossible. In May 1991, President Lee officially abolished the "Temporary Provisions during the Period of Mobilization against the Communist Insurgency" and, in effect, announced that the CCP is no longer a "bandit" organization and the P.R.C. no longer an "illegitimate" government.

The above measures and actions reflect KMT's rapid policy adjustment in response to Taiwan's changing political reality and the rapidly growing cross-strait economic and civilian exchanges. The aim of the adjustment is to develop a peaceful coexistence with Beijing, while unification is not so urgent and therefore the negotiation on it should wait until the peaceful coexistence is achieved. In September 1992, the MAC finally issued the long-awaited report on "Issues and Prospects of Direct Transportation Links across the Taiwan Strait." The report states that the R.O.C. is willing to open direct air and sea links with China, on the condition that the CCP renounces the threat of force against Taiwan and recognizes the R.O.C. as an equal political entity. The opening of direct transportation links has been repeatedly proposed by the P.R.C. since 1979. This report indicates that Taipei's baseline of reunification is equal recognition.

At the same time, while working hard to make Beijing negotiate on the unification issue on equal terms, Taipei is well aware of the importance of military might in determining the game.[44] Hence, although the defence budget has steadily decreased since the 1950s, it still amounted to around 25% of the total government budget during the past five years.[45] Apart from the regular budget, there is also a special budget line called "Procurement of High Performance Fighters." In 1993 and 1994, this budget amounted to 4.38% and 3.75% of the total government budget respectively.[46] With this huge military investment and help from the U.S. Government, Taiwan

---

[44] Martin L. Lasater, *Policy in Evolution: The US Role in China Unification* (Boulder: Westview Press, 1989).

[45] *The Republic of China 1995–1996 National Defence Report* (Taipei: Li Ming Cultural Enterprise Co. Ltd., 1996).

[46] *The Republic of China 1992 National Defence Report* (Taipei: Li Ming Cultural Enterprise Co. Ltd., 1992), p. 126.

has successfully updated its military defence system.[47] In September 1992, the U.S. Government even agreed to sell 150 F-16 aircraft to Taiwan. At almost the same time, a similar deal of 60 French Mirage 2000-5 fighters was concluded with the French Government. These two deals have greatly strengthened Taiwan's future defence capability, thereby enhancing Taipei's ability to withstand the military pressure from Beijing amid its search for more national autonomy.

Besides, in order to increase the people's confidence in the military, Taipei has also stepped up the nationalization and depoliticization of the military, including cutting greatly the power of the Garrison Command headquarters and passing the National Security Bill to institutionalize the supervision and management of the military.[48] In 1992, the KMT government also published for the first time *The Republic of China 1992 National Defence Report*. The motive behind the publication was not only to channel the pressure from the DPP[49] or to democratize by increasing the transparency of the military, but also to make known Taipei's new defence policy to its people as well as to the P.R.C. The report contains at least four key points about Taipei's current defence policy:

1. Taiwan has abandoned the use of military means to achieve unification.
2. The locus of Taiwan's defence policy is protection, not aggression.
3. Taiwan will strengthen its defence capability in accordance with the P.R.C.'s military development.
4. The main objective of Taiwan's military development is to develop a modernized, self-sufficient security system; it will focus on quality instead of quantity.

---

[47] Richard C. Bush, "The Role of the United States in Taiwan–PRC Relations," in *Taiwan: Beyond the Economic Miracle*, edited by Denis Fred Simon and Michael Y. M. Kau, p. 352.

[48] E. A. Feigenbaum, *Change in Taiwan and Potential Adversity in the Strait*, p. 19.

[49] The Taiwan Research Fund, which has a close relationship with the DPP, published *The White Paper on National Defence* in 1989. The *White Paper* explores in detail Taiwan's strategic circumstances and the national defence policy Taiwan should pursue. Its main points had had a significant impact on the later official report. This again can show the convergence of the official and non-official views on Taiwan's national security.

The National Defence Report is biannual. It has been published three times already, and the views expressed are basically identical to those of the first publication.[50]

While seeking equal recognition from the P.R.C. and strengthening its defence capability, Taipei has also launched the so-called "pragmatic diplomacy" to break its current international isolation, as well as to define the cross-strait relations through participating in the international community. Taipei's calculation is that if it can obtain diplomatic recognition from the international community, it is difficult for Beijing to negate the political existence of Taipei. Moreover, no matter how small the chance to gain international recognition may be, the very action of pragmatic diplomacy itself should help internationalize the question of Taiwan. In 1993, Taipei openly expressed its interest in re-entering the UN. This idea was first put forward by the DPP in 1988. At that time, the KMT refused to entertain the proposal because it was considered unrealistic and conflicted with the policy of "One China." After five years of rapid democratization, the KMT radically changed its position on the question, and this, to a certain extent, reflected the great impact of party politics on the formation of state policies. It also signified the emergence of a popular state in Taiwan rallying for its own identity and autonomy. In June 1993, President Lee endorsed the idea by referring to the models of Germany and Korea, arguing that the R.O.C.'s changed position was not inconsistent with the policy of one China. At about the same time, Taipei's Foreign Ministry successfully mobilized seven Latin American states to sponsor a resolution to admit Taiwan in the name of the R.O.C. on Taiwan into the UN as one of the two independent states in a divided nation. However the resolution was vetoed by the UN General Committee before reaching the General Assembly. Since then, the rally for returning to the UN has become ritualized as one of Taipei's most important annual internationalizing activities. Though the effort has not made any significant breakthrough, it has not stopped.

Apart from the bid to re-enter the UN, Taipei also actively pursues the so-called "vacation diplomacy" by sending government leaders to visit

---

[50] For the first and third publications please see Notes 45 and 46. The second one is *The Republic of China 1993–94 National Defence Report* (Taipei: Li Ming Cultural Enterprise Co. Ltd., 1994).

countries which have no diplomatic ties with Taiwan.[51] In December 1993, Premier Lien Chan spent his "private vacation" in Singapore and met a number of Singaporean officials. Then in February 1994, President Lee took a bolder step visiting Thailand, Indonesia and the Philippines. During the visits, Lee signed a number of trade and investment agreements with the host countries. In May 1994, Lee extended his international tour to visit Nicaragua, Costa Rica, South Africa and Swaziland — four of the then 29 countries that officially recognized the R.O.C. on Taiwan. Lee met more than 20 of the foreign leaders who attended Mandela's Inauguration, most of them from countries with no formal ties to Taipei.[52] In April 1995, Lee directed his "vacation diplomacy" to the Middle East, visiting the United Arab Emirates and Jordan. In June, he even visited the Cornell University in the United States.[53]

Taipei's new state policy is systematically explained in its official *White Paper on Relations with the Mainland* issued on 5 July 1994 and

---

[51] Apart from enhancing Taiwan's international space, through "vacation diplomacy," Taipei also wants to direct part of the Taiwan investments from mainland China to Southeast Asia and other areas, strengthen Taiwan's economic potentials in those regions, and lessen the political risks of Taiwan's undue heavy economic dependency upon mainland China. This is generally called the "southward approach," as opposed to the "westward (mainland China) approach." Theoretically, Taipei's "vacation diplomacy" and "southward approach" are complementary. The former can develop investment opportunities for the latter, while the latter can strengthen the former's international ties. Yet, it is unrealistic to say that the "southward approach" and "westward approach" are contradictory. Nor does Taipei really attempt to render the two approaches in a mutually exclusive way. Considering that the undue "westward approach" will weaken Taiwan's influence and development in the Asia-Pacific region and make Taiwan undesirably rely on mainland China, the real motive of Taipei's "southward approach" is obviously to strike a balance with the "westward approach," instead of replacing it.

[52] *Far Eastern Economic Review*, 9 June 1994, p. 18.

[53] In terms of raising international attention, Taipei's pragmatic diplomacy should be considered very successful. But in terms of its rally for returning to the United Nations, it is obviously strategic rather than practical. First of all, among the 30 countries that have diplomatic ties with Taiwan, only South Africa has some influence in international politics. Second, as the permanent member of the UN

the six points made by President Lee (hereafter the Lee's Six Points) at the National Unification Council on 8 April 1995. Both documents conclude the major current views on unification Taipei had developed and articulated in recent years. On the whole, the *White Paper* contains seven points:

1. The present split of China across the Strait is a result of the establishment of the P.R.C. in October 1949 and the subsequent retreat of the R.O.C. government from Nanjing via Guangzhou to Taipei. Since then, the two governments have maintained separate rule over the two sides of the Taiwan Strait.

2. The existence of a divided China is not simply a power struggle between the KMT and CCP; it has been heavily shaped by international politics and external ideological domination, both of which eventually gave rise to the confrontation between a Nationalist China and a Communist China.

3. Taiwan has relinquished the use of force as a means of reunification.

4. The model of "one China, two equal political entities," not "one country, two systems," should be employed to resolve the present R.O.C.–P.R.C. conflicts. The R.O.C.–P.R.C. relations are neither international nor purely internal to a sovereign nation.

5. The model of "one country, two systems" proposed by the P.R.C. does not work, because "one country" means annexation of the R.O.C. by the P.R.C. and "two systems" implies subjecting Taiwan to the P.R.C.'s arbitrary determination.

6. R.O.C.–P.R.C. relations should be based upon the principles of reason, peace, equality and reciprocity.

7. If the P.R.C. moves to practise democracy, people in Taiwan will support unification rather than separation. Conversely, if Beijing

---

Security Council, Beijing has the power to veto any country applying to join the UN. In fact, Beijing repeatedly states that it will not allow Taipei to join the UN in any form. Nevertheless, Taipei's strategy seems to be that the very action of rallying for joining the UN can help internationalize the so-called "Taiwan question" and open international discussion on its policy of dual recognition.

continues to use the threat of force and to isolate Taiwan internationally, it will only provoke separatism in Taiwan.

The Lee's Six Points includes:

1. Taiwan and mainland China are under the rule of two separate political entities, which constitute the current divided rule across the Strait. Both entities therefore should base upon the reality of a divided nation to search for a viable method for reunification.
2. Both sides should use the Chinese culture as a base to strengthen cross-strait exchanges in general and to promote information, academic, technological and sports cooperation in particular.
3. Both sides should deepen economic and trade exchanges and develop a mutually beneficial, complementary relationship.
4. Both sides should have equal rights to join international organizations, and their leaders should meet in international arenas, so as to lessen political confrontation and promote a harmonious atmosphere for exchanges.
5. Both sides should insist on solving their conflicts through peaceful means.
6. Both sides should jointly work to preserve the prosperity and to promote democracy in Hong Kong and Macau.

Putting the viewpoints of the *White Paper* and Lee's Six Points together, it is obvious that Taipei's current national policy holds that the existing China is divided; if both sides want reunification, they must return to the reality of separation and conduct peaceful negotiations on equal terms. Military and international pressure will but push the Taiwan people to support separatism. Under this policy baseline, it is natural for Taipei to reject reunification through the "one country, two systems." Also natural is to rally for equal recognition in cross-strait political relations and for equal participation of Taiwan as a sovereign state in the international community. In other words, what Taipei is currently concerned about is the objective sovereign status of Taiwan before its unification with the mainland. When Taipei stresses that the R.O.C. on Taiwan is a sovereign state, and that it can coexist with the P.R.C. on the mainland in the international community on equal terms, the logical conclusion is undoubtedly that the Chinese sovereignty can be split and shared across the Strait. Taipei even believes that the normalization and peaceful reunification of Taiwan and mainland China must take place on the foundation of the progressive process from "sovereignty split" to "sovereignty unification."[54] On the other hand, Taipei also emphasizes the needs to deepen cross-strait economic and cultural exchanges, partly because of practical reasons, and partly because of the desire to soothe the cross-strait political tension. Nevertheless, due to political and security considerations, Taiwan is still unwilling to develop direct transportation links with the mainland.

Taipei's new state policy has not changed much since 1993, though between July 1995 and March 1996 Taipei's pragmatic diplomacy was seriously threatened by Beijing verbally and through repeated military exercises near Taiwan. In his Presidential Inauguration on 20 May 1996, President Lee reiterated that Taipei would continue to pursue the two-fold state policy of equal recognition and pragmatic diplomacy, though he also indicated some conciliatory gestures by saying that Taipei is willing to negotiate with Beijing to end the cross-strait hostility and that he is willing to visit the mainland. It appears that Taipei has firmly held that "one China is only an ideal,"[55] and Taiwan's current position is that "there are two Chinas at the present stage and Taiwan is moving towards one China as its ultimate goal."[56] As there are two Chinas before unification, Taiwan and the mainland should be equal, and have the same sovereign status and rights to participate in the international community.

Beijing's Response to Taiwan's New State Policy

All the time, Beijing regards the R.O.C. in Taiwan as a local regime only, which has not yet been eliminated or incorporated. The P.R.C. instead has successfully inherited the sovereignty over the whole China since 1949. It is the only legal representative of China, and Taiwan does not have any sovereign status. As such, it is irrelevant to speak of sovereignty split or the question of Taiwan's return to the UN as a split sovereign state. Upon this understanding, while cross-strait relations have turned out to be assuasive since the 1970s, Beijing has laid out "one country, two systems" as the proper model for unification with Taiwan. This unification model attempts to deny Taiwan a political status equal to mainland China and

---

[54] Shi Chi-yu, *The Chinese Consciousness of Contemporary Taiwan* (Taipei: Chungcheng Bookstore, 1993), pp. 154–60.

[55] *United Daily News*, 10 August 1994.

[56] *United Daily News*, 20 November 1993.

insists on a vertical unitary state structure in which Beijing is the central government, while Taiwan is a local regime with a high degree of autonomy.[57]

Obviously, Taipei's new state policy in recent years runs against Beijing's principles of "one China" and "one country, two systems." More importantly, Beijing believes that the motive behind Taipei's new state policy, including its insistence on no direct transportation links with the mainland, its pragmatic diplomacy and its rally for equal recognition, is not to promote unification but to objectify and eternalize the cross-strait separation. Obstructing direct transportation links is to discourage the development of the positive forces of unification; rallying for equal recognition and launching the pragmatic diplomacy are to split China peacefully and therefore to pursue Taiwan's independence in a hidden form. From Beijing's perspective, once it accepts Taipei's theory of equal recognition and sovereignty split, Taiwan will become a truly independent sovereign state, while unification will lose its necessity. At that time, there will be no difference between the R.O.C. on Taiwan and an independent Taiwan, not to mention the huge negative impact the acceptance might have on Chinese national integration.[58]

To counter, apart from carrying out actions to isolate Taiwan internationally and not giving up the threat of force, Beijing issued the *White Paper on the Question of Taiwan and Chinese Unification* on 31 August 1993, systematically criticizing Taipei's policy changes in recent years. The *White Paper* comprises four major points:

1. Since any sovereign state is entitled to use any means it deems necessary, including military ones, to uphold its sovereignty and territorial integrity, Beijing will never give up the use of force in the pursuit of reunification as demanded by Taipei.

2. As Taiwan is part of China and has no independent sovereignty, Beijing strongly opposes Taipei's bid to return to the UN in any

---

[57] Byron S. J. Weng, "One Country, Two Systems," in *The Future of Taiwan*, edited by F. K. Guo and Zhao Fu-shan (Beijing: China Friendship Publishing Co., 1986), p. 351.

[58] Beijing always worries that allowing Taiwan to go for independence will create a demonstrative effect on the minorities and local regimes on the mainland, thereby posing a severe challenge to its existing unitary state structure.

form, including the German and Korean models. The question of Taiwan is purely an internal affair of China, which is different from the questions of Germany and Korea under international agreements after World War II. The international community — especially the United States — should not attempt to interfere in China's reunification without facing serious political and other consequences.

3. Besides UN organizations, Taipei is ineligible for membership in other categories of intergovernmental organizations without Beijing's prior approval.

4. "One country, two systems" is the paramount principle of cross-strait peaceful unification. The central government is in Beijing. Under the "One China" principle, mainland China's socialism and Taiwan's capitalism will coexist and develop together. Taiwan will become a special administrative region and enjoy a high degree of autonomy.

On 30 January 1995, the P.R.C. President Jiang Zemin further concluded eight points (hereafter Jiang's Eight Points) on Beijing's current position on unification with Taiwan. They are:

1. "One China" principle is the basis and prerequisite for the realization of peaceful unification. Beijing thus strongly opposes such theories as "Taiwan's independence," "split sovereignty and divided rule" and "transitional stage of two Chinas."

2. Beijing does not oppose Taiwan developing civilian, economic and cultural relations with foreign countries, but it rejects Taiwan conducting such activities to "expand international survival space" with the aim to promote "two Chinas" or "one China, one Taiwan."

3. Both Beijing and Taipei should enter negotiation and reach a peace agreement to end their hostility under the "One China" principle.

4. Beijing will not promise to abandon the use of force in order to prevent Taiwan's independence and foreign interference in the unification of China.

5. Both sides should step up their direct links, and negotiate a civilian agreement to protect the rights and interests of Taiwan's investments in mainland China for mutual benefit.

6. Both sides should use the Chinese culture as a major foundation for their peaceful unification.

7. Beijing welcomes Taiwan's political parties and groups to

foresightedly and constructively promote the development of cross-strait relations.

8. Beijing welcomes Taiwan's leaders to visit the mainland in an appropriate capacity; mainland China's leaders are also willing to visit Taiwan by invitation.

Both the *White Paper* and Jiang's Eight Points reiterate Beijing's opposition to Taipei's new policy of equal recognition and pragmatic diplomacy, fearing that it will make the cross-strait split an objective fact. They also emphasize the appropriateness of using military force. Yet, Jiang's Eight Points does not emphasize the central status of Beijing in "one country, two systems," and this leaves some room for Taipei to manoeuvre. Moreover, Jiang's other proposals, such as Beijing's willingness to negotiate with Taipei to end their hostility and sign a civilian agreement to protect Taiwan's investments in mainland China, and its welcoming of leaders of both sides to exchange visits, also reflect Beijing's will to make a rapprochement. Since Beijing had a very high expectation from Taipei about its goodwill, it believed that Taipei should reciprocate actively. However, Beijing suffered a serious setback when Lee's Six Points still insisted on divided rule and pragmatic diplomacy, responding to Jiang's call for negotiation on ending the cross-strait hostility by requesting Beijing to relinquish the use of force as a precondition. The worst was yet to come when President Lee made a high profile visit to the United States.[59] Perhaps because of frustration with the setback, along with the enhanced, mutually reinforced possibilities that the United States might interfere in the Chinese unification and that Taiwan might further slide towards independence after Lee's visit, Beijing swiftly decided to intimidate Taipei through a series of military exercises in the Taiwan Strait. For Beijing, the military exercises at least served three purposes: (1) to

---

[59] The frustration with the setback is expressed rather directly in the Chinese Premier Li Peng's speech, "To Accomplish the Reunification of Our Country is the Common Will of all the Chinese," presented at an anniversary seminar of the Jiang's Eight Points on 30 January 1996. Li said: "Jiang's Eight Points represents the CCP's sincerity to solve the Taiwan question.... But since the Taiwan authorities still have not slightly changed its plan to divide the mother country, they not only did not actively respond the above proposals (Jiang's Eight Points), but also requested unrealistic preconditions, creating various barriers to the cross-strait negotiations." See *Wen Wei Po*, 31 January 1996.

avenge Taipei's "return of evil for goodwill"; (2) to warn the United States and the international community not to interfere in the Chinese unification; and (3) to stop the menacing development of separatism in Taiwan.[60] Especially with regard to the third purpose, it appears that Beijing attempted to use military pressure to bring Taiwan back from a peaceful split to peaceful unification.[61]

The Effect of Cross-Strait Tension on Hong Kong

Since Taiwan and mainland China split in 1949, their ties with Hong Kong have long been crucial to cross-strait relations. As a British colony ceded from China, Hong Kong is a major arena for Taipei and Beijing to keep in touch with each other. Especially after the early 1980s when economic and civilian exchanges across the Taiwan Strait began to increase rapidly, Hong Kong's mediation has become even more crucial. Owing to political considerations, today Taipei still insists on no direct transportation links with the mainland. As a result, cross-strait economic and civilian exchanges are largely mediated through Hong Kong. In 1995, the Taiwan–Hong Kong trade totalled US$27.9 billion, of which it is estimated that 70% belongs to cross-strait trade. The trade accounted for 13% of Taiwan's total trade in the same year, second only to that with the United States. Taiwan also enjoyed from it a favourable balance of over US$23 billion.[62] With the prosperous Hong Kong–Taiwan trade and the rising mediatory role of Hong Kong in cross-strait relations, the passenger flow between Hong Kong and Taiwan has also been increasingly rapidly, from 616,513 in 1987 to 2,087,947 in 1995. The rapid increase has mainly been constituted by Taiwan passengers. Since the mid-1980s, the number of passengers from Taiwan to Hong Kong has risen dramatically, from 345,195 in 1987 to 1,761,111 in 1995.[63] It suffices to say that until cross-strait relations are

---

[60] Timothy Wong, "Missile Tests: The Objective and Risk of Gambling," *Sing Tao Daily*, 8 March 1996.

[61] Qi Xin, "Rational Thinking under the Predicament of Current Cross-Straits Relations," *United Daily News*, 25–26 July 1995.

[62] *The Republic of China Statistical Yearbook 1995.*

[63] *The Republic of China Statistical Yearbook*, various years; *Hong Kong Statistics Monthly*, February 1996.

normalized, Hong Kong is a necessary channel for Taiwan people to visit relatives as well as to conduct business in mainland China.

As Hong Kong is so involved in cross-strait relations, any cross-strait tension is likely to strain Hong Kong's future development. In fact, right after the cross-strait tension emerged following Lee Teng-hui's visit to the United States, Beijing cancelled all its talks with Taipei over the transition of Hong Kong–Taiwan ties after 1997. In early March 1996, when Beijing announced resumption of military exercises near Taiwan, Hong Kong's stock market also experienced a severe plunge of about 8% in a day. As Hong Kong–Taiwan ties are largely established on indirect cross-strait ties, it is not difficult to imagine that the cross-strait tension would naturally do some damage to both, even though exact statistical figures are unavailable.

More importantly, on 22 June 1995, China's Vice-Premier Qian Qichen represented the State Council to unilaterally announce seven basic principles and policies that govern Hong Kong–Taiwan relations (hereafter Qian's Seven Points). The announcement indicates the resolution of Beijing as the sovereign to forge a formal and concrete scope, in the form of a central policy, for the Hong Kong–Taiwan ties. It signifies Beijing's will to represent Hong Kong in dealing with Taiwan, and constrains Taipei's activities in Hong Kong in the future. The Qian's Seven Points is divided in two parts: one is for the people-to-people interaction between Hong Kong and Taiwan, and the other is for Taipei's official activities in Hong Kong. On the people-to-people interaction, Qian's Seven Points is positive and encouraging, but on Taipei's official activities in Hong Kong, it is restricted. First, as the fifth point makes clear: "In the name of whatever, to make official contacts, hold talks, sign agreements and set up organizations with the Taiwan region, the Hong Kong Special Administrative Region must report to the Central People's Government, and seek a sanction from it or the Special Administrative Region Chief Executive authorized by the Central People's Government." That is to say, any official activities between Taipei and Hong Kong after 1997 must be under the full control of Beijing; the Government of the Special Administrative Region is not allowed to have independent decision-making power. Secondly, the fourth point stipulates: "On the entry of Taiwan residents into Hong Kong, the Central People's Government will make arrangements for their documents and the other problems they have." This point further shows Beijing's attempt to steer the cross-strait civilian exchanges. Thirdly, the seventh point says: "Taiwan can preserve their existing organizations and personnel in Hong Kong. Their behaviours must strictly abide by The Basic

Law of the Hong Kong Special Administrative Region of the P.R.C.; they cannot violate the principle of 'One China'; they cannot carry out activities which harm the stability and prosperity of Hong Kong and deviate from the work as stipulated in their registrations." On surface, this point gives the green light for Taipei to carry its organizations in Hong Kong through 1997. But it indeed forces Taipei to succumb to Beijing's "One China" principle. As everyone knows, though Taipei's organizations in Hong Kong are registered as civilian organizations, their activities are official in nature. If Taipei could accept "One China," which obviously refers to the P.R.C. in the linguistic context of Qian's Seven Points, there would be no cross-strait conflicts anymore. Under this point as interpreted by Beijing, even though Taipei's organizations can survive in Hong Kong, their room for manoeuvre in the future will be hardly comparable with that before 1 July 1997.

We do not know with certainty whether Taipei will follow what Qian's Seven Points defines or will withdraw from Hong Kong altogether. If the latter happens, it will probably inflict damage on all the three parties — mainland China, Taiwan and Hong Kong, since their interests are so closely connected. In any case, before a decision is made, the Hong Kong–Taiwan ties will be clouded with uncertainty, which in turn will complicate the Hong Kong's 1997 transition.

Structural Constraints on the Radicalization of Taiwan's State Policy

After the presidential election in March 1996, the evolution of the state in Taiwan is close to completion and has set its shape. A democratic R.O.C. located in the Taiwanese indigenous society has successfully replaced the authoritarian one aimed at unifying China. Given this new state structure and Beijing's serious criticisms against President Lee in the past year, will Taiwan's future state policy move towards a more radical end and push the cross-strait conflicts onto the dead-end road of military clashes, thereby seriously damaging Hong Kong's development as well as development on both sides of the Strait? As history is open, the question would not have definite answers. What can however be pointed out is that there are at least six structural constraints that deeply prevent Taipei's state policy from further radicalization (i.e. to openly declare Taiwan's independence).

The first structural constraint is Beijing's military pressure. Though Beijing's military exercises near the Taiwan Strait between July 1996 and

March 1997 could not promote unification and might have even deepened the Taiwan people's alienation from and confrontation with mainland China,[64] as Beijing repeatedly emphasized, the military exercises were to stop Taiwan's independence and they definitely generated tremendous pressure on the pro-independence advocators and supporters. In fact, the presidential election result shows that the pro-independence DPP candidates only captured 20% of the popular vote, which was significantly less than what the DPP got (on an average, 30%) in previous elections.[65] During the period of Beijing's military exercises, many public opinion polls also indicated that the support for Taiwan's independence tended to decline.[66] In other words, when faced with the real danger of military clashes, especially when considering the potential disaster the clashes might bring to Taiwan's export-oriented economy, it is definitely not easy for any of Taiwan's political leaders to persuade the Taiwan people to accept any radical policy which pursues the *de jure* independence of Taiwan.

The second constraint is electoral politics. In Taiwan, the major impetus of democratic development is the frequently held elections. Indeed, as the central and local regimes are divided into many tiers (e.g. central, provincial, county, city, town), the electoral cycle of Taiwan is very short. Since 1991, there have been central or local elections held every year. Besides, the various tiers of regimes are overlapping, making even the lowest level of elections carry some crucial political significance. Thus, regardless of the level of elections involved, the ruling and opposition parties must compete with each other with all their efforts and resources. As a result, the public policies (including the mainland one) of the parties or candidates must stand against the voters' "referendum" over and over again. For most of Taiwan's voters, though very dissatisfied with Beijing's

---

[64] K. S. Liao, "The CCP's Missile Tests and the Development of Cross-Straits Relations," in *The Interaction and Integration of Mainland China, Taiwan, Hong Kong and Macau*, edited by Timothy Wong, Sun Tung-wen and K. S. Liao, p. 213.

[65] It must be pointed out that there were many factors that could be attributed to the low support rate the DPP candidates received, including Lee Teng-hui's personal charisma and the KMT's financial and organizational strengths. The DPP's pro-independence position might play a role, but its real impact is yet to be determined.

[66] *China Times*, 16 July 1995, 28 July 1995; *United Daily News*, 24 August 1995.

tough Taiwan policy, are quite clear about Beijing's determination to resort to force if Taiwan does go for *de jure* independence. Hence, through electoral politics, the voters' pragmatic tendency to seek peace and avoid turmoil has naturally constrained Taipei's mainland policy from turning radical, as reflected by the low percentage of popular vote the DPP received in the 1991 National Assembly elections and the 1997 presidential election. In these two elections, Taiwan's independence was the DPP's main platform, which was discarded by the voters. The voters were rather afraid of the colossal disaster that the radical call for independence might bring to Taiwan. On the other hand, in recent years, though the KMT has been troubled by money politics and scandals about its close association with secret societies, many voters still cast votes in its favour mainly because they find its relatively moderate mainland policy more acceptable. If the KMT adopts a more radical, pro-independence policy and if Beijing does not change its current Taiwan policy, whether the KMT can still win the voters' support is questionable. Especially under electoral pressure every year, in order to remain in power, the ruling party will inevitably tend to strive to preserve the status quo rather than make radical policy shift to scare off the voters.

The third constraint is the pluralization and localization of the Taiwan society. First of all, today's Taiwan is no longer an agrarian society. It is instead composed of numerous interest groups which are expanding, diversifying and configuring autonomously. In such a situation, though the ruling KMT still retains its dominant position, it has been checked by the opposition parties as well as other autonomous social and political groups. Outside the domain of party politics, various social groups also have their own interests, not necessarily compatible with the parties' political ethos. For example, some of the KMT and DPP members have already built up close economic ties with mainland China; they even criticize or reject the parties' mainland policy. Second, today the most important political arena in Taiwan is the Legislative Yuan. But paradoxically, owing to the reality of the "multiple seats, single vote" electoral system, most of the Legislative Yuan candidates not only have to compete with each other with different party backgrounds, they also have to compete with fellow candidates from the same party. In order to win in the election, the candidates must take care of their own interests, establishing personal networks in their own constituencies and seeking support therefrom. As a result, the party loyalty of those winners is inevitably weakened, and their complicity with the local interests has become the nightmare of their respective parties. A good example is that in the newly elected Legislative Yuan since December 1996, the KMT and DPP have suffered from the revolts of their fellow legislators over several important political and other issues. The revolts, as widely reported in Taiwan, involved heavy conflicts of interests.[67] With all these pluralized and localized interests in society and politics, it is therefore simply not easy to reach any consensus over radical policy moves that would severely endanger Taiwan's immediate interests, both collective and individual.

The fourth constraint is the Taiwan economy's heavy dependence upon export-oriented trade. Taiwan's economic development has been basically relying on export, which has contributed a huge foreign reserve of over US$90 billion in Taiwan. In the 1970s and 1980s, the United States was Taiwan's major export market, but it has been gradually replaced by mainland China in the 1990s. In 1995, the cross-strait trade amounted to over US$20 billion, of which Taiwan's enjoyed a US$14.5 billion favourable balance, far above its US$7 billion favourable balance in the overall trade.[68] In other words, if trading is seriously disturbed by the cross-strait political conflicts, Taiwan will surely suffer a serious economic setback. Realizing the political risk of its heavy economic dependency upon mainland China, Taipei has in recent years tried very hard to promote the "southward policy" (encouraging Taiwan's business people to invest in Southeast Asia), with the intention to check the capital flow into mainland China. Taipei has also actively launched a plan of developing Taiwan into the "Asia-Pacific Operations Centre" to step up Taiwan's economic transformation as well as to strengthen its economic autonomy and internationalization. Taipei's efforts, however, have not made any significant breakthroughs so far, due to a number of reasons: (1) mainland China's cultural affinity with Taiwan naturally makes the mainland a more attractive investment area as compared with the Southeast Asian countries; (2) the relatively backward financial institutions in Taiwan need some time to be modernized; (3) the inadequacies of financial and other experts as well as of the infra-structure inevitably slow down the plan of economic transformation and internationalization; (4) Beijing is unwilling to cooperate. On the other hand, the cross-strait trade keeps growing, while Taiwan's economic restructuring moves very slowly. It can be anticipated that in the short and

---

[67] *United Daily News*, 12 February 1996; *China Times*, 17 February 1996.
[68] *The Republic of China Statistical Yearbook 1995.*

intermediate period, especially before Taiwan can reverse its dependency upon the mainland market, Taipei must keep its mainland policy moderate in order to avoid undesirable economic consequences. As Taiwan's economy has suffered from considerable losses under Beijing's repeated military threats over the past year,[69] Taiwan's various political forces should have realized the importance of the cross-strait *détente* to Taiwan's economic survival.

The fifth constraint is the transition problem of Taiwan–Hong Kong ties resulting from Hong Kong's 1997 sovereignty transfer to the P.R.C. As mentioned above, cross-strait economic and civilian exchanges are largely mediated through Hong Kong. When the current cross-strait tension emerged, Taiwan's huge economic interests in Hong Kong were deeply shaded by Beijing's unilateral snapping of its negotiations with Taipei over the transition of Taiwan–Hong Kong relations as well as its subsequent announcement of the restrictive Qian's Seven Points. Unless Taipei prefers to withdraw from Hong Kong after 1997, it will surely avoid any radical mainland policy move in order not to further agitate Beijing and create more obstacles to the transition of Taiwan–Hong Kong ties.

The last constraint is the rising influence of Beijing in the international community, which has rendered all of Taipei's radical policy moves on cross-strait relations fruitless, unrealistic and costly. First, Beijing is one of the five permanent members in the UN Security Council, having the decisive veto power over Taiwan's bid to return to the UN as an independent sovereign state. Second, even if Taiwan wants to bypass the Security Council and directly seek support from the UN General Assembly, it still faces serious obstacles, as Beijing has diplomatic relations with 159 countries in the UN. It is very difficult, if not impossible, for Taipei to garner enough votes to solve its predicament in the foreseeable future. Third, in today's post-Cold War era, since Russia, eastern European countries and some Asian and African countries are still politically unstable, the U.S.-led capitalist West still needs China's cooperation in many areas to maintain international stability. The Western countries, therefore,

---

[69] From July 1995 to March 1996, Taiwan's stock market dropped one-third of its market value, and Taiwan's foreign reserve decreased by over US$10 billion. A Taiwanese economist even estimated that Beijing's military exercises costed about 1% of Taiwan's GNP growth rate. See Tuo Jia-pok, "Taiwan's Economy Hit Hard under the Cross-Straits Tension," *China Times*, 8 May 1996.

will not easily break with Beijing by actively interfering in the cross-strait affairs, especially by supporting Taiwan to join the UN. That explains why the United States quickly reiterated its "One China" policy and its refusal to support Taiwan's return to the UN after Beijing reacted strongly against the Clinton Government allowing Lee Teng-hui to visit the United States by withdrawing its U.S. ambassador and cancelling all high-level official exchange visits between China and the United States. Fourth, as China's overall state capacity (especially economic and military) keeps rising, and China potentially becomes the strongest regional power in Asia, along with the additional strength to be added by the return of Hong Kong after July 1997,[70] it is unthinkable for any pragmatic country like the United States to give up China for Taiwan, supporting Taiwan's independence by engaging themselves in a surely long and bitter confrontation with Beijing.

Conclusion

This chapter has analysed how Taiwan's democratization in recent years has changed its state structure, and from this angle, discussed the formation of Taiwan's new state policy and its impact on the cross-strait relations. The chapter argues that today's Taiwan has established a libertarian-civic state driven by indigenous popular support, which is radically different from the past one under the KMT authoritarianism. The former emphasizes Taiwan's autonomy and independence, believing that Taiwan is no longer representative of the whole China, and unification should hinge upon the evolution of the cross-strait ties. The latter upholds the "One China" principle and sees unification as a necessity. Owing to this radical change in state position, Taipei pushes forward its new state policy to pursue equal recognition in cross-strait relations and its pragmatic diplomacy in the international community. However, Beijing suspects that Taipei is attempting to objectify and eternalize the cross-strait split, and this suspicion

---

[70] Now there are 30 countries which have diplomatic ties with Taiwan, of which 13 have their consular office in Hong Kong. Since Hong Kong will return to China's sovereignty after 1997, if these countries want their offices to continue operation after that time, they must negotiate with Beijing for a proper arrangement. As Beijing does not accept dual recognition, and if a few of these 13 countries eventually choose Beijing over Taipei, Taipei's existing diplomatic space will be definitely under tremendous pressure.

eventually developed into the cross-strait confrontation in 1996 in which Beijing resorted to military threats as revenge for Taipei's changed state policy. The confrontation not only caused a serious crisis across the Taiwan Strait unseen in many years, but also created uncertainty over Hong Kong's 1997 transition in which Hong Kong–Taiwan relations occupy an important position.

Despite this unprecedented cross-strait confrontation, there are several structural factors that serve to constrain Taipei from taking an even more radical state position and policy, including Beijing's threat of force, the short electoral cycle of Taiwan, Taiwan's pluralized and localized social and political interests, Taiwan's heavy economic dependency upon the mainland, the huge economic interests of Taiwan in Hong Kong which will be reverted to mainland China in 1997, and the rising influence of Beijing in the international community.

These structural factors, however, can at most define the structural limits for Taiwan's state policy making at the macro level; they cannot actually resolve the cross-strait conflicts. After all, apart from openly declaring Taiwan independent, Taipei still has a lot of room to manoeuvre, and by doing so, it can properly gain the identification from its people who are increasingly autonomous in dealing with Taiwan's relationship to the mainland. For example, while Taipei insists that the R.O.C. on Taiwan is an independent sovereign state and that pragmatic diplomacy is to find a way out for the R.O.C. to the international community, is this policy discourse not different from an independent Taiwan, widely supported in the Taiwan society, and yet infuriating Beijing? Indeed, with the development of radical separatism being strained, the problem Beijing really faces in the future should be how to define Taipei's extremely challenging new state policy discourse which supports neither an early unification nor an immediate *de jure* independence.

As said before, a major reason for Beijing's military threats following Lee's visit to the United States is to bring Taiwan back from peaceful split to the road of peaceful unification. For Beijing, Lee's visit was only a threshold over which Taipei was judged to have crossed towards a peaceful split from mainland China. What is important is Taipei's radical state policy change in recent years, which is the nexus of the current cross-strait conflicts. Driven by democratization, Taipei has given up competing with Beijing over the sovereignty of China, and at the same time has been trying to seek equal recognition with Beijing and the peaceful coexistence of mainland China and Taiwan in the international community under the theory of split sovereignty and divided nation. Taipei argues that its policy change does not attempt to abandon its long-time position of a unified China; rather it only wants to make Beijing recognize the reality of the cross-strait split, and then search for a mutually acceptable foundation for the normalization of the cross-strait relations as well as the eventual unification of China. Taipei even believes that though its state policy change is in direct conflict with Beijing's "One China" principle, it is a rational and pragmatic choice of compromise between Beijing's "one country, two systems" and the radical separatists' call for Taiwan's *de jure* independence.

Nevertheless, even if Taipei has the real intention to unify with mainland China, it has to face a dilemma which has aroused Beijing's deep suspicion. After democratization when Taiwan retreats from the competition for the sole representative of the whole China to the rallying for the objective recognition of Taiwan's split sovereignty in a divided China, how can Taipei convince Beijing that the objective recognition of the cross-strait split is only a means to unification in the transitional period, but not an end itself? In fact, before Taipei can convince Beijing with concrete actions that it is committed to future unification, given Taiwan's existing constitutional-political structure, it is impossible for Beijing to stop Taipei from declaring independence through peaceful ways. A simple example is that if the ruling KMT can push the National Assembly to change the name of the R.O.C., what can Beijing do, apart from military action? Beijing may feel even more powerless if Taipei obtains a UN membership and is under the UN protection. This is why when Taipei makes use of the momentum of democratization to push Beijing to recognize the cross-strait split as a precondition for unification talks, it inevitably arouses Beijing's suspicion that Taipei is preparing for the eternalization of the cross-strait split, i.e. Taiwan's independence. On the other hand, today Taiwan has become a libertarian-civic state; unification with mainland China is only a choice, not a necessity. More importantly, even if Taipei chooses unification, its open and autonomous state system is unlikely to allow any political leaders in Taiwan to accept a unification arrangement that will relegate Taiwan to a local government. Otherwise, the political leaders will be abandoned by the voters. For Taipei, if it fails to seek an objective recognition from Beijing or from the international community, owing to the fact that Taiwan is extremely small relative to the mainland in terms of overall state capabilities, it will probably find it difficult to hold peace talks with Beijing.

This is precisely the most important conflict between Beijing and

Taipei. On the one hand, Taipei believes that an objective political status in the international community is a realistic need for Taiwan as well as a necessary precondition for peaceful unification. Given the new political reality (like popular sovereignty and the R.O.C. on Taiwan), Taipei has to push its pragmatic diplomacy to seek an international breakthrough. On the other hand, Beijing thinks that what Taipei is doing is to invite foreign interference in the cross-strait relations, and that with foreign support, a peaceful split from China will become even easier. Hence, Beijing must warn Taipei that the cost of a peaceful split is simply no peace at all, i.e. the threat of force.[71] In fact, both possibilities are equally valid. The key is whether Taipei and Beijing can find a way out between these two possibilities, instead of going to the extreme and letting their confrontation escalate.

In this regard, that Beijing used enormous military pressure to force Taipei to give up its pragmatic diplomacy after President Lee's visit to the United States surely has deeply upset the Taiwan people, but it certainly reflects Beijing's profound distrust of Taipei. For Beijing, what Lee's visit highlights is not merely Taipei's international survival space but also the possible alliance between Taiwan's separatist forces and the international anti-Chinese forces in obstructing Chinese unification. Hence, the necessity for Beijing to take action in advance. Beijing's actions, however, have further deepened Taiwan's anxiety over its intention to use its military might to subordinate Taiwan to its domination. In Taipei's view, given that pragmatic diplomacy is a crucial means to counter Beijing's pressure, as well as an articulation of the Taiwan people's growing desire to join the international community, how can Taipei be so easily submissive to Beijing's intimidation? If it gives up, what does it have to bargain with Beijing?

In fact, the cross-strait policies of Beijing and Taipei derived from their mutual suspicion contain great limitations. Beijing's military threat may suppress Taiwan's call for independence, but it cannot promote unification, because even if military forces take over Taiwan, they cannot conquer the hearts of the 21 million Taiwan people. Besides, military threat of any kind contains a spillover effect. It will damage the economies of Hong Kong and mainland coastal provinces which have close ties with Taiwan. The damage is detrimental to Hong Kong's transition in particular and mainland China's

---

[71] Qi Xin, "Rational Thinking under the Predicament of Current Cross-Straits Relations."

modernization in general. On the other hand, Taipei's pragmatic diplomacy may internationalize the question of Taiwan and win international sympathy, but it cannot really enhance Taiwan's international space, because international politics is mainly based upon might, not ethical correctness. Which pragmatic countries are willing to antagonize the rising mainland China just for the sake of ethical correctness?

Hence, a more reasonable and comprehensive way to solve the current cross-strait conflicts should be not to allow each side to go its own way and step up confrontation. Instead, both sides should work together to form a mutually binding agreement that will give Taiwan an objective political status in return for its concrete commitment to unification. It is an agreement under which the two competing states in the divided China can transit to an "agreed-upon autonomous unification," i.e. a unified Chinese sovereignty with two governing regimes which do not overlap with each other.[72] It is only under this kind of arrangement that Beijing can withdraw, with composure, its threat of force on Taiwan, that Taipei can freely pursue its reasonable international space without fearing the intervention of foreign powers in the cross-strait affairs, and that both Beijing and Taipei can fundamentally solve the tension between "peaceful split" and "peaceful unification," and actually move from "peaceful split" towards "peaceful unification."

Finally, we should add that although Hong Kong has been helplessly squeezed by the political conflicts between mainland China and Taiwan, and although it will come under Beijing's sovereignty after 1997, it deserves a place in the development of links with Taiwan after 1997. No doubt, London does not recognize the political status of Taiwan in the international community, but it does tolerate Taipei's various activities in Hong Kong and allows Hong Kong to develop close, non-political relations with Taiwan. As the relations are essentially non-political, they should not violate the principle of "One China" in the "one country, two systems." To keep its ties with Taiwan which are important for Hong Kong's prosperity, Hong Kong should admit with no hesitation that such ties are part of "Hong Kong people ruling Hong Kong," and put forward the demand to Beijing. It is only by doing so that Hong Kong can maintain its prosperity and continue to play a mediatory role in cross-strait relations.

---

[72] Timothy Wong, *Democratization and Separatism*, pp. 26–29; Qi Xin, *A New Horizon of Culture* (Beijing: Huayi Publishing Co., 1996), pp. 282–85.

11

China, the United States, and the Future of Hong Kong

Ting Wai

Introduction

Both China and the United States (U.S.) attach great importance to the future of Hong Kong, as this capitalist enclave is important to their interests in the fast-developing Asia-Pacific region. Although numerous works have been published on Sino-American and China–Hong Kong relations, how the interactions between the two nations affect the future development of Hong Kong have been less studied. With the return of sovereignty of Hong Kong from Britain, a faithful ally of the U.S., to China in 1997, the crucial problem, judging from an international relations perspective, is whether the city could remain useful in promoting and sustaining the political and economic interests of the Western world, while at the same time continuing to play a dominant role in facilitating the modernization of China. In the past, Hong Kong's geopolitical position has been peculiar. Despite the continual ideological/political conflict between socialist China and the capitalist West since 1949, Hong Kong caught in the middle of the conflict continues to grow and prosper, irrespective of all the vicissitudes in the forty years of the Cold War era. Since the relations between the West and China are not yet cleared of conflicts and competition, would its "change of camp" from the West to China witness the emergence of a different Hong Kong? Will the Sino-American disputes make it a pawn for both sides? The political variables, such as the interplay among the great powers, that is, the U.S., China, the United Kingdom and Japan, the phenomenon of complex interdependence in geo-economics, and the political uncertainty in China which would put Hong Kong in a precarious position, will largely govern the future development of the Special Administrative Region (SAR).

During the Cold War era, the conflicts and confrontation between the People's Republic of China (P.R.C.) and the U.S. had no detrimental effects on the political order and economic prosperity of Hong Kong. Rather the opposite is true. Although the survival of Hong Kong depended on the great powers, Hong Kong survived well. This chapter aims to study whether the change of sovereignty would bring political difficulties for Hong Kong in the post-Cold War period, with the continual Sino-U.S. conflict arising from their mutually damaging perceptions and policy orientations.

U.S.–Hong Kong Relations: Harmony in Doubt?

Although not a sovereign state, Hong Kong has always been treasured by the US for its open economy which has adopted a *laissez-faire* and free trade policy and has bred generations of successful entrepreneurs. Hong Kong is the thirteenth largest trading partner of the U.S., while the U.S. is Hong Kong's second largest trading partner. As an entrepôt, Hong Kong handles 68% of China's exports to the U.S. and 32% of U.S. exports to China.[1] There are more than 1,000 American companies operating in Hong Kong, with a total cumulative direct investment which amounted to US$13.8 billion at the end of 1995, primarily in wholesale trade, banking and finance, and manufacturing. In comparison, China absorbed US$10.7 billion of American direct investment between 1979 and 1995. The U.S. is Hong Kong's third largest investor after China and Britain, and its second largest direct investor in manufacturing, just after Japan. Hong Kong serves as the base in the Asia-Pacific region for the regional offices or head-quarters of 414 American companies,[2] while more than 2,300 foreign

---

[1] See Stuart Eizenstat, Undersecretary of Commerce for International Trade, "Revoking China MFN Would Hurt Hong Kong, US," *Economic Policy Backgrounder*, USIS, 7 June 1996, p. 4.

[2] See "The US Presence in Hong Kong," The American Chamber of Commerce in Hong Kong, July 1996. In comparison, the total assets of Chinese state enterprises in Hong Kong amount to US$42.5 billion at the end of 1994. See *Hong Kong Economic Journal*, 18 November 1995, p. 6. See also *Report on the 1996 Survey of Regional Representation by Overseas Companies in Hong Kong* (Hong Kong Government Industry Department, December 1996), pp. 11 and 16.

companies in total had set up their regional headquarters there by the end of 1996. The total number of American citizens residing in Hong Kong has reached 36,000, even more than the British. Currently there are 14,000 Hong Kong students studying in the U.S.,[3] and around 60,000 citizens of Hong Kong have completed their studies in the U.S. Hong Kong serves as a bridge for the U.S. in the expansion of its economic activities in the Asia-Pacific region. Winston Lord expresses very clearly the wish to maintain the characteristics of Hong Kong as follows:

> Our public and private statements reiterate the themes key to Hong Kong's continued autonomy: access to free markets and an open investment regime; a solid legal system and independent judiciary; non-interventionist economic policies; continued protection of civil liberties and cultural and academic freedoms; an open and aggressive press; and open and accountable democratic institutions.[4]

Thus, it is in the interest of the U.S. Government and business people to defend the status quo of Hong Kong; to protect the "rules of the games" in its socio-economic system, in terms of free and fair competition, the rule of law, and the healthy practice of business ethics; and to support the proper functioning of Hong Kong's institutions, such as the independent judiciary and the competent and non-corrupt civil service. American multinational companies do rely on Hong Kong as their Asian headquarters to coordinate their investments in the P.R.C. and the whole Asia-Pacific region. As it is difficult to find a replacement, it is no surprise that the U.S. Government's policy *vis-à-vis* Hong Kong is so clearly defined, that the rule of law, civil rights, and freedom of speech should be maintained, and the development of more democratic political institutions should be encouraged. Negative changes in Hong Kong like rampant corruption, deteriorating business environment in which favouritism prevails over competition, and freedom of information becoming questionable, may lead to the withdrawal of American multinational companies from Hong Kong. If the U.S. interests are at stake, the crucial question is whether Washington would adopt a tougher attitude to deter Chinese interference and to help safeguard the present character of Hong Kong.

---

[3] See Winston Lord, Assistant Secretary of State for East Asian and Pacific Affairs, in testimony before the Senate Foreign Relations Subcommittee on East Asian and Pacific Affairs, 18 July 1996, *Foreign Policy Backgrounder*, 19 July 1996, p. 7.

[4] *Ibid.*, p. 8.

Hong Kong in China: Autonomy in Disarray?

Despite the interminable guarantee made by Chinese officials on such sacrosanct principles as "high degree of autonomy," "Hong Kong people ruling Hong Kong," and "capitalism in Hong Kong remaining unchanged for 50 years," we have already witnessed a series of changes even during the period of transition. The increasing participation of Chinese state enterprises in Hong Kong, of which some are even listed in the Stock Exchange of Hong Kong, have aroused serious reflections on how the political-economic system of Hong Kong is adversely affected.[5] These enterprises are controlled by the party-state. Participation of these actors in the Hong Kong market would imply state penetration, or intervention of political power in the proper functioning of the market. This may disrupt the rules of the game of the market, in which only competition, protected by the supporting institutions, can prevail in principle. Not many are suspicious of the sincerity of Chinese leaders in maintaining the stability and prosperity of Hong Kong. However, good intentions alone are not enough. While increased participation of mainland Chinese in Hong Kong affairs is inevitable with the eventual return of sovereignty to China, would it also bring along the Chinese communist influence and the Chinese style and mentality of doing business? And all kinds of peculiar features which are products of "socialism with Chinese characteristics"?

Hong Kong people worry not only about the possible direct political intervention from Beijing, but also the increasing Chinese influence which brings along the "Chinese way" of doing things.[6] If the great "institutional pillars" of Hong Kong, including the independent judiciary, freedom of speech, and the so-called capitalist rules of the game (the rule of law, free competition, spirit of contract, etc.) are also affected, then it could be said that Hong Kong has been "transformed" in a way which no Hong Kong and foreign citizens residing in Hong Kong would welcome.

Scepticism about the degree of autonomy that Hong Kong may enjoy and the possibility of Chinese interference in Hong Kong's political and

---

[5] See, for example, Ting Wai, "Les Entreprises Chinoises à Hong Kong," *Perspective Chinoises*, Vol. 31 (September–October 1995), pp. 22–27.

[6] For a more detailed analysis, see Chan Hing-lin, "Chinese Investment in Hong Kong: Issues and Problems," *Asian Survey*, Vol. 35, No. 10 (October 1995), pp. 941–54.

economic affairs can be illustrated by the debate initiated in 1996 on the formation of the 400-member Selection Committee for the First Government of the Hong Kong SAR by the 150-member Preparatory Committee. The National People's Congress passed a resolution requesting the establishment of a Provisional Legislative Council after 1 July 1997, which is also to be formed by the 400-member Selection Committee. As it is not prescribed in the Basic Law, the legality of such a Provisional Legislative Council is questionable to the Hong Kong people. The people of Hong Kong worry about the possibility of laws being enacted by this provisional legislative body to curb their freedom and rights according to the whims of China. Although it is open to the public to compete for these 400 positions, the method to be adopted by the Preparatory Committee for choosing from among the 5,791 Hong Kong citizens who have filed their applications remains unknown.[7] The complicated process in lieu of universal suffrage lacks transparency and arouses suspicion of political interference. The U.S. Government has made its position very clear:

> Because of our support for the development of open, accountable, and democratic institutions, and for the sake of continuity and stability in Hong Kong, the United States believes current LegCo members should be allowed to serve through the transition.[8]

Although both the U.S. and the European Union insist that they have no intention of intervening in the domestic affairs of Hong Kong, they are doubtful whether Hong Kong can really have a high degree of autonomy in political matters. It is still debatable whether a more accountable government in a democratic set-up could facilitate stability and prosperity in Hong Kong. A strong authoritarian tradition which opts for consensus among the

---

[7] See *Wen Wei Po*, 26 September 1996, p. A10.

[8] See *United States–Hong Kong Policy Act Report* as of 31 March 1996, as required by Section 301 of the United States–Hong Kong Policy Act of 1992, 22 U.S.C. 5731 as amended, p, 23. The European Union has expressed the same regret, as expressed by Etienne Reuter, Head of the Office of the European Union in Hong Kong, "this Legco is a democratically constituted body which forms the backbone of a legal and governmental system.... The prospect of a dismissal of the elected legislators on 1 July 1997 is therefore the wrong signal. It is also psychologically counter-productive." See Etienne Reuter, "Hong Kong and the European Union," *East–West Dialogue*, Vol. 1, No. 1 (June 1996), p. 9.

social classes rather than polarization and contestation still exists in Hong Kong society.

Sino-American Relations: Limited Conflicts and Cooperation

The Chinese perception of U.S. policy regarding China is based on the following views. On the one hand, there is the argument that the U.S. seeks to "contain" China. On the other hand, some Americans want more dialogues and contacts with China. However, it is estimated in China that the latter view has been more favoured recently, as evidenced by a more conciliatory attitude of Washington towards China in granting it the Most-Favoured-Nation (MFN) status without conditions, concluding an agreement on Intellectual Property Rights (IPR), the visit of Anthony Lake to China in July 1996, and the resumption of military contacts,[9] particularly the visit of Chi Haotian, the Chinese Minister of Defence to the U.S. in December 1996.

There is no need to reiterate the Chinese attack on the so-called U.S. theory of "Chinese threats." According to some Chinese strategists, the idea of containment of China originates in the false assumption that the P.R.C. starts to threaten other nations as it becomes prosperous. However, the opinion in Washington is not uniform. It is generally agreed that China should conform to international norms and the U.S. should, in its interest, foster changes in China. But the approaches are different.[10] The first is a moderate posture towards China, characterized by the policy of "engagement" initiated by the Clinton administration. It is based on the assumption that China would move in the right direction. The second approach is less accommodating in that it advocates the use of military force as a counterweight to the rising China and requires Washington to be firm in all disputes with China. The third approach lays no hope on the present communist regime of China. It believes that with no change in the political system in China, there is no hope for a constructive relationship between

---

[9] See Sin Di, "The Two Opinions of US Policy towards China," *Wide Angle Monthly* (August 1996), p. 18.

[10] See Robert Sutter and Kerry Dumbaugh, "China–United States Relations," *CRS Issue Brief*, updated 18 May 1995, Order Code IB 94002, pp. 9–10.

the U.S. and China. Apparently, the last two approaches are viewed by China as promoting the "Chinese threat" theory.

Although the containment policy is supported by some American officials and Congressmen, many do not think that a richer and stronger China would automatically become a nationalist trouble-maker. They welcome a more prosperous China, but argue that it should be open and responsible. This view can be seen in a report made by U.S. China Policy Task Force of the Center for Strategic and International Studies, Washington, D.C., and by Kenneth Lieberthal who argues:

> The United States strongly welcomes and supports a strong, stable, prosperous China, which is open and not divided, and is integrated as a full, responsible, and constructive member of the international community.[11]

> On balance, China is likely to act constructively in the future if it is secure, cohesive, reform-oriented, modernizing, stable, open to the outside world, and able to deal effectively with its problems.[12]

Nobody can stop China from becoming more prosperous and powerful. Further, the opening up of China would help to facilitate its integration into the global community. What the West and the neighbours of China are afraid of is whether a richer China will become less stable domestically due to its multiple social problems, and become irresponsible in its external behaviour. It is not merely the military build-up of China that alarms its neighbours in the Asia-Pacific region. If the Chinese communist regime loses its authority and legitimacy, and if China moves towards disintegration and destabilization, the resulting social disorder will bring troubles for the neighbours also. If that happens, the party-state would camouflage the domestic problems by diverting the attention of its people to the perceived threat from the outside. If the regime, in order to remedy its loss of legitimacy and to unify its people, adopts a nationalist and even jingoistic position, strong anti-foreign sentiments that develop thereafter would certainly be detrimental to the interests of neighbouring nations. What are the neighbouring nations to think, when the People's Liberation Army

---

[11] See *Developing a Consensus for the Future: A Report of the CSIS US China Policy Task Force* (Washington, D.C.: The Center for Strategic and International Studies, 1996), p. 10.

[12] Kenneth Lieberthal, "A New China Strategy," *Foreign Affairs*, Vol. 74, No. 6 (November/December 1995), p. 36.

increases its defence expenditure, and simultaneously gains financial strength for its modernization through the weapons trade and other business activities? Thus, potential political instability blending with strong nationalist feeling and military strength is the real reason for others' anxiety and suspicion.[13]

Under the banner of "comprehensive engagement," the policy of the Clinton administration suffers from zigzags due to a lack of vision and consistency. In the *New York Times* President Clinton conceded this fault in foreign policy, but stressed that eventually his policy on China would be on the right track.[14] A careful reappraisal of the relative importance of different U.S. foreign policy imperatives in the post-Cold War era shows that for the U.S., military security and economic exchanges have proved to be more important than ideological issues such as the democratization and human rights conditions in China. The following U.S. policies are listed in order of importance:

1. The stability of the Asia-Pacific region — The U.S. does not want to see a militarily strengthened China that would provoke an arms race among the East Asian countries. Thus Chinese exports of missiles and strategic materials to build weapons of mass destruction (WMD) are of primary concern. Peaceful means to solve conflicts between China and other powers is regarded as a long-term U.S. policy.

2. U.S. economic interests — Washington welcomes further opening up of China, but wants it to abide by international norms in its external economic behaviour, and to establish the necessary financial regulations and legal provisions for coping with its rapid economic growth. The two memoranda signed in 1992 on copyright and market access, and the agreement on the Protection

---

[13] Chinese analysts argue that the U.S. only wants to have a poor and disintegrated China because it does not want to see the increasing influence and success of the "Chinese model." Emphasis on "Chinese threat" is aimed at creating hostility between China and its neighbours. See especially Lu Qichang, "Some Arguments on the US's China Policy," *Contemporary International Relations*, Vol. 71 (September 1995), p. 4.

[14] See *New York Times*, 29 July 1996. p. A16.

of Intellectual Property Rights signed in February 1995, are considered by the U.S. as a success in this domain.

3. Domestic politics of China and the prospect for democracy — Although the U.S. has the lofty goal of seeing political democratization in China accompany increasing social and economic pluralism, its intention and capability of fostering democracy is rather limited. Engaging China economically in the hope of forming a solid social foundation for democratization is the means adopted.

4. Human rights in China — Perennial disputes are going on between China and the West on whether there exists universal value of human rights, but the role of the U.S. in improving human rights conditions in China is very limited.

China would like to integrate into the global economic system, but it declines to become part of the world order dictated by the U.S. An increasingly prosperous China with a regime losing its legitimacy would become more and more self-assertive when facing the challenges and pressure from the West.[15] How can Hong Kong, being constantly squeezed between the big powers, live under the sovereignty of China, and re-position itself, so as to be beneficial to all the powers concerned, and in return be treasured by them?

Complex Interdependence and Possible Political Manoeuvres

A brief review of the three bilateral relationships shows that, despite the importance of Hong Kong as an international financial and services centre and with a GNP one-fifth of China's, it has a very limited role in international relations or in deciding its own fate as it is not a sovereign entity. China will be the predominant power which decides the fate of this city. Since the interests of the U.S. are at stake, the superpower can also

---

[15] The American attitude can be illustrated by a report in *Newsweek*, "economic growth could feed China's nationalism and assertiveness as much as its democracy. The prospect is chilling." See Robert J. Samuelson, "Trading with the Enemy," *Newsweek*, 1 April 1996. p. 40. The Chinese reaction can be witnessed by the popularity of the book *China Can Say No* since summer 1996.

check and balance the behaviour of China and its possible impact upon the functioning of Hong Kong.

Winston Lord stresses that the issue of Hong Kong was raised in almost all official high-level meetings with the Chinese leaders.[16] He made no attempt to disguise his views regarding the internal affairs of Hong Kong. He made it very clear that Beijing did make a mistake in its decision to dissolve the legislature elected in 1995:

> It's a serious mistake to thwart the elected will of the Hong Kong people and their elected legislature ... I've been very careful ... not to give a legal interpretation, but from a psychological and policy impact, in terms of autonomy, in terms of freedom of expression.[17]

The same kind of high-profile attitude has already been illustrated by the United States–Hong Kong Policy Act of 1992 enacted by the U.S. Congress. The U.S. pledges to play an active role in maintaining Hong Kong's confidence and prosperity. It respects Hong Kong's status as a separate customs territory which will be treated as fully autonomous from China in economic and trade matters. In other words, after 1997, the policy of the U.S. towards Hong Kong will also be "one country, two systems"! The Act also requires reports to be submitted by the Department of State periodically on the state of transition of Hong Kong. Since then, three reports have been produced on Hong Kong in 1993, 1995 and 1996.

Congressional hearings in June or July each year bring out the worries of Congressmen on judicial independence, press freedom and political stability of Hong Kong. They are, in general, dissatisfied with the lack of assurance by Beijing on the high degree of autonomy and the rule of law. The Chinese reaction is the usual verbal guarantee that in Hong Kong situation is fine and that American intervention is not welcome.[18] Lord explicitly points out that Chinese leaders may not fully comprehend the importance of the rule of law in attracting and maintaining investments in the territory.[19] Former Consul General of Hong Kong, Richard Mueller

---

[16] Lord's 18 July statement before the Senate Foreign Relations Subcommittee on East Asian and Pacific Affairs: Questions and Answer, p. 23.

[17] *Ibid.*, p. 30.

[18] See *Far Eastern Economic Review*, 6 July 1995, p. 26.

[19] *Supra* Note 16, p. 22.

stressed that the U.S. will continue to support Hong Kong's participation in international institutions and to maintain bilateral agreements provided it has a "genuine" degree of autonomy after 1997.[20] Again, the opinion in the U.S. is divided on whether a strong policy should be adopted towards Hong Kong. Some may want a strong U.S. concern about Hong Kong, but avoid "direct pressure on China unless conditions deteriorate notably." Some opt for a more assertive U.S. policy: to suspend benefits for Hong Kong after 1997 if Beijing infringes too much upon the autonomy of Hong Kong.[21] If the U.S. makes it very clear that deterioration of the situation in Hong Kong will lead to the imposition of such "sanction," China has to be more careful when thinking of using a strong arm tactics in the domestic affairs of Hong Kong. The possibility of such sanction, and the withdrawal of American investors in the event will act as a deterrent against Chinese interference.

Despite this kind of high-profile attitude, even researchers in the American Congress agree that the ability of the U.S. to directly affect the 1997 transition "seems marginal unless it decides to confront Beijing more directly over the Hong Kong issue."[22] If the U.S. Government wishes to use "sanctions" against China for its interference in the autonomy of Hong Kong, the Chinese Government may also retaliate by using Hong Kong as an instrument. It has recently been reported that a bill is being drafted by the Hong Kong Government that allows the Chief Executive in the future to implement economic sanctions against other countries upon the instruction of the sovereign state that governs Hong Kong.[23] Although the attitude of China remains unknown, this has aroused serious concern of business people and democrats in Hong Kong. They worry about the possibility of China's infringement upon the economic autonomy of Hong Kong, and the possibility of using Hong Kong for imposing sanctions whenever disputes arise between Beijing and other countries. If the U.S. imposes economic sanctions or threatens to withdraw its investments or "benefits" (such as trade quotas, immigration quotas, and technology

---

[20] *Supra* Note 18.

[21] See James Casey Sullivan and Robert Sutter, "Hong Kong's Political Transition: Implications for US Interests," updated 30 August 1995, *CRS Issue Brief*, p. 8.

[22] *Ibid.*, p. 7.

[23] See *South China Morning Post*, 18 August 1996, p. 1.

transfer) from Hong Kong, and if China retaliates by ordering Hong Kong to reciprocate, then Hong Kong would be dragged into the great power conflict and become a pawn in it. The Chinese leaders have been consistently reiterating that while internationalization of Hong Kong in the economic area is allowed, political internationalization is out of question. During the Cold War era, the difficult relationship between China and the West did not threaten the survival of Hong Kong. With the tacit consent of China, Hong Kong continued to prosper, although it had been always considered as part of the Western world. It was in the interest of China to have a "window" at the border. But will Hong Kong continue to be fortunate enough to evade the great power conflicts in the post-1997 political order which is to be dictated by China?

The complex economic interdependence can also be demonstrated by the issue of MFN status and its impacts upon the Greater China region. Now the debate is over as both the Democrats and Republicans have agreed that an isolated China would be disastrous to Hong Kong and that China should be encouraged to open up further. The opening up of such a big potential market is definitely in the interests of American entrepreneurs. However, at present the Chinese benefits more from the American market than vice versa. The American market is extremely important to China, as Chinese exports to the U.S. are about a third of its total, while U.S. exports to China are only about 2% of total U.S. exports.[24] Apart from the fact that the MFN status has been used in a subtle manner to demand concessions from China regarding the improvement of human rights conditions, it has helped to facilitate economic integration of Taiwan and Hong Kong to the mainland. If China were to lose the MFN status, most industrialists in Hong Kong who invested in China would withdraw and put their capital in other parts of Asia.

Economic development of both Hong Kong and Taiwan are virtually tied to the mainland. A few years ago some might have been optimistic that economic integration would lead to political integration (reunification by "conquering" the mainland). But now the crucial fact is that the two territories are dependent upon the mainland, especially the southern coastal areas, for their economic growth. Economic dependency may become a

---

[24] See *Newsweek*, 1 April 1996, p. 40.

political instrument for Beijing. President Lee Teng-hui has warned that Taiwan should not be over-dependent on China or else trade and investment would be used by the Chinese Government as a political weapon against the island.[25] As a result, he has recently requested the business people in Taiwan not to invest too heavily in China. On the political level, how can a democratic Taiwan, or Hong Kong living under the rule of law, "cohabit" peacefully with an authoritarian China, while being closely linked economically to each other? Would the changing central-local relations in China lead to a weaker central authority that allows more autonomy for Hong Kong and its neighbouring regions? Or would the opposite become true, that is, the central government exercises an even tighter control over Hong Kong, in view of its background as a British colony where the adversaries of China (Britain and the U.S.) still have enormous vested interests? Chinese leaders are ever fearful of Taiwan and Hong Kong being separated from the mainland through the instigation of the "imperialists." It is not surprising if the focus of attention of China's Asia-Pacific policy in the next few years will be on Taiwan and Hong Kong, while the Spratly Islands and Diaoyu island issues will only be its "secondary contradiction." China is not only mindful of the compatriots in both Taiwan and Hong Kong holding different views, but also of the "imperialist intrigues" behind them.

It is quite clear that the U.S. Government wants to help consolidate an area in which it can make a contribution: the rule of law in Hong Kong. The U.S. is anxious to ensure that the bilateral agreements that apply to Hong Kong would be continued beyond 1997. But arrangement has to be made with China through the Sino-British Joint Liaison Group (JLG). Some agreements are awaiting the approval of the JLG, including a new extradition treaty and an air services agreement. Other agreements that are being negotiated between Hong Kong and the U.S. include a bilateral mutual legal assistance agreement, a bilateral prisoner transfer agreement, and an investment protection agreement.[26]

On the other hand, the U.S. Government likes to assist other countries in reinforcing their law enforcement mechanism and institutions. Hong Kong will be no exception if there is deterioration in the rule of law. With

---

[25] *South China Morning Post*, 15 September 1996, p. 6.

[26] *Supra* Note 8, *United States–Hong Kong Policy Act Report* as of 31 March 1996, p. 7.

the return of sovereignty, the U.S. is even expanding its law enforcement presence in Hong Kong. In 1995, a representative from the FBI arrived in Hong Kong. In 1996, an office of the U.S. Secret Service was opened to "work on credit card fraud and US banknote counterfeiting."[27] Representatives from the U.S. Immigration and Naturalization Service have also been working with the Hong Kong Government in preventing the smuggling of Chinese aliens to the U.S. The U.S. Government also cooperates with Hong Kong in the operations against drug trafficking, money laundering, organized crimes and the export of pirated goods from China. Although Washington appreciates Hong Kong's efforts in these operations, it is questionable if the same level of efficiency and effectiveness would be maintained in the future. When China comes to power, would the Hong Kong Government be able to exercise its law enforcement function in a rightful manner? Will it be troubled by pressure from the central authorities, and will it be infiltrated by corruption? Will cooperation with the U.S. Government suffer as a result?

Apart from law enforcement, what the U.S. is most concerned about is whether the export control mechanism of Hong Kong would remain effective after 1997. The crucial problem areas in Sino-American relations, namely the U.S. trade deficit, Intellectual Property Rights, human rights and proliferation of WMD, are not problems at all in U.S.–Hong Kong relations. The U.S. enjoys a trade surplus; human rights is not a problem in Hong Kong; the customs office of Hong Kong is effective in its operations against pirated products from China; and exports and imports of the sensitive strategic goods are under strict control. The 1955 Import and Export (Strategic Commodities) Ordinance of Hong Kong controls exports and imports of weapons, nuclear and chemical products. Owing to Hong Kong's good record, since 1992 it has "benefited from the license-free import of most controlled high technology dual-use items under section 5(k) of the US Export Control Act."[28] Export control consultations and training are carried out with the U.S. Despite its high regard for Hong Kong's efforts in export control, the U.S. Government is worried about whether the 1955 Ordinance will undergo a smooth transition and become part of the law after 1997. Although China has signed the

---

[27] *Ibid.*, p. 6.
[28] *Ibid.*, p. 19.

Nuclear Non-proliferation Treaty and is willing to abide by the Comprehensive Test Ban Treaty and the Missile Technology Control Regime, the alleged transfer of WMD from China (to Pakistan, Iran and Syria) is always a source of dispute in Sino-American relations. It will be in the interest of Hong Kong not to involve itself in any of these disputes. But, as one of the most important ports in Asia, would it not be dragged into the conflict if used by China for such transfer of WMD?

Whether Hong Kong would be dragged into power politics will depend, to a large extent, on the attitude, behaviour and judgement of China. Chinese leaders always insist that Hong Kong is prosperous because its people put their energies in economic activities, not in political games. The P.R.C. will definitely react strongly against any "foreign intervention" in its domestic affairs. However, as Western political influence is inevitable due to its economic presence, Hong Kong without Western presence is no longer the same, and a different Hong Kong might not be beneficial to China. Would the economic benefits rendered to China by Hong Kong suffice to deter Beijing from overreacting and involving Hong Kong in Sino-American disputes? As D. Shambaugh said, threats to its internal political stability are considered by Chinese leaders as threats to its national security.[29] If China adopts a heavy-handed approach against the democrats in Hong Kong, it is not only because of their democratic cause, but also because China believes that intrigues of the "imperialists" are involved. For the Chinese leaders, the most effective weapon is to make use of the "united front" strategy based on nationalist sentiments to unite as much people as possible, including those who are hostile to the regime. It has been reported recently that Beijing will make use of the 1997 transition and the increasing cross-strait economic integration to strengthen the national identity of all the Chinese in the three regions. China believes that a strong national cohesive force in domestic politics and an improving relationship with Southeast Asian nations are factors that can counterbalance the American threat and disrupt the "flexible diplomacy" of Taiwan.[30] The growing dissatisfaction of the Hong Kong Chinese towards

---

[29] See David Shambaugh, "The Insecurity of Security: the PLA's Evolving Doctrine and Threat Perceptions towards 2000," *Journal of Northeast Asian Studies*, Vol. 13, No. 1 (Spring 1994), p. 6.

[30] See Ai Hongren, "Sino-American Relations and the Strategy of Zhongnanhai regarding Taiwan," *Wide Angle Monthly* (August 1996), p. 18.

the Japanese claim on Diaoyu islands provides a chance for the Chinese communists to carry forward their united front strategy. Establishing linkages even with hostile elements based on nationalist sentiments is, in the eyes of Chinese leaders, helpful in consolidating its rule over Hong Kong. The common anti-Japanese feeling does provide a way to break the barrier between the democrats in Hong Kong and the Chinese Government. Continual emphasis on patriotism will be used to lure Hong Kong citizens on to the "right track." But the effectiveness of this strategy on the people of Hong Kong who have a more global outlook remains doubtful. However, the pragmatism of Hong Kong people may render partial success in the Chinese united front strategy.

Concluding Remarks

It is difficult to predict the political future of Hong Kong after it becomes part of China, because political development in China is full of uncertainties. It is inconceivable to see a rapid decline of Hong Kong, though institutional infrastructure will continue to buttress the social and economic order. Although scepticism exists if the high degree of autonomy of Hong Kong is infringed upon by China, Western countries including the U.S., Britain and Japan could help to check and balance the behaviour of the P.R.C. Their presence in Hong Kong due to enormous economic interests not only helps to "internationalize" Hong Kong, but also safeguards the character and proper functioning of this international city. However, the mere change of sovereignty raises a geopolitical concern. Although in the Cold War era Hong Kong remained relatively insulated from power politics under the tacit "cooperation" of Britain and China, whether the same insulation will continue to exist remains to be seen. Beijing insists that the internationalization of Hong Kong should only be economic, but not political, thus making it clear that Hong Kong will not be allowed to become a centre of international conflicts. But, if the U.S. adopts a strong posture against Chinese excessive interference in Hong Kong and threatens to withdraw special arrangements or "benefits" accorded to Hong Kong, how will China react? The vehemently nationalist attitude of China could only add to the worries of foreign investors.

What the West in general and the U.S. in particular are worried about is whether the civil service of Hong Kong will remain competent and honest in law enforcement and will safeguard the capitalist rules of the game, especially competition and the rule of law. With Chinese state enterprises increasingly participating in Hong Kong's economy, the power background of these companies would create difficulties for the SAR Government. Whether it can resist pressure from the central authority would be a test of its degree of autonomy.

The international character of Hong Kong will fade away if foreigners do not regard the SAR as the former Hong Kong. Losing Western presence will be detrimental. To a large extent, this depends on the sensibility of the Chinese leaders when they resort to nationalist feelings in appealing to the people, and whether they can understand the importance of the rule of law in the functioning of the socio-economic system in Hong Kong. While the West still needs an international city in Asia for their economic interests, it is wise for China as well as Western nations to adopt a more conscious attitude not to involve Hong Kong in their political conflicts.

Acknowledgements

The author wishes to thank Miss. Carmen Chung for her research assistance in the preparation of this chapter. He is also grateful to Dr. Herbert Yee, Dr. Gerald Chan, and Dr. Lam Lai-sing for their helpful comments on an earlier version of this chapter.

12

Europe, Hong Kong and the 1997 Transition

Brian Bridges

On 1 July 1997 the British territory of Hong Kong will be handed over to mainland China. The 1984 Sino-British Joint Declaration and the 1990 Basic Law for the Hong Kong Special Administrative Region (HKSAR) are intended to ensure the maintenance of a free economic system, a high degree of autonomy, and a form of democratic political system for Hong Kong. This unprecedented hand-over will create a new situation not only for Hong Kong and the two sovereign powers directly concerned, but also for the broader international community, including Europe.

After decades of either ignoring Asia or seeing it primarily as an economic "threat," Europe has recently become more interested in Asia. The European Commission's strategy paper on Asia in 1994 and the Euro-Asia Summit in Bangkok in March 1996 symbolize the new European commitment to Asia. China is seen by Europe as being a central player in the Asian scene, in economic, political and security terms and, indeed, was the subject of a separate European Commission policy paper in 1995. But Hong Kong is important, not only to Britain, whose flag will be folded up on 30 June 1997, but also to its fellow members of the European Union (EU).

European Commission officials envisage that the "principle of continuity" will govern the EU's relations with Hong Kong even after the 1997 hand-over. However, Hong Kong itself cannot easily be maintained in aspic; it has changed since the Sino-British Joint Declaration of 1984 and it will continue to evolve before and after July 1997. The nature and direction of the evolution and the role that China plays in encouraging or obstructing that evolution will affect the implementation of the principle of continuity.

Hong Kong is of course important to China in a number of ways.[1] On the positive side, it has acted and would continue to act as an agent of modernization by being a source of and a conduit for inflows of technology and capital, whether from Europe or elsewhere. It serves as a gateway to the "Greater China" network of overseas Chinese entrepreneurs, to other Asia-Pacific traders and to the wider world, including Europe. Hong Kong also serves as a symbol of Chinese national unity and sovereignty, and its "return" is designed to be a model for both Macau and Taiwan. Although the Chinese drew on their negotiating experience with the British over Hong Kong in setting up Macau's reversion in 1999, the main objective was and still is Taiwan. But, drawing on their experiences of 1989, some Chinese leaders fear that Hong Kong can act more negatively, as a source of "subversive" ideas which could ultimately undermine communist party power inside the rest of China. This mix of motives and the shifting balance of their relative importance conditions the Chinese policy towards Hong Kong during the transition period.

This chapter endeavours to focus on the implications for European economic and political interests in the transition being undertaken by Hong Kong. After an overview of the main European economic and political interests in Hong Kong, this chapter outlines the broad parameters of the continuing political transition, and then examines in detail a number of key political issues which will be important for Europe. It concludes with an assessment of Hong Kong's future role in Sino-European relations.

European Economic Interests

Britain, as the departing colonial power, clearly has a considerable stake in the political and economic stability of Hong Kong in the remaining months up to the hand-over and afterwards and Hong Kong has indeed been one of the most critical issues in Britain's relations with China since the early 1980s. But many of the other members of the EU are also heavily involved in Hong Kong, at least commercially. For them the post-1997 Hong Kong may actually rise in importance in the context of their own

---

[1] See Michael Yahuda, *Hong Kong: China's Opportunity* (London: Routledge, 1996) for an extended discussion.

relations with China. In the modern world, where interdependence is growing, it is becoming increasingly difficult to separate economics from politics. Nonetheless, an attempt will be made to discuss first the economic stake and then the political stake of the Europeans in Hong Kong.

A few simple statistics can give some idea of the European economic stake in Hong Kong.[2] There are hundreds of European companies operating in Hong Kong; over 90 manufacturing companies, over 40 banks and the same number again of insurance companies. European investment, at US$800 million, accounted for 15% of all manufacturing foreign direct investment (FDI) in Hong Kong in 1994, with Britain, Germany and the Netherlands as the leaders of the European pack. European net assets in the non-manufacturing sector had reached an estimated US$34 billion by the end of 1994. A total of 115 European companies are involved in the construction of the new international airport and its adjacent infrastructure. Over 50,000 EU citizens reside and work in Hong Kong and over a million Europeans visited Hong Kong in 1995.

Bilateral trade has been growing at an average annualized rate of 15% during the 1991–1995 period, reaching US$44 billion in 1995. Hong Kong is one of the EU's major trading partners and the EU is Hong Kong's third largest trading partner. In recognition of this economic importance, a European Commission office was opened in Hong Kong in 1993.

Hong Kong, of course, acts as a gateway to China, especially southern China. European investment in Hong Kong has been important since the 1960s. But European investment in China is still a comparatively recent phenomenon. In 1993 the utilized FDI by the four largest European investors in China was still only roughly equivalent to that of all the EU countries in Hong Kong. Many European companies, especially the small and medium-sized companies, see joint ventures with Hong Kong companies as a useful way into the China market. This "stepping stone" approach becomes clear from Hong Kong Government surveys over the past few years which show a slowdown in the growth of manufacturing FDI from Europe but an increase in the establishment of regional offices or

---

[2] The data used in the following two paragraphs are drawn from a variety of sources, but primarily from materials produced by the European Commission office in Hong Kong.

headquarters in the territory.[3] Hong Kong, not only plays a role as a financial and service centre for European companies doing business with China but also with the broader Asia-Pacific region.

Clearly of paramount importance to European commercial interests is the need for Hong Kong to retain its open, market economy system, which facilitates the free flow of capital. Hong Kong has been one of the most liberal trade and investment regimes in the world. Although outsiders occasionally might have felt that British companies are more equal than others, the awarding of government contracts is widely recognized as being fair and open. Europeans, well aware of the growing predominance of Chinese companies in several important sectors of the Hong Kong economy, still hope that a similar degree of impartiality will be displayed in public sector projects during the post-transition period.

European Political Interests

The West European countries do have a general interest in peace and stability in the Asia-Pacific region. But they no longer have vital interests in the sense of interests which, if threatened, would directly or indirectly affect their own survival, or interests which they would defend or promote by force of arms if no other means were adequate. Hong Kong is no exception to this rule.

Clearly, stability and democracy within the territory figure as the most important European political interests in Hong Kong. The Europeans appreciate that the responsibility for the implementation of a stable or smooth transition to the "one country, two systems" format lies with the present sovereign, Britain, and the new sovereign, China. A number of specific issues in the political domain remain crucial to this endeavour; these are discussed briefly below.

High Degree of Autonomy

The Joint Declaration allows for a "high degree of autonomy" for Hong Kong after 1997, but as some constitutional experts have pointed out, the

---

[3] Paul Whitla, Brian Bridges and Howard Davies, *European and American Investment in the Chinese Economic Area* (Unpublished Report for JETRO Hong Kong, 1995).

concept of autonomy lacks a "clear definition." Examples from other parts of the world suggest a wide variation in the powers available to autonomous regions in practice.[4] The Joint Declaration on paper does grant a range of powers which seem to be more extensive than is usually the case for autonomous regions.

The test, of course, lies in the implementation of these powers after 1997. While it is true that the Chinese Government has made a number of practical concessions which should allow Hong Kong a greater autonomy than is to be found in any other region of China, historically China has not only strongly insisted on the inviolability of its sovereignty but also has a long tradition of exercising strong central control. Within China, of course, the economic reforms begun in the late 1970s have helped to encourage decentralization in economic decision making and China's provinces have, on balance, become more independent as policy actors.[5] But this devolution of economic powers has not been accompanied by the same degree of loosening of political control. The Chinese would like to try to assert political control over Hong Kong, partly to prevent any "Greater Hong Kong" regionalist aspirations and partly to prevent other regions of China trying to exploit the wealth of Hong Kong. As Article 12 of the Basic Law points out, the HKSAR will be a "local administrative region ... directly under the Central People's Government."

Rule of Law

The continuance of Hong Kong laws and the existing legal system after 1997 will be a key factor in Hong Kong's ability to maintain its promised high degree of autonomy. As Governor Christopher Patten has repeatedly tried to emphasize, particularly to doubting business people, the "rule of law" is necessary for Hong Kong to maintain its position as a major international commercial centre. European business people, like business people elsewhere, need to be sure that the courts can be relied upon to uphold contracts and impartially enforce commercial laws and regulations. In general, there is concern that Hong Kong courts, at all levels, will enjoy

---

[4] Michael Davis, *Constitutional Confrontation in Hong Kong* (New York: St. Martin's Press, 1990), pp. 131–35.

[5] See David S. G. Goodman and Gerald Segal, *China Deconstructs* (London: Routledge, 1994).

less independence under the HKSAR than they do now and that the "economic legality" which underpins the economic system in Hong Kong will be weaker.[6] This will have deleterious implications for European commercial interests.

Human Rights

Civil and human rights tread into the sensitive area of a country's internal affairs. Although some European governments, notably the Dutch, have long been vocal on these issues, the majority of European states have only begun to highlight these issues very recently.[7] Nonetheless, the declared policy of the Europeans, as laid down in the European Commission's 1994 Asian strategy paper, has been to start from the assumption that "economic development could bring about the progressive construction of civil society and thus improve the exercise of human rights, which in their turn could also be an important factor for development."[8] The European record on human rights inside China may be some guide to future action over human rights in Hong Kong. Since the 1989 Tiananmen Square incident, which led to sanctions against China which were only completely lifted in 1995, the European Community has endeavoured to raise human rights issues within China regularly with Chinese officials. The Chinese have adopted a dual-pronged response: resisting specific accusations as being unwarranted interference in China's internal affairs and using the carrot of commercial orders combined with the stick of economic reprisals to undermine European unity.[9] Consequently, European governments have displayed and

---

[6] David Newman and David Weimar, "The Credibility of the PRC Commitment to a Market Economy in Hong Kong: Hypotheses and Evidence" (unpublished paper, January 1996). See also Bruce Bueno de Mesquita, David Newman and Alvin Rabushka, *Red Flag over Hong Kong* (New Jersey: Chatham House Publishers, 1996).

[7] Francois Godemont, "Europe and Asia: The Missing Link," in *Asia's International Role in the Post-Cold War Era, Part II* (London: IISS-Brassey's, 1992, Adelphi Paper No. 276), pp. 97–98.

[8] European Commission Communication, "Towards a New Asia Strategy," July 1994.

[9] Peter Ferdinand, "Economic and Diplomatic Interactions between the EU and China," in *The European Union and China: A European Strategy for the*

will almost certainly continue to display varying degrees of enthusiasm for raising human rights issues with China. Undoubtedly, the onus will fall on Britain to take the lead. However, there may be little in practice that Britain can do to guarantee the future of determined but exposed campaigners for democracy and human rights such as Martin Lee, the leader of the Democratic Party.[10]

Related to the future human rights situation in Hong Kong is the issue of passports and whether Hong Kong citizens may be easily able to travel to, and crucially, reside in European states should they feel the need to leave Hong Kong after 1997. Under current European legislation, granting the right to live in Britain means, in practice, the right to work, at least, anywhere within the EU. British Prime Minister John Major's pronouncements in March 1996 on visa-free access to Britain for HKSAR passport holders is intended to set the trend for other European governments, but despite endorsement of the move by Sir Leon Brittan, the Commission Vice-President, to date no other EU member country has followed suit. Immigration is a contentious issue in Europe, and, although Portugal has taken a relatively liberal approach to the right of abode for the people of Macau, most EU member states are cautious about opening their doors to Hong Kong residents.

Democratic Institutions

Europeans frequently speak on the virtues of open, accountable and democratic institutions. Developing such institutions does take time, but

---

Twenty-First Century, edited by Richard L. Grant (London: The Royal Institute of International Affairs, Asia-Pacific Programme, 1995), p. 38. French Prime Minister Alain Juppe dropped a planned banquet speech after Chinese Premier Li Peng's aides objected to an intended reference to human rights in China. *Eastern Express*, 15 April 1996.

[10] Sir Percy Cradock, a senior British Foreign Office "China hand," has argued that "it is unrealistic to think we can give them a kind of immunity." House of Commons Foreign Affairs Committee [hereafter HCFAC], *Relations between the United Kingdom and China in the Period up to and beyond 1997* (London: HMSO, 1994),Vol. II, p. 126. When asked what Britain could do if legislators such as Martin Lee were arrested after 1997, Governor Patten replied, "make one hell of a fuss." *Sunday Morning Post*, 5 May 1996.

the pace at which Britain moved during the past decade or two has clearly been far too leisurely. Even the proposals put forward by Governor Christopher Patten in 1992 were, in his own words, "fairly modest,"[11] but at least the September 1995 Legislative Council elections did constitute the first entirely elected legislature in Hong Kong's history.

The other European governments have largely watched from the sidelines, neither taking any particular step to urge Britain to introduce more democratic institutions earlier in the 1980s nor committing themselves publicly and explicitly to the Patten proposals subsequently.[12] In part, this apparent European indifference stemmed from the view that Hong Kong was after all primarily a British problem; Britain, for too long, did indeed try to go it alone. In part, it may also have been reinforced by Britain's own poor record, under Mrs. Margaret Thatcher, of sensitivity to European concerns on other issues and by a perception of Hong Kong as an overly successful commercial competitor.[13]

After 1997, however, Britain may well be more aggressive in seeking EU support and public opinion in Europe may be, as it was at least briefly in 1989, once again a significant factor.

Hong Kong's Role as an International Actor

The future Europe–Hong Kong–China relationship also needs to be considered within the context of their interactions in the regional and international system. In principle, the HKSAR Government will not be given authority over foreign and defence affairs, but the Basic Law does allow it, under the name of "Hong Kong, China," to carry out external contacts and negotiations in trade, financial and monetary, shipping, communications, tourism, cultural and sports aspects. EU member states, like other

---

[11] *Relations between the United Kingdom and China*, Vol. II, p. 195. See also Li Pang-kwong, "Elections, Politicians and Electoral Politics," in *The Other Hong Kong Report 1995*, edited by Stephen Y. L. Cheung and Stephen M. H. Sze (Hong Kong: The Chinese University Press, 1995).

[12] An Italian diplomat interviewed in May 1996 commented that the Italian approach to post-1997 political developments would be one of "standing at the window watching."

[13] Gerald Segal, *The Fate of Hong Kong* (London: Simon and Schuster, 1993), pp. 182, 191.

states which maintain diplomatic relations with China, will be able to maintain their consulates in Hong Kong after 1997.

In theory, Hong Kong should in future have more independent authority to negotiate treaties and agreements on issues such as bilateral taxation and investment protection, a situation that will be to Europe's advantage. Sir Leon Brittan, on his visit to Hong Kong at the end of May 1996, said that EU policy would be to "underscore the autonomy and the market economy of the SAR."[14] In particular, he raised the possibility of a trade and cooperation agreement to parallel that concluded with Macau in 1992.

Although China recognizes that European — just as much as non-European — states do have legitimate commercial interests in Hong Kong and that there are distinct economic advantages to Hong Kong continuing to enjoy international privileges and treatment in various international economic bodies, it is determined not to allow what it describes as the "internationalization" of Hong Kong. In other words, China does not want issues such as the right to emigrate, nationality and civil liberties to be raised by external powers either bilaterally or multilaterally within regional or global organizations. External support for Hong Kong (or for Macau, Taiwan and Tibet, for that matter) is usually seen by China as support for disintegration. Of course, Hong Kong is "already internationalized";[15] indeed, Hong Kong's success has been founded on its role as an international city. China will find it difficult to prevent the Europeans from feeling that they have a stake in its future.

The Future of Europe–Hong Kong–China Relations

Business people and government officials, whether from Europe, Hong Kong or China, display an aura of confidence in the future. A survey conducted among the member companies of the British Chamber of Commerce in the spring of 1996 showed that 98% of those companies

---

[14] Sir Leon Brittan, "Europe and Hong Kong: Prospects for Cooperation into the Next Century," speech in Hong Kong, 31 May 1996.

[15] Brian Hook, "The External Relations of Hong Kong," in *The Other Hong Kong Report 1991*, edited by Sung Yun-wing and Lee Ming-kwan (Hong Kong: The Chinese University Press, 1991), p. 511.

expected to be operating in Hong Kong in the year 2000.[16] Italian commercial officials perceived a bright future and remarked that a few Italian companies pulling out are leaving for strategic economic reasons rather than political uncertainties. But, as Sir Leon Brittan remarked recently, confidence can be a fickle creature, even though Hong Kong always seems to bounce back after every hiccup.

For the future, Hong Kong has the potential to act both as a positive catalyst in Euro-Chinese relations, as a facilitator, and as a source of conflict — a spoiler.

The EU's long-term strategy towards China has two basic objectives: to involve China as a full and responsible partner in the international community and to develop business opportunities for Europe in China's vast market. Clearly Hong Kong can play a positive role in both these undertakings.

China will continue to grow stronger, both economically and militarily, and its sheer size and geographical position will ensure its deep involvement in regional issues. Its irredentist claims, whether to Taiwan or to the South China Sea, coupled with its arms sales, can cast it in a destabilizing role. The death-watch associated with Deng Xiaoping had prolonged China's own political transition and is certainly working to encourage greater nationalist sentiment. However, ultimately it will be the internal challenges, socio-economic as much as political, which will define its regional role. Generational change, socio-economic stabilization and increasing openness to the outside agencies could bring a new leadership more confident of itself and more aware of the advantages of integration over antagonism.

Although some Chinese leaders do see Hong Kong as itself being a destabilizing influence on social and political order within China, increased contact with and exposure to the outside world through Hong Kong could help to encourage others who are more open to a moderate approach to international affairs.

Similarly, although other regional cities aspire to Hong Kong's mantle (most clearly Shanghai within China and Singapore in the broader Asian region), Hong Kong is likely to continue to play its multiple roles as a

---

[16] *Britain in Hong Kong*, July/August 1996. A majority of the interviewees, however, expected corruption to increase and bureaucratic efficiency to deteriorate after 1997.

commercial facilitator for China's modernization and by extension as a positive conduit for European commercial activity. But to facilitate continuation of these roles, the principles laid down in the Joint Declaration and the Basic Law designed to maintain the free market system have to be faithfully implemented, and a favourable attitude towards business retained. In practice, European companies will have to adapt to the fact that many sectors of Hong Kong business will be dominated by China-controlled companies after 1997; it remains to be seen how far China might restrict competition in order to protect its investments. Regardless of the degree of Chinese interference, however, the continued opening up of China in all directions would inevitably mean that Hong Kong will no longer be quite so pre-eminent in the China market by the early twenty-first century as it is now, but its role — and its importance in Sino-European trade — will certainly not disappear overnight.

But we also need to be aware that political issues inside Hong Kong can intrude into the Sino-European relationship after 1997. In large part, the extent to which these issues disrupt the Sino-European relationship will depend on the attitudes of the Chinese leadership at both the central and the local levels towards Hong Kong's autonomy and on British/European willingness, and ability, to defend the provisions of the Sino-British agreements.

The official line of British officials, even Governor Patten, at the moment is that the Chinese, having signed up to the Joint Declaration, should be trusted to carry out their obligations; and that the discussion of "breaches" can only be hypothetical.

During the post-transition period, Britain, as a signatory of the Joint Declaration, clearly has the right to raise directly with the Chinese any cases where it believes the Joint Declaration has not been "properly implemented."[17] The Sino-British Joint Liaison Group will indeed remain in operation until the end of 1999 to help facilitate resolution of difference of views. British Prime Minister Major, on his March 1996 visit to the territory, stated that "if there were breaches of the Joint Declaration, the British government would have a duty to pursue every legal and other

---

[17] See the comments by Foreign Office Minister of State, Alistair Goodlad, in HCFAC report on *Relations between the United Kingdom and China*, Vol. II, p. 30.

avenue available to us and that is precisely what we would do."[18] It is less clear what "avenues" are available which would have a demonstrable effect on the Chinese. Moreover, the British Government has been publicly non-committal about what precise steps it would take.

One recourse for the British would be to call on its European partners. But, if the British failure to insert a section on Hong Kong into the final communiqué at the June 1996 Florence European Council meeting is any indicator, Britain clearly has to work hard through formal and informal channels to build a European consensus on the post-1997 Hong Kong situation. Better appreciation of growing Portuguese concern over Macau would certainly be one way of deepening support. At the broader European level, use would have to be made of the emerging common foreign and security policy (CFSP). But, despite the efforts now under way, through the recently started Inter-Governmental Conference (IGC) process, to reform and improve foreign policy coordination and coherence, Britain may find it difficult to forge a strong common position on action against China if things were to go wrong in Hong Kong after 1997. Yet, clearly a concerted European approach would carry far more weight with China.

The hand-over of Hong Kong to China is an unprecedented experience for both China and Britain. Both China and Britain (and, by extension, Europe) have clear economic and political interests in making Hong Kong work after 1997. Chinese actions towards Hong Kong in the remaining months of British rule and in the early years of Chinese rule will be seen by the Europeans, and indeed by the Americans and other states in Asia, as an important litmus test of China's intentions to act responsibly in the international system. Since the EU's IGC is expected to wind up its work in mid-1997, the Hong Kong issue may also become one of the first tests of character of the EU's aspirations for a new common foreign policy.

---

[18] *Eastern Express*, 5 March 1996.

Towards the Establishment of a New Order

Joseph Y. S. Cheng

Samuel Huntington argued that while governments are often categorized as democratic or undemocratic, they can also be divided into effective and ineffective governments.[1] Hong Kong, with its spectacular economic growth in the postwar era as a British colony, obviously has an effective but undemocratic system of government. The colonial government has won its legitimacy by results. Even in the 1980s and early 1990s, opinion surveys consistently revealed that Hong Kong people had a higher degree of trust in the British administration in Hong Kong than in the British and Chinese Governments. When Sino-British negotiations on the territory's future formally began in 1982, most Hong Kong people wanted the main-tenance of the status quo, i.e. the continuation of the British colonial administration.

The Chinese leadership could not accept an extension of the colonial administration. It considered that once the issue of Hong Kong's future had been raised publicly, it had no choice but to take back the territory in 1997. Deng Xiaoping introduced the creative idea of "one country, two systems," promising Hong Kong people that they could retain their freedoms, life-styles and existing systems. In addition, the Chinese leadership offered the community "self-administration" (*gangren zhigang*). By the initialling of the Sino-British Joint Declaration in September 1984, Hong Kong people

---

[1] Samuel P. Huntington, *Political Order in Changing Societies* (New Haven and London: Yale University Press, 1968), p. 1.

had to accept that as colonial rule was to be terminated in 1997, and none of the parties concerned wanted the future Hong Kong Special Administrative Region (HKSAR) to be directly administered by Beijing, the establishment of a HKSAR Government with a high degree of autonomy, as stipulated in the Joint Declaration, would be a natural development. Such a government would also help to guarantee the maintenance of the status quo in Hong Kong for the transition period of fifty years after 1997.

The Constitutional and Political Order

The Sino-British Joint Declaration indicated that the People's Republic of China (P.R.C.)'s basic policies regarding Hong Kong, as stated in the Joint Declaration and elaborated in its Annex I, "will be stipulated, in a Basic Law of the Hong Kong Special Administrative Region of the People's Republic of China, by the National People's Congress (NPC) of the People's Republic of China, and they will remain unchanged for 50 years." The Joint Declaration further pointed out that the Chinese Government's decision to establish the HKSAR was "in accordance with the provisions of Article 31 of the Constitution of the People's Republic of China."

Article 31 of the P.R.C. Constitution states: "The state may establish special administrative regions when necessary. The systems to be instituted in special administrative regions shall be prescribed by law enacted by the National People's Congress in the light of specific conditions." In line with this, the Constitution grants the NPC the power "to decide on the establishment of special administrative regions and the systems to be instituted there."

The drafting of the Basic Law was therefore China's domestic affair. It is a "mini-constitution" defining the respective authorities of the central government in Beijing and the HKSAR Government, the political system of the HKSAR and the rights and obligations of Chinese citizens in the HKSAR. The political system of the HKSAR was probably the most controversial issue in the drafting of the Basic Law, partly because while the Sino-British Joint Declaration promised that Hong Kong's "capitalist system and lifestyle shall remain unchanged for 50 years," the colonial political system obviously had to be replaced. Moreover, the Sino-British Joint Declaration and its annexes did not provide for a political system for the HKSAR.

Lee Yee, editor-in-chief of *The Nineties*, a respectable local monthly, asked Lu Ping, then secretary-general of the State Council's Hong Kong and Macau Affairs Office, during his visit to the territory in January 1986, "Will Hong Kong after 1997 retain only its capitalist economic system, and not the capitalist political system?" Lu Ping's answer was very reassuring. "Certainly not. The Sino-British Joint Declaration stipulates the maintenance of the capitalist social system, this includes the economic system as well as the political system. The economy is the base, politics is the superstructure."[2] Many people in Hong Kong believed in the sincerity of Chinese leaders, who had taken much trouble to negotiate the Sino-British Joint Declaration and draft the Basic Law. But they and Chinese officials responsible for Hong Kong affairs were accustomed to socialism and a one-party state. While they might accept some form of economic pluralism, it would certainly be difficult for them to accept political pluralism, social pluralism and freedom of expression, or to realize that those things were essential to the functioning of the pluralistic capitalist economy in Hong Kong.

Since the beginning of the Sino-British negotiations on the territory's future in the early 1980s, the Chinese authorities have initiated a learning process to study what makes Hong Kong tick. This learning process has been largely successful. The Sino-British Joint Declaration and the Basic Law, short of a democratic system of government, largely offered what Hong Kong people wanted. At the same time, the Chinese authorities have also started a process to educate the community the limits of "one country, two systems."

After the release of the Hong Kong Government's *Green Paper on the Further Development of Representative Government in Hong Kong* in July 1984, the Chinese Government promptly indicated that it would not assume responsibility for political reform initiated by the British administration. On 9 September 1984, Xu Jiatun, director of the Hong Kong branch of the New China News Agency, addressed the University Graduates' Association. Xu stated: "Hong Kong after 1997 will not be a dependent territory of Britain, and will not be any 'independent political entity.' Instead it will become a highly autonomous SAR under the Chinese Government, a part of the great Motherland." Answering questions afterwards, Xu explained: "Being 'highly autonomous,' Hong Kong still remains a part of the Chinese Government, while an 'independent political entity' is independent of

---

[2] Lee Yee's communications with the author in January 1986.

China. On this question, there is a view and a tendency that is worthy of your attention."[3]

Beijing remained unhappy about London's intention to leave the issue of political reform to the people of Hong Kong. From mid-October 1985 onwards, Ji Pengfei, director of the State Council's Hong Kong and Macau Affairs Office, frequently received visitors from Hong Kong, and the main theme of the conversations was that "if changes could be avoided, then they should not be initiated." At the end of October 1985, when Timothy Renton, minister of state at the British Foreign Office in charge of Hong Kong Affairs, visited Hong Kong, he declared that Britain would neither play a leading role in the territory's political reform nor introduce an appropriate political system, and that the local people should develop a suitable political system on their own. Under these circumstances, it was reported that the Chinese authorities had asked to discuss Hong Kong's political reform at the second round of meetings of the Sino-British Joint Liaison Group, scheduled for the end of November 1985 in Beijing. This request was turned down. Beijing then felt that Xu Jiatun should issue a public warning.

In his first press conference in Hong Kong on 21 November 1985, Xu indicated that he "did not want to see major changes in the twelve years [to come], transforming the fundamental system in Hong Kong, and then no more changes in the following fifty years." Xu further pointed out that the key to the maintenance of Hong Kong's stability and prosperity lay in "following the text [of the Sino-British Joint Declaration]"; and he warned: "Now we cannot help noticing a tendency of doing things deviating from the Joint Declaration. If there are unexpected changes, I think one should pay attention to questions of this kind."[4]

On 19 January 1997, the legal sub-group of the Preparatory Committee made its final recommendations to repeal sixteen of Hong Kong's laws and modify nine others, including key provisions in the Bill of Rights. The sub-group considered that these statutes were inconsistent with the Basic Law.[5] This was in line with the Chinese authorities' position since November 1985: the British administration must not introduce major changes in the transition period without their consent; they would only

---

[3] See all major newspapers in Hong Kong on 10 September 1984.

[4] See all major newspapers in Hong Kong on 22 November 1985.

[5] *South China Morning Post*, 20 January 1997.

maintain the status quo in Hong Kong as it stood in 1984 when the Sino-British Joint Declaration was concluded. The Chinese authorities also wanted to retain for the HKSAR Government all the draconian powers enjoyed by the colonial government without dilution. Like the traditional colonial government, they wanted the HKSAR Government to be well prepared for all contingencies. They therefore looked upon attempts by the British administration and the elected Legislative Council to revise existing statutes to improve the protection of human rights as British conspiracies.

On 30 November 1985, Ji Pengfei's visit to Hong Kong was disclosed by the Chinese authorities. On the same day, Ji's most recent statements on Hong Kong were also released by *Liaowang*, a Beijing weekly. Ji was quoted as follows on the development of representative government in Hong Kong: "The question of Hong Kong's political system after 1997 will be decided by the Basic Law. Reforms of Hong Kong's political system in the transition period have to take into consideration convergence with the Basic Law."

By the end of 1985, the British Government accepted the Chinese authorities' position on convergence with the Basic Law.[6] It also meant that the drafting of the Basic Law would be in the hands of the Basic Law Drafting Committee responsible to the NPC. The British Government and the British administration in Hong Kong could only influence the work of the Basic Law Drafting Committee by diplomatic channels and indirectly through public opinion in Hong Kong and that of the international community.

When membership of the Basic Law Drafting Committee was announced in July 1985, it was clear that the Chinese Government placed top priority on the stability and prosperity of the territory and that radical political reforms would be unlikely. There were twenty-three members from Hong Kong on the committee with fifty-nine members, most of them prominent business people and leading professionals. The interests of the Establishment in Hong Kong apparently were assured, as the Chinese authorities were keen to retain Hong Kong's attractiveness to investors.

The Chinese authorities' demand for the final say was reflected in the powers of interpreting and amending the Basic Law. Article 158 of the

---

[6] See the author's "Hong Kong: The Pressure to Converge," *International Affairs* (London), Vol. 63, No. 2 (Spring 1987), pp. 271–83.

Basic Law provides that "the power of interpretation of this Law shall be vested in the Standing Committee of the National People's Congress." Article 159 also provides that the "power of amendment of this Law shall be vested in the National People's Congress," while the "power to propose bills for amendments to this Law shall be vested in the Standing Committee of the National People's Congress, the State Council and the Hong Kong Special Administrative Region."

Regarding the political system, both the Sino-British Joint Declaration (Annex I, Article 1) and the Basic Law (Articles 45 and 48.5) provide the Central People's Government with the power to appoint the Chief Executive and the principal officials of the HKSAR Government. It had been anticipated that such an appointment would be a mere formality to demonstrate China's sovereignty over Hong Kong. Chinese officials responsible for Hong Kong affairs, however, indicated that the power of appointments would be a "substantial" one, implying a veto power in the hands of the Central People's Government.

The Basic Law also stipulates that the Chief Executive "shall be accountable to the Central People's Government and the Hong Kong Special Administrative Region in accordance with the provisions of this Law" (Article 43). It is significant that the Chief Executive's power of appointing and dismissing the principal officials of the HKSAR Government is quite limited. He may nominate them and report such nominations to the Central People's Government for appointment and may propose to the Central People's Government the removal of the principal officials (Article 48.5).

According to the Constitution of the P.R.C., local people's congresses, at their respective levels, "elect, and have the power to recall, governors and deputy governors, or mayors and deputy mayors, or heads and deputy heads of counties, districts, townships and towns" (Article 101). The Constitution further provides that "the standing committee of a local people's congress at and above the county level ... decides on the appointment and removal of functionaries of state organs within the limits of its authority as prescribed by law" (Article 104). In actual practice, the Communist Party of China controls the appointment of local government personnel at all levels, without much regard for the constitutional powers granted to the local people's congresses. Since the Party is not expected to exercise explicit control of all the important appointments in the case of the HKSAR Government, then the Central People's Government will have to assume that ultimate control.

The HKSAR political system as outlined in the Basic Law enables the

Chief Executive to be a very strong leader within the local government. The Chief Executive has powers and functions similar to the United States President, though the former probably has even larger powers *vis-à-vis* the legislature. For example, the Chief Executive may dissolve the Legislative Council when the latter refuses to pass the budget or other important bills and consensus cannot be reached after consultation (Article 50).

The strength of the Chief Executive and the weakness of the Legislative Council are further demonstrated by the Chief Executive's power "to approve the introduction of motions regarding revenues or expenditure to the Legislative Council" (Article 48.10) and "to decide, in the light of security and vital public interests, whether government officials or other personnel in charge of government affairs should testify or give evidence before the Legislative Council or its committees" (Article 48.11). If the Chief Executive can, without having to give reasons, reject any motion presented to the Legislative Council regarding revenues and expenditure, then the Legislative Council can only respond to the Chief Executive's proposals regarding revenues and expenditure. It is not sufficiently clear whether the Legislative Council can reject certain items of the budget, though it does not appear likely. The Chief Executive's power to exempt government officials or other personnel in charge of government affairs from testifying or giving evidence before the Legislative Council or its committees will severely hamper the latter's function as a watchdog of the Chief Executive and the executive authorities.

Further, regarding bills relating to government policies, members of the Legislative Council may only introduce them with the prior written consent of the Chief Executive (Article 74). Obviously there will be a danger that "government policies" may by defined so broadly as to render members of the Legislative Council almost powerless to introduce Bills.

In sum, the political system outlined in Chapter IV of the Basic Law presents an "executive dominant" system in which the Chief Executive will have powers similar to those of the previous British Governor. The Legislative Council will only have limited powers.

There seemed to have been an attempt to retain the political structure of the existing colonial government as both Beijing and the conservative business community accepted it as part of the foundation of Hong Kong's economic success and political stability. A statement by the former Chairman of the Hong Kong Stock Exchange, Ronald Li, at an international investment conference in June 1987, perhaps reflects the conservative business community's attitude. Li declared: "Hong Kong is a colony. It is a dictatorship, although a benevolent one. It is and has been a British colony, and it's going to be a Chinese colony, and as such it will prosper. We do not need free elections here." The colonial government in Hong Kong was certainly a benevolent one; there was ample liberty in the territory and the rule of law was observed. The colonial government, however, had to be accountable ultimately to a democratic government willing to defend freedom and the rule of law. This was the guarantee of its benevolence, but this guarantee disappeared after June 1997.

In both the election of the first Chief Executive and that of the provisional legislature in late 1996, the Chinese authorities wanted to make sure that nothing would go wrong. The formation of the Selection Committee had been critical and the process well demonstrated the style of "election with Chinese characteristics." In the first place, the Preparatory Committee rejected the proposal that various important interest groups in the territory would be allowed to nominate a number of representatives to the Selection Committee. Instead, people who wanted to join the Selection Committee had to take part on an individual basis. They, therefore, did not have to be accountable to the organizations to which they belonged. In drawing up the final list of candidates, the Preparatory Committee's Presidium had ample discretionary power. Finally in the voting process, one could assume that the fifty-six mainland China members in the Preparatory Committee had voted alike, and hence they would have wielded a decisive influence on the outcome of the elections.

The Chinese authorities, therefore, expected no surprises from the Selection Committee, and the question of whether the Chinese leadership had designated a candidate for the post of the first Chief Executive would have been insignificant. Similarly, in the election of the provisional legis- lature, when Qian Qichen appealed for support for those candidates with experience in legislative affairs,[7] the Selection Committee got the message and returned thirty-three incumbent Legislative Councillors plus eight former Legislative Councillors.[8] Among the sixty members of the provisional legislature, fifty-one were members of the Selection Commit- tee; and thirty three of them were members of the Selection Committee as well as members of pro-Beijing political groups. Only six of them were

---

[7] *Ming Pao*, 13 December 1996.

[8] For analyses of the election to the provisional legislature, see all major newspapers in Hong Kong on 22 December 1996.

neither members of the Selection Committee nor affiliated to pro-Beijing political groups. Lau Siu-kai, a Preparatory Committee member heavily involved in the design of the political system of the HKSAR, observed that the Chinese authorities were satisfied with the outcome of the provisional legislature election. He noted that since no political party could dominate the provisional legislature, the executive would not be restrained by the provisional legislature.[9] At the same time, the pro-Beijing camp clearly controls a stable majority in the provisional legislature. With the exception of the four members of the Hong Kong Association for Democracy and People's Livelihood and one or two independents, one can hardly expect any dissident voices.

China's Role in the HKSAR

The Chinese authorities began publicly building their Hong Kong community network and influence in 1985 when the Hong Kong branch of the New China News Agency opened three district offices on Hong Kong Island and in Kowloon and the New Territories. Pro-Beijing political forces mounted a campaign to block the introduction of direct elections to the Legislative Council in 1988. They also mobilized their supporters, identified candidates and isolated political opponents in the district board elections in March 1988.

The pro-Beijing united front suffered a severe setback because of the Tiananmen incident, and this was reflected in the sweeping electoral victory of the pro-democracy political groups in the 1991 elections to the Legislative Council.[10] Since then, the pro-Beijing political groups have gradually recovered. These groups did not perform well in the 1995 Legislative Council elections in terms of seats won, but they altogether secured 34% of the vote and their mobilization power was impressive in a number of ways. Most important of all, public opinion revealed a lot of sympathy for the

---

[9] Wong Wai-kwok, "The Provisional Legislature Directs the Legislative Council?" *Yazhou Zhoukan* (a Hong Kong Chinese weekly magazine), Vol. 11, No. 1 (30 December 30 1996 to 5 January 1997), p. 30.

[10] See the author's "Hong Kong's Legislative Council Elections: Review of 1991 and Planning for 1995," in *25 Years of Social and Economic Development in Hong Kong*, edited by Benjamin K. P. Leung and Teresa Y. C. Wong (Hong Kong: Centre of Asian Studies, The University of Hong Kong, 1994), pp. 291–313.

leaders of the Democratic Alliance for Betterment of Hong Kong (DAB) who lost to the candidates of the pro-democracy groups. Many Hong Kong people felt that the former had been doing a good job in serving the public, and their presence in the legislature would contribute to the well-being of the community and the development of representative government.

The DAB's performance in the elections showed that in the long run, the community service offered by the pro-Beijing groups would be rewarded. Given their financial resources, they would be able to gradually expand their grassroots network. Moreover, the pro-Beijing united front can also reward their supporters with honours such as memberships of the NPC, the Chinese People's Political Consultative Conference and their provincial counterparts as well as appointments as members of the Preparatory Committee for the HKSAR, Hong Kong Affairs Advisors and District Affairs Advisors. By the mid-1990s, the Chinese authorities had already established their system of honours for the Hong Kong community. Such efforts and resources have laid a good foundation for the pro-Beijing political groups. With a more favourable electoral system and the support of the pro-business groups, the Chinese authorities can hope to secure a reliable majority support in the legislature even after the 1998 elections. Willingness to accept elections will maintain the Chinese authorities' attempts to seek legitimacy for the HKSAR Government and encourage them to be responsive to public opinion in the territory.

The DAB also demonstrated, however, that in order to win elections, it could not afford to toe the Beijing line closely all the time. The Chinese leadership's sense of insecurity regarding Hong Kong since the Tiananmen incident and the Sino-British confrontation did not allow the DAB too much room for manoeuvre. Signs of disagreement between the DAB and the Chinese officials responsible for Hong Kong were apparent. In the appointments to the Preparatory Committee for the HKSAR announced at the end of 1995, the DAB received four seats, while other pro-Beijing groups which had been far less effective in elections but which had been faithful in supporting the Beijing line were much more handsomely rewarded.

On the basis of the Preparatory Committee's membership, it seemed that the Chinese authorities had planned to cultivate a number of pro-Beijing groups and avoid dependence on one single political organization.[11]

---

[11] For an analysis of the membership of the Preparatory Committee for the HKSAR, see *Ming Pao*, 27–28 December 1995.

This may well be a sign that the Chinese officials responsible for Hong Kong want to strengthen control of the united front, and to prevent the emergence of possible checks and balances as well as the further development of political parties with strong mass support.

The Chinese authorities have been very successful in winning over the elites in the territory. In the approach to 1997, Hong Kong's Establishment, in order to protect its vested interests, had been eager to indicate its support for China's Hong Kong policy. About 6,000 people wanted to join the Selection Committee. With the exception of the pro-democracy groups, these 6,000 people more or less covered the elites in all important sectors. This fact certainly bestowed considerable legitimacy on the Selection Committee as well as the first Chief Executive and the provisional legislature it elected.

Since the conclusion of the Sino-British Joint Declaration in 1984, Chinese leaders have been according top priority to the cultivation of the business community in the territory. Their rationale is simple and straightforward. Hong Kong must remain attractive to investors. If investors stay, the stability and prosperity of the territory will be maintained. From the membership of the Basic Law Drafting Committee to those of the Preparatory Committee for the HKSAR and the Selection Committee for the first government of the HKSAR, it has been clearly demonstrated that business leaders dominate.[12] The business community in return firmly supported the Chinese Government in the Sino-British conflict. It has confidence in China's economic reforms and its opening up to the outside world. The momentum picked up very quickly after the Tiananmen crackdown. Business people believe that the trend is irreversible. Hence they have been very bullish about the economic future of China and Hong Kong's role in China's development.[13] Since Chinese enterprises invest substantially in the territory, and most major Hong Kong firms have businesses in China, it is only natural that the latter have been eager to establish their *guanxi* (relationship) networks in China. Emphasis on *guanxi* means that fair competition cannot be maintained; and fair competition has been an important factor for Hong Kong's success.

---

[12] For an analysis of the membership of the Selection Committee, see *Sing Tao Daily*, 3 November 1996.

[13] See, for example, Bruce Gilley, "Red Flag over Hong Kong," *Far Eastern Economic Review*, Vol. 158, No. 49 (7 December 1995), pp. 72–78.

In terms of political participation, local business leaders enjoy access to top Chinese leaders. When the latter visit Guangdong, they typically would arrange to see some of the richest Hong Kong tycoons. Local business leaders believe that their interests will be respected by the future HKSAR Government and they consider that the best way to articulate their interests is to cultivate and maintain good relations with the Chinese leadership. The most effective means of achieving this end appears to be major investments in China and generous donations.

While visiting Singapore in June 1996, Lu Ping, head of the Hong Kong and Macau Affairs Office, revealed that provincial governments had been called to a meeting recently "to deepen their understanding" of China's policy towards Hong Kong. They were reminded that they should not think of "stretching out their hands too far into Hong Kong."[14] Similar messages had also been passed on to the central ministries, and many attempts had been made to encourage Chinese cadres to study the Basic Law. But the Guangdong provincial leadership saw the approach of 1997 as a godsend. The special privileges given to Guangdong and its special economic zones in the 1980s had been fast eroded by the spread of "national treatment" partly in response to the demand for such privileges by other provinces and partly in response to international pressure in the process of preparing China for admission to the World Trade Organization (WTO). The governor, Lu Ruihua, in an interview with the New China News Agency, stated that Hong Kong and Guangdong "are set to integrate to become the most dynamic economic hub throughout the Asia-Pacific region."[15] Guangdong academics also argued that the province should make good use of the capital markets in Hong Kong to raise funds for its infrastructure projects.[16] Shenzhen, in its city planning which covered the period up to 2010, has already involved Hong Kong, anticipating a relationship of equal partnership with the future SAR.[17] The Shenzhen Government expects that up to one million people would work and live in Shenzhen after 1997.[18]

---

[14] *South China Morning Post*, 12 June 1996. See also *Renmin Ribao* editorial, 30 June 1996.

[15] *South China Morning Post*, 21 June 1996.

[16] *Ming Pao*, 16 August 1996.

[17] *Ibid.*, 21 June 1996.

[18] *Ibid.*, 26 November 1996.

In the approach to 1997, China's policy towards Hong Kong involved many *xitongs* (policy systems), as reflected by the affiliations of the fifty-six mainland China members on the Preparatory Committee. The People's Liberation Army, for example, believed it had an important interest in the territory. Observers of the Sino-British negotiations in the recent two years or so noticed that the Hong Kong and Macau Affairs Office kept a lower profile and took a longer time to respond to various agenda items. One plausible explanation was that its director, Lu Ping, had to consult many central ministries. He not only had to report to Qian Qichen, who chaired the Preparatory Committee, but also top Chinese leaders who probably paid attention to the situation in Hong Kong too, as the return of the territory to China had a bearing on their status in Chinese history. In sum, there might be many "grannies" who demanded a say in China's Hong Kong policy as they believed they had an interest at stake in the territory's future.

The Hong Kong and Macau Work Committee probably has an important role to play in the relationship between the central government and the HKSAR. Its views are likely to be sought by the State Council or the Secretariat of the Party Central Committee, which will make the final decisions. The Hong Kong and Macau Work Committee is the organ of the Communist Party of China in Hong Kong and Macau, and its status is equivalent to that of a provincial Party committee. Ever since the 1950s, the director of the Hong Kong branch of the New China News Agency has also served as the secretary of the Committee. Xu Jiatun, the former director of the Hong Kong branch of the New China News Agency, was first secretary of the Jiangsu Provincial Party Committee and a member of the Party Central Committee before he took up his post in Hong Kong. It was considered that, given the presence of a considerable number of senior Chinese cadres in Hong Kong working in places like the Bank of China's Hong Kong branch, a cadre with Central Committee membership would be required to coordinate the various lines of activities of the Party and the state administration in Hong Kong. What kind of influence such a high-ranking Party cadre would have on the HKSAR Chief Executive is difficult to assess at present. Xu Jiatun, however, indicated to a group of Hong Kong journalists at an off-the-record briefing in June 1987 that the future role of the Party in Hong Kong would be "to assist the Special Administrative Region Government."

The Chinese authorities have been very sensitive to foreign interference in Chinese domestic affairs. One of the most important conspiracy theories in the Chinese leadership's perception of Hong Kong is that the pro-democracy groups in the territory are in collaboration with the United States, Britain and Taiwan to bring about "peaceful evolution" in China.

The U.S. State Department's expression of a "significant interest" in protecting civil liberties in the territory after its return to China has created an area of potential conflict.[19] Since 1992, the State Department has been required by law to report to the Congress on Hong Kong, and criticisms are expected on China's policy towards the territory. Chinese leaders usually raise the issue of sovereignty, arguing that the criticisms made by the U.S. Government or Congress constitute interference in China's domestic affairs. When the U.S. Republican Congressman, Jim Kolbe, visiting China commented that China was unlikely to win permanent most-favoured-nation (MFN) status in 1997 because the United States would be concerned whether China would keep its promise to Hong Kong and respect its autonomy, Chinese officials responded by warning the United States not to link the granting of permanent MFN trading status to the way Beijing handled the transfer of power in Hong Kong.[20]

In testimony before the House International Relations Subcommittee on Asia and the Pacific on 13 February 1997, Jeffrey Bader, Deputy Assistant Secretary of State for East Asian and Pacific Affairs, stated that the United States would "play a strong supportive role to ensure that our own interests are protected."[21] In response, C. H. Tung, the Chief Executive-designate, said that he welcomed constructive concern from the international community, but not if it stemmed from "misleading" information.[22] It is expected that such exchanges would be repeated many times after 1997. In general, the Chinese authorities believed that the Clinton administration would respect Beijing's vital interests and value a stable bilateral relationship, but there would be frequent strong criticisms from the U.S. Congress.

The Chinese authorities sternly rejected the statement of the British Foreign Secretary, Malcolm Rifkind, suggesting the adjudicating of the legal status of the provisional legislature by the International Court of

---

[19] *South China Morning Post*, 20 April 1996.

[20] *Ibid.*, 17 January 1997.

[21] *Ming Pao*, 15 February 1997 and *Foreign Policy Backgrounder* released by the U. S. Consulate General in Hong Kong on 14 February 1997.

[22] *South China Morning Post*, 17 February 1997.

Justice.[23] Chinese leaders usually adopt a very strong stand against the British Government's attempts to play "the international card."[24] They could feel quite assured though that Western governments had reacted mildly against the provisional legislature. Both the European Union and Canada merely stated that they hoped to see the election of the legislature taking place soon after the establishment of the HKSAR Government to replace the provisional legislature.[25] Former British Deputy Prime Minister and Foreign Secretary, Sir Geoffrey Howe, while defending the British moral responsibility to monitor the implementation of "one country, two systems" in Hong Kong after the transfer of power, admitted frankly that British influence would be limited, and that it would be foolish to think otherwise.[26] Similarly, in his brief visit to Hong Kong in February 1997, Malcolm Rifkind conceded that there was little the British Government could do to reverse the Chinese authorities' decisions to establish a provisional legislature and repeal laws related to human rights.[27] It is interesting to note that 1996 witnessed a severe decline in the number of British expatriates in Hong Kong from 34,500 in February to 25,500 in December. The decline was largely due to a reduction in the "floating population" of British backpackers, students and specialist consultants working on various infrastructure projects.[28]

Hong Kong's relations with Taiwan will surely be closely watched by the Chinese authorities. Taiwan was the third largest source of imports for Hong Kong in 1995; it was at the same time the seventh largest market for Hong Kong's domestic exports. After China and Japan, Taiwan is also an important source of Hong Kong's re-exports.[29] Taiwan has considerable investments in Hong Kong, which has also been serving as a staging post for Taiwanese investments in China. The Mainland Affairs Council in

---

[23] *Ming Pao*, 24 December 1996.

[24] New China News Agency dispatch on 25 December 1996; see *Ming Pao*, 26 December 1996.

[25] *Ibid.*, 24 December 1996.

[26] *Ibid.*, 7 January 1997.

[27] *South China Morning Post*, 17 February 1997.

[28] *Ibid.*, 3 February 1997.

[29] Bob Howlett, Information Services Department, *Hong Kong 1996* (Hong Kong: Government Printer, 1996), pp. 93 and 447.

Taipei anticipated that the approach of 1997 would not affect the economic exchanges and trade between Taiwan and Hong Kong.[30] In June 1995, Chinese Vice-Premier and Foreign Minister, Qian Qichen, announced seven basic principles governing Beijing's handling of Hong Kong's relations with Taiwan after 1997.[31] Qian's seven points guaranteed that existing non-government exchanges between Hong Kong and Taiwan would not be affected. However, all official contacts between Hong Kong and Taiwan would have to go through the central government. If the HKSAR allows Taiwan to set up semi-official organs in the territory, would it demand reciprocity? Under such circumstances, it would be difficult for the Taipei Government to resist Beijing's attempts to set up semi-official organs in Taiwan. In short, Chinese leaders may exploit Taiwan's lucrative economic ties with the HKSAR to exert pressure on Taiwan. Moreover, Hong Kong may well have a more significant intermediary role in the relationship across the Taiwan Strait; and it seems that Chinese officials responsible for Taiwan affairs are ready to take some measures in this direction.

The Mainland Affairs Council naturally hoped to maintain the status quo regarding Taiwan's organs in Hong Kong. After the return of Hong Kong to China, all such organs would come under the Mainland Affairs Council as one single unit. Taipei had hoped that the status of Taiwanese agencies in the territory would be discussed in the second meeting between Koo Chen-fu and Wang Daohan, i.e. the highest-level meeting between the Straits Exchange Foundation and the Association for Relations Across the Taiwan Strait. Owing to the deterioration in relations between Beijing and Taipei since President Lee Teng-hui's informal visit to the United States, the meeting had been postponed. Hence Taipei's intention to further strengthen its activities in the territory would simply be wishful thinking. Taipei has stated that, in view of the present impasse and the lack of negotiations, Taiwan's organs in Hong Kong would continue their existing mode of operation. It has also indicated that it would not alter the present arrangements governing Hong Kong people's applications for visas to visit Taiwan; furthermore, it would welcome the establishment of an office in Taiwan by the HKSAR. Taipei considered that the Asia-Pacific Economic

---

[30] *Ming Pao*, 19 January 1997.

[31] Julian Baum and Louise do Rosario, "Studied Ambiguity — Beijing Gives Its Line on Taipei — Hong Kong Links," *Far Eastern Economic Review*, Vol. 158, No. 27 (6 July 1995), p. 21.

Cooperation Forum and the WTO could be well utilized to consolidate its relations with Hong Kong. There were also suggestions that a private foundation or research institute might be set up in the territory to monitor the implementation of "one country, two systems."[32]

The Economic and Social Order

The Chinese leadership's determination to maintain Hong Kong's prosperity has convinced all parties concerned that the economic order will largely remain intact, as guaranteed by the Sino-British Joint Declaration and the Basic Law. In the process of drafting the Basic Law, the business community enjoyed the trust of Chinese officials responsible for Hong Kong who believed that the two parties had common objectives regarding the future of the territory. As can be expected, Chapter V of the Basic Law which deals with the economy proves to be satisfactory to the local business community.

If Hong Kong had been ready to develop a genuine system of representative government, the local business leaders would have been prepared to imitate their counterparts in the West and form political parties to articulate their interests. In 1984–1985, two members of both the Legislative and Executive Councils, Maria Tam and Allen Lee, made preparations to form political groups which were intended to develop into political parties. Such political groups were to include the central figures in the Establishment as well as representatives from the established rich families and major business conglomerates. Maria Tam even formally launched the Progressive Hong Kong Society.[33] Nevertheless, by the mid-1980s, business leaders discovered that despite the promise of "self-administration" (*gangren zhigang*), the Chinese authorities had no intention of allowing a fully democratic system in Hong Kong. They, therefore, did not form political parties to defend their interests. They considered their interests safeguarded well by their access to Chinese leaders who also displayed a genuine concern for the protection of investors' interests.

Article 107 of the Basic Law states: "The Hong Kong Special

---

[32] *Ming Pao*, 28 January 1997 and *Sing Tao Daily*, 2 February 1997.

[33] See the author's "The Present Situation of the Development of Hong Kong's Political Forces," *Hong Kong Economic Journal Monthly*, Vol. 9, No. 2 (May 1985), pp. 25 and 34 (in Chinese).

Administrative Region shall follow the principle of keeping expenditure within the limits of revenues in drawing up its budget, and strive to achieve a fiscal balance, avoid deficits and keep the budget commensurate with the growth rate of its gross domestic product." This fiscal conservatism has been most reassuring for Hong Kong's business people. In the mid-1980s, they worried that the development of a system of representative govern-ment would prompt politicians into making promises of "free lunches" to the electorate, i.e. increasing government expenditure on social services. This ultimately would lead to higher taxation for the wealthy. Chinese leaders also agreed to Hong Kong's joining the WTO before China, in contrast to their insistence that Taiwan's admission to the WTO must follow that of China. It is significant that Hong Kong's economic interests take precedence over sovereignty considerations.

With the approach of 1997, different types of interest groups have to respond to the new challenges and devise strategies to ensure their effective articulation of their interests. Interest groups such as the Hong Kong General Chamber of Commerce must shed their image of enjoying a special status under the British administration and their leadership being dominated by the British hongs. In recent years, the Chamber has elected leaders who can communicate well with the Chinese authorities, and their recognition has been affirmed by appointments to the Preliminary Working Committee and Preparatory Committee. In 1995, the Chamber, for the first time, joined other established business groups in the celebration of the National Day of the People's Republic of China.

Similar changes have taken place in a number of important professional associations too. Access to the Chinese authorities has been considered an important factor in their leadership contests, while expatriates, voluntarily or involuntarily, adopt a lower profile. Most professional associations would like to persuade the Chinese authorities to allow them to retain their role in determining their respective professional qualifications in the ter-ritory. With the rapid expansion of economic exchanges between Hong Kong and China since the late 1970s, professional firms with an early start in the China market tend to do well and their status and influence within the respective professions have been rising correspondingly. Heads of these firms often receive appointments and honours from the Chinese authorities too, and they obviously have a vested interest in maintaining good relations with Beijing and avoid antagonizing it.

Christopher Patten's political reform package and the political struggles of the pro-democracy camp failed to force the Chinese authorities to make concessions. The local business community instead considered it a wiser strategy to accept China's Hong Kong policy, gradually building up Chinese leaders' trust for the territory, reducing their sense of insecurity, and, on this basis, negotiating for more relaxed arrangements for Hong Kong. The difficulty of this approach was that little weight was attached to Hong Kong people's basic rights. Similarly, Chinese leaders' tolerance for the rule of law would then be based on utilitarian considerations, and not out of a genuine acceptance and appreciation of it.

According to official, but unnamed, sources in China quoted in *China Economic News*, assets of China-funded enterprises in Hong Kong reached US$42.5 billion by the end of 1994. Hence, by the end of 1996, the figure should well exceed US$50 billion. Investments by or through Hong Kong into China amounted to US$66 billion at the end of 1994, which were about one-third more than the investments from China in the territory.[34] It is estimated, however, that at least 40% of Hong Kong's investments in China come from China-related enterprises in the territory, so it is most likely that China is a net exporter of capital to Hong Kong if capital is classified according to legal ownership.[35] At any rate, China is currently the most important source of overseas investment in Hong Kong.

In late 1995, it was said that the Bank of China Group (HK) controlled 28% of local deposits, and that China-controlled enterprises, including H-shares and red chips, accounted for about 5% of the Stock Exchange of Hong Kong. In addition, China-owned interests were estimated to possess 5% of the territory's property.[36] Normura Research Institute believes that by 1997, Chinese concerns would control at least one-third of the territory's banking, property and transport sectors.[37]

In terms of trade, China surpassed the United States and became the most important destination for Hong Kong's domestic exports, amounting to HK$44,987 million (28.7% of the total) in the first nine months of 1996,

---

[34] See Ian Perkin, "Estimates Fall Short of Mainland Assets in HK," *Sunday Morning Post*, 20 October 1996.

[35] Hsueh Tien-tung and Woo Tun-oy, "The Development of Hong Kong-China Economic Relationship," in *25 Years of Social and Economic Development*, edited by Benjamin Leung and Teresa Wong, p. 705.

[36] See Bruce Gilley, "Great Leap Southward," *Far Eastern Economic Review*, Vol. 158, No. 47 (23 November 1995), p. 62.

[37] *Ibid.*

despite a decline of 5.5% compared with the corresponding period in 1995. When re-exports are taken into consideration, China's significance is even more prominent. In the first three quarters of 1996, China absorbed HK$349,471 million (33.8%) of the territory's total exports, compared with 21.3% taken up by the United States. Regarding imports by main suppliers, China was again the most important supplier for the territory, providing HK$422,129 million (37.2%) of Hong Kong's imports in the first nine months of 1996.[38] The substantial trade flows reflect the level of integration between the two economies.

In October 1995, heads of thirty large Chinese state-owned firms in Hong Kong met in Shenzhen to discuss increasing investments in the territory's businesses and real estate to boost confidence in the economy and to guarantee a smooth transfer of power in 1997.[39] In the third quarter of 1995, Hong Kong's economic growth fell to 4.2%, the lowest level in nearly six years; the unemployment rate also reached a ten-year high of 3.5%.[40]

In November 1996, *Ta Kung Pao* reported the remarks of Zheng Wentong, deputy director of the United Front Work Department of the Communist Party of China, to the effect that a multi-billion rescue fund had been established in Beijing to prop up the local financial markets in case of "unforeseen circumstances" after the return of the territory to China.[41] This was probably another classic example of how good intentions on the part of the Chinese authorities could become counter-productive. Dai Xianglong, Governor of the People's Bank of China, in a visit to Hong Kong soon afterwards, had to reassure the territory that the bank would step in only at the request of the Hong Kong Monetary Authority and that any action taken would be in accordance with the Basic Law and market practices.[42] The episode reminds Hong Kong people that while many Chinese officials responsible for Hong Kong affairs understand what makes Hong Kong tick, most cadres in China do not know Hong Kong well and

---

[38] *Hong Kong External Trade* (Census and Statistics Department, Hong Kong Government), September 1996, pp. 3–6.

[39] Gilley, "Great Leap Southward," p. 60 and *Ming Pao*, 6 November 1995.

[40] *South China Morning Post*, 6 February 1996.

[41] See Chris Yeung, "Let's Have Quiet from the North," *Sunday Morning Post*, 17 November 1996.

[42] *South China Morning Post*, 14 November 1996.

are not familiar with the working of an administration and economy guided by the philosophy of positive non-interventionism.

On the other hand, apparently China would not allow foreign interests to dominate key sectors of Hong Kong's economy after 1997. At the end of April 1996, Swire Pacific sold some of its shares in Cathay Pacific Airways and Dragonair to two major Chinese companies. CITIC Pacific planned to spend HK$6.3 billion for new shares of Cathay to increase its stake in the airline from 10% to 25%. At the same time, Swire's share in Cathay would drop from 52.6% to 43.9%. In a more complex transaction, China National Aviation Corporation, a subsidiary of the Civil Aviation Administration of China, put up HK$2 billion to acquire 35.9% of Dragonair from Swire, Cathay, CITIC Pacific and the family of K. P. Chao, Dragonair's founder. China National Aviation Corporation would also merge its China Hong Kong Airlines into Dragonair.[43] All parties concerned seemed to have been satisfied with the deal, despite the political overtone of the transactions. At the end of 1996, there was some speculation that Hong Kong Telecom International Limited was looking for a similar arrangement. Instead in late January 1997, CITIC Pacific announced that it would spend HK$16.3 billion to acquire 20% of China Light & Power, the territory's biggest electricity producer.[44]

The economic order of the HKSAR will probably face two significant challenges in the years ahead. To the business community, the market economy of Hong Kong is probably still the freest in the world and experiences the least interference from the government. In the past, the freedom of the market economy had been effectively protected by government officials.[45] To a large extent, senior officials of the British administration in Hong Kong were a neutral administrative elite without direct ties to the business community. Appointed by the British Government, they were constitutionally accountable to the British Government. In practice, the British administration had encountered little interference from London.

[43] Michael Westlake, "A Wing And a Prayer," *Far Eastern Economic Review*, Vol. 159, No. 19 (9 May 1996), p. 67.

[44] Emily Thornton, "The Power of Two," *Far Eastern Economic Review*, Vol. 160, No. 7 (13 February 1997), pp. 40–42.

[45] See Norman J. Miners, *The Government and Politics of Hong Kong*, 4th edition (Hong Kong: Oxford University Press 1986), Chapter 4, "Economic Constraints and the Government's Ideology."

The postwar economic development in Hong Kong differed from that in the other "little dragons of Asia" (Singapore, Taiwan and South Korea). The major enterprises in the territory had not received any direct assistance from the government. Part of their capital came from the Chinese entrepreneurs (mostly from Shanghai) who fled to Hong Kong in 1949–1950, and the rest from the banking system in Hong Kong in which a firm foundation had been established when the territory served as an entrepôt, as well as from the subsequent accumulation of the enterprises themselves. On the other hand, much of the capital of the major corporations in Taiwan and South Korea came from government-owned financial institutions, and the corporations maintained close ties with the respective governments and ruling parties.[46] The governments in Taipei and Seoul assumed a considerable guidance role in their respective market economies. The business communities were forced to maintain cordial relations with the government officials, and it was not uncommon to offer political donations in exchange for favoured treatment from the government authorities. Even in Singapore, the guiding hand of the government was obvious in the market economy: the priority accorded to the "strategic industries" of electronics, petrochemicals, etc. in the early 1970s is a good example.

In Hong Kong, a basic separation between economics and politics had been maintained, and the business community had full confidence in the government's observance of the operational principles of a free market economy. Though the free market economy led to a concentration of wealth and an unequal distribution of income, yet in a colonial political system, power had been highly concentrated in the senior officials of the colonial government and had not been affected by economic development. This separation of political power and wealth in fact constituted a form of checks and balances. The considerable gap between the rich and the poor too had not paved the way for a strong labour movement.

The above fine tradition has been seriously challenged by a number of trends. In the first place, business people in Hong Kong have been keen to establish their *guanxi* networks in China. For example, in July 1996, the

---

[46] Regarding the situation in South Korea, see, for example, Mark Clifford, "Filing for Divorce" and "Playing the Game," *Far Eastern Economic Review*, Vol. 140, No. 16 (21 April 1988), pp. 58–60.

Sino-British Joint Liaison Group reached an initial agreement on the issuing of six Personal Communication Services licences which would probably revolutionize Hong Kong's mobile telephone network.[47] It was an open secret in the local business community that almost every serious bidder had engaged in lobbying in Beijing. Further, the Chinese authorities have been actively cultivating local business leaders in their united front strategy. Hong Kong people generally believe that the local business community has an important influence on China's Hong Kong policy and the HKSAR Government's policies. Business leaders too have become more interested in politics, and some second-generation business leaders from prominent families have become legislators. Finally, senior civil servants have found second careers in the business sector an increasingly attractive option, and this has cast doubt on their neutrality.

The HKSAR Government may be tempted to adopt a more active role in the territory's economic development. Hong Kong is concerned with the erosion of its competitiveness due to high costs and the move of its manufacturing industries to mainland China. Development of high-tech industries may be the answer. C. H. Tung, the Chief Executive-designate and another candidate in the election, Peter K. C. Woo, endorsed the idea of promoting the development of high-tech industries with government support. In subsequent interviews after his election, C. H. Tung often commented on the need to enhance Hong Kong's competitiveness and to spend its wealth for this purpose.

The HKSAR Government's accumulated wealth is impressive indeed. In 1996–1997, the accumulated fiscal reserve reached HK$150,190 million. Upon the transfer of power, the HKSAR Land Fund was consolidated into the General Revenue Account and the total reserves reached HK$321,960 million. By the year 2000, the reserves are estimated to amount to HK$365,990 million.[48] Chinese officials responsible for Hong Kong have been worrying that the British administration may spend all the reserves before its departure. They would not like to see it spending more to improve social services too, not only because such spending may result in heavy

---

[47] *South China Morning Post*, 27 July 1996; and *Hong Kong Economic Journal*, 27 July 1996.

[48] See Lau Pui-king, "Managing the Public Finance," in *The Other Hong Kong Report 1997*, edited by Joseph Y. S. Cheng (Hong Kong: The Chinese University Press, 1997).

financial burden for the HKSAR Government, but also because the generosity of the British administration may reflect badly on the HKSAR Government. These considerations no longer apply after June 1997, and there is considerable public opinion pressure on the HKSAR Government to spend its reserves on the territory's future development.

In the 1990s, in almost every major policy area, new approaches and new policy programmes are called for. In public housing, for example, the government has promised a new initiative to satisfy the demand of the sandwiched-income class. What is the responsibility of the government or the Housing Authority in meeting the demand for home ownership of the young middle-class families? In the field of medical care, some kind of medical insurance scheme is called for to ensure the long-term standards of medical and hospital care. How should this scheme be introduced so as to protect those who may not be covered, namely, the old and the under-privileged? In education, the territory now has an oversupply of places in tertiary institutions, but the government has very limited responsibility in child care and kindergarten education. Meanwhile, the community has become more concerned with the quality of education and the morale of teachers in primary and secondary schools.

Many years have been wasted on the Sino-British negotiations on the transfer of power. C. H. Tung in his election campaign promised to thoroughly review the British administration's housing and education policies. Undeniably, new policy programmes are required to meet the demand for quality social services in the increasingly affluent society, new funding arrangements should also be explored to tap the resources of those who can afford to pay. C. H. Tung repeatedly emphasized that Hong Kong had become overly politicized. The best way to achieve depoliticization is perhaps to focus the community's attention on livelihood issues. This is probably also the best approach for the HKSAR Government to strengthen its legitimacy and win the support of Hong Kong people.

How to prepare for the approach of 1997 remains a divisive issue among many interest groups outside the Establishment. Arguments and differences of views, for example, became apparent in the Christian com-munity, and to a lesser extent, in the Catholic Church in mid-1996.[49] The

---

[49] See Melana K. Zyla, "Devil of a Dilemma — Churches Ponder How Close to Get to Beijing," *Far Eastern Economic Review*, Vol. 159, No. 31 (1 August 1996), p. 17.

Catholic Church, for example, wanted to serve as "the conscience of society," but it ran a large number of schools, hospitals and charities which depended very heavily on government funding. The Catholic Church leaders appreciated the need to maintain a good relationship with the incoming HKSAR Government. Among the Christian groups, quarrels became open over the issue of church commemoration of China's National Day. Apparently the Lutherans and Methodists have been most amenable to cooperating with the Chinese authorities. Some of their leaders argued that "Hong Kong is returning not only to China but to the People's Republic of China." On the other hand, the local evangelical churches, which have strong links to China's secret "house churches," are moving underground.[50] In contrast to the 1970s and 1980s, some social workers and grassroots activists are disappointed with the lack of progress in the democratization process. Hence they are often tempted to adopt a confrontational approach, resulting in further polarization among grassroots political groups and social workers. Many small radical groups have emerged in recent years and they have been keen on protest activities against the Chinese authorities.

At the end of December 1996, a State Education Commission official indicated that the Tiananmen incident was an event of the past, and it should not be discussed in the schools in Hong Kong. The latter should work on the strengthening of patriotic education, including the Taiwan question, with emphasis on the preservation of state sovereignty and reunification of the country.[51] This has been the line articulated by the pro-Beijing united front and Preparatory Committee members responsible for education policy. No concrete changes have yet been introduced by the Hong Kong Government. The Education Department, however, is now reviewing the syllabus of the history subject at the junior secondary school level, but it has given no indication whether sensitive issues such as the Tiananmen incident will be excluded from the syllabus.

Hong Kong's journalistic profession is among the least optimistic in the community. It probably has its reasons. In October 1996, in an interview with the *Asian Wall Street Journal*, Chinese Vice-Premier Qian Qichen indicated that local activities to commemorate the Tiananmen incident

---

[50] *Ibid.*; and *Hong Kong Economic Journal*, 15 June 1996.
[51] *Ming Pao*, 28 December 1996.

would be prohibited after 1997. Qian said that "in the future, Hong Kong should not hold political activities which directly interfere in the affairs of the Mainland." He further stressed that the media could "put forward criticisms, but not rumours or lies," "nor can they put forward personal attacks on Chinese leaders."[52] The community generally believed that activities commemorating the Tiananmen incident and personal attacks on Chinese leaders should be regulated within the existing legal framework, and it found Qian's statements intimidating. It was speculated that China was going through a critical stage in the leadership succession process, and the Chinese Communist regime was tightening its control over the media and the ideological sphere. Qian's statements were made in this context.

The journalistic profession in the territory has indeed been disturbed by the phenomenon of self-censorship. A series of surveys of the profession from the end of 1993 to 1995 revealed that about 90% of the respondents considered that self-censorship existed. About 60% indicated that self-censorship existed where they worked; and over 50% said self-censorship came from the pressure of their superiors.[53] Less than 10% of those surveyed thought that they would work until retirement. In June 1996, it was reported that about 60% of the staff of Radio Television Hong Kong worried that it would lose its editorial independence after 1997.[54]

The vast majority of Hong Kong people have, to some extent, accepted the substitution of stability and prosperity for democracy. They have lowered their expectations of democracy because they realize that this is not a realistic goal and they value the high living standards which the territory has been offering them. They, and especially the middle class, are also aware that there are no greener pastures outside Hong Kong. Hence the community has adopted a very accommodating attitude regarding its future. But where do Hong Kong people get their satisfaction from?

There is a view that children of the increasingly affluent middle class will find it difficult to attain a sense of achievement. In general, the postwar generation in Hong Kong had a hard time in its childhood. Members of this generation often suffered various economic hardships before completing their education. But their career development and Hong Kong's

---

[52] *Asian Wall Street Journal*, 16 October 1996; *Ming Pao* and *South China Morning Post*, 17 October 1996.

[53] *Ming Pao*, 5 August 1995.

[54] *Ibid.*, 13 June 1996.

economic growth have brought them much satisfaction through job advancement and improvement in living standards. On the other hand, young people from middle-class families today will probably have to endure a decline in living standards when they become independent, and they will have to work for many years before they can catch up with their parents. To them, a sense of satisfaction and achievement will be more difficult to come by.

Professional ethics somehow appears to be one of the casualties of the uncertainty of the future. Hong Kong people's trust of professionals has been in decline. When advised by a doctor to have an operation, very often there is strong suspicion that the advice is based on greed rather than medical grounds. Young professionals are overeager to establish their own practices before building adequate clientele. They are therefore under pressure to relax their professional standards and engage in work in "grey areas" or even illegal activities. About 72% of the respondents in a poll in October 1995 believed that the 1997 question would lead to an increase in corruption.[55]

In the past decade and more, the gap between the rich and the poor in the territory has been widening. As the economy matures, demand for manual labour falls and the creation of job opportunities also slows down. A survey of labourers in September 1996 revealed that 51.3% of the respondents believed that wage levels would deteriorate after 1997, and only 8.3% believed that they would improve; 52% thought that the unemployment situation would deteriorate after 1997, and only 18.6% considered that it would improve; further, 45.6% of the respondents believed that social welfare would deteriorate after 1997, and only 8.3% thought that it would improve.[56] Middle-class families too reveal some worry about decline in real income and the job situation, especially employment opportunities for their children.

It is small wonder that C. H. Tung would like to appeal to Confucianism. More realistically, there may well emerge a new type of neighbourhood groups. Given the acute need for emotional support in a highly competitive society where work pressure is substantial, a sense of loneliness and alienation is widespread. Single parents, retirees, young people

---

[55] *Ibid.*, 14 October 1995.
[56] *Ibid.*, 15 September 1996.

who are well educated and ready for some voluntary work, etc. form a substantial pool of potential members ready to group together in service of the neighbourhood. These people are distinct from members of the existing grassroots groups in that they are financially better off and do not plan to seek help directly from the government. They do not intend to take an active part in politics, but they want a meaningful interaction with the community through which they seek mutual help, emotional support and satisfaction through service. Today, religious organizations come closest to satisfying this demand, but obviously there is much room for similar secular groups to develop.

Conclusion

In 1997, both Chinese leaders and Hong Kong people have much more confidence in a stable transfer of power compared with, say, eight years ago. Even the death of Deng Xiaoping does not pose a threat, as people accept that the post-Deng era has already begun. This improvement in confidence has been achieved by a number of factors. Hong Kong people appreciate that Chinese leaders value the territory, and have been working hard to retain investors. It is obvious that China's economic reforms and opening to the outside world are irreversible.

The worry of a major shock by 1997 has been diluted to a concern for a slow erosion of the rule of law, the freedoms now enjoyed and, indeed, the Hong Kong way of life. It also means that the Chinese authorities have gained time. They now have been given the benefit of the doubt to make "one country, two systems" work. They have been given a vote of confidence by local and international investors. The number of Hong Kong residents who emigrated in 1996 fell to pre-Tiananmen incident level. The emigration flow reached a peak in 1992 and showed a marked decline in 1995 and 1996, as reflected in the following figures given by the Security Branch of the Hong Kong Government: 42,000 in 1989; 61,700 in 1990; 59,700 in 1991; 66,200 in 1992; 53,400 in 1993; 61,600 in 1994; 43,100 in 1995 and 40,300 in 1996.[57] The return flow of former emigrants has also been expanding as Hong Kong approaches 1997. It was reported that for

---

[57] *South China Morning Post*, 15 February 1997.

every 100 emigrants leaving Hong Kong in 1995, 60 former emigrants returned to the territory from overseas. The corresponding proportions in previous years were 27.9% in 1994, 29.1% in 1993, 16.2% in 1992, 7.7% in 1991 and 7.2% in 1990.[58]

Despite some doubts on the legality of the provisional legislature, Hong Kong people have come to accept it as a political reality. After all, the community cannot countenance the scenario of having an illegal legislature in July 1997. Declaring a legislature illegal means that the laws it passes are illegal, the taxes it imposes are illegal, etc., and Hong Kong people do not want a very chaotic situation. In the end, the legitimacy of the HKSAR Government will have to depend on its ability to deliver the goods. An opinion survey showed that Hong Kong people's trust for C. H. Tung rose from 4.9 to 5.7 on a ten-point scale after he had secured a through-train arrangement for all Chinese senior civil servants. Assessment of his competence also climbed from 5.2 to 5.9.[59]

The Chinese leadership's top priority in its policy towards Hong Kong has been the maintenance of the territory's stability and prosperity. It is similar to the Chinese leadership's domestic disposition in the immediate post-Deng era: *wending yadao yiqie* (stability is more important than anything else). Given Hong Kong people's traditional political values, fear of major changes and concern for the economy and employment, there is no incentive to challenge the Chinese authorities. Order is established through gradually reducing the gap between the expectations and objectives on the part of Beijing and those on the part of Hong Kong people. Maintenance of the existing economic order has paved the way for the community to adjust to the changes in the political and social order.

Most economists forecast healthy growth for Hong Kong's economy till 1999. The HKSAR Government also has substantial fiscal reserves to enhance Hong Kong's competitiveness, improve its infrastructure and raise the quality of its social services. The government's task has been made easier because uncertainty has lowered people's expectations. In the longer term, however, it still has to provide satisfaction to a very hard-working community.

---

[58] *Ming Pao*, 11 September 1996.
[59] *Ibid.*, 26 February 1997.